iOS Development with Swift

iOS Development with Swift

CRAIG GRUMMITT

MANNING
SHELTER ISLAND

For online information and ordering of this and other Manning books, please visit
www.manning.com. The publisher offers discounts on this book when ordered in quantity.
For more information, please contact

    Special Sales Department
    Manning Publications Co.
    20 Baldwin Road
    PO Box 761
    Shelter Island, NY 11964
    Email: orders@manning.com

 Recognizing the importance of preserving what has been written, it is Manning's policy to have
the books we publish printed on acid-free paper, and we exert our best efforts to that end.
Recognizing also our responsibility to conserve the resources of our planet, Manning books
are printed on paper that is at least 15 percent recycled and processed without the use of
elemental chlorine.

Manning Publications Co.
20 Baldwin Road
PO Box 761
Shelter Island, NY 11964

Development editor:	Helen Stergius
Review editor:	Aleksandar Dragosavljević
Technical development editor:	Doug Sparling
Project editor:	Kevin Sullivan
Copyeditor:	Katie Petito
Proofreader:	Katie Tennant
Technical proofreader:	Doug Warren
Typesetter and cover design:	Marija Tudor

ISBN 9781617294075
Printed in the United States of America
1 2 3 4 5 6 7 8 9 10 – EBM – 22 21 20 19 18 17

brief contents

contents

preface

It seems everyone has a brilliant idea brewing for an iOS app these days, though not many actually do the work to see it to fruition. Even putting potential revenues aside, the prospect of making your own app and seeing people download and appreciate your work is exciting. This book should send you on the way to building your first app using Swift.

What is Swift?

Swift is the modern language created by Apple for iOS that got the Apple developer world buzzing back in June 2014—but why was Swift created in the first place?

While loved by many iOS developers, Objective-C was seen by some as an out-moded language. More than 30 years old and based on C, it had a verbose and peculiar syntax, with an unsafe type system. Built as a modern alternative to Objective-C, Swift was designed with specific enhancements in mind, specifically:

- *Safety*—Swift introduced several programming concepts to reduce some common programmer mistakes. These include *strong typing, optionals,* and *error handling.*
- *Performance*—Apple introduced internal optimizations to ensure that Swift runs fast. Xcode also provides warnings to encourage you to write code that ensures your app is running optimally.
- *Expressiveness*—Expressive code maintains the right balance between clarity of meaning and succinctness. Swift draws on lessons learned from Objective-C and other languages to introduce several concepts that may be new at first, but in time you'll wonder what you did without them!

Why learn Swift?

You can still develop in iOS using Objective-C, and many developers do. In fact, according to RedMonk's programming language rankings guide (http://mng.bz/ zQNT), Objective-C is still ranked higher than Swift (but only just!). A common question for a new iOS developer is, should I learn Swift or Objective-C?

Enhanced safety, performance, and expressiveness seem like significant qualities! Combine those with a reputation for being relatively easy to learn, and Swift looks like a pretty good choice. In an interview with Accidental Tech Podcast (http://atp.fm/ 205-chris-lattner-interview-transcript/), Chris Lattner (creator of Swift) summed up Swift's benefits with the term "programmer productivity." After all, it *is* called Swift!

Swift has enjoyed a meteoric rise in popularity since its unveiling. It's regularly ranked as one of the most loved programming languages on Stack Overflow. According to RedMonk, "There is no debate that Swift is growing faster than anything else we track." According to the freelancing platform Upwork, Swift is the second-fastest-growing tech skill desired by employers (http://mng.bz/R12L).

But what are other iOS developers doing?

Many developers embraced Swift from the outset. Popular iOS tutorial site https://raywenderlich.com fully transitioned all new and previous tutorials to Swift, while other iOS developers such as Natasha the Robot (https://natashatherobot .com/) blogged about their experiences exploring this new syntax.

On the other end of the spectrum, it's true that some iOS developers resisted the change. *More than Just Code* (http://mtjc.fm/) podcaster Tammy Coron said this:

> *In the early adoption of Swift I was very anti-Swift.... But the more I started to use it, the more I was forced to use it, the more I liked it.... It feels like I've got cooties all over me whenever I have to write in Objective-C! Every project that I start now is a Swift project, and it feels so natural. Granted, I'm forty years old, I didn't really want to learn something new. I was using Objective-C, and having a good old time with it. Who wants to learn another language? But I'm all for Swift now, and I feel bad I dogged it from the beginning.*

Resisting change can be instinctive. Change can feel as though you're abandoning your accumulated knowledge and reputation and entering the unknown. I've experienced this myself several times over my development career as one skill or tool became outmoded or redundant and others gained favor in the industry. But when you apply yourself to exploring new technologies, you can find yourself discovering once again the excitement of learning something new. My hope is that you, too, will find that passion as you go through this book.

It's also clear that Swift is the future for iOS development. If your plans in iOS development involve maintenance of a codebase, you may need to know Objective-C. But in general, Swift is the way forward, and the consensus these days among iOS professionals is that if they were learning iOS now, they'd do it in Swift.

Of course, learning iOS development with Swift doesn't prevent you from also learning Objective-C at some point in the future. Regardless of the language you're programming in, the underlying frameworks are nearly identical except for tweaks to the syntax. Learning iOS development with Swift doesn't mean planting your flag firmly in the Swift camp. You can use Objective-C code in your Swift project, or vice versa. Learning Swift is just a good place to start, and you'll find exploring Objective-C easier with Swift experience behind you.

On the one hand, there are some significant differences between the languages. For example, Objective-C has very different approaches from Swift in regard to class headers, type safety, nil values, and error handling. On the other hand, some differences are really just a matter of syntax. See the following listing for a comparison of the same code in Swift and Objective-C.

Comparison of Swift and Objective-C

```
UIView.animate(withDuration: 1) {
    self.yellowView.alpha = 0            Swift
}

[UIView animateWithDuration:1.0 animations:^{
    self.yellowView.alpha = 0.0;          Objective-C
}];
```

Swift isn't necessarily limited to iOS app development, either. Swift is used in all Apple platforms, from macOS to iOS to watchOS, and the concepts you learn in Swift will be useful when you migrate to these platforms. And now it isn't limited to only Apple products. Apple stunned everyone in 2015 when they announced that Swift was going open source. IBM was one of the first adopters of the new language, making Swift available to enterprise app developers on IBM Cloud. There's no lack of enthusiasm from Apple on this front. In the same podcast, Chris Lattner suggested that going open source was a major step toward "world domination" for Swift!

Whatever your plans in iOS development, this book should have you well on the way to building your first app using Swift.

acknowledgments

In this book, I share many things I've learned over the years, and for that, I am in turn deeply indebted to those who've shared their guidance, experience, and knowledge with me, including those involved with producing the extremely helpful online resources out there—sites, blogs, and podcasts such as Ray Wenderlich, NSHipster, Use Your Loaf, AppCoda, Natasha The Robot, iOhYes, and More Than Just Code. I also thank fellow mentors at Thinkful for their inspiration, and those who are kind enough to share their knowledge on Stack Overflow.

A big thanks goes to Manning and the wonderful staff who have helped make this book as good as it could be. Thank you Helen Stergius for your tireless efforts, support, and energy—this book is a million times better for your advice. Thanks go to Doug Sparling and Doug Warren for their meticulous work in editing from a technical perspective. Thanks also go to the many others at Manning for their assistance and support in marketing and production: Candace Gillhoolley, Christopher Kaufmann, Aleksandar Dragosavljević, Ana Romac, Katie Petito, Katie Tennant, Kevin Sullivan, and Marija Tudor.

I thank the reviewers who offered their time to read my manuscript at various stages and whose feedback was invaluable: Amit Lamba, Andrea Prearo, Becky Huett, Doniyor Ulmasov, Ghita Kouadri, Karolina Kafel, Laurence Giglio, Luis Moux-Dominguez, Maksym Shcheglov, Stephan Heffner, and Žarko Jovičić.

Finally, I thank my wife Chris for her support, encouragement, and understanding as I spent long days in front of the computer while there was a wedding to plan! I love you.

about this book

In this book, we'll look at building native iOS apps using Swift. iOS is the operating system launched 10 years ago (how time flies!) by Apple for their range of "i" products: iPhones, iPads, and iPod Touches. A native iOS app can take advantage of Apple's built-in user interface frameworks to present a UI that looks and acts consistently with what users are accustomed to in iOS apps.

To build iOS apps in iOS 11, you'll use the current version of Apple's powerful development software, Xcode 9. Because Xcode comes directly from Apple, you can be confident that apps you build will be native, and the tools and frameworks will be up to date. Developers new to Xcode should be sure to read the first chapter to familiarize themselves with it.

You'll also be programming in Swift 4. This book dedicates two chapters to get you up to speed on Swift, and you'll find other Swift tidbits where relevant throughout the book. Of course, if you already have experience in Swift, feel free to skip or skim these chapters.

In this book, you'll learn how to build up and lay out your app's interface in code or using a storyboard. You'll learn how to structure your code and respond to user input.

You'll also learn how to work with data: how to pull data down from a web service, how to deal with data in your code, and how to store data on the device and in the iCloud. We'll look at how to then display data within the app.

We'll also look at solving common problems, best practices for structuring your code, and what to do when things don't go to plan.

There's a good chance you're reading this because you want to publish an app. Throughout the book, we'll be building up a demo app, and to finish off, we'll go over the process of publishing an app to the App Store.

Who should read this book

iOS Development with Swift is intended for those with some experience in programming (you should probably have some familiarity with object-oriented programming, for example) interested in learning about developing for iOS. Perhaps you're curious and want to dip your toe in the iOS waters to test them out, or perhaps you want to dive right into a career change and build apps for a living! Don't worry if you haven't played with mobile development before—novices to this area should have no problem following along.

How this book is organized

The book has four parts that cover 17 chapters.

Part 1 introduces you to Xcode and gives a brief but solid overview of Swift.

- Chapter 1 covers an introduction to iOS development using Xcode. You'll set up an Xcode project, add visual elements in the storyboard, and run an app on the simulator.
- Chapter 2 takes a look at what's new, different, and exciting in the Swift language. Using the Xcode playground, we look at type safety and inference in Swift, collection types, higher-order functions, closures, tuples, and optionals.
- Chapter 3 takes our discussion of Swift deeper by looking at creating objects from classes or structures. It examines Swift's approach to methods and properties, initializers, and extending types and operators, and you'll see what the buzz is all about with protocol-oriented programming.

Part 2 has you building up your app's interface using views.

- Chapter 4 looks at how apps are structured, from how model-view-controller works in iOS to the view hierarchy. It also explains how view controllers work, and how you connect views from the storyboard to your code using outlets.
- Chapter 5 introduces user interaction to your views by overriding touch methods, using gesture recognizers, and connecting controls in the storyboard to actions in your code.
- Chapter 6 discusses solutions for adapting your layout to different environments (for example, different device resolutions or orientations) such as applying rules to a layout with auto layout constraints.
- Chapter 7 takes adaptive layouts further, using size classes to make more-substantial changes to a layout based on its environment, and using stack views to apply general rules to a layout and managing constraints.
- Chapter 8 describes solving a real-world problem: moving the interface up when the user selects a text field and the iOS keyboard appears onscreen, and dismissing the keyboard when the user finishes editing the text field.

Part 3 explores some topics that are vital for building many apps, such as displaying, storing, and downloading data, navigating between scenes, dealing with media, and debugging.

- Chapter 9 introduces displaying data in a table view, and explores navigation to a second form view to add or edit data in the table.
- Chapter 10 demonstrates displaying data in a collection view, and looks at manipulating the data via sorting and searching. It also looks at navigating between view controllers using a tab bar.
- Chapter 11 covers storing data on the device using a variety of techniques, from the more basic state preservation and user defaults to the more complex SQLite and Core Data.
- Chapter 12 looks at storing data in Apple's iCloud using CloudKit. It also looks at threads and queues, activity indicators, and alerts.
- Chapter 13 covers adding icons and images to your app with the asset catalog. It also looks at taking photos, selecting photos from the photo library, detecting patterns in images, drawing in a view, and playing audio.
- Chapter 14 examines connecting your app with web services and downloading data such as text or images. It also discusses parsing JSON and using dependency managers.
- Chapter 15 discusses some vital techniques for debugging your app, from the console and breakpoints to gauges and instruments. We'll also take a look at applying unit tests to ensure your code is doing what it's intended to do, and UI tests to ensure that your app's interface is working as expected.

Part 4 covers the next steps required for a successful application release.

- Chapter 16 describes in great detail the process of distributing your app to beta testers using TestFlight, and then distributing your app to the wider world on the App Store.
- Chapter 17 finishes up with a quick look at what you can do to continue your journey of learning iOS development.

At the close of the book, two appendixes provide additional information to help you find your way around Xcode and Swift.

- Appendix A looks in detail at configuring your app with project settings.
- Appendix B helps you to adjust to programming in Swift with several Swift cheat sheets.

This book covers building a real iOS app from initial layout in chapter 6 to launching in the App Store in chapter 16. My hope is that watching the app develop over these chapters, and considering and solving problems that inevitably present themselves, will be an interesting and illuminating process for new iOS developers.

About the code

This book contains many examples of source code both in numbered listings and in-line with normal text. In both cases, source code is formatted in a `fixed-width font` `like this` to distinguish it from ordinary text. Sometimes code is also **in bold** to highlight code that has changed from previous steps in the chapter, such as when a new feature adds to an existing line of code.

In many cases, the original source code has been reformatted; I've added line breaks and reworked indentation to accommodate the available page space in the book. In rare cases, even this was not enough, and listings include line-continuation markers (➥). Additionally, comments in the source code have often been removed from the listings when the code is described in the text. Code annotations accompany many of the listings, highlighting important concepts.

Source code for the examples in this book is available in a GitHub repository at https://github.com/iOSAppDevelopmentwithSwiftinAction/. It is also available on the publisher's website at https://manning.com/books/ios-development-with-swift, and at the author's website for the book at http://iosdevelopmentwithswift.com/.

Note to print book readers

Some graphics in this book are best viewed in color. The eBook versions display the color graphics, so they should be referred to as you read. To get your free eBook in PDF, ePub, and Kindle formats, go to https://manning.com/books/ios-development-with-swift to register your print book.

Book forum

Purchase of *iOS Development with Swift* includes free access to a private web forum run by Manning Publications where you can make comments about the book, ask technical questions, and receive help from the author and from other users. To access the forum, go to https://forums.manning.com/forums/ios-development-with-swift-grummitt. You can also learn more about Manning's forums and the rules of conduct at https://forums.manning.com/forums/about.

Manning's commitment to our readers is to provide a venue where a meaningful dialogue between individual readers and between readers and the author can take place. It is not a commitment to any specific amount of participation on the part of the author, whose contribution to the forum remains voluntary (and unpaid). We suggest you try asking the author some challenging questions lest his interest stray! The forum and the archives of previous discussions will be accessible from the publisher's website as long as the book is in print.

about the author

CRAIG GRUMMITT is an interactive developer with more than 20 years of experience, from museum touchscreens to games, and from online learning to mobile apps. He has multiple successful apps in the iOS and Android App Stores under the moniker Interactive Coconut. He has a passion for mobile development and finding simple and concise ways to explain complex topics.

about the cover illustration

The caption for the illustration on the cover of *iOS Development with Swift* is "A Page of the Grand Signior." The illustration is taken from a collection of costumes of the Ottoman Empire published on January 1, 1802, by William Miller of Old Bond Street, London. The title page is missing from the collection, and we have been unable to track it down to date. The book's table of contents identifies the figures in both English and French, and each illustration bears the names of two artists who worked on it, both of whom would no doubt be surprised to find their art gracing the front cover of a computer programming book … 200 years later.

The collection was purchased by a Manning editor at an antiquarian flea market in the "Garage" on West 26th Street in Manhattan. The seller was an American based in Ankara, Turkey, and the transaction took place just as he was packing up his stand for the day. The Manning editor didn't have on his person the substantial amount of cash that was required for the purchase, and a credit card and check were both politely turned down. With the seller flying back to Ankara that evening, the situation was getting hopeless. What was the solution? It turned out to be nothing more than an old-fashioned verbal agreement sealed with a handshake. The seller proposed that the money be transferred to him by wire, and the editor walked out with the bank information on a piece of paper and the portfolio of images under his arm. Needless to say, we transferred the funds the next day, and we remain grateful and impressed by this unknown person's trust in one of us. It recalls something that might have happened a long time ago. We at Manning celebrate the inventiveness, the initiative, and, yes, the fun of the computer business with book covers based on the rich diversity of regional life of two centuries ago, brought back to life by the pictures from this collection.

Part 1

Introducing Xcode and Swift

Many people have ideas for awesome apps, but *you* have decided to do something about it, take the plunge and learn iOS app development. Congratulations and good luck on your journey!

Before you get too deep into the ins and outs of app development, you need to focus on foundation skills. In this part, you'll explore the development environment and learn about Apple's language for development in iOS, Swift.

In chapter 1, you'll examine Xcode, Apple's own software for building iOS apps. Then, in chapters 2 and 3, you'll take a lightning tour of what's new, different, and exciting in Swift. Chapter 2 focuses more on different syntax and data types, while chapter 3 takes a look at objects in Swift. You'll explore Swift in Xcode playgrounds, a tool that helps you focus purely on programming, without concerning yourself with app development.

Your first iOS application 1

This chapter covers

- Exploring the iOS SDK
- Creating a project in Xcode
- Exploring the Xcode interface
- Using Interface Builder and storyboards
- Running your app

In this chapter, you'll take your first look at *Xcode*, Apple's software for building iOS apps. You'll also build a basic first app, launch it on the iOS simulator, and then take a sneak peek at an app you'll build throughout this book.

1.1 *Exploring iOS SDK*

An app wouldn't be much use without access to the device. Storing files, playing sounds, displaying information on the screen, receiving touch events from the user—it's all achieved via the iOS SDK. Your app never directly accesses the hardware; instead, the iOS SDK provides abstraction layers for apps to access the underlying hardware.

Figure 1.1 shows the abstraction layers of the iOS SDK, from the higher-level services and features to the lowest-level interfaces. Table 1.1 has more details about what's contained in each layer.

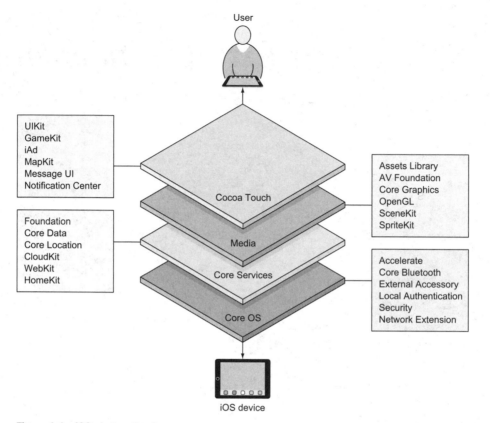

User

UIKit
GameKit
iAd
MapKit
Message UI
Notification Center

Cocoa Touch

Assets Library
AV Foundation
Core Graphics
OpenGL
SceneKit
SpriteKit

Foundation
Core Data
Core Location
CloudKit
WebKit
HomeKit

Media

Core Services

Accelerate
Core Bluetooth
External Accessory
Local Authentication
Security
Network Extension

Core OS

iOS device

Figure 1.1   iOS abstraction layers

Table 1.1   iOS SDK abstraction layers

Layer name	Description
Cocoa Touch	The Cocoa Touch layer provides the highest-level abstraction, and you'll use it frequently in iOS development. You can use frameworks in the Cocoa Touch layer to ■ Display, layout and animate your views ■ Recognize user touches and gestures ■ Recognize device motion ■ Display and lay out text ■ Display maps ■ Display user photos ■ Display web content ■ Send and receive push notifications ■ Share content

Table 1.1 iOS SDK abstraction layers

Layer name	Description
Media	The Media layer provides a lower level abstraction of graphics, video, and audio technologies. You can use frameworks in the Media layer to ■ Record and play back audio and video ■ Access and manipulate user photos ■ Display and animate 2D and 3D graphics
Core Services	Core Services goes even lower level, giving you access to features such as ■ Working with data in the cloud ■ Multi-threading ■ In-app purchases ■ Local data storage such as Core Data and SQLite ■ File sharing ■ HTML content
CoreOS	CoreOS provides the lowest-level layer. You're less likely to use this layer directly, but will use it indirectly frequently because other layers frequently traverse this layer to access the underlying hardware.

To access features in the iOS SDK in your code, you'll need to import the appropriate framework. Common frameworks available in each of the layers are listed in figure 1.1.

These are two commonly used frameworks in iOS app development:

- *UIKit framework of the Cocoa Touch layer*—Among the many features it provides are the basic architecture for your app and a library of standardized views and controls, and it manages user input. The UIKit is often imported by default, which in turn imports the Foundation framework by default.
- *Foundation framework of the Core Services layer*—Provides additional features and functionality for basic data types. Foundation also adds basic classes and utilities, such as URLs, timers, formatters, and notifications.

1.2 Creating an Xcode project

Now that you have an idea where everything fits together in the iOS SDK, how about using that information to create your first app?

To develop iOS apps, you first need to get your tools together:

- You need a Mac.
- You need to download Xcode (https://itunes.apple.com/us/app/xcode/id497799835?mt=12) for free from the App Store. Xcode is the integrated development environment (IDE) for building software for Apple products, including iOS apps.
- If you'd like to distribute your app on the App Store, you also need to join the Apple Developer Program (https://developer.apple.com/programs/).
- For testing purposes, you'll also probably want an iOS device such as an iPad or iPhone.

That's it! Let's get started exploring Xcode and building your first project!

To build an app in Xcode, the first thing you need is an Xcode project. An Xcode project is where you keep all your related source code, storyboards, frameworks, images, and resources related to the app.

Open Xcode and select Create a New Xcode Project on the Welcome to Xcode window, or select File > New > Project (see figure 1.2).

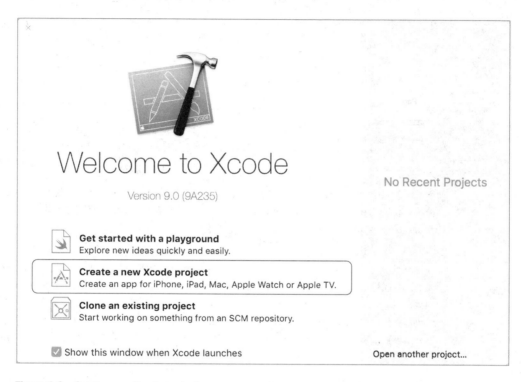

Figure 1.2   Create your Xcode project.

1.2.1   *Templates*

Similar to the way Microsoft Word has templates for resumes and letters or blank documents, Xcode provides templates for common app types. See figure 1.3.

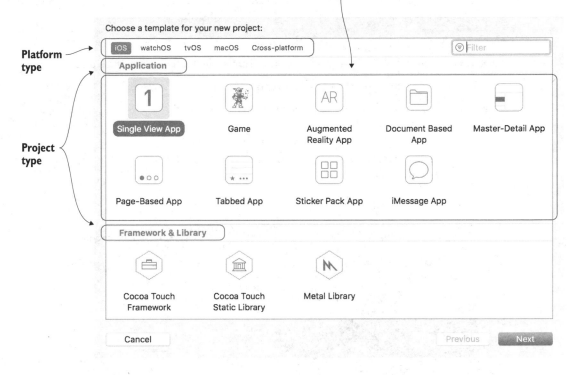

Figure 1.3 Xcode iOS templates

Using Xcode, you can build apps for iOS (iPads, iPhones, and iPod Touch), watchOS (Apple Watch), tvOS (Apple TV), or even macOS (Mac programs). Table 1.2 lists the application types available for your convenience.

Table 1.2 iOS application templates

Template type	Description
Single View Application	The simplest template available for iOS; the equivalent of a blank document in Word.
Game	Leads you down a different path, configuring your app to use one of several game frameworks built into iOS
Augmented Reality Application	Sets up your app to blend live video from the camera with animated objects using augmented reality
Document Based Application	Demonstrates loading a document using the document browser
Master-Detail Application	Configures your app with a split view, one way of customizing the presentation of your app's content, depending on whether you view it on an iPhone or iPad

Table 1.2   iOS application templates *(continued)*

Template type	Description
Page-Based Application	Adds a storybook design to the app with animated page turns
Tabbed Application	Adds a tab bar to the bottom of the app with two tabs preconfigured
Sticker Pack Application	Provides a sticker pack for use in iMessage
iMessage Application	Template for a sticker pack with additional features such as in-app billing

See figure 1.4 for examples of the applications some of these templates can help produce.

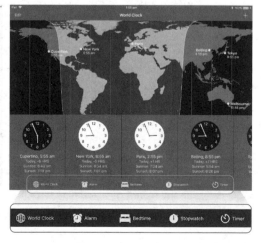

Figure 1.4   Applications from iOS templates

In this book, we'll focus on iOS development. To understand the inner workings of app development, we'll always start with a Single View Application. Not to worry, you can add pages, tabs, and master detail later. You can even use a Single View Application to create a game. Using this approach, you'll build up the boilerplate setup yourself and get a clearer understanding of what's happening under the hood!

Your next step is to select Single View Application, and then select Next.

1.2.2 *Project options*

Before you get to the fun part of playing with a project, you first have to set up its options. Fill in your project options similar to the example in figure 1.5. Table 1.3 explains these options in detail.

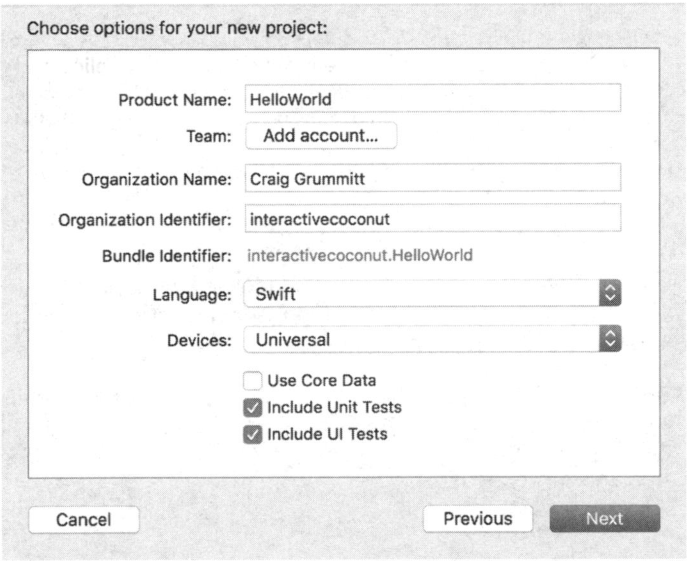

Figure 1.5 Xcode project options

Table 1.3 Project options

Option	Description
Product Name	Any name will do, but for a first project HelloWorld is tradition, after all.
Team	Even if you're a solo developer, your developer account with Apple is referred to as your *team*. You'll need a team later to test your app on your device and pay to join the Apple Developer Program for your app to use special services such as iCloud or distribute your app on the App Store. You're welcome to set up your Apple Developer account now if you like, but if you're keen to get stuck into playing with Xcode, feel free to leave this option. We'll look at teams and the Apple Developer Program in detail in chapter 16.
Organization Name	This is used to generate copyright strings in your code.

Table 1.3 Project options *(continued)*

Option	Description
Organization Identifier	This and the product name are used to generate the bundle identifier. By convention, to ensure it's unique, many developers use a reverse domain name for their organization identifier. More on the bundle identifier appears in the final chapter.
Language	You can still choose to develop your app in Swift's predecessor, Objective-C, for the foreseeable future. Choosing Swift or Objective-C doesn't preclude using the other; it's more an indication of which you're intending to use predominantly. In this book, we'll focus exclusively on development in Swift.
Devices	You can choose to develop only for iPad or iPhone, but if you want your app to work on both, you should choose Universal.
Core Data	Core Data is a framework for persisting complex data. Selecting it here adds boilerplate code that otherwise isn't necessary. Let's leave it deselected.
Unit/UI Tests	Selecting Include Unit and UI Tests sets up your project with targets to conveniently test your app's source code and interface. Taking advantage of these test targets to ensure your code is bug free and your app works as expected is a good habit to get into, especially as your apps become more complex. Let's leave these selected.

Project targets

An Xcode project contains one or more targets. An Xcode target contains all the specifications for building a specific product. A common target is an app. You can also have other targets for unit and UI testing.

Most commonly, one Xcode project contains one app target, but an Xcode project can have more. Pro and Lite versions of an app are a good example of where it would make sense for an Xcode project to contain two app targets, because the apps share many of their resources and codebase.

Move on to the next screen by selecting Next. Select a path for your project. You can check Create Git Repository on My Mac to enable version control for your application. This can be useful for keeping a record of revisions you make to your app, as well as later, when linking this repository to an online Git-hosting service such as GitHub.

Well done! You've created your first project! Now let's explore a little more.

1.3 *Exploring the Xcode interface*

When you first open Xcode, you can feel overwhelmed. It's a large and complex piece of software. You could work in Xcode for years and still discover new features. This book doesn't comprehensively cover Xcode, but it will get you well on the way on your journey of discovery, and to publishing your first app!

To keep things simple, let's divide the Xcode workspace into five parts (see figure 1.6). Let's briefly explore each of them.

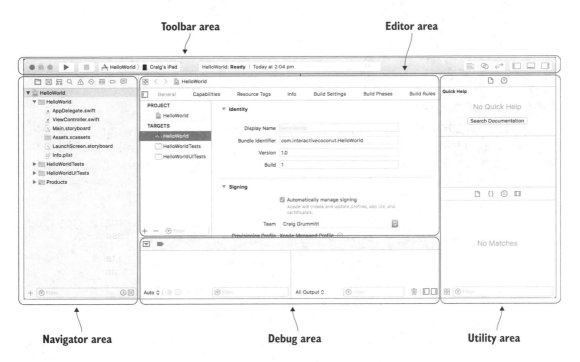

Figure 1.6   The Xcode interface

1.3.1   *Toolbar area*

The top bar of the Xcode window is known as the toolbar.
In the toolbar, you'll find

- View selector for showing or hiding views
- Editor selector for customizing the editor area
- The activity viewer for information about the current state of currently executing tasks and status messages
- App execution controls for playing and stopping your app, and for selecting the scheme to run and the simulator or device

See figure 1.7 for the Xcode toolbar.

Figure 1.7   The Xcode toolbar

1.3.2   Utility area

On the right, you'll find the utility area. The utility area includes the inspector pane and the objects pane. We'll look at these in more detail later in this chapter when we learn about Interface Builder.

1.3.3   Navigator area

On the left is the navigator area. Notice the eight icons in the bar at the top of the panel. These icons represent eight types of navigators that you can open in this area.

Tap on the icons now and check out each of the navigators. Table 1.4 briefly describes the navigators.

Table 1.4   Navigators

Navigator	Icon	Description
Project Navigator		Manage and navigate to files in your project
Source Control Navigator		Manage your project's source control repository
Symbol Navigator		Convenient way to navigate to classes, functions, and other objects in your project
Find Navigator		Find text anywhere in your project
Issue Navigator		Information on any current build warnings or build errors
Test Navigator		Information on any current unit tests or UI tests
Debug Navigator		Information on the current state of an app when execution is paused
Breakpoint Navigator		Navigate to and modify breakpoints
Log Navigator		A log of past builds of your app

You'll find yourself using certain navigators much more than others. Let's look now at the navigator you'll probably use the most, the Project Navigator. We'll come back to other navigators in later chapters.

PROJECT NAVIGATOR

The Project Navigator looks straightforward enough—it's like Finder, right? Well, not exactly. While it's true that you can navigate the files in your project using the Project Navigator, the files in the Project Navigator can be simplified versions of the file structure on disk. To illustrate this, right-click on the project name at the top of the Project Navigator and select Show in Finder to open your project in a Finder window (see figure 1.8).

For example, if you explore the Assets.xcassets icon in Finder, you'll see it has subfolders for each media asset it contains. Similarly, the LaunchScreen.storyboard and

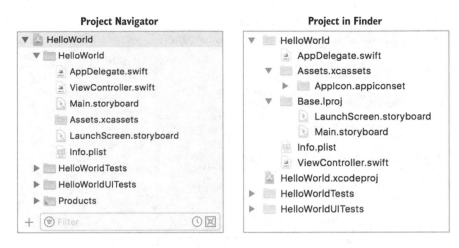

Figure 1.8 Project Navigator versus Project in Finder

Main.storyboard are contained in a special folder in Finder called Base.lproj. If you add other translations of your app, they will be contained in another folder.

You decide what files make up your project. Xcode starts off your project a certain way by default, but now you're in control of the structure of your project. The yellow icons in the Project Navigator are called *groups*. You can (and should) group related items in your Project Navigator to keep your project neatly organized. As your project grows, a well-organized project becomes more and more essential!

> **NOTE** In previous versions of Xcode, there was a disconnect between the groups contained in the Project Navigator and folders in Finder. Since Xcode 11, groups in the Project Navigator are by default synced with folders on disk. If you open a project set up in a previous version of Xcode, you may see a triangle in the corner of a group icon, indicating that it's not synced to a folder in Finder.

To practice organizing your project, right-click on ViewController.swift, and select New Group from Selection. Name the group ViewControllers.

1.3.4 Editor area

Focus now on the big panel in the center of the screen, called the editor area. The editor area looks different depending on what you have selected in the Project Navigator. When you create your project, the project itself is selected, which takes you straight to the project editor. We'll look at the project editor in more detail in appendix A, but for now, select other items in the Project Navigator and note the different types of editors that appear in the editor area. These editors include the following:

- *Project editor*—Use to edit settings for your project and target
- *Source editor*—Use to edit source code, such as Swift

- *Property list editor*—Use to edit property lists, recognizable by the .plist extension
- *Interface Builder*—Use to edit storyboards and nibs
- *Asset catalog editor*—Use to modify or add images in your app

Figure 1.9   Editor areas

See figure 1.9 for the appearance of some editor area types. (We'll look at Interface Builder in more detail shortly.)

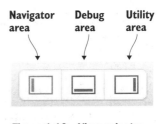

Figure 1.10   View selector

A lot goes on in the editor area. Press Command-0 and Option-Command-0 to hide the navigator and utility areas of the screen. Hiding these areas can be especially useful if you have limited screen space. If you prefer, you can also open and close these areas by tapping the relevant button in the view selector, at the right of the toolbar (figure 1.10). Open the navigator area again by clicking the Navigator toggle button.

> **TIP** You can find and customize all of the keyboard shortcuts in Xcode inside the Xcode > Preferences > Key Bindings menu.

You'll find that many panels in the Xcode interface have similar toggle buttons, including the debug area.

1.3.5   Debug area

If you select the Debug toggle button, a debug area opens below the editor area. The debug area contains controls for running your app, a pane where you can view variables, and a console for displaying output from your app or interacting with the debugger. You can also open and close the debug area with the keyboard shortcut Command-Shift-Y. We'll discuss debugging in more detail in chapter 15.

1.4   *Editing your app's interface*

You can edit your app's interface in code, but the easiest way to edit an interface is to build it up visually.

Click on Main.storyboard in the Project Navigator to open the main storyboard in the editor area.

1.4.1   *Storyboards and nibs*

Storyboards are used to visually define your app's user interface (UI) and the flow of navigation within your app. A storyboard contains scenes—screens or pages in your app. You can use one storyboard, or if you have a more complicated app, set up several interconnected storyboards.

The storyboard that's generated by default in a Single View Application couldn't be simpler—it only contains one scene. Most apps contain several interconnected scenes. These connections will be represented in the storyboard.

You may remember seeing another storyboard in your Project Navigator called LaunchScreen.storyboard. This storyboard represents a basic scene that displays while your app is loading. To ensure your launch screen loads quickly, this scene can't *do* anything other than display static images.

A related concept to the storyboard is the nib. A nib also represents a UI in a visual way, but only a single scene or view. It's typically instantiated from code. In general, storyboards have replaced the older nib approach.

1.4.2   View controllers and views

Everything that you see in your scene is a type of view (or is rendered within a view). Text fields, labels, buttons, switches, and images are all examples of types of views. Views can contain other views and be contained within other views. At the root of a scene is one parent view that contains everything visual in your scene.

If you have experience in programming, you'll most likely have come across the design pattern Model-View-Controller, where the view is separated from the model and the controller. We'll come back to this concept in chapter 4 when we look at models, but for now let's consider the view and the controller.

In iOS, the controller of your scene is called a *view controller*. The view controller is responsible for managing your scene's views. These responsibilities include the following:

- *Interaction with views*—The user can interact with particular view types, such as buttons and text fields. The view controller is responsible for responding to this interaction. In the login scene for the Facebook app, the view controller is responsible for responding when the user taps the Log In button. After successfully validating the login details, the view controller initiates navigation to the Facebook news feed scene.
- *Updating views*—Several view types, such as image views or table views, display content that might need updating from a data source. The view controller is responsible for updating these views. The Facebook news feed is an example of a view that would need updating.

We'll take a closer look at view controllers and views in chapter 4.

1.4.3   Interface Builder

Storyboards and nibs at their rawest are XML files. Unlike HTML, iOS developers rarely work directly with these XML files and instead use Interface Builder, a visual environment that Apple provides for editing your storyboards and nibs.

Close the navigator area on the left again (Command-0) and open the utility area on the right (Command-Alt-0) to fully appreciate the Interface Builder options available to you. Your screen should look something like figure 1.11.

When you first open your Single View Application storyboard, you'll see one scene on the canvas, represented by a view controller.

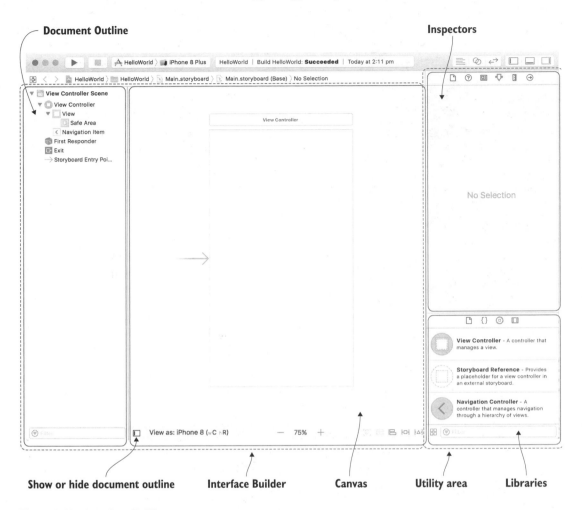

Document Outline

Inspectors

Show or hide document outline   Interface Builder   Canvas   Utility area   Libraries

Figure 1.11   Interface Builder

1.4.4   *Object Library*

On the right, you'll find the utility area. At the bottom of the utility area, you'll find the libraries pane. Open to the library you'll most likely use the most, the Object Library. (This is the third icon at the top of the libraries pane, and looks like a square inside a circle ). The Object Library contains a variety of different objects that you can add to the storyboard, including these:

- User interface elements
- View controllers
- Visual effects
- Gesture recognizers

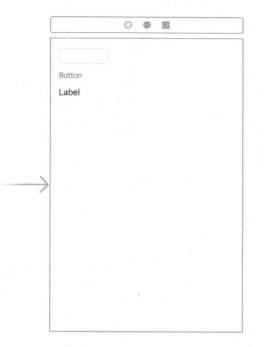

For fun, drag a text field, a button, and a label to the main scene's view, similar to figure 1.12. Notice blue guidelines appear to guide you. Try to follow these guidelines where possible, because they're recommendations from Apple about scene margins and distances between objects.

Figure 1.12   Simple interface

1.4.5   Document Outline

On the left of Interface Builder, you'll find the Document Outline. This gives you a representation of the hierarchy of all the elements in your storyboard (see table 1.5).

Table 1.5   Storyboard elements

Element	Description
View controller	Manager for a scene's views.
View	Visual components of your interface.
Safe area	An area of the root view that you can be confident is not obstructed by special views such as navigation bars. You can use safe area layout guides to help you lay out your views. (More on the safe area when we discuss auto layout in chapter 5.)
Constraint	Rules that define the layout of the views in a scene. (We'll discuss constraints more in chapter 5, too.)
Gesture recognizers	Helpers that detect common gestures. (We'll come back to these when we discuss user interaction in chapter 4.)
First responder	A first responder is the view in your scene that will be the first to receive any app events. Tapping on a text field, for example, will make it first responder. Use the first responder icon in Interface Builder to connect an action from a control to an action on the current first responder.
Exit	Customize behavior when exiting a scene. We'll explore this further when we learn about navigation in chapter 9.
Storyboard entry point	Indicates the initial scene for the storyboard.

If you added the objects in the previous section, your document outline should look something like figure 1.13. The elements you see in the main view are similar to layers in a Photoshop document, but with a difference—the top layer is shown at the bottom in the Document Outline. In our example, if the label and the button overlapped, the label would obscure part of the button. You can drag views around within the Document Outline to reorder them.

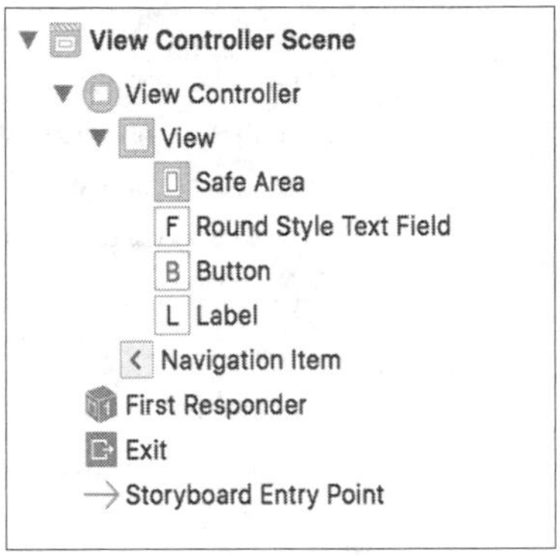

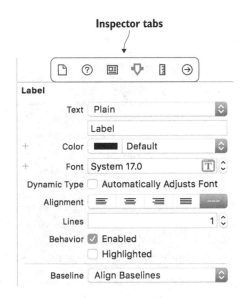

Figure 1.13   Document Outline

When your storyboard or UIs start to become complex and unwieldy, the Document Outline is a handy place to find and select views and view controllers. You can show or hide the Document Outline by clicking the relevant button at the bottom left of the canvas (), as you saw in figure 11.11.

1.4.6   Inspectors

At the top of the utility area on the right is where you'll find the inspectors. Similar to the navigator area, use the tabs at the top to select different inspectors. See figure 1.14.

These are not only useful in the storyboard; you'll find relevant inspectors available in all file types. With the storyboard open, you have the following inspectors available.

Figure 1.14   Inspectors

FILE INSPECTOR

Here, you can manage the metadata for the file, including which target it belongs to, whether it has been modified, and whether it has been localized.

Be sure to select one of the views in your scene so that you can see the details in the remaining inspectors.

HELP INSPECTOR

This inspector gives you context-specific help information about the element that's currently selected. It usually contains links to open the documentation if you want more-detailed reference information. Try it now—select the button in the scene and quick help should appear in the Help Inspector.

Select Class Reference (at the bottom of the documentation text, next to the label More) to open more-detailed information in the documentation. UIButton is the name of the class underlying all standard buttons, provided to you by Apple in the UIKit framework. You'll find the UIKit framework ubiquitous in iOS development—it's essential for working with the views, view controllers, events, animation, and a myriad of other functions within iOS.

Notice the detailed information in the documentation for UIButton:

- *Overview*—A description of how to use UIButton, including attributes you can configure in Interface Builder and accessibility and internationalization information.
- *Symbols*—Methods and properties available for UIButton, divided into related sections.
- *Relationships*—Classes that UIButton inherits from, and protocols that UIButton conforms to. Note that UIButton inherits from UIControl, which in turn inherits from UIView. We'll come back to controls in chapter 5, but for now it's sufficient to know that objects that expect user interaction, such as buttons, pickers, switches, and sliders, generally subclass UIControl. As you saw earlier, UI objects at their base are views, which is why they, in turn, subclass UIView.

> **TIP**   The File and Help Inspectors are always open regardless of the file you currently have open.

IDENTITY INSPECTOR

This is similar to the File Inspector, but in the Identity Inspector, you manage the metadata for the selected element in your storyboard. This includes the class name associated with the object, the ID, and accessibility details.

Select a view in the scene, and look at the class field in the Identity Inspector. Notice that the class name is grayed out, and begins with the prefix *UI*. This indicates that it isn't a custom class; rather, it's a class provided to you by Apple in the UIKit framework.

Now, select the view controller either in your Document Outline or by clicking on the yellow circle with a white square inside at the top of the scene in your storyboard.

Notice that the view controller class name is in a darker font, and doesn't begin with a prefix. This indicates that this element has been associated with a custom class that you can modify. This custom `ViewController` class subclasses Apple's built-in `UIViewController` class and comes as a default in the Single View Application template. You can find it in the ViewController.swift file in the Project Navigator. Don't worry if this isn't clear yet; it'll make more sense when we look further at subclassing `UIViewController` in chapter 4.

ATTRIBUTES INSPECTOR

In the Attribute Inspector, you can modify the attributes of an object, beyond the default values. For example, you could modify the text, font, alignment, and number of lines of a label. Try out the Attribute Inspector now by modifying the text of the label to "Hello World."

Select the button now and examine the attributes available to you. Notice that the attributes are divided into sections, following the same hierarchy you saw in the documentation earlier. First, attributes that are specific to buttons are listed, followed by attributes relevant to all controls, followed by attributes relevant to all views. Note that all views have the same attributes, such as background, alpha, tint, and whether it's hidden.

SIZE INSPECTOR

In this inspector, you can adjust the position and dimensions of an object. You can also modify any layout constraints you've applied to the object. We'll look more at constraints and auto layout in chapter 6.

CONNECTIONS INSPECTOR

Here, you'll find connections made between the storyboard and your view controller. These connections are called *outlets* and *actions*. We'll investigate these concepts further in chapters 4 and 5.

Building interfaces in Interface Builder vs. code

Interface Builder is a convenient tool for building up interfaces rapidly and visually. It has limitations, however, so many iOS developers often prefer to build their interfaces in Swift. There have been many discussions over the years about which is the best approach. Be aware when reading over any older posts on this topic online that Apple has improved many limitations with storyboards and Interface Builder over the last few years. Here are several pros and cons of both approaches.

Building interfaces in Interface Builder

Pros:

- Simple and fast to use.
- Easier to build interfaces visually.
- Apple's recommended approach.

Cons:

- Resolving conflicts in revision control can be a headache.
- Some dynamic designs are impossible in Interface Builder.

Building interfaces in code

Pros:

- Greater control, making dynamic designs more possible.
- Resolving conflicts in revision control is less of a problem.

Cons:

- Interfaces need to be built without visual feedback.
- More complicated and time consuming.

In the end, the approach you take is up to your personal preferences and the best solution for each specific situation. We'll look at building up views in code in more detail in chapters 6 and 7.

Xcode is the main tool you'll use to build apps in iOS, and it's a good idea to begin familiarizing yourself with it. One short chapter can't cover all facets of this huge and complex program, but after investing some time in exploring Xcode while going through this book, you should develop a level of comfort in the tool and be building apps of substance. You'll get there soon!

1.5 Running your app

Now that you've created an app and are more familiar with the Xcode interface, let's run the app to see what it looks like!

You have two broad options for where to run your app: on a device or the simulator.

1.5.1 Running your app on a device

Nothing beats running your app on the device, for several reasons:

- *True interaction*—It's in your hand! You can touch, swipe, and pinch your app the way your users will—with their fingers.
- *True experience*—These days, simulators reproduce the iOS environment quite well, but never perfectly. On the device, you can be sure you're seeing how a real-world environment responds to your app, including memory and CPU restrictions.
- *Necessity*—Certain features are unavailable or unreliable on a simulator, such as the accelerometer, camera, microphone, push notifications, and external accessories. To test these features you need to use a physical device. For a full and up-to-date list, check "API Differences" and "Hardware Differences" on Apple's Testing and Debugging in Simulator page (https://developer.apple.com/library/content/documentation/IDEs/Conceptual/iOS_Simulator_Guide/Testingon-theiOSSimulator/TestingontheiOSSimulator.html).

It's a good idea to invest in at least one device, if you haven't already. Before submitting your app to the App Store, it's imperative to experience your app the way the end user will.

1.5.2 Running your app in the simulator

It's also important to run your app in different environments. From iPhone 4S to iPad Pro, you have many points of difference to test, including dimensions, Retina and non-Retina, CPU speed, and memory availability. At the time of writing, 18 iOS simulators are available by default for testing your app in different simulated environments. If you want to be thorough, it's quite an investment to get your hands on all possible physical devices.

Simulators make testing your app in a variety of different environments, and even iOS versions, as easy as choosing an option in a menu. The simulator is indispensable for getting quick feedback as to how your app looks and operates in different device environments.

1.5.3 *Running your app*

In the Xcode workspace toolbar, you'll find the Run and Stop buttons. Tapping the Run button automatically builds the selected scheme in the selected destination (see figure 1.15).

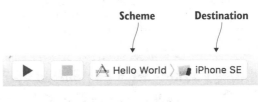

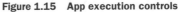

Figure 1.15   App execution controls

The scheme specifies which target you wish to test, along with any other configuration of the build. Your project comes with a scheme preconfigured to test your project's main target.

The destination is where you can choose a device or a simulator to test your app. You can also add an additional simulator in the Devices window. Xcode comes preconfigured with a simulator for every available device in the latest version of iOS. If you'd like to test your app in an earlier version of iOS, you can add a simulator specifying iOS version. You need to download the sizable simulator app for that version.

1.5.4 *Simulator features*

Though hardware-specific features such as accelerator and gyroscope aren't available on the simulator, other features are available either in the Simulator menu or as keyboard shortcuts.

When you open the Simulator and select the Hardware menu, you'll find several actions available that would otherwise be difficult to perform on a simulator, such as rotating the device, shaking the device, or tapping the device's Home button. You can connect your Mac's keyboard in the Hardware menu for convenience rather than using the simulator's software keyboard. You can even simulate two fingers in the simulator by holding down Alt (great for simulated pinching).

Run your app in the simulator now. Leave the scheme and the simulator at their defaults and select the Play button. You should see the objects you created in Interface Builder appear in the simulator. Success, you've made your first (albeit basic) app! See figure 1.16. (Depending on your Mac's screen resolution, you may need to reduce your app's scale in the simulator's Window menu to see it all at once.)

Figure 1.16   Your first app in the simulator!

This app doesn't *do* anything yet. To add more complexity to your apps, you'll first need to add code, and in this book we'll do that with Swift. Let's peek at a completed app.

1.6   *Peeking at a completed app*

How awesome are books? Well, you must agree, you're reading one right now! I don't know about you, but I find it difficult to keep track of my books. What books do I have again? Where is that Jostein Gaarder book I read in university? In the bookcase in the lounge room? Stored in the attic? Did Albert borrow it? Or maybe I imagined the whole thing?

Throughout this book, you're going to build an entire app from start to finish that will help users keep track of their books. Users will enter the author's name, book title, and notes about each book, or—and this is where it gets fancy—they'll use the handy barcode scanning feature, which will automatically generate the details for each book. We'll call this app *Bookcase*. Let's take a sneak peek of what the finished app looks like right now. We'll also peek at programming in Swift by making a small change to the code.

1.6.1   *Checking out a repository in Xcode*

To download the app, you'll use Xcode's version control, which is built right into the IDE.

You can easily download (or *check out*) a project repository (or *repo*) from an online source such as GitHub. Check out the finished Bookcase app with the following steps:

1 Select Source Control > Clone.
2 Enter the URL of the repository in the text field. In this case, paste in https://github.com/iOSAppDevelopmentwithSwiftinAction/Bookcase.git.
3 Navigate to where you'd like to download the repo locally, and select Clone.

Easy, right? The repo should now open up in Xcode and be available on your local drive.

> **NOTE**   Watch for *Checkpoint* callouts distributed throughout this book. These are points where you can either download a project already set up for you or compare your code with mine at the same point.

1.6.2   *Peeking at the completed app's storyboard*

Let's peek at the Bookcase app's storyboard. Select the Main.storyboard file in the Project Navigator and the storyboard should appear in Interface Builder (see figure 1.17). At a glance, you can get an idea of the flow of navigation, that the app has a tab bar controller and several navigation controllers; you can see that one scene contains a table view, and get an idea of the UI.

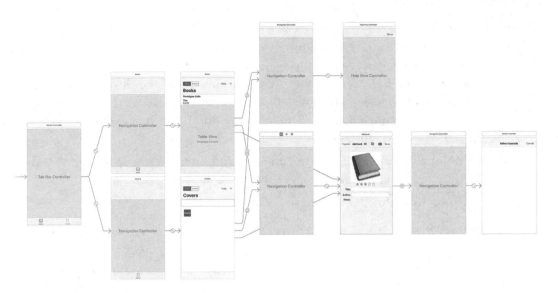

Figure 1.17   Bookcase app storyboard

1.6.3   Tweaking the code

Sometimes, when you're working on an application, you might make use of test data to get an idea of how the app will look in the real world after the user enters real data. Because this app is finished now, it's time to remove this test data. See figure 1.18 to see how the first scene of the app looks with the test data, and how you want it to look when it's published to the App Store.

Figure 1.18   The app with and without test data

Let's remove the test data and take our first peek at Swift code in action:

1 Open the Project Navigator and notice the Model group. This is where code that manages all data in the application is kept.

2 Open the BooksManager.swift file. This file contains Swift code that's responsible for managing the book data.

3 Find the sampleBooks method. This method returns the sample data. (Methods start with the keyword `func`.)

When the app is published to the App Store and a new user opens the app for the first time, this method should no longer return sample data.

4 Modify the method to return a blank array:

```
func sampleBooks()->[Book] {
    return []
}
```

Run the app for the first time in the simulator. If all has gone to plan, it should open with a clean slate, ready for the user to enter their own books into the app.

> **NOTE** Because this app stores its data locally, this change to the sample data only affects the user experience the first time they run the app. If you've already run the app on the simulator and want to simulate running it again for the first time, you can either delete the app or select Simulator > Reset Content and Settings.

✔ **CHECKPOINT** If you'd like to compare your project with mine at this point, you can check out mine in the Chapter1.2.Complete branch. To change branches, open the Source Control Navigator, and find the remote branch in Remotes/Origin. Right-click (or two-finger tap if you're using the trackpad), and select Checkout. If you've made changes in this branch, Xcode will request that you either commit or discard those changes before changing branches. Select Source Control > Discard all Changes to discard your changes.

Well, that's given you a small taste of Swift in an Xcode project. In the next two chapters, we'll cover a crash course in Swift, and the best place to do that is the playground!

1.7 *Summary*

In this chapter, you learned the following:

- The iOS SDK contains several abstraction layers of services and features, including the Cocoa Touch layer.
- The abstraction layers of the iOS SDK contain frameworks that Apple provides, such as the ubiquitous UIKit.

- The Xcode interface includes the navigator area, editor area, and the utility area, which is composed of libraries and inspectors.
- Use Interface Builder to edit a storyboard.
- Everything you can see in a scene is a type of view or rendered within a view.
- View controllers manage views, interact with them, and update them.
- Use the simulator to test your app quickly on a variety of different device types, but be sure to test your app on a device as well.

Introduction to Swift playgrounds

This chapter covers

- Exploring Xcode playgrounds
- Using type safety in Swift
- Understanding simple Swift data types
- Working with collections and tuples in Swift
- Working with optionals

Swift isn't JavaScript without the semicolons or Objective-C without the square brackets. Swift is inspired by new philosophies and approaches to programming that have driven its design and evolution.

Even the most experienced programmers will encounter new concepts and syntax in Swift. In this chapter and the next, I assume that you have experience in programming and are mainly interested in what's new, different, and exciting about Swift. I'll also discuss how concepts in Swift relate to shifts in programming philosophy.

After looking at data types and collection types in Swift, we'll look at a type that may be new to many: the optional. The optional, tied closely to the idea of type safety in Swift, can be unfamiliar at first, but do stick with it—the optional is essential to understanding programming in Swift.

There's much to look at in Swift, but don't worry; as you progress in the book, or for those of you who may already have some experience with Swift, you can always refer to the cheat sheets in appendix B. This chapter is summarized in the first two pages of the cheat sheets.

2.1   Xcode playground

When Apple introduced Swift, they also introduced a special environment in Xcode called the Swift Playground. In a playground, you can experiment and play with Swift concepts and syntax, without the distractions of peripheral concerns such as the architecture of your project, storyboards, or the simulator.

A programmer new to Swift has new syntax and concepts to discover and explore. In addition to the current body of Swift concepts, updates to the language occur reasonably frequently, with more to learn and discover.

An Xcode project can be an unwieldy environment if all you want to do is explore a new Swift concept. As you've seen, a project comes by default with all sorts of additional files, and if you want to see the result of a short code block, you first need to build your project and run it on either a simulator or a device. If, for example, all you want to do is explore how dictionaries work in Swift, this process is overkill. Playgrounds solve this problem by simplifying the environment.

Create a playground now by selecting either Get Started With a Playground on the Xcode welcome screen, or by selecting File > New > Playground.

You should see a playground appear with default code (see figure 2.1).

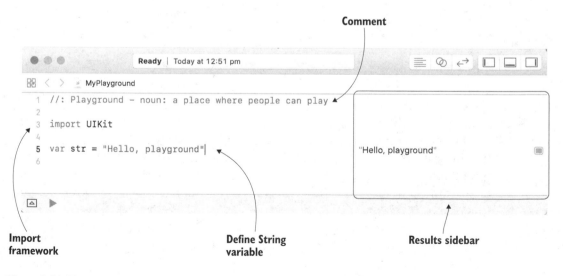

Figure 2.1   Playground

You'll notice the value of your `str` variable, `"Hello, playground"`, appears in the area on the right side of the playground. This area shows the result of each line of code, and is called the results sidebar.

2.1.1 Results sidebar

The results sidebar is a feature playgrounds have that Xcode projects don't—use it to view the result of every line of your code. In the default playground, you can see the result of initializing the "Hello, playground" string in the sidebar. If you aim your mouse pointer at the line containing the result, you'll see two additional buttons that give you two additional techniques for viewing the result.

QUICK LOOK

If you tap the eye button, the result appears in a bubble pop-up called a Quick Look. This obviously isn't necessary for the default string, but could in other circumstances give you additional information that isn't available or doesn't fit in the limited space in the sidebar (see figure 2.2).

"Hello, playground"   Hello, playground

Figure 2.2   Quick Look

SHOW RESULT

If you tap the filled, rounded, rectangle button a result view is anchored directly below the line of code. Tap the same button to remove the Show Result view again.

Quick Look and Show Result go beyond text information that you see in the sidebar, giving you useful visual representations of the result. You can display UI views and controls, visualize images and colors, and graph numeric calculations in `for` loops.

See figure 2.3 for examples of visual result views.

Result views of URL variables even give you a preview of the web page at that URL! Add a URL variable to your playground, with your own URL:

```
var url = NSURL(string: "http://www.craiggrummitt.com")
```

Note how the string of the URL appears in the results sidebar.

Tap the Quick Look and Show Result buttons and note how your actual website is rendered in the Show Result view.

**Graph of for
loop calculation**   **Representation
of color**

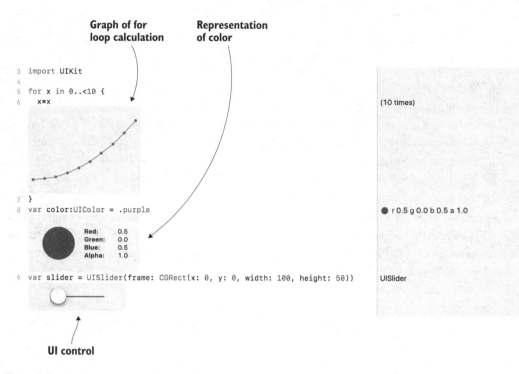

```
3  import UIKit
4
5  for x in 0..<10 {
6     x*x



7  }
8  var color:UIColor = .purple


   Red:    0.5
   Green:  0.0
   Blue:   0.5
   Alpha:  1.0


9  var slider = UISlider(frame: CGRect(x: 0, y: 0, width: 100, height: 50))
```

(10 times)

● r 0.5 g 0.0 b 0.5 a 1.0

UISlider

UI control

Figure 2.3   Examples of visual result views

2.1.2   *Automatic compiling*

Note how the results automatically appeared in the results sidebar, and you didn't have to request the playground to run. By default, playgrounds automatically compile and run after every change you make, meaning you don't need to do anything to see the results of your code immediately. Occasionally, in a large or complex playground, these constant compilations can cause your playground to slow down or even crash Xcode. If you prefer to manually request your playground to run, hold your mouse button down over the Play button, and choose Manually Run. The Play button toggles to an outline, and the playground switches to run only when you press Play (see figure 2.4).

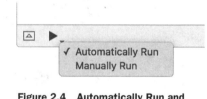

✓ Automatically Run
   Manually Run

Figure 2.4   Automatically Run and Manually Run

2.1.3   *Console*

As with Xcode projects, playgrounds have access to a console. If you'd like to go old-school when visualizing the results of your code, you can use the console, for example, to display results of the `print` function. Use the `print` function to display the `str` variable:

```
print(str)
```

Tap the arrow in a rectangle at the bottom left of the playground to open (or close) the console. You should see the value of the string in the console (see figure 2.5).

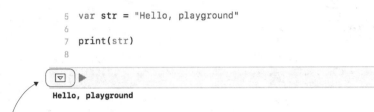

Show/Hide console

Figure 2.5   Playground console

Occasionally, a runtime error can occur that isn't anticipated by the compiler and leaves your playground unresponsive or not working as expected. In these cases, it pays to check the console to see if an error was reported there.

Now that you're more familiar with playgrounds, you're ready to use them to begin exploring Swift concepts.

Where we explore Swift concepts in this book, you'll find links to playgrounds to follow along with the text. You can also experiment in your own playground. No need to worry about saving playgrounds, Xcode keeps them saved automatically!

Let's get started!

2.2   *Type safety and type inference*

One of the key philosophies of Swift is safety, and one of the key components of safety in Swift is type safety. Type safety ensures that all variables are defined with a specific type. After a variable is defined as a specific data type, it can't later store values of a different data type. A `String` variable, for example, can never contain an `Int` value.

> ✓ **CHECKPOINT**   You might prefer to examine the code listings in this section in the TypeInference.playground. You can download all the code for this chapter by selecting Source Code > Clone and entering the repository location: https://github.com/iOSAppDevelopmentwithSwiftinAction/Chapter2.

But wait—when you create a playground, by default you have a variable `str` containing a string value, but the data type isn't mentioned in the definition. How could this be?

If you leave the data type out of the definition, Swift determines the data type of the variable using a process called *type inference*. If Swift has enough information to infer the correct type, this is as safe as specifically defining the data type. You can confirm the type that has been inferred for your variable by holding down the Alt key and clicking on the variable (see figure 2.6).

```
5   var str = "Hello, playground"
        Declaration   var str: String
        Declared In   MyPlayground.playground
```

Variable definition

Figure 2.6   Press Alt and click on the variable to see an inferred variable's data type.

Usually you can leave out the data type when you define a variable and let Swift infer the data type for you—in fact, it's good practice. There are cases, however, where you'll need to define a variable's data type.

- Sometimes, you want to declare a variable without passing a value to it yet. Xcode doesn't have a value to infer the variable's data type, so it needs to be specified in the definition:

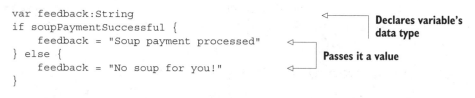

```
var feedback:String
if soupPaymentSuccessful {
    feedback = "Soup payment processed"
} else {
    feedback = "No soup for you!"
}
```

Declares variable's data type

Passes it a value

- Sometimes, the data type that Xcode infers isn't the data type you intended. For example, if you define a number without a decimal component, it will be inferred to be of data type `Int`. You may prefer it to be defined as a number with a decimal component, known as `Double`, so that you can easily perform calculations with other decimal numbers.

  If you declare the data type, Xcode will better understand your intention:

Clarifies data type as Double

```
var quantitySoup:Double = 2
var priceSoup = 2.99
var total = quantitySoup * priceSoup
```

Double is inferred

This example explicitly specifies that you want the data type of quantity to be inferred as a Double. If you don't do this, quantity is automatically inferred to be an Int, and calculations between an Int and a Double aren't permitted without converting the data type of one of the variables.

> **TIP** An alternative to clarifying the data type in the declaration is giving extra hints in the value as to the data type to be inferred. In the code snippet, you could have declared the quantity as 3.0, and it would have been inferred as a Double.

2.2.1 Converting numeric types

Because performing calculations between numbers of different types isn't permitted, sometimes data type conversion is necessary. To divide an Int from a Double, for example, you first need to convert the Int to a Double, as shown in the following listing.

Listing 2.1 Convert Int to a Double

```
var restaurantRent = 809.10      ⟵─── Inferred as Double
var daysInMonth = 31
var dailyRent = restaurantRent / daysInMonth          ⟵── Error. Double can't be divided by Int.
var dailyRent = restaurantRent / Double(daysInMonth)  ⟵── Converts Int to Double to divide it
```

Inferred as Int → (applies to `restaurantRent` and `daysInMonth`)

Here's a question for you: in the following listing, what's the value of slicesPer-Person?

Listing 2.2 How many pizza slices per person?

```
var totalPizzaSlices = 8
var numberOfPeople = 3
var slicesPerPerson = totalPizzaSlices / numberOfPeople
```

Try it out in the playground. You'll find that slicesPerPerson is equal to 2. All I can say is that I hope I'm third in line for pizza slices, and I get whatever's left!

Be aware of this common pitfall. The result of an equation will be the same data type as the data types in the equation. If you divide one Int from another Int, your answer is an Int. If you want the answer to be a Double, you need to ensure you first convert your Int variables to Doubles:

```
var slicesPerPerson = Double(totalPizzaSlices) / Double(numberOfPeople)
```

> **NOTE** Several other number data types are available. For example, you'll also find an unsigned integer data type called UInt, and a data type called Float that has a decimal component, but with much smaller precision than Double. Unless you have a good reason to do otherwise, it's best to use an Int and Double for compatibility and to minimize data type conversion.

2.2.2   *Concatenating strings*

You may be used to using the addition symbol to generate a `String` from two values.

```
var name = "Jerry"
var message = "Welcome " + name
```

As Swift is type safe, concatenating `Strings` in this way only works if every element being concatenated is a `String`. A `String` and a `Double`, for example, by default don't concatenate. In the following example, `cost` is inferred to be a `Double`, so concatenating it with a `String` produces an error:

```
var cost = 3.50
var message = "Your meal costs $" + cost          ◁── Error
```

You have two options to generate a `String` with mixed types:

- *Convert a data type*—In any situation where you want two different data types to interact, you can convert one of them to be the same data type as the other. In the following code, you can add the `cost` variable by converting it to a `String`:

  ```
  var message = "Your meal costs $" + String(cost)
  ```

- *String interpolation*—A much cleaner and easier-to-read approach is a technique called string interpolation. Using string interpolation, you can integrate variables or expressions into the body of your `String`, surrounding it with a backslash and a pair of parentheses:

  ```
  var message = "Your meal costs $\(cost)"
  ```

2.3   *Collections*

Swift has three main data types for storing different types of collections: arrays, sets, and dictionaries. In keeping with Swift's type-safe philosophy, collections are only permitted to store values of a specific data type. You can either specify the type when you declare the collection, or let Swift infer the type by analyzing all its elements when you instantiate it.

> **OPEN** Follow along in the Collections.playground.

2.3.1   *Arrays*

An `Array` stores values of the same data type in an ordered list. The following listing shows common `Array` syntax in Swift.

> **NOTE** Constants are declared with the `let` keyword.

Listing 2.3 Using arrays

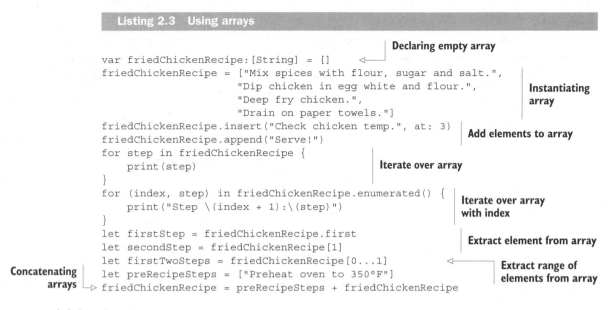

```
var friedChickenRecipe:[String] = []          ⟵  Declaring empty array
friedChickenRecipe = ["Mix spices with flour, sugar and salt.",
                      "Dip chicken in egg white and flour.",         Instantiating
                      "Deep fry chicken.",                           array
                      "Drain on paper towels."]
friedChickenRecipe.insert("Check chicken temp.", at: 3)
friedChickenRecipe.append("Serve!")            Add elements to array
for step in friedChickenRecipe {
    print(step)                                Iterate over array
}
for (index, step) in friedChickenRecipe.enumerated() {   Iterate over array
    print("Step \(index + 1):\(step)")                   with index
}
let firstStep = friedChickenRecipe.first
let secondStep = friedChickenRecipe[1]         Extract element from array
let firstTwoSteps = friedChickenRecipe[0...1]  ⟵  Extract range of
let preRecipeSteps = ["Preheat oven to 350°F"]    elements from array
friedChickenRecipe = preRecipeSteps + friedChickenRecipe
```

Concatenating arrays

2.3.2 Sets

A `Set` stores values of the same data type in an unordered list. As the items in a `Set` have no order, `Array` concepts such as subscripts, indices, and duplicate values are meaningless. After instantiating a `Set` of values, take note in the results sidebar that the elements are probably not displaying in the order they were defined, further illustrating that `Sets` don't maintain a defined order. The following listing shows common `Set` syntax.

Listing 2.4 Using sets

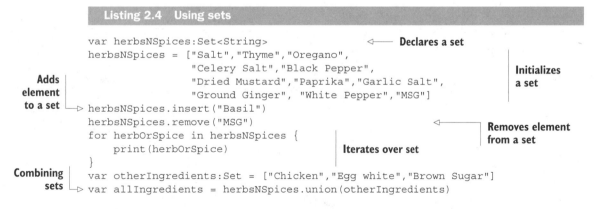

```
var herbsNSpices:Set<String>                   ⟵  Declares a set
herbsNSpices = ["Salt","Thyme","Oregano",
                "Celery Salt","Black Pepper",          Initializes
                "Dried Mustard","Paprika","Garlic Salt",   a set
                "Ground Ginger", "White Pepper","MSG"]
herbsNSpices.insert("Basil")
herbsNSpices.remove("MSG")                     ⟵  Removes element
for herbOrSpice in herbsNSpices {                 from a set
    print(herbOrSpice)
}                                              Iterates over set
var otherIngredients:Set = ["Chicken","Egg white","Brown Sugar"]
var allIngredients = herbsNSpices.union(otherIngredients)
```

Adds element to a set

Combining sets

In addition to union, `Sets` can be combined in creative ways, with the `intersection`, `symmetricDifference`, and `subtracting` methods.

2.3.3 Dictionaries

Like sets and arrays, a `Dictionary` stores a series of values. Where the values in an `Array` are referenced by an index, the values in a `Dictionary` are referenced by a key. For example, a series of language names could be referenced by a three-letter language code. Like a `Set`, a `Dictionary` is unordered.

Listing 2.5   Using dictionaries

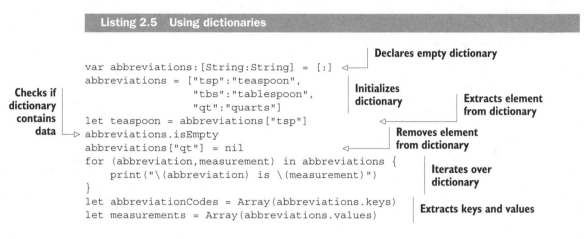

```
var abbreviations:[String:String] = [:]          Declares empty dictionary
abbreviations = ["tsp":"teaspoon",
                 "tbs":"tablespoon",             Initializes
                 "qt":"quarts"]                  dictionary        Extracts element
let teaspoon = abbreviations["tsp"]                                from dictionary
abbreviations.isEmpty
abbreviations["qt"] = nil                         Removes element
for (abbreviation,measurement) in abbreviations { from dictionary
    print("\(abbreviation) is \(measurement)")    Iterates over
}                                                 dictionary
let abbreviationCodes = Array(abbreviations.keys)
let measurements = Array(abbreviations.values)    Extracts keys and values
```

Checks if dictionary contains data

Concatenating two dictionaries is, strangely, not available in Swift. In the next chapter, you'll add this functionality to Swift by extending the `Dictionary` type.

2.4 Control Flow

As you'd expect, Swift has several standard approaches for controlling the flow of a program. Several, such as the `if` statement, or `while`, should be familiar enough, as you can see in the following code listing.

OPEN   Follow along in the ControlFlow.playground.

Listing 2.6   `if`, `else`, and `while` statements

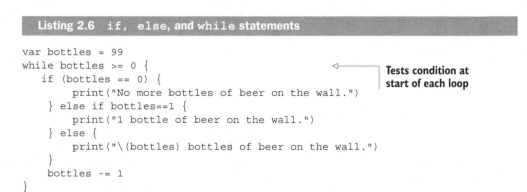

```
var bottles = 99
while bottles >= 0 {                                      Tests condition at
    if (bottles == 0) {                                   start of each loop
        print("No more bottles of beer on the wall.")
    } else if bottles==1 {
        print("1 bottle of beer on the wall.")
    } else {
        print("\(bottles) bottles of beer on the wall.")
    }
    bottles -= 1
}
```

NOTE You can also test a condition at the end of each loop with the `repeat-while` loop. Note also that parentheses around the condition of an `if` statement are optional. Braces around an `if` statement's block of code, on the other hand, are never optional in Swift.

Other control-flow approaches, such as `for-in` and `switch`, may be worth taking a closer look to familiarize yourself with any differences in Swift.

2.4.1 *for-in*

Swift has two main `for-in` loop approaches. You've already seen that you can use a `for-in` loop to iterate over the elements of a collection. A second type of `for-in` loop can loop over a range, using the `range` operator, as shown in the following listing.

Listing 2.7 `for-in` **loop with** `range`

```
for index in 1...3 {
    print("\(index) banana")
}
```

You saw the `range` operator earlier, when you used it to extract a range of elements from an `Array`. You'll explore another use of `range` in a `switch` statement in a moment.

There are two main types of ranges, as explained in table 2.1.

Table 2.1 Ranges

Type	Example	Description
Closed	`1...3` (1,2,3)	A range of values, including the second number
Half-open	`1..<3` (1,2)	A range of values, excluding the second number

The easiest way to remember the difference is that the half-open range ends when it's less than (<) the second number.

To reverse a range, you need to call its `reversed` method. For example, `(0..<100).reversed()` creates a range from 99 down to 0.

You can also omit one side of the range to make a *one-sided* range that will continue as far as possible on the side with the omitted value. This can be useful for iterating over elements of a collection, for example, until the final element in the collection.

```
var numbers = [0,1,2,3,4]
for i in numbers[3...] {        ⟵———  Iterates until final element
  print(i)                      ⟵———  Prints 3 and 4
}
```

Wait, isn't something missing?

In addition to what's in Swift, you might be interested to know what's *not* in Swift that you may be accustomed to in other languages.

Two missing operators that might surprise you are the increment (++) and decrement (--) operators. Swift is an evolving language, and these operators weren't forgotten; they were intentionally removed from Swift in Swift 3. You can read the arguments for their removal in the Swift evolution document at https://github.com/apple/swift-evolution/blob/master/proposals/0004-remove-pre-post-inc-decrement.md.

Similarly, you may be accustomed to the C-style `for` loop in other languages. For simplicity, this type of `for` loop was deprecated in Swift 3:

```
for(var i=0;i<10;i++)        ◁──────  RIP C-style for loop
```

Again, if you're interested, you can read the evolution proposal for this change at https://github.com/apple/swift-evolution/blob/master/proposals/0007-remove-c-style-for-loops.md.

2.4.2   *switch statement*

Most likely, you're also familiar with the `switch` statement, which is used for comparing one value against multiple values. Note the several points of difference, though, between `switch` statements in Swift and in many other languages:

- Swift by default *does not* drop down to the next case. This means that the `break` statement after every case isn't necessary in Swift.
- Every case *must* contain executable statements. If you want two cases to share the same executable statements, you can make a compound case by separating the cases with a comma.
- You can compare a value in a case to a range; this is called *interval matching*.
- Switches must be exhaustive. If you want a case to signify "the rest" to make the case exhaustive, use the `default` keyword, as shown in the following listing.

Listing 2.8   `switch` statement

```
for bottle in (0..<100).reversed() {
    switch bottle {
    case 0:
        print("No more bottles of beer on the wall.")      ◁────  No break necessary
    case 1:
        print("1 bottle of beer on the wall.")
    case 2...100:                                           ◁────  Interval
        print("\(bottle) bottles of beer on the wall.")            matching
    default:
        print("Something went wrong! ")                     ◁────  Default makes the
    }                                                              switch exhaustive
}
```

2.5 Functions

Functions in Swift are defined with the `func` keyword, followed by a list of parameters in parentheses, and an optional return value indicated by an arrow (hyphen and right angle bracket), as shown in the following listing.

 OPEN Follow along in the Functions.playground.

> **Listing 2.9 Function syntax**

```
func serve(drink: String, customer: String) -> String {
    return("\(customer), your \(drink) is served")
}
```

Now that you have a `serve` function, you can call it by passing it a drink and a customer:

```
print( serve(drink: "beer", customer: "Billy") )
```

Note that by default you need to pass in the names of the parameters when calling the function. It's possible, however, to modify these names.

2.5.1 Modifying external parameter names

Sometimes, you might want your parameter names when calling the function to be different from the parameter names within the function. Swift makes this possible by distinguishing between local and external parameter names.

In listing 2.9, for example, you could make it extra clear to someone calling the function that they're serving the drink *to* the customer by renaming the external parameter name `to`. In addition to reasons of clarity, this has the added benefit of satisfying the Swift API design guidelines that method and parameter names should preferably use "grammatical English phrases."

Local and external parameter names are the same by default. To split the parameter name into two, specify the external parameter name followed by the local parameter name, as in the following listing.

> **Listing 2.10 Modify external parameter name**

```
func serve(drink: String, to customer: String) -> String {
    return("\(customer), your \(drink) is served")
}
```

While the customer parameter within the function would continue to be referred to as `customer`, the call to the function is now much closer to grammatical English:

```
print( serve(drink: "beer", to: "Billy") )
```

But wait—you wouldn't say "Serve *drink* beer to Billy," would you? This function call could sound even closer to grammatical English by omitting the drink parameter name.

2.5.2 *Omitting external parameter names*

If you prefer a function to be called without specifying a parameter name, you can replace the external parameter name with an underscore: _.

An explicit external parameter name for the drink parameter is probably not necessary. Remove it with an underscore before the parameter, as follows.

Listing 2.11 Omit external parameter name

```
func serve(_ drink: String, to customer: String) -> String {
    return("\(customer), your \(drink) is served")
}
```

Your call to your function now sounds much cleaner:

```
print( serve("beer", to: "Billy") )
```

If you read it back, it now sounds close enough to grammatical English: "Serve beer to Billy." Nice!

2.5.3 *Default parameter names*

Billy is such a regular at your restaurant that you could save time and make him the default. In fact, he always drinks beer, so let's make that the default too.

Function parameters can define default values, as in the following listing.

Listing 2.12 Default parameter name

```
func serve(_ drink: String = "Beer",
        to customer:String = "Billy") -> String {
    return("\(customer), your \(drink) is served")
}
```

A parameter with a default value can be left out of the function call, and the default value will be assumed:

```
print( serve() )
```

We'll look more closely at types of functions in the next chapter. For now, we've had a bit too much to drink with Billy, so we should be ready to discuss metaphysical philosophy! Let's enter the realm of *optionals*.

2.6 *Optionals*

It sounds like a Seinfeld routine, but imagine being well known as the inventor of nothing.

That's the plight of Sir C. A. R. Hoare (Tony Hoare), who implemented the null reference into a language called ALGOL W in 1965. In 2009, he called it his "billion-dollar mistake":

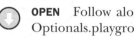 **OPEN** Follow along in the Optionals.playground.

> *My goal was to ensure that all use of references should be absolutely safe, with checking performed automatically by the compiler. But I couldn't resist the temptation to put in a null reference, because it was so easy to implement. This has led to innumerable errors, vulnerabilities, and system crashes, which have probably caused a billion dollars of pain and damage in the last forty years.*

As mentioned earlier, a key component of Swift is type safety. A variable defined as a `String`, for example, can never contain a value that isn't a `String`.

If you have experience in other languages, you're probably familiar with the absence of value—this concept is known in Swift as `nil`.

But wait, I said "a variable defined as a `String` can never contain a value that isn't a `String`." `nil` isn't a `String`. Therefore, a variable defined as a `String` can never contain `nil`! Figure 2.7 illustrates what happens if you try to assign `nil` to a `String`.

```
5  var str = "Hello, playground"
6  str = nil                          ⊘ Nil cannot be assigned to type 'String'
7
```

Figure 2.7 Strings can't be `nil`.

The question is this: what sort of variable can be equal to `nil`? Swift introduces the optional type to address this question—and the billion-dollar mistake.

Imagine you have a box with the word "CAT?" written on it (see figure 2.8). You're 100% certain that this box contains either a cat or no cat. You can't know which without unwrapping the box.

What you've imagined is a cat optional!

An optional contains either

- A thing of a certain type (for example, a cat)
- `nil` (that is, no cat)

Figure 2.8   A cat optional

So, a `String` optional, for example, contains either

- A String
- `nil`

Using an optional to represent a variable that may or may not be equal to `nil` is how Swift stays type safe while allowing the concept of `nil`.

When would you declare a variable as an optional? You should declare a variable as an optional if it may be equal to `nil` at some point in its lifetime. Perhaps the variable is declared before it can be defined; perhaps a function can fail and needs to be able to return `nil`; or perhaps a property of an object may or may not exist, and this needs to be expressed in code.

2.6.1   *Declaring an optional*

Declaring an optional is straightforward. You're unlikely to pass a value to your optional when declaring it, so type inference won't be possible. Explicitly declare its type, followed by a question mark to indicate it's an optional. Here's a `String` optional:

```
var main:String?
```

Initializing an optional later is no different from initializing a non-optional.

```
main = "Steak"
```

Let's say you want to print your main meal in uppercase. Where an optional is different is in how to retrieve its value. You can't access an optional like any other variable:

```
print("Your \(main.uppercased()) is served!")        ◁—— Error
```

As with the cat in the box, you need to *unwrap* your main optional to access its contents.

2.6.2   *Unwrapping an optional*

Unwrapping an optional refers to extracting its contents. There are two main techniques available for unwrapping an optional: forced unwrapping assumes the optional can't contain `nil`, while optional binding (combined with an `if` or `guard` statement) performs a check.

FORCED UNWRAPPING

I'm a little reluctant to go into forced unwrapping. It's a powerful feature, but used incorrectly, we're right back at the billion-dollar mistake that Tony Hoare bemoaned.

Okay, you've twisted my arm—here's the secret. Add an exclamation mark after the optional, and the optional will be unwrapped with the expectation that it will be the appropriate data type (that is, *not* `nil`).

```
print("Your \(main!.uppercased()) is served!")
```

Use forced unwrapping with caution—you must be 100% certain that the variable can't equal `nil` or you'll cause a runtime error. How can you be certain that your variable isn't equal to `nil`? Well, one way is to surround your forced unwrapping of an optional with an `if` statement verifying first that your optional contains a value:

```
if main != nil {
    print("Your \(main!.uppercased()) is served!")
}
```

This structure is so common that an alternative syntax has been developed to unwrap your optionals called *optional binding*.

OPTIONAL BINDING

Use optional binding with an `if` statement to bind the value in an optional to a variable, if it exists. The previous `if` statement could be rewritten as

```
if let mainValue = main {
    print("Your \(mainValue.uppercased()) is served!")
}
```

I've used two names to indicate which is which. The `if` statement checks if the `main` optional contains a value. If it does, its value is extracted to the `mainValue` variable and execution continues inside the `if` block.

Commonly, the same name is used for the bound variable and the optional. The extracted value will override the optional inside the `if` block:

```
if let main = main {
    print("Your \(main.uppercased()) is served!")
}
```

Sometimes, you may want to perform optional binding on several optionals. Prior to Swift 1.2, this situation grew in infamy, as the nested `if let` statements could go on and on, forming a triangular shape. This became known as the optional pyramid of doom (see the following listing).

Listing 2.13   Pyramid of doom

```
var drink:String? = "Malbec"                 ◁──────┐  Declares another
if let main = main {                                │  optional for drink
    if let drink = drink {
        print("Your \( main.uppercased() ) pairs well with
        ➥\( drink.uppercased() )")
    }
}
```

This scenario was resolved with Swift 1.2. Finally, multiple variables could be optionally bound in the same line, as shown in the following listing.

Listing 2.14   Multiple optional binding

```
if let main = main, let drink = drink {
        print("Your \( main.uppercased() ) pairs well with
        ➥\( drink.uppercased() )")
}
```

One drawback of optional binding is that the variable that contains the extracted value is only available inside the `if` block. If you need to use your optional later in the code, you need to unwrap it again. The `guard` statement resolves this problem.

GUARD STATEMENT

While an `if` statement performs a block of code if a condition is met, a `guard else` statement performs a block of code if a condition is not met.

The `serve` function in the following listing serves a drink based on the `drink` argument. It ensures that the `drink` argument is not Kool-Aid before continuing.

Listing 2.15   The `guard` statement

```
func serve(drink: String) -> String {
    guard drink != "Kool-Aid" else {
        return("Don't drink the Kool-Aid!")
    }
    return("Your \(drink) is served")
}
```

There's another key difference between the `guard` and `if` statements. After `if` or `if else` blocks, program execution can continue in the current scope. If a program enters a `guard else` block, when it exits the block it *must* exit the current scope. For example, it could `return` out of a function, `continue` to the next cycle of a loop, `break` out of a block of code, or `throw` an error.

You can use this knowledge to combine the `guard` statement with optional binding to ensure a variable stays valid for the remainder of the current scope. With the `guard` statement, what gets bound in the scope, stays in the scope, so to speak.

Let's say your `serve` function can accept an optional `drink` parameter that defaults to `nil`, making this parameter truly optional (see listing 2.16).

You can then extract the `drink` value through the process of optional binding. If no `drink` parameter is passed into the function, this is trapped by a `guard` statement, and a message is returned. If a `drink` parameter is passed in, the function continues to the original `guard` statement checking that the `drink` isn't Kool-Aid.

Listing 2.16   The `guard let` statement

```
func serve(drink: String? = nil) -> String {        ◁── Optional function
    guard let drink = drink else {                        parameter
        return("No drink for you!")
    }
    guard drink != "Kool-Aid" else {
        return("Don't drink the Kool-Aid!")
    }
    return("Your \(drink) is served")
}
```

If you like, you can merge these two `guard` statements together, as shown in the following listing.

Listing 2.17   Merge `guard` statements

```
func serve(drink: String? = nil) -> String {
    guard let drink = drink, drink != "Kool-Aid" else {
        return("No drink for you!")
    }
    return("Your \(drink) is served")
}
```

UNWRAPPING WITH OPERATORS

You're probably familiar with the ternary conditional operator that gives you shortcuts where `if` or `guard` statements would be used:

> *condition ? if true do this : if false do this*

You could use the ternary conditional operator to unwrap an optional, by doing the following:

> *optional != nil ? optional! : alternative value*

If an optional doesn't contain `nil`, the optional is force unwrapped. If the optional does contain `nil`, an alternative value appropriate to the data type is suggested.

Let's say that unless there's been a special request, martini cocktails are generally mixed by stirring. In the following listing, you'll use the ternary conditional operator to determine how the martini should be prepared. (The ternary conditional operator is in bold.)

> Listing 2.18   The ternary conditional operator

```
var defaultMix = "Stirred"
var specialMix:String?                         Defines string optional
specialMix = "Shaken"                                          Sets optional
let prepareMartini = specialMix != nil ? specialMix! : defaultMix
```

When setting the `prepareMartini` constant, we first check if the `specialMix` optional contains `nil`. If `specialMix` doesn't contain `nil`, the ternary conditional operator force-unwraps `specialMix`. If `specialMix` does contain `nil`, it uses the `defaultMix`.

This approach is so common that an alternative operator syntax is available within Swift that makes the above syntax even more succinct, called the `nil` coalescing operator. That's quite a mouthful, but don't worry, the concept is simple. The syntax is the following:

> *optional if not nil ?? alternative value*

If the optional doesn't contain `nil`, it's automatically unwrapped. If it does, the alternative value is used.

Let's prepare another martini, but this time using the `nil` coalescing operator, as shown in the following listing. (The `nil` coalescing operator is in bold.)

> Listing 2.19   The `nil` coalescing operator

```
let prepareMartini = specialMix ?? defaultMix
```

IMPLICITLY UNWRAPPED OPTIONALS

Occasionally, you may need to make a variable an optional because you don't have access to all the necessary information to initialize it when it's defined. But you may have 100% confidence that the variable will be initialized by the time it's needed.

In these cases, unwrapping the optional whenever you need to access it can seem unnecessary. Instead, you can indicate to the compiler that an optional should be implicitly unwrapped by using an exclamation mark instead of a question mark when defining it.

Let's make your first optional example implicitly unwrapped, as shown in the following listing.

Listing 2.20   Implicitly unwrapped optional

```
var main:String!                              ⟵─────────  Implicitly unwrapped optional
main = "Steak"
print("Your \(main.uppercased()) is served!")          ⟵─────────  No error now!
```

As with forced unwrapping, be extra careful with your use of implicitly unwrapped optionals. Accessing one before it has been initialized will cause a runtime error.

2.6.3   *Optional chaining*

Any object or data type could have optional properties or methods that return optionals. Arrays, for example, have an optional `first` property, which will return the first value in the array. If the array is empty, the `first` property returns `nil`.

Imagine you have nine tables in your restaurant in a 3-by-3 grid. You have a two-dimensional array (for those who came in late, that's fancy talk for an array of arrays) of `Bool`s that represent whether each table is reserved for tonight's dinner:

```
var reserved = [[true,  true,   false],
                [false, false, false],
                [true,  true,   false]
]
```

Imagine now that you'd like to display a message if your favorite table (first row, first table) is available. You could extract this info using Array's `first` property and multiple optional binding, as you saw earlier:

```
if let firstRow = reserved.first, let firstTable = firstRow.first {
    let reservedText = firstTable ? "reserved" : "vacant"
    print("Best table in the house is \(reservedText)!")
}
```

But you have a more succinct and legible alternative when traversing multiple optionals in a chain, called *optional chaining*. You can chain together multiple optionals into one optional binding statement.

```
if let firstTable = reserved.first?.first {
    let reservedText = firstTable ? "reserved" : "vacant"
    print("Best table in the house is \(reservedText)!")
}
```

Your chain could keep going! You just need to append optionals with a question mark that you traverse en route to the optional you're binding.

2.6.4 *Final comments on optionals*

At first, optionals may appear strict, and the syntax may seem new and unfamiliar. They represent a new approach to ensuring the safety of your variables that can take some getting used to. But many who have worked with Swift do find that going back to languages without optionals can feel strangely unsafe.

Optionals are an integral part of the Swift language, and it's worth investing time in becoming comfortable working with them. They're trying to solve a billion-dollar problem, after all!

2.7 *Tuples*

A tuple is a strange beast—it's a group of related data, but it is not a collection. Sounds a bit like an array or a dictionary on the surface, but a tuple differs from other collections in three important ways:

OPEN Follow along in the Tuples.playground.

- The number of items in a tuple is defined when it's instantiated. While the number of elements in an array can grow or shrink, if a tuple is defined as a group of three items, it will never contain more or fewer items.
- Elements in a tuple are related, but aren't necessarily of the same data type. A tuple could contain an `Int` and a `String`, for example, and that's fine.
- Though a tuple maintains a group of related data, it isn't a `Collection`, and therefore doesn't have access to the higher-order functions mentioned in the last section.

The types of data you might use tuples for are different as well. Tuples are a good fit for finite related data. Examples of tuples:

- A geolocation with two `Doubles` representing latitude and longitude
- A dice-roll of two dice, with two `Ints` representing the top face of each individual die
- A playing card, with an `Int` representing the number and a `String` representing the suit

Declare a variable as a tuple with parentheses, with the data type of every element specified. The following listing demonstrates standard syntax for initializing a tuple and setting and retrieving tuple values.

Listing 2.21 Using tuples

Declares a tuple. Specifies data types of elements.

Initializes a tuple. Infers data types.

Set/Get tuple elements with index numbers

```
var meal1:(String,Double)
var meal2 = ("Turkey chili soup",2.99)
print("\(meal2.0) costs \(meal2.1)")
```

```
var meal3:(name:String,price:Double)
var meal4 = (name:"Bread",price:2)
meal4.price = 3
```

Optionally gives elements of tuple a name

You can also initialize tuple with names.

Set/Get tuple elements with names if available

2.7.1   *Tuples as return values*

Tuples can be useful when you have small pieces of data that you need to return from a function. You could, for example, return a tuple of the number and suit of a card from a function:

```
func chefSpecial() -> (name: String, price: Double) {
    return (name:"Crab bisque",price:3.99)
}
var meal = chefSpecial()
```

If you plan to use a tuple frequently, it can be a good idea to set up a *type alias*. A type alias lets you define an alias for a type. A type alias for the meal tuple we've been working with would look like this:

```
typealias Meal = (name: String, price: Double)
```

You could then rewrite the chefSpecial method definition as

```
func chefSpecial() -> Meal {
```

2.7.2   *Tuple magic*

If you're not yet impressed with tuples, here are several magic tricks tuples can perform that could convince you that tuples are worth looking into.

INITIALIZING VARIABLES BASED ON A TUPLE

You can initialize variables inside a tuple, retrieving values from another tuple. The following initializes a soupName and a soupPrice variable based on the elements of a tuple variable called soup:

```
var soup = (name:"Jambalaya",price:2.99)
var (soupName,soupPrice) = soup
```

DEFINING TWO VALUES AT ONCE USING A TUPLE

Similarly, you could define two values at once using a tuple structure:

```
var (soupName,soupPrice) = ("Tomato soup",1.99)
```

This effectively becomes shorthand for

```
var soupName = "Tomato soup"
var soupPrice = 1.99
```

SWAPPING TWO VALUES USING TUPLES

Using this knowledge, you can easily swap two values. Say you have a variable representing a meal in your left hand and another variable representing a meal in your right hand:

```
var mealLeftHand = "Fish and chips"
var mealRightHand = "Burger and fries"
```

Believe it or not, swapping the variables is as easy as

```
(mealLeftHand, mealRightHand) = (mealRightHand, mealLeftHand)
```

Shazam! The meals have switched. Now go and impress your friends!

2.8 *Higher-order functions*

Higher-order functions are functions that can receive functions as parameters. This can result in more succinct and highly optimized code, and can be a powerful weapon for your program-

> **OPEN** Follow along in the Higher-OrderFunctions.playground.

ming arsenal. Because every `Array`, `Set`, and `Dictionary` is a `Collection`, they have support for a number of shared higher-order functions. Let's look at one now, the `map` function.

2.8.1 *map*

Say you have an `Array` of all the prices of the soup in your restaurant:

```
var prices = [3, 1.99, 2, 1.99, 1.70]
```

One day, you realize that you've been undercharging for soup and need to add 10% to all your prices. One solution could be to set up a `for-in` loop to generate the second array:

```
var updatedPrices:[Double]=[]
for price in prices {
    updatedPrices.append(price * 1.1)
}
```

Not bad, but a little verbose. Let's look at an alternative solution, using the `map` higher-order function. The `map` function is a powerful tool that allows you to perform an action on every element of a collection and return a new collection.

First, create a function that returns one updated price. The following function receives a `price` argument, calculates the updated price, and returns the value:

```
func updatePrice(price: Double) -> Double {
    return price * 1.1
}
```

Now that you've created this function, you can pass it into the map higher-order function.

```
var updatedPrices = prices.map(updatePrice)
```

The map function uses the updatePrice method to calculate a new price on every element of your prices Array and return a new Array with updated prices.

Great! That works fine, but it isn't any more succinct. An alternative approach is to pass a *closure* into the map function.

2.8.2   *Closures*

A closure is a block of functionality. You can think of a closure as a function without a name. In reality, it's the other way around—a function is a type of closure with a name! Like functions, closures can accept arguments and return values.

CONVERTING A FUNCTION TO A CLOSURE

The syntax for closures is a little different from functions, and it can be difficult to remember initially. There are ways to make the syntax of a closure more succinct (we'll get into that in a moment), but converting a function to a basic closure isn't bad if you follow two simple steps.

Let's explore the two steps now while you convert the updatePrice function to a closure.

1 Remove the keyword func and the function name:

```
(price:Double)->Double {
    return price * 1.1
}
```

2 Move the brace to the beginning and replace where it was with the keyword in:

```
{ (price:Double)->Double in
    return price * 1.1
}
```

That's it! As I mentioned, in certain cases you can make your closure more concise, but you've arrived at the base structure of a closure.

SIMPLIFYING A CLOSURE

The updatePrice closure can now be passed directly into the map function:

```
var updatedPrices = prices.map(
    { ( price:Double ) -> Double in
            return price * 1.1
    }
)
```

This still doesn't look too succinct. Fortunately, there are several improvements you can make:

■ As the type of the price parameter and the closure return value can be inferred by the type of the prices Array, these types don't need to be specified.

After shedding the data type, you can also remove the parentheses around the parameter:

```
var updatedPrices = prices.map( { price in return price * 1.1 } )
```

- If you leave out argument names in a closure, you're provided with default argument names. The first argument is $0, the second is $1, and so on. With this knowledge, you can make your code even more concise.

```
var updatedPrices = prices.map( { return $0 * 1.1 } )
```

- Believe it or not, you can go further! If the closure contains only one line of code, Swift can infer that you want to return the result of this line, so you can remove the `return` keyword.

```
var updatedPrices = prices.map( { $0 * 1.1 } )
```

That's it! Compare that line of code with the `for-in` loop we began with:

```
var updatedPrices:[Int] = []
for price in prices {
    updatedPrices.append(price * 1.1)
}
```

Note the difference in conciseness without sacrificing clarity. The line still clearly returns a version of the `updatedPrices` array that has been doubled.

The `map` function is a powerful tool. All the higher-order functions are great examples of Swift's expressiveness and performance. In addition to the `map` higher-order function, `Collections` have access to many more, including `filter`, `reduce`, and `sorted`.

2.8.3 *filter*

The `filter` function extracts the elements of a collection that satisfy a condition. It accepts a closure that receives an element to check, and returns a `Bool`.

Perhaps you might want to filter only meal prices that are greater than $5, to put on the specials board:

```
var filteredPrices = prices.filter( { $0 >= 5 })
```

2.8.4 *reduce*

Use the `reduce` function to generate a single value by performing an operation on every value of a collection.

Maybe you're interested to know how much you would make if someone came into your restaurant and ordered everything on the menu:

```
var totalPrice = prices.reduce(0, {$0 + $1})
```

2.8.5   *sorted*

The `sorted` method accepts a closure that determines which of two elements should come first in the order. The closure receives two elements to compare and returns a `Bool`.

Say you're interested in seeing the prices of meals in your restaurant by sorting them from largest to smallest:

```
var sortedPrices = prices.sorted(by: { $0 > $1 } )
```

2.9   *Summary*

In this chapter, you learned the following:

- Xcode playground is a useful environment for experimenting with new Swift concepts and syntax.
- Variables in Swift are type safe, but their type can be inferred.
- Variables of different types need to be converted to the same type to interact.
- Use `for-in` loops to loop through the elements of a collection.
- Use higher-order functions on your collections for succinct and optimized code.
- Use closures to pass functionality to a function.
- Use tuples to pass multiple values around.
- Use optionals to store variables that may equal `nil`.
- Unwrap optionals with optional binding (`if let` or `guard let else`) or the `nil` coalescing operator.
- Only unwrap optionals with forced unwrapping or implicit unwrapping if you are 100% sure an optional contains a value.

Swift objects 3

This chapter covers

- Exploring objects, methods, and parameters in Swift
- Initializing properties
- Comparing inheritance with protocols
- Differentiating between classes and structs
- Exploring ways to extend your code

It's impossible to do anything in iOS development without using objects. Views are objects, view controllers are objects, models are objects—even basic data types such as `String`, `Int`, and `Array` are objects in Swift!

An object in Swift is a specific instance of a type of thing. In this chapter, we'll look at different ways of building up and structuring these types of things in your code. From experience in other languages, you may know this "type of thing" (or type) as a class. While it's true that types can be represented by classes in Swift, they're not the only type of thing in Swift—other types called structures and enumerations also exist. We'll come back to those, but first let's look at classes.

Don't forget, you can refer to the Swift cheat sheets in appendix B. This chapter is summarized on the last page of the cheat sheets.

3.1 Classes

One approach for creating objects in Swift is with a class. A class defines what a type does with methods. A method is a function defined within a type. Along with methods, a class defines what a type is with properties. Properties are variables or constants stored in a type.

Let's say you've decided to build a distance converter app. Your app will accept distances in miles or kilometers, and will display the distance in either form of measurement, too.

You decide the best approach is to build a type that stores distances, regardless of the scale. You could create a distance with a miles or kilometers value, update the distance with a miles or kilometers value, or use the distance type to return its value as miles or kilometers (see figure 3.1).

Figure 3.1 Distance type

3.1.1 Defining a class

Let's start by defining a simple `Distance` type with a class. In this chapter, you'll build up this class to contain a distance using different measurement types.

1 Create a new playground to follow along, and call it Distance. Classes are defined with the `class` keyword followed by the name of the class and the rest of the definition contained within curly brackets.

2 Create a `Distance` class.

```
class Distance {

}
```

3 Now that you have a class, you can create (or instantiate) your class with the name of the type, followed by parentheses, and assign this object to a variable:

```
var distance = Distance()
```

You might recognize the parentheses syntax from the previous chapter as an alternative syntax for creating or instantiating simple data types.

Now that you have a class definition for `Distance`, you can add properties and methods to it.

3.1.2 *Properties*

Variables that we've looked at so far have been global variables—defined outside the context of a class or function. Variables that are defined within a class are called properties, and fall into two broad categories: type properties and instance properties.

TYPE PROPERTIES

Type properties, also known as static properties, are relevant to all things of a certain type. It isn't even necessary that an instance of a type exist to access type properties. Type properties are connected to the type rather than the object. You instantiate a type property with the `static` keyword followed by a normal declaration of a variable.

For example, maybe you'd like to store the number of kilometers in a mile in a type property in your `Distance` class. In this case, a constant would make more sense, because the number of kilometers in a mile won't be changing any time soon. Use the keyword `let` instead of `var` to define a constant.

1 Add a type property constant to your simple `Distance` class:

```
class Distance {
    static let kmPerMile = 1.60934
}
```

You could then retrieve or set this type property directly on the type.

2 Print to the console using the type property you created:

```
print ("2 miles = \(Distance.kmPerMile * 2) km")
```

INSTANCE PROPERTIES

Instance properties are relevant to specific objects or instances of a type.

Because the `miles` value will be relevant to specific instances of `Distance`, add `miles` as an instance property to your `Distance` class.

```
class Distance {
    static let kmPerMile = 1.60934
    var miles:Double
}
```

Whoops! If you're following along in the playground, you'll notice that this triggers a compiler error. Tap the red dot to see more information on the error (see figure 3.2). A pop-up appears below the line that describes the error along with Xcode's suggested fix.

```
5  class Distance {
6      static let kmPerMile = 1.60934   ⊘ Class 'Distance' has no initializers          ✕
7      var miles:Double                    Stored property 'miles' without initial value prevents synthesized initializers   Fix
8  }
```

Figure 3.2   Non-optional variable can't equal `nil`

As we explored in the previous chapter, non-optionals can never equal `nil`. The `Distance` class can't contain a `miles` property that's equal to `nil`.

You have three possible alternatives to get rid of that red dot.

- One option is to give the property a default value. This is what Xcode suggests. If you tap Fix Button, Xcode will resolve the problem in this way for you.

  But a default value for the `miles` property doesn't make sense. There's no reason why 0 or any other value should be a default value for `miles`. Press Command-Z to undo this fix.

- Another option is to make the `miles` property an optional. This is easy to do; all you need to do is add a question mark:

  ```
  var miles:Double?
  ```

  This removes the error, but isn't appropriate for this example either. If you define a `Distance` object, you want it to have a value for miles! A distance with a miles value of `nil` doesn't make sense. Undo this fix too.

- You could pass a value to the `miles` property in an initializer. What's an initializer?

3.1.3   *Initializers*

An initializer is a special type of function that sets up a type. You can use an initializer to pass in values when you instantiate the type.

You can create an initializer with the `init` keyword followed by any parameters you want to pass in to initialize the instance properties.

1. Add an initializer to the `Distance` class to pass in a value to initialize the `miles` property.

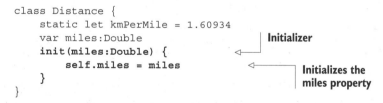

As you can see, you can use the keyword `self` to differentiate between the instance property (`self.miles`) and the parameter (`miles`) that's passed in to the initializer.

Now that the `miles` property is set in the initializer, the requirement that all non-optionals should contain non-nil values is satisfied, and the red dot should go away.

2. You can now instantiate a `Distance` object by passing in a value for miles.

```
var distance = Distance(miles: 60)
```

NOTE By default you need to pass in the names of the arguments in initializers and functions. We'll look at this in more detail shortly.

3 Now that you have a `Distance` class, you could introduce a `km` property if you like, and initialize it in the initializer calculated from the `miles` value and the `kmPerMile` type property.

```
class Distance {
    static let kmPerMile = 1.60934
    var miles:Double
    var km:Double                                    ◁─┐ Adds km
    init(miles:Double) {                                │ property
        self.miles = miles
        self.km = miles * Distance.kmPerMile     ◁─┐ Calculates km
    }                                                │ from miles
}
```

In case we need to calculate kilometers again, it may make sense to move this calculation to a method.

NOTE If all properties of a class have default values, Xcode will synthesize a default initializer automatically for you with no arguments.

3.1.4 Methods

Functions defined inside a class are called methods. Like variables and properties, methods can be divided into *instance methods* or *type methods*.

Instance methods are methods that are relevant to an instance of a type, whereas type methods apply to the type itself.

INSTANCE METHODS

Instance methods are relevant to each instance of a type.

In the future, you might want your `Distance` class to return a nicely formatted version of its data. Because the response will be different for each instance of `Distance`, this would be more relevant as an instance method.

1 Add an instance method to your `Distance` class that returns a nicely formatted miles string.

```
func displayMiles()->String {
    return "\(Int(miles)) miles"
}
```

2 You can call your instance method now using a `Distance` object.

```
var distance = Distance(miles: 60)
print(distance.displayMiles())
//prints "60 miles" to console
```

You currently calculate kilometers from miles in the `Distance` initializer. Let's refactor this calculation into a reusable method. You might be tempted to use an instance method, but you'll find this approach causes an error.

3 Add an instance method that calculates kilometers from miles, and call it from the initializer.

```
class Distance {
    static let kmPerMile = 1.60934
    var miles:Double
    var km:Double
    init(miles:Double) {
        self.miles = miles
        self.km = toKm(miles:miles)          ◁──┐  Call instance method;
    }                                           error here
    func toKm(miles:Double)->Double {
        return miles * Distance.kmPerMile       Instance method
    }
}
```

Curious! Why does calling an instance method in the initializer cause an error?

Until an initializer has fulfilled its duties to provide initial values for all non-optionals, the instance isn't designated as safe and therefore its instance properties and methods can't be accessed.

To solve this problem, one solution could be to ensure that all properties have values before using the instance method:

```
init(miles:Double) {
    self.miles = miles
    self.km = 0                    ◁──┐  Provides default
    self.km = toKm(miles:miles)        value
}                                                  ◁─── No error now!
```

But stepping back from the problem, converting miles to kilometers could be as easily set up as a useful utility method on the type. Let's refactor our toKm method as a type method.

TYPE METHODS

Like type properties, type methods (also known as static methods) are methods that can be called directly on the type, rather than individual instances of the type.

1 Use the static keyword to refactor the toKm method as a type method. Type methods have implicit access to type properties, so we can remove the class name Distance before kmPerMile:

```
static func toKm(miles:Double)->Double {
    return miles * kmPerMile
}
```

Similar to the way you used type properties, call a type method by prefacing it with the type. For example, here's how you could call the toKm method we set up on the Distance class:

```
print(Distance.toKm(miles: 30))
```

Because type methods are called on the type and don't depend on an instance of a type, they can be used to initialize properties in the initializer.

2 Call your new static method in the initializer for `Distance`.

```
init(miles:Double) {
    self.miles = miles
    self.km = Distance.toKm(miles:miles)
}
```

OVERLOADING

It can be strange to developers new to Swift that it's completely valid in Swift to have two functions with the same name, as long as the names or types of the parameters are distinct. This is called *overloading* a function. "Overloading a function"—even the name sounds a little scary! Don't worry, this is standard practice in Swift and a useful tool.

At the moment, the `Distance` class has a static method called `toKm` that calculates kilometers from miles. What if later you find you need to calculate kilometers from another form of measurement, for example, feet? You'll probably want to name that method `toKm`, too. Well, in Swift you can do this by overloading the function by defining two functions with different parameter names, as shown in the following listing.

Listing 3.1 Overloading a function with different parameter names

```
static let feetPerKm:Double = 5280

static func toKm(miles:Double)->Double {
    return miles * kmPerMile
}
static func toKm(feet:Double)->Double {
    return feet / feetPerKm
}
```

Which method you use depends on the parameter name you pass:

```
let km = Distance.toKm(miles:60)    //96.5604
let km2 = Distance.toKm(feet:100)   // 0.03048
```

Similarly, perhaps in the future you want your `Distance` class to accept an `Int` value for `km` in your `toMiles` method. This time, you could overload the function by defining two functions with the same name that expect different data types, as shown in the following listing.

Listing 3.2 Overloading a function with different parameter data types

```
static func toMiles(km:Double)->Double {
    return km / kmPerMile
}
static func toMiles(km:Int)->Double {
    return Double(km) / kmPerMile
}
```

Again, the method you use depends on the data type of the parameter you pass. Initializers can be overloaded as well.

1 Add a second initializer for the `Distance` class to initialize the object based on kilometers. You'll need to add a type method to calculate miles from kilometers as well.

```
class Distance {
    static let kmPerMile = 1.60934
    var miles:Double
    var km:Double
    init(miles:Double) {
        self.miles = miles
        self.km = Distance.toKm(miles:miles)
    }                                                    Overloaded
    init(km:Double) {                                    initializer
        self.km = km
        self.miles = Distance.toMiles(km:km)
    }
    static func toKm(miles:Double)->Double {
        return miles * kmPerMile
    }                                                    New type
    static func toMiles(km:Double)->Double {             method
        return km / kmPerMile
    }
}
```

2 You can now use miles or kilometers to instantiate a `Distance` object:

```
var distance1 = Distance(miles: 60)
var distance2 = Distance(km: 100)
```

The `Distance` class is shaping up, but it has a bit of redundancy to it. Whether you store the distance in miles or kilometers, you're storing the same distance twice using two different measurement units. Shortly, we'll look at how to clean up that redundancy with computed properties.

Convenience initializers

The initializers we've looked at so far have been *designated* initializers—the main initializer for the class that ensures that all instance properties have their initial values. *Convenience* initializers are alternative initializers that add the keyword `convenience`, and, by definition, must ultimately call `self`'s designated initializer to complete the initialization process. Instead of overloading the initializer in the `Distance` class, we could have added a convenience initializer.

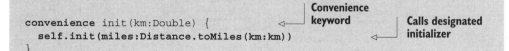

```
convenience init(km:Double) {                    Convenience      Calls designated
    self.init(miles:Distance.toMiles(km:km))     keyword          initializer
}
```

3.1.5 *Computed properties*

Computed properties are properties that calculate their values from other properties.

As you saw earlier, there might be a point in the future when you want to add additional measurements to your `Distance` class—centimeters, feet, inches, cubits, yards, furlongs, nautical miles, light years, you get the idea. Should you keep all these versions of the same distance in memory? Probably not.

One solution to avoid this redundancy is to decide on one core property that will store the distance—in our `Distance` class, this could be `miles`. Then the other properties, rather than storing values, will calculate their value from the `miles` property. These types of properties will be computed properties.

Computed properties lie somewhere between properties and methods—they're methods implemented with the syntax of properties. They act similarly to getters and setters in other languages.

The computed property itself doesn't store any data. Rather, when the property's value is retrieved, the getter calculates a value to return. Calculations are performed in curly brackets {} and the value is returned using the `return` keyword.

1. To avoid redundancy, convert the `km` property to a read-only computed property. The `km` property will no longer store data; rather, it will calculate kilometers from the `miles` property at the moment it's requested. The initializers will no longer need to set the `km` property and will set the miles property directly.

```
class Distance {
    static let kmPerMile = 1.60934
    var miles:Double
    var km:Double {
        return Distance.toKm(miles:miles)
    }
    init(miles:Double) {
        self.miles = miles
        self.km = Distance.toKm(miles:miles)
    }
    init(km:Double) {
        self.km = km
        self.miles = Distance.toMiles(km:km)
    }
    static func toKm(miles:Double)->Double {
        return miles * kmPerMile
    }
    static func toMiles(km:Double)->Double {
        return km / kmPerMile
    }
}
```

2. Confirm that the km property can continue to be retrieved like a normal property.

```
var distance = Distance(km: 100)
print ("\(distance.km) km is \(distance.miles) miles")
```

This solves the redundancy, but unfortunately there's a problem. You want to be able to update a distance object by setting the kilometer value.

3 Check what happens when you update the `km` property.

```
distance.km = 90          ◁—— Error
```

Because `km` is a read-only property, attempting to update it causes an error.

Computed properties can optionally also implement a setter. A setter is a block of code that's called when a computed property is set. Because the computed property doesn't store any data, the setter is used to set the same values that derive the computed property's value in the getter.

The getter approach used in the previous example uses shorthand syntax to implement the getter. The longhand syntax uses a `get` keyword followed by curly brackets `{ }`.

4 Convert the `km` computed property to use the longhand syntax.

```
var km:Double {
    get {                                    ◁—— Explicit getter syntax
        return Distance.toKm(miles:miles)
    }
}
```

The `set` syntax is similar to the `get` syntax, with the exception that the set syntax receives a variable representing the new value.

5 Convert the `km` computed property so that it now can be "set," as per the following code snippet:

```
class Distance {
    static let kmPerMile = 1.60934
    var miles:Double
    var km:Double {
        get {
            return Distance.toKm(miles:miles)
        }
        set(newKm) {
            miles = Distance.toMiles(km:newKm)
        }
    }
    init(miles:Double) {
        self.miles = miles
    }
    init(km:Double) {
        self.miles = Distance.toMiles(km:km)
    }
    static func toKm(miles:Double)->Double {
        return miles * kmPerMile
    }
    static func toMiles(km:Double)->Double {
        return km / kmPerMile
    }
}
```

As you can see, setting the `km` property doesn't store the value of kilometers. Instead, it calculates and stores a value in the `miles` property.

6 Confirm you can now update a distance object using either miles or kilometers:

```
var distance = Distance(km: 100)
distance.km = 35
distance.miles = 90
```

7 Confirm you can also retrieve the values of either miles or kilometers:

```
print("Distance is \(distance.miles) miles")
print("Distance is \(distance.km) km")
```

Mission complete!

DOWNLOAD You can check your `Distance` class with mine in the Distance.playground. Download all the code for this chapter by selecting Source Code > Clone and entering the repository location: https://github.com/iOSAppDevelopmentwithSwiftinAction/Chapter3.

CHALLENGE Confirm in the results sidebar that the distance object is instantiating, updating, and displaying correctly using miles or kilometers.

3.1.6 Class inheritance

If you're experienced in object-oriented programming (OOP), class inheritance and subtyping will most likely be a familiar topic. In Swift, multiple classes can inherit the implementation of one class through subclassing, forming an is-a relationship.

NOTE If you're familiar with class inheritance, you can skim through to the section called "Pros and cons."

Classes and subclasses form a hierarchy of relationships that looks like an upside-down tree. At the top of the tree is the base class from which all classes inherit, and every subclass inherits the methods and properties of its superclass and can add on implementation.

Let's explore inheritance by building up a class structure representing telephones. Different types of telephones exist—from older rotary phones to the latest iPhones, but they all share common functionalities: to make calls and to hang up.

See figure 3.3 for a simplified representation of the hierarchy of relationships of different types of telephones. At the base (top) of the tree is an abstract telephone, which can initiate and terminate calls. This branches into landline and cellular phones. Both landlines and cellular phones inherit the telephone's ability to initiate and terminate calls, but the cellular phone adds the ability to send an SMS. The various types of phones that inherit from landlines and cellular phones add (among other things) different input techniques. The various types of smartphones add their own implementation of an operating system.

NOTE   This example isn't intended to be comprehensive. If I listed everything a smart phone could do, I'd be here all day!

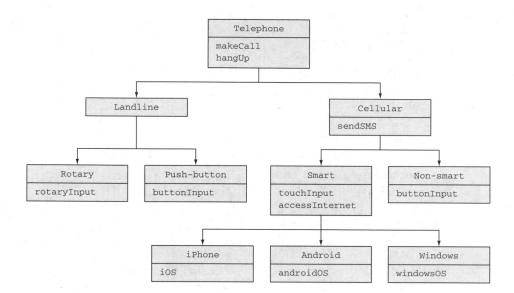

Figure 3.3   Telephone inheritance

You could model these relationships with classes. Subclasses indicate their superclass with a colon after their name, as shown in the following listing.

Listing 3.3   Class inheritance

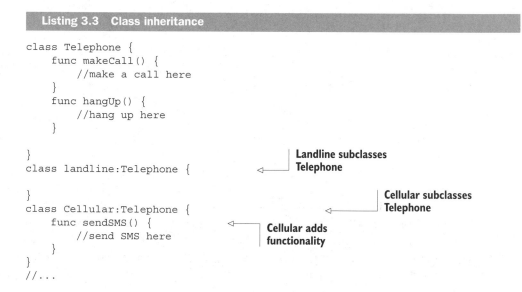

```
class Telephone {
    func makeCall() {
        //make a call here
    }
    func hangUp() {
        //hang up here
    }

}
class landline:Telephone {          ◁──┐ Landline subclasses
                                        Telephone
}
class Cellular:Telephone {          ◁──┐ Cellular subclasses
    func sendSMS() {                      Telephone
        //send SMS here        ◁──┐ Cellular adds
    }                              functionality
}
//...
```

After modeling this hierarchy, a method could receive a `Telephone` parameter, and regardless of whether the parameter passed is an Android, iOS, or even a rotary phone, the method knows that it can tell the telephone to `makeCall()` or `hangUp()`:

OPEN Explore the rest of the code in the Telephone-ClassInheritance.playground.

```
func hangUpAndRedial(telephone:Telephone) {
    telephone.hangUp()
    telephone.makeCall()
}
```

OVERRIDING

In addition to inheriting the implementation of a superclass, a subclass can override this implementation.

The `Cellular` class probably wants to implement its own version of making a call on cellular networks. It can do this by overriding the `makeCall` method, as shown in the following listing.

Listing 3.4   Override method

```
class Cellular:Telephone {
    override func makeCall() {
        //make cellular call
    }
    func sendSMS() {
        //send SMS here
    }
}
```

Overriding a method will, by default, prevent the superclass's implementation of that method from running. Sometimes, a subclass might want to add to the superclass's implementation rather than replace it. In this case, the subclass can use the `super` keyword to first call the method on the superclass, as shown in the following listing.

Listing 3.5   Call `super`

```
override func makeCall() {
    super.makeCall()
    //make cellular call
}
```

PROS AND CONS

Class inheritance is used extensively throughout Apple frameworks. For example, as you saw in chapter 1, the `UIButton` class subclasses the `UIControl` class, which, in turn, subclasses `UIView`.

Inheritance is a powerful technique for expressing relationships and sharing implementation between classes and lies at the heart of object-oriented programming.

Inheritance has issues, however, that are worth noting.

- *Swift only permits inheritance from one class.* iPhones aren't simply telephones any more. They're game consoles, e-readers, video players, compasses, GPS devices, step counters, heart rate monitors, fingerprint readers, earthquake detectors, and the list goes on. How can an iPhone share common functionality and implementation with these other devices? According to the simple inheritance model, they can't.

- *Sharing code can only happen between subclasses and superclasses.* Non-smart phones and push-button phones both have push-button input, but neither of them inherits from each other. iPads have iOS too, but they aren't telephones. These common implementations couldn't be shared, according to the pure inheritance model.

- *Sometimes it's not so clear which identity is the most relevant to subclass.* Should you have subclassed smartphones by operating system or by manufacturer? Both are important and could potentially contain different functionality or properties.

The trend in pure Swift has moved away from class inheritance and toward implementation of protocols.

3.1.7 *Protocols*

Protocols are similar to interfaces in other languages. They specify the methods and properties that a type that adopts the protocol will need to implement.

Protocol methods only indicate the definition of the method and not the actual body of the method, for example:

```
func makeCall()
```

If you rewrote the abstract `Telephone` class as a protocol, it would look like the following code snippet:

```
protocol Telephone {
    func makeCall()          Protocol methods
    func hangUp()
}
```

A type adopts a protocol with syntax similar to inheritance—a colon after the type name. As the methods in a protocol don't contain any implementation, a class that adopts the protocol must explicitly implement these methods. If you rewrote the `Landline` class to adopt the `Telephone` protocol, it would look like the following code snippet:

```
class Landline:Telephone {               Adopts the Telephone
    func makeCall() {                     protocol
        //make a landline call here
    }                         Implements the
    func hangUp() {           protocol methods
        //hang up a landline call here
    }
}
```

Protocol properties only indicate whether a property can be retrieved or set. For example, if you add a phone number property to `Telephone`, it looks like the following code snippet:

```
protocol Telephone {
    var phoneNo:Int { get set }        ◁──┐  Protocol
    func makeCall()                        │  property
    func hangUp()
}
```

The protocol only specifies that the `phoneNo` property needs to exist in an adopting type, and that the property needs to get or set. Implementing the property is left to the adopting class.

```
class Landline:Telephone {             │  Adopts the
    var phoneNo:Int              ◁─────┘  protocol property
    init(phoneNo:Int) {
        self.phoneNo = phoneNo            Initializes the property
    }
    func makeCall() {
        //make a landline call here
    }
    func hangUp() {
        //hang up a landline call here
    }
}
```

PROTOCOL EXTENSIONS

Okay. I have a confession to make.

I've been suggesting that protocols don't contain implementation, and that's not entirely true. Protocols are blessed with the magical ability to be *extended* to add actual functionality, which types that adopt the protocol will have access to.

In the previous example, the functionality of making a call and hanging up could be implemented in the `Telephone` protocol through use of an extension, as shown in the following listing.

Listing 3.6 Extending a protocol

```
protocol Telephone {
    var phoneNo:Int { get set }
    func makeCall()
    func hangUp()                      Extension
}                                      of protocol
extension Telephone {            ◁──┘
    func makeCall() {
        print("Make call")
    }                                  Implementation of
    func hangUp() {                    methods in protocol
        print("Hang up")
    }
}
```

```
class Landline:Telephone {
    var phoneNo:Int
    init(phoneNo:Int) {
        self.phoneNo = phoneNo
    }
}
```

Because these methods are now implemented in the `Telephone` protocol, they no longer need to be implemented in a class that adopts that protocol. Note that the `Landline` class no longer implements the `makeCall` or `hangUp` methods.

Extended protocols still can't store properties, but because computed properties don't store properties, computed properties can be implemented in extended protocols.

PROTOCOL RELATIONSHIPS

This integration of protocols and protocol extensions into the Swift language made different and complex approaches possible for structuring relationships between types. This is due to several factors:

- Like classes, protocols can inherit other protocols.
- Types can adopt multiple protocols.
- Protocols can represent different types of relationships.

Class inheritance places the emphasis on is-a relationships. As you've seen, protocols can represent this relationship as well. When protocols represent an is-a relationship, the convention is to use a noun. In our example, `Landline` is-a `Telephone`.

But protocols aren't limited to identity or is-a relationships. Another common relationship that is represented is capabilities, or can-do. A common convention for protocols that represent a can-do relationship is to suffix its name with "able," "ible," or "ing."

Relationships in the real world are often not as simple as a pure inheritance model can handle. Complexity and nuance need to be addressed, and protocols and protocol extensions are useful for this.

Let's look again at telephones, converting subclasses to is-a and can-do protocols. Figure 3.4 illustrates one way you could redraw their relationships.

In this example, a protocol called `PushButtonable` could be written to handle the capability of button input. This protocol could then be adopted by both the push-button landline and the non-smart cellular phone. Despite not having an inheritance relationship, the two classes could still share implementation through the `Push-Buttonable` protocol extension.

The iPhone no longer inherits all its *smart* characteristics through the `Smart` class. Rather, it adopts specific capabilities through protocols such as `Touchable` or `Internetable`. In this way, it could go beyond traditional telephone capabilities and adopt protocols and share implementation through protocol extensions with completely different devices. Maybe it could share `VideoPlayable` along with `Television`, `Navigable` along with `GPSDevice`, or `GamePlayable` along with `GameConsole`.

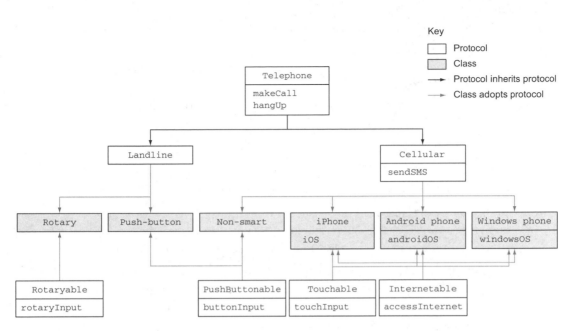

Figure 3.4 Telephone using protocols

Using protocols to structure the relationships in your code has been coined protocol-oriented programming. Sure, you could continue to program in Swift using familiar object-oriented programming techniques, but it's worth exploring the possibilities with protocols.

OPEN Explore the protocol relationships in code in the TelephoneProtocols.playground.

> **CHALLENGE** Add a `Television` type that shares a `VideoPlayable` protocol with iPhones, Androids, and Windows phones.

3.2 Structures

Classes aren't the only "type of thing" in Swift. An alternative approach to creating objects in Swift is with a structure.

Structures have many similarities to classes. For example, they can

- Have properties
- Have methods
- Have initializers
- Adopt protocols

Define a structure with the `struct` keyword, for example:

```
struct Telephone {

}
```

Instantiation of a structure is identical to that of a class:

```
var telephone = Telephone()
```

3.2.1   *Structures vs. classes*

Structures have three main differences from classes worth noting:

- Structures can't inherit.
- Structures can have memberwise initializers.
- Structures are value types.

Each of these is explained in the following sections.

STRUCTURES CAN'T INHERIT

Structures can't inherit other structures. They can indirectly inherit functionality, however, by adopting protocols, which, as you've seen, can inherit other protocols.

MEMBERWISE INITIALIZERS

If you don't set up an initializer for a structure, an initializer that accepts all the structure's properties as parameters will automatically be generated for you. This automated initializer is called a memberwise initializer.

As you saw earlier in the chapter, when the `Distance` class didn't initialize its `miles` property, an error appeared. If you change the definition of this class to a `struct`, a memberwise initializer is automatically generated and the error disappears:

```
struct Distance {
    var miles:Double
}
```

You can now instantiate this structure using the memberwise initializer:

```
var distance = Distance(miles: 100)
```

STRUCTURES ARE VALUE TYPES

An important distinction between structures and classes is how they're treated when they're assigned to variables or passed to functions. Classes are assigned as *references*, and structures are assigned as *values*.

Look at the following listing. Predict the value of `color1.name` that will be printed to the console.

Listing 3.7   Changes to reference types

```
class Color {
    var name = "red"
}
var color1 = Color()
var color2 = color1
color2.name = "blue"
print(color1.name)
```

If you predicted `"blue"`, pat yourself on the back! Because classes are reference types, when `color1` was assigned to the `color2` variable, `color2` was assigned the reference to the underlying `Color` object (see figure 3.5).

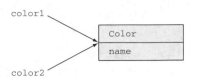

Figure 3.5   Reference types

In the end, both `color1` and `color2` refer to the same object, and any changes to `color2` are reflected in `color1` (and vice versa).

In Swift, core data types such as `String` are value types. Look at the following listing and predict the value of `letter1` that will be printed to the console.

Listing 3.8   Changes to value types

```
var letter1 = "A"
var letter2 = letter1
letter2 = "B"
print(letter1)
```

If you went with `"A"`, you're right. This time, when `letter2` was assigned to the `letter1` variable, `letter2` was assigned the *value* of `letter1`, instantiating a new String object. You're left with two String objects, as in figure 3.6.

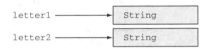

Figure 3.6   Value types

Because you now have two separate String objects, making a change to one of them doesn't affect the other.

Like `Strings`, when a structure is assigned to a new variable, it's copied. Let's look at the `Color` example again, but tweak one thing—it's now a structure rather than a class (to be clear, let's also rename it `ColorStruct`). Now, what is the value of `color1.name` that will be printed to the console in the following?

```
struct ColorStruct {
    var name = "red"
}
var color1 = ColorStruct()
var color2 = color1
color2.name = "blue"
print(color1.name)
```

If you predicted `"red"`, you're paying attention! Because structures are value types, when `color2` was assigned `color1`, only the value of `color1` was copied, two `Color-Struct` objects now exist, and any changes to `color2` aren't reflected in `color1`. Try it out in a playground and see for yourself!

Since Swift went open source, it's been fascinating to explore how the language looks "under the hood." One thing you'll discover if you look at the source of Swift is that many of the core data types are implemented as structs, explaining why types such as `String` are value types. Incidentally, this represents a change in direction from Objective-C, where many types are implemented as classes (though references are implemented differently).

CONSTANTS

We've looked at constants in brief, but now's a good time to look at them a little closer.

You undoubtedly are familiar with constants—they're a special type of variable that will never be reassigned. In Swift, a constant is declared using the `let` keyword instead of `var`.

For example, if you assign an instance of a `Person` type to a constant, you can't later assign another instance of the `Person` type to the same constant:

```
let person = Person(name: "Sandra")          Error—can't
person = Person(name: "Ian")        ◁───┘    reassign constant
```

> **TIP**   If a variable is never reassigned, for performance reasons you should declare it a constant.

Here's a tricky question for you: is it permissible to modify a property of a constant of the `Person` type? For example:

```
person.name = "Ian"
```

If your answer was a confused expression and a shrug of the shoulders, you're right!

Whether a property of a constant can be modified depends on whether you have a value type or a reference type, and I wasn't clear in the question about whether `Person` was defined as a class or a structure. I did warn you it was going to be tricky!

For value types, the identity of the constant is tied up with the properties it contains. If you change a property, the variable is no longer the same value. For value types such as structures, it isn't permissible to modify a constant's properties.

For reference types, the identity of the constant is a reference to an object. There could be other constants or variables that point to that same object. For reference types such as classes, it's permissible to modify a constant's properties.

WHICH OBJECT TYPE?

After learning the differences between classes and structures, the next question most people want the answer to is this: which should I use, and when?

To arrive at an answer of that complex question I find it helps to break it down into smaller questions:

- *Does the type need to subclass?* The choice may be clear—sometimes your type needs to subclass; therefore, you need a class.
- *Should instances of this type be one of a kind?* If you're storing data in a type, and want any changes to that data to be reflected elsewhere, it might make sense to use a class.
- *Is the value tied to the identity of this type?* Consider a `Point` type that stores an x and a y value. If you have two points that are both equal to (x:0, y:0), would

they be equivalent? I suggest that they would. Therefore, the value is tied to its identity and it should probably be implemented as a structure.

Now, consider an `AngryFrog` type that among other properties also contains an x and a y value. If you have two angry frogs that both are positioned at `(x:0, y:0)`, would they be equivalent? I suggest probably not, because they're probably two distinct entities, maybe traveling in different directions, or may be controlled by different players. The identity of an `AngryFrog` would be tied to a reference to a specific instance rather than the current values of its properties, and therefore it should probably be implemented as a class.

For a visual representation of this decision process, see figure 3.7.

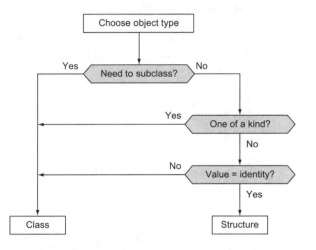

Figure 3.7 Structure or class decision

A complex codebase may have additional factors to consider, but I find these three questions a handy guide to arrive at an answer to the structure or class decision.

Let's practice this decision process with the `Distance` type you worked with earlier in the chapter:

- Does the `Distance` type need to subclass? No, it doesn't.
- Should there be only one `Distance` object? No, there can be more than one.
- Is the value equivalent to its identity? If you had two 100 km `Distance` objects, they should be treated as equivalent, so yes, the value is equivalent to identity.

Therefore, the `Distance` type should probably be implemented as a structure. Fortunately, changing a class to a structure or vice versa is straightforward. Swap the `class` keyword over for `struct`, and that's often all that's necessary. Go ahead and change the `Distance` class to a structure now.

We still haven't looked at all the object types available in Swift. To make things even more interesting, you have yet another alternative to classes and structures, called enums. We'll cover enums in chapter 10.

3.3   Extensions

We've looked at protocol extensions to add functionality to protocols. Extensions can also be used to add functionality to classes and structures.

There's much that extensions can do, but they do have limitations:

- Extensions can't override functionality.
- Extensions can add computed properties, but can't add stored properties.
- Extensions of classes can't add designated initializers.

3.3.1   Extensions of your type

When we looked at the `Distance` class earlier in the chapter, we considered that at a later point we may want to add additional measurements. Well, the time has come! Let's add feet to the `Distance` structure.

1 Open your Distance playground again.

2 Create an extension of your `Distance` structure.

```
extension Distance {
}
```

3 Add a feet computed property.

```
static let feetPerMile:Double = 5280
```

4 Add type methods to your extension to convert to miles and kilometers from feet, or back again to feet from miles.

```
static func toMiles(feet:Double)->Double {
    return feet / feetPerMile
}
static func toKm(feet:Double)->Double {
    return toKm(miles:toMiles(feet:feet))
}
static func toFeet(miles:Double)->Double {
    return miles * feetPerMile
}
```

5 You can set up a computed property now for feet.

```
var feet:Double {
    get {
        return Distance.toFeet(miles:miles)
    }
    set(newFeet) {
        miles = Distance.toMiles(feet: newFeet)
    }
}
```

6 Finally, create an initializer for the `Distance` structure.

```
init(feet:Double) {
    self.miles = Distance.toMiles(feet:feet)
}
}
```

Your `Distance` structure can now be initialized with `feet` and updated by setting `feet`.

 OPEN Compare your `Distance` extension with mine in the Distance-Extensions.playground.

CHALLENGE To confirm it's now possible, create a new instance of `Distance` using feet, update this value, and then print this value to the console. Then extend the DistanceExtensions playground to include another form of measuring distance.

3.3.2 *Extensions of their type*

You aren't limited to extending your own code. You can also extend classes, structures, or protocols of third-party code, or even of Apple frameworks or the Swift language!

As you saw in the previous chapter, the dictionary doesn't contain a method to join with another dictionary. Let's rectify this situation!

1 Create a new playground, and call it Extensions.

2 Add an extension to `Dictionary` so that it can add to another dictionary.

Extends Dictionary →
```
extension Dictionary {
    func add(other:Dictionary)->Dictionary {
        var returnDictionary:Dictionary = self
        for (key,value) in other {
            returnDictionary[key] = value
        }
        return returnDictionary
    }
}
```
Defines new method to extend Dictionary

3 To confirm your new extension works, create two sample dictionaries ready to add together:

```
var somelanguages = ["eng":"English","esp":"Spanish","ita":"Italian"]
var moreLanguages = ["deu":"German","chi":"Chinese","fre":"French"]
```

4 Now use your new method to join the two dictionaries:

```
var languages = somelanguages.add(other:moreLanguages)
```

From now on, whenever you want to join two
dictionaries in a project that contains this
extension, the add method is available to you.
Because this method is defined directly on the
Dictionary structure, you didn't need to
define the datatypes of the key and value, making this method available for all
Dictionary types.

OPEN Compare your code
in this section with mine in
the Extensions playground.

3.3.3   *Operator overloading*

I'm not completely happy with the add method. It's not intuitive that you're returning
the union of the two dictionaries, rather than adding one dictionary directly to the
other. I think it would be clearer if you'd used the add (+) operator, the way you can
with Arrays. Fortunately, Swift makes it possible to define or redefine operators!
Redefining functionality for an operator is called *operator overloading*.

The + operator function receives a left and right parameter and returns a value
of the same type.

1   Redefine the add method in a Dictionary extension as an overloading of the
+ operator.

```
func +(left: [String:String], right:[String:String]) -> [String:String] {
    var returnDictionary = left
    for (key,value) in right {
        returnDictionary[key] = value
    }
    return returnDictionary
}
```

Apart from how it's defined, not much has changed from the body of the
method. The data types of the key and value need to be specified because
you're no longer defining a generic Dictionary inside a Dictionary extension. Apart from that tweak, the code is similar, and you now can add two
Dictionarys (with key/value String/String) with the plus (+) operator,
which is much more intuitive!

2   You'll still need two sample dictionaries to add together:

```
var somelanguages = ["eng":"English","esp":"Spanish","ita":"Italian"]
var moreLanguages = ["deu":"German","chi":"Chinese","fre":"French"]
```

3   Add the two dictionaries together again, but this time use your overloaded add
operator:

```
var languages = somelanguages + moreLanguages
```

CHALLENGE   Overload the == operator to determine whether two Distance
objects are equivalent. Tip: The == operator returns a Bool value.

3.3.4 *Generics*

It's a shame, however, that this new overloaded operator will only "operate" on a specific type of Dictionary—one with a key that's a String, and a value that's a String. What if you had another Dictionary with a key/value of Int/String? You'd need to define an overloaded operator again, for each combination of keys/values! How tiresome.

This is where a concept called *generics* is super useful. A generic can be substituted in a function for any type, but must consistently represent the same type. It turns a function that deals with a specific data type to a generic function that can work with any data type.

Pass in a list of generics between angle brackets <>, after the function or operator name. Like function parameters, generics can be given any name you like.

1 Make the overloaded + operator for adding Dictionarys generic for any datatype for key or value.

```
func +<Key,Value>(left: [Key:Value], right:[Key:Value]) -> [Key:Value]
{    var returnDictionary = left
     for (key,value) in right {
         returnDictionary[key] = value
     }
     return returnDictionary
}
```

2 Again, you'll need two sample dictionaries to add together.

```
let somelanguages = ["eng":"English","esp":"Spanish","ita":"Italian"]
let moreLanguages = ["deu":"German","chi":"Chinese","fre":"French"]
```

3 Check your generic method still adds these dictionaries of with a String key and String value.

```
var languages = somelanguages + moreLanguages
```

Great, it still works! But will it add dictionaries of another type?

4 Create two sample dictionaries of another type to check. Let's try dictionaries with an Int key and String value:

```
let someRomanNumerals =
  [1:"I",5:"V",10:"X",50:"L",100:"C",500:"D",1000:"M"]
let moreRomanNumberals = [1:"I",2:"II",3:"III",4:"IV",5:"V"]
```

5 Confirm your overloaded operator can now join this different type of Dictionary.

```
var romanNumerals = someRomanNumerals + moreRomanNumberals
```

Generics are another powerful tool to add to your programmer's arsenal. The Swift team themselves use them to define Arrays and Dictionarys, which is why you didn't need to define the data type of the `Dictionary` when you extended it. You were already using this powerful feature!

3.4   Summary

In this chapter, you learned the following:

- Use classes or structures to represent types.
- Classes are reference types; structures are value types.
- Use initializers to initialize values.
- Use computed properties as getters and setters.
- Consider protocols to share functionality between classes or structures.
- Use extensions to add functionality to classes and structures.
- Use operator overloading to redefine operators.
- Use generics to make functions more flexible.

Part 2

Building your interface

Now that you have a good understanding of Xcode and Swift, you're probably anxious to dive into building apps! In this part, you'll explore building basic apps, with a focus on building up the interface.

In chapter 4, you'll get to know the building blocks of iOS apps—view controllers and views. You'll use these concepts to build a basic app.

In chapter 5, you'll take this basic app a little further, examining different ways to integrate user interaction into your app.

In chapter 6 and 7, you'll work on laying out more-complicated interfaces, and use various techniques for ensuring that your interfaces adapt to different devices, orientations, and multitasking modes.

In chapter 6, you'll also be introduced to *Bookcase*, a more complex app that you'll build over the course of this book from a concept to a finished app, ready to publish to the App Store.

Chapter 8 takes a different approach: you'll solve a complex, real-life problem. You'll look at dismissing the software keyboard and what to do when the keyboard obscures part of the interface. Along the way, you'll encounter all sorts of topics such as first responders, notifications, scrolling, and animation.

View controllers, views, and outlets

4

This chapter covers

- Exploring the view controller life cycle
- Creating views
- Modifying properties of views
- Connecting views in the storyboard with code

Now that you're familiar with Xcode and how to create a project, and you've explored Swift, the language you'll use to build apps, you're ready to start building an app.

In this chapter, you'll use view controllers and views, the basic building blocks of building any app, to build two example apps:

- You'll build a basic "Hello World"-style interface purely in code in an app called ViewsInCode.
- You'll then build views into an interface in Interface Builder in a distance converter app. Using the Distance structure that you built in chapter 3, the distance converter app will convert distances from miles to kilometers.

In the next chapter, we'll look at integrating user interaction with the distance converter app. In later chapters, we'll look at techniques for laying out an interface. But first, we need to look a little closer at the view hierarchy.

4.1   *View hierarchy*

As mentioned in chapter 1, everything you can see in your app is either a view or contained within a view. Examples of views are labels, images, or plain vanilla—views! Controls such as buttons, date pickers, and switches are types of views, too.

All the views in your app could be represented in a hierarchy—views can contain other views. Right at the top of every view hierarchy of an iOS app is a special view called the window.

The window represents the entire area taken up visually by your app. You're familiar with the concept of a window from desktop computers.

With enhancements of multitasking in iOS 9, the similarity with windows on desktop computers is even closer, because multiple apps can now be visible on the screen simultaneously. App windows no longer necessarily take up the entire dimensions of the screen. We'll look more at the implications this has on layout in chapter 6.

Though the app window is also a type of view (subclassing `UIView`), it doesn't display any content on its own. Rather, it contains another view, called its *subview*. Don't get subviews confused with subclasses—a subview is a view contained in another view, while a subclass is a class that inherits its implementation from another class.

In a simple interface, an app window's subview could be the root view for a scene. This root view would then contain subviews for every element in the interface. Subviews could be text fields, buttons, images, or other simple views. Subviews can then contain further subviews, and so on.

The distance converter app you'll build later in the chapter will allow the user to enter a distance in miles or kilometers and perform a conversion. See figure 4.1 for the view hierarchy of the distance converter app.

In the distance converter example, the app window has a subview that's the root view for the converter scene. The root view covers the available space in the window.

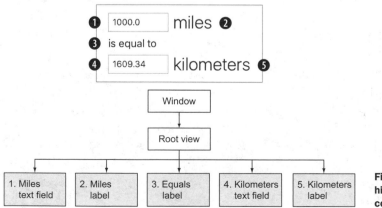

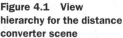

Figure 4.1   View hierarchy for the distance converter scene

Underneath this root view are all the views of the scene—the text fields and labels that make up the app's interface.

4.2 *Model-view-controller*

To ensure good code design in iOS, it's highly recommended you follow the model-view-controller (MVC) design pattern. Objects in your code are conceptually divided into three broad categories: model, view, and controller. Using the MVC pattern keeps your code organized and easily manageable as you maintain or extend your app:

- *Model* objects maintain the data for an application and handle any manipulation of that data. Model objects know nothing about the visuals of the scene they're used in; they're only interested in the data. A model object in the distance converter app could be the `Distance` structure that contains distance data and performs conversions.

- As you've seen, *views* are the visual components of an app. They can also provide visual feedback on interaction and report on user interaction. They're typically generic and reusable. Apple provides many views for you in the UIKit that are ready to go, such as labels, images, and switches. You've already seen that the distance converter app will contain a root view that then contains standard label and text field views.

- Every scene contains a controller called the *view controller*. The view controller is a Swift object that you can customize to coordinate between the view and model objects. You could think of the view controller as the director of a scene.

The main scene of the distance converter app will be connected to a main view controller, which will coordinate between the text field views and distance data. The view controller will generate a distance model object with a default value, and use it to update the text field views with the current distance.

When you make the distance converter truly interactive in the next chapter, these text fields will notify the view controller when the user makes a change and the view controller will in turn update the distance model object.

The model in your distance converter app will only be updated by the view controller, but in certain apps it may also be updated by an external source, such as a web service. In these cases, the model should then notify the view controller of this change, so that the view controller can perform any necessary tasks, such as updating the view.

See figure 4.2 for a look at how the MVC pattern works in iOS, in relation to the distance converter app.

Figure 4.2   Model view controller in distance converter app

As you can see, in iOS, the model and view are both self-contained units. They know nothing about each other, nor do they know about the scene they're in. The view controller contains references to the model and view objects and is in the middle of the communication between objects.

> **NOTE** If the view and model objects don't have a reference to the view controller, how can they communicate with it? iOS has alternative solutions to solve this dilemma. In the next chapter, we'll explore three approaches commonly used with view objects: target-action, events, and delegation (also often used with model objects). Later in the book, we'll look at notifications and bindings, approaches more commonly used with model objects.

Let's look more closely at the view controller and see it in operation in a sample app.

4.3   *View controller*

View controllers have several important responsibilities, such as

- Responding to communication from view objects (such as from user interaction)
- Configuring, laying out, and updating view objects for a scene
- Responding to communication from model objects (such as from network calls)
- Communicating with and updating the data in the model

As you've seen, every scene has a root view, which contains all the views in the scene, and a view controller, which is responsible for managing all the views in the scene. The view controller automatically contains a reference to the scene's root view. Figure 4.3 shows how the view controller fits into the distance converter scene view hierarchy.

The views themselves are already built to do what they do: the label will display text, and the text field will display the software keyboard and accept user input. But it's up to the view controller to react to your specific app's needs.

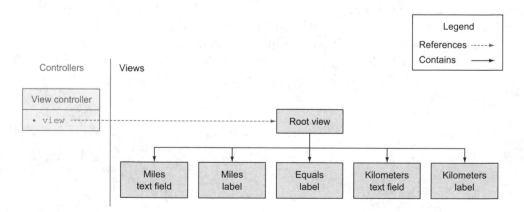

Figure 4.3   Distance converter scene

4.3.1 *Creating a custom view controller*

Most of the time, the default behavior of views in a scene isn't sufficient. Code needs to be written to customize the behavior of the scene. This custom behavior is performed by the view controller.

For example, in the completed distance converter app, the view controller will respond when the user enters a value in miles or kilometers, convert to the appropriate measurement, and display the result to the user. But how do you create a custom view controller? You can write the custom behaviors of your view controller by subclassing the `UIViewController` class and connecting this class with the scene.

Let's put the distance converter app aside for the moment—you'll build that later in the chapter. For now, you'll build a basic app that displays views in code.

Create a new Single View Application Xcode project following the steps you went through in chapter 1. Call this project "ViewsInCode." As the name suggests, the Single View Application template sets up an app with one scene created and ready to use.

Follow these steps to find where the class connected to a scene's view controller is defined:

1 Select the view controller for the app's scene in Interface Builder.
2 In the Inspector area, select the Identity Inspector (third icon).
3 In the Custom Class field, you'll find that this view controller is already connected to a custom class, or subclass, unimaginatively called `ViewController`.
4 Because the Swift file name is usually the same as the name of the class it defines, you know to find the Swift file containing the `ViewController` class in the ViewController.swift file in the Project Navigator.

See figure 4.4 to help you navigate these steps.

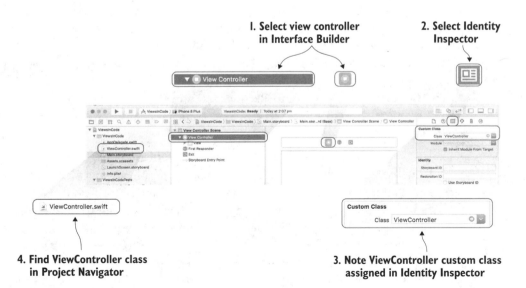

Figure 4.4   Subclassing the view controller

Open the view controller subclass now. You can either select ViewController.swift in the Project Navigator or, for convenience, you can click the arrow next to the custom class in the Identity Inspector (see figure 4.5).

Custom Class

Class ViewController

Module ViewsInCode

4.3.2 *Customizing a UIViewController subclass*

Figure 4.5   Jump to class

When you open the file, you'll find that the ViewController class is by default pre-populated with two methods, overridden from its superclass UIViewController (see figure 4.6).

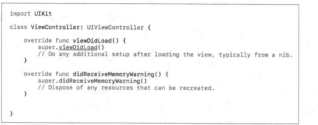

```
import UIKit

class ViewController: UIViewController {

    override func viewDidLoad() {
        super.viewDidLoad()
        // Do any additional setup after loading the view, typically from a nib.
    }

    override func didReceiveMemoryWarning() {
        super.didReceiveMemoryWarning()
        // Dispose of any resources that can be recreated.
    }

}
```

Figure 4.6   Default
UIViewController

During the lifetime of a view controller, it will go through certain life events. At these special times in its life, certain view controller methods will be called. When you subclass UIViewController, you can override these methods to provide custom implementation in these moments.

You'll see viewDidLoad and didReceiveMemoryWarning in the default ViewController subclass. You can override many more methods, and we'll look at more shortly. But for now, viewDidLoad is a great place to start, because it's triggered after the root view, and all of its subviews have loaded.

To prove that you automatically have access to the root view of the scene at this point, let's change the background color of the view in code to yellow.

The variable in the view controller that references the root view has a name that's simple enough to remember: view. You could test this out with simple code completion.

1 In the line following super.viewDidLoad(), begin typing view.

Code completion suggestions should appear automatically. With only the first two characters entered, the view property should appear as the second suggestion, with the V icon beside it indicating it's an instance variable. (Other icons you'll see frequently are L for local variable, S for static variable, and M for instance method.) Beside the suggestion, you'll see that the suggested view property is an implicitly unwrapped UIView optional (UIView!). You can also see a description of the suggestion at the bottom of the suggestion window. You can scroll or use your cursor keys to explore possible suggestions. See figure 4.7.

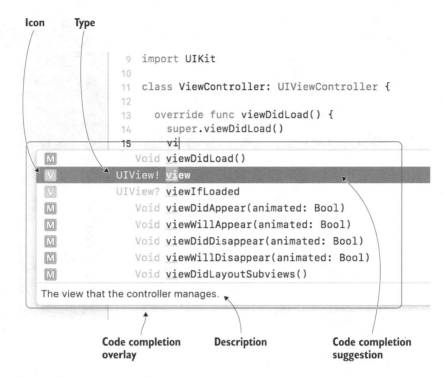

Figure 4.7 Code completion

2 Select the `view` property from the code completion suggestions.

Where does this variable come from? You definitely haven't set up a `view` property in your `ViewController` class. The most obvious candidate is `View-Controller`'s immediate superclass `UIViewController`, but it could have come from a superclass of `UIViewController`. Who knows, it could even be a computed property in a protocol extension that `UIViewController` or one of its superclasses implements.

You can find out where this property comes from by looking at the documentation. You can bring up the Help Inspector by moving the cursor inside the `view` in your code and selecting the help icon in the inspector panel. Curiously, the Help Inspector doesn't tell you which class the property is declared in, so you'll need to select Property Reference at the bottom of the property description in the Help Inspector to open documentation for this property. The documentation will indicate that this property is declared in the `UIViewController` class.

Now that you have a reference to the root view, let's change its background color. You know that the `view` property is a `UIView`, so you could scan through the documentation for `UIView`, but let's see if you have any luck with code completion.

3 Add a period(.) after `view`, and type *color* to see what Xcode suggests. First on the list of suggestions is a `backgroundColor` property—that must be it!

The `backgroundColor` property is defined as a `UIColor` optional. If you look at `UIColor` in the documentation, you'll find that it contains shorthand type methods that return common colors—let's use one now to set the view's background color.

4 Add the following line to the `viewDidLoad` method after calling the super method:

```
view.backgroundColor = UIColor.yellow
```

5 Run the app on the simulator. You should see a blank app with a yellow background (see figure 4.8).

4.3.3   *Initial view controller*

Not many apps have one scene. To illustrate, let's temporarily add a second scene to the ViewsIn-Code app.

Figure 4.8   Blank app with a yellow background

1 Open the main storyboard by selecting Main.storyboard in the Project Navigator.

2 Drag in another view controller from the Object Library beside the other. Now, the storyboard contains *two* view controllers. How does the app know which scene to display first?

Look closer at the left of the view controllers in the storyboard, and notice that one of them has an arrow pointing to it. Select each of the view controllers (not the view), and examine the Attributes Inspector. Notice the "Is Initial View Controller" attribute is selected for the original view controller.

3 Select this checkbox for your new view controller. Notice the arrow now appears before that new view controller, and the storyboard entry point changes in the hierarchy too (see figure 4.9).

You can also drag this arrow directly to the left of a view controller.

4 Drag the arrow back to the original view controller to identify it once again as the initial view controller.

When you're finished experimenting, delete the new view controller and make sure the original view controller is set once again as the initial view controller. If

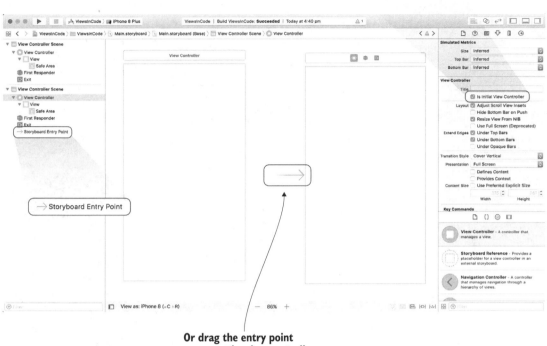

Select to make a view controller the initial scene (or storyboard entry point).

☑ Is Initial View Controller

Or drag the entry point arrow to the view controller.

Figure 4.9   Initial view controller

there's no initial view controller, all you'll see when you run your app is a black screen!

iOS performs the following steps between launching your app and seeing the root view of your initial view controller:

1   iOS instantiates the app window.

2   iOS loads the main storyboard and instantiates its initial view controller.

3   A reference to the initial view controller is passed to the app's window, which keeps track of the view controller currently at the root in the `rootView-Controller` property.

4   This triggers the initial view controller's root view to be added as the window's subview.

5   This triggers the initial view controller to load its root view (usually from the storyboard).

6   The window becomes visible and the root view appears.

In the end, you'll have relationships between the app window, initial view controller, and the root view that look like figure 4.10.

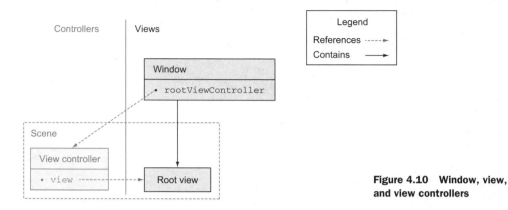

Figure 4.10   Window, view, and view controllers

View controller life cycle

To know how to subclass a `UIViewController` object, you need to know which methods to override and when. To do this, you need to examine the steps a view controller goes through in its life cycle.

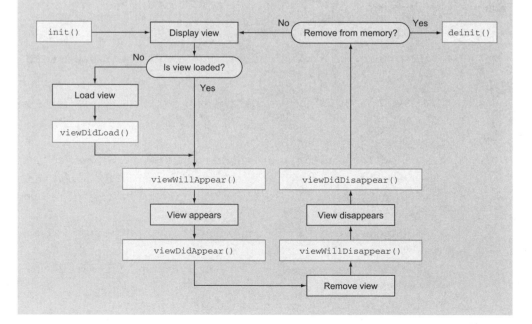

Initializing a view controller

As is the custom in any Swift type, the view controller starts off life with an initializer. The initializer doesn't have access to the root view, so configuring the views in the scene often occurs later in the life cycle.

Loading a view

If the root view isn't yet loaded, the view controller needs to load it. Wait—how could a root view already be loaded? Well, when one scene navigates to another scene, the originating view controller stays in memory. When returning to the originating view controller, its root view will display but doesn't need to load again and the `viewDid-Load` method won't be called.

The most common and recommended way for a view controller to load its root view is via the storyboard. However, a view controller can also get its root view in other ways. It can load its root view from a nib file (like a storyboard with one scene), or alternatively instantiate it in code by overriding the `UIViewController`'s `load-View` method.

After a root view and all of its subviews are loaded, the `viewDidLoad` method is called. This method is commonly overridden to perform any additional one-off setup that your root view requires. As you did earlier, you could modify the properties of the root view itself. Alternatively, you could modify the properties of its subviews, or instantiate and add new subviews to the root view.

Displaying a view

Whether the root view needed to be loaded or not, the `viewWillAppear` method will be called before the view displays. This method is commonly overridden if you want to update the root view or its subviews every time you navigate to this scene.

Imagine the main menu scene of a game that displays a top score field. When the user navigates to the game itself and then returns to the main menu, the top score should be updated in case the player beats it! The top score field should then probably be updated in the `viewWillAppear` method.

The `viewDidAppear` method is called after the root view is displayed. This method is commonly overridden to initiate processor-intensive work that otherwise could cause sluggishness in presenting the view. This could include starting an animation, playing a sound, or making a network call.

Removing a scene's root view

Notice in the figure that the `UIViewController`'s methods for displaying its root view have companion methods for removing its root view.

For example, if your app navigates to a second scene, the root view for the first scene would disappear. Before this view is removed, the `viewWillDisappear` method is called. After the view is removed, the `viewDidDisappear` method is called. Override these methods to perform any final tidying up when the view disappears. Perhaps you want to stop a sound file, stop a perpetual animation, remove notification observers, or store a state.

(continued)

Deinitializing a view controller

When any object is removed from memory in Swift, a special `deinit` method is called. Implement the view controller's `deinit` method if you want to perform any additional cleanup right before this view controller is destroyed.

Releasing memory

One method that didn't make the life cycle chart is `didReceiveMemoryWarning`. You might remember seeing this method in the autogenerated custom view controller code. With modern devices, the need to free up memory is unlikely, but if your app does have high memory expectations (for example, perhaps it's storing many images in a cache), overriding this method is where you could free up that memory.

4.4   *Managing views*

Now that you know more about view controllers, let's look at how to use a view controller to manage views. Views can be built up in code or in Interface Builder. Let's first look at building up views in code.

4.4.1   *Managing views in code*

Open your ViewsInCode project again. You've demonstrated you had access to the view controller's root view by editing its background color in the subclassed view controller's `viewDidLoad` method.

Now that you have access to the root view, you can add subviews to it in code. Let's add a red view that fills the width of the root view, but only half the height (see figure 4.11).

ADDING A VIEW IN CODE

In the `ViewController` class, define an implicitly unwrapped `UIView` object called `redView` above the `viewDidLoad` method.

```
var redView:UIView!
```

To instantiate a `UIView`, you need to pass in the view's frame dimensions using a structure type called `CGRect`. Get the width and height of the root view with view's `bounds` property. You can then set its background color to red and add it to the scene's root view.

1   Add the following to the end of the viewDid-
    Load method:

Figure 4.11   Add red view

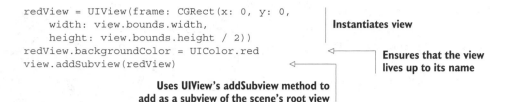

```
redView = UIView(frame: CGRect(x: 0, y: 0,
    width: view.bounds.width,
    height: view.bounds.height / 2))
redView.backgroundColor = UIColor.red
view.addSubview(redView)
```

Instantiates view

Ensures that the view lives up to its name

Uses UIView's addSubview method to add as a subview of the scene's root view

2 Run the app again, and you should see a red rectangle appear in the top half of the interface. Great!

Frame vs. bounds

Both the `frame` and `bounds` of a view refer to a rectangle, defined by a `CGRect` object that contains the `size` (`width` and `height`) and `origin` (`x` and `y`) of the view. The `origin` of a `CGRect` object usually refers to the upper-left corner.

The difference between `frame` and `bounds` is that `frame` is seen from the perspective of the view's superview coordinate system, and `bounds` is seen from the perspective of the view's own coordinate system. As you can see in the view in the example, the `size` of the `bounds` is often the same as the `size` as the `frame` of a view. The `origin`, on the other hand, often differs, depending on the perspective.

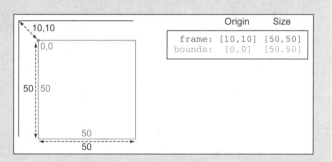

If you apply any transformations to the rectangle, however, such as scaling or rotation, the size of a view can look different from the perspective of a view's own coordinate system or its superview's. Scale a view 50% such as in the example, and the `size` of its `bounds` won't change, but from the perspective of its superview, the `size` of its `frame` has shrunk by half.

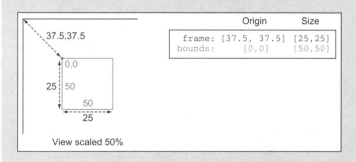

View scaled 50%

We'll explore transformations further in the next chapter.

ADDING A LABEL IN CODE

Well, that's all fine for basic views, but how about more complex views such as labels? Let's add a label to the view halfway down, as in figure 4.12.

You can instantiate a label the same way as with a view, but using the `UILabel` class.

Let's position the label halfway down the root view with 20-point margins and give it an arbitrary width and height of 20 points.

Hello World

Figure 4.12   Adding a label

What's the point?

Don't worry, I'm not down in the dumps!

Points are how coordinates and distances are measured in iOS and are distinct from the actual pixels in the screen of the device. The intention of points is to have consistency of scale across different devices, especially Retina and non-Retina devices. In the main, the underlying pixels are irrelevant, and you'll measure distances and coordinates in points.

---

1   First, as before, add the definition of the implicitly unwrapped label above the `viewDidLoad` method:

```
var label:UILabel!
```

Now, instantiate the label code. Because `UILabel` subclasses `UIView`, you can use `UIView` properties such as `backgroundColor`. Give the label a temporary background color so you can see it clearly. Display text in the label with `UILabel`'s `text` property, and use `UILabel`'s font property to adjust the font size.

2   Add the following listing code after the `redView` code in the `viewDidLoad` method.

Listing 4.1   Add label

```
label = UILabel(frame:
         CGRect(x: 20, y: self.view.bounds.height / 2,
         width: 20, height: 20))
label.backgroundColor = UIColor.orange
```

```
view.addSubview(label)
label.text = "Hello World"
label.font = label.font.withSize(40)
```

3 Run the app, and you'll see a small orange rectangle appear where the text field should go.

Obviously, the text field needs more space to display, but what should the width and height be? `UIView` has a handy method for setting the width and height to its ideal dimensions to fit its contents, called `sizeToFit`.

4 Run `sizeToFit` on the label, and run the app again.

```
label.sizeToFit()
```

Success! You can remove the orange background now if you like, and you should now see something similar to figure 4.12.

✔ **CHECKPOINT** If you'd like to compare, you can check out my project at https://github.com/iOSAppDevelopmentwithSwiftinAction/Views-InCode.git (1.DisplayingViews branch).

You can close the ViewsInCode project; we'll come back to it later. But now, let's use Interface Builder to manage views in a scene in the storyboard.

4.4.2 Managing views in Interface Builder

In the remainder of this chapter, you'll build the interface for the distance converter app that we looked at earlier in this chapter. In the next chapter, this app will convert

distances the user enters, but for now you'll specify a miles distance in code for the app to convert to kilometers and display in the text field (see figure 4.13).

This time, we'll explore building an interface using Apple's visual tool for building interfaces, Interface Builder.

1 First, create another Xcode project and call it "DistanceConverter."

✔ **CHECKPOINT** If you want to skip the initial setup, you can download it from https://github.com/iOSAppDevelopmentwith-SwiftinAction/DistanceConverter.git (1.Initial-Setup).

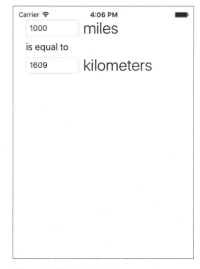

Figure 4.13   Distance converter app

2   Click on the main storyboard in the Project Navigator to construct the interface of the initial scene. Drag on text fields and labels to make the interface you see in figure 4.14.

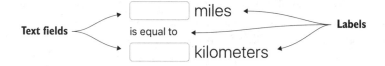

Figure 4.14   Distance converter storyboard

Earlier, you set the text and adjusted the font size of a label in code. This time, you'll use Interface Builder's Attribute Inspector.

3   Select a label and find the text attribute in the Attribute Inspector. By default, it will say "Label." Enter the text "miles," "kilometers," and "is equal to" for the three labels.

4   Adjust the font size for the miles and kilometers labels. Find the font attribute and click on the arrow, to edit the font (see figure 4.15).

Use the custom font type if you want to specify the font family—otherwise, the default font family for a font style will be used. In iOS 9 and later, for example, the system font is San Francisco. In general, if you want a consistent look with other iOS apps, use Apple's built-in font styles.

5   For the miles and kilometers labels, use the built-in Title 1.

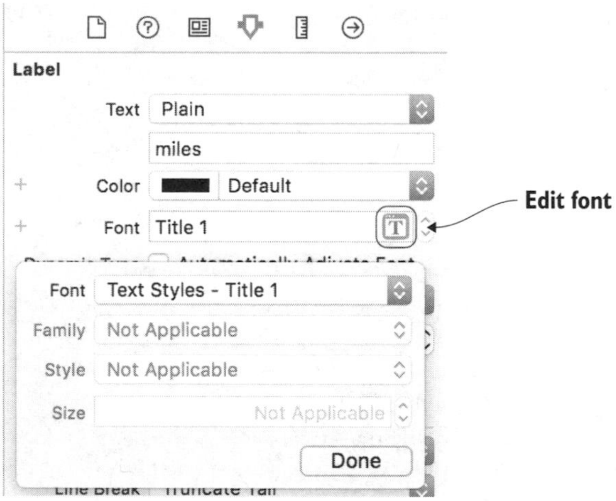

Figure 4.15   Editing the font in the Attribute Inspector

You'll use the `Distance` structure from the previous chapter as a model in this app.

TIP When you modify the text of a label or change its font size, you might find that it's no longer big enough to contain its content, indicated by an ellipsis (…). You can resize a view to its content by selecting a view, and then selecting Editor > Size to Fit Content. Frustratingly, you might find after running the app that Xcode has slightly misjudged the new size, and you'll need to add a few extra pixels in Interface Builder. You can do this by dragging the width handle or adjusting the width in the Size Inspector. After resizing, you might also find you need to reposition the view.

6 Create a Distance.swift file by selecting File > New > File, and select the Swift File template.

TIP You have alternative approaches to creating a file. You could also right-click on the group in the Project Navigator where you want to create the file, select New File, and select the appropriate template. Alternatively, you could find the file template you want in the File Template library in the library area, and drag it where you want it in the Project Navigator. Too many options!

7 Paste in the `Distance` structure you worked on in chapter 3. You can also find it at https://github.com/iOSAppDevelopmentwithSwiftinAction/Distance-Converter /blob/1.InitialSetup/DistanceConverter/Distance.swift.

8 In the custom `ViewController` class, add a `distance` variable that stores a `Distance` object. I'm going to instantiate mine with 1,000 miles; you can instantiate yours however you like.

```
var distance = Distance(miles: 1000)
```

> ✓ **CHECKPOINT** If you'd like to download the project at this point, you can check it out at https://github.com/iOSAppDevelopmentwith-SwiftinAction/DistanceConverter.git (1.InitialSetup).

Now that you have a `distance` object, the challenge is to display its `miles` property in the miles text field and its `km` property in the kilometers text field. As you saw earlier in the chapter, following the MVC pattern, it's the view controller's job to update text field views from the model.

For the view controller to update the text field views, it will need a way of referencing them in code.

CONNECTING VIEWS TO OUTLETS

The easiest way to get a reference to a view in the storyboard in your custom view controller class is to use what's called an *outlet*. An outlet is a variable in your code that's connected behind the scenes with a view in Interface Builder. Let's set up outlets for the two text fields now.

Open the main storyboard. To set up your outlets, you'll first need to open the Assistant Editor.

Using the Assistant Editor

Opening the Assistant Editor splits the editor area into two editor panes, most commonly with the standard editor on the left and the Assistant Editor on the right. The two editor panes could be the same type of editor, such as two Swift files, or they could be different types, such as the storyboard on the left and a related Swift file on the right.

Open the Assistant Editor by selecting the Assistant Editor selector at the top right—that's the button in the middle of the three editor selectors that looks like two rings.

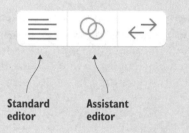

Standard
editor

Assistant
editor

When you want to close the Assistant Editor, leaving only the standard editor open, select the editor selector on the left that looks like a paragraph of text.

As you've seen, if you select a file in the Project Navigator, the standard editor pane will open that file in the appropriate editor. How do you open a file in the Assistant Editor pane?

An alternative way to open a file in either editor pane is by using the jump bars at the top of the editor panes. The jump bars display a hierarchical path of where what you're currently editing fits into the project. The hierarchy of the jump bars spreads on the left from the project itself, to your current location in the file on the right. Use the jump bars to jump to a different file or location within a file.

In the Assistant Editor, the left of the jump bar gives you additional modes for navigating to a file. The Manual mode gives you the same hierarchy you've seen in the standard editor's jump bar. But the real magic of the Assistant Editor lies in other automated modes that open files related to your selection in the standard editor. If you have Interface Builder open in the standard editor, for example, the Automatic mode becomes available and automatically opens the source file for the object you select in Interface Builder.

If, for example, you select the view controller in the storyboard, your custom `View-Controller` class will automatically open in the Assistant Editor pane, if you have Automatic mode selected.

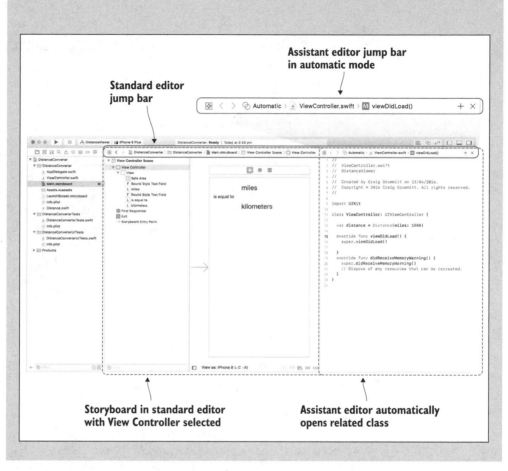

Now, you should have the storyboard open in the standard editor, and the Assistant Editor open to the view controller source file.

1 Find the text field before the label that says "miles." Hold down the Control key and drag from the text field to your view controller source file below the declaration of `distance`.

2 A connection menu appears. Give the outlet the name "milesTextField" and select Connect.

**1. Control-drag the text field to
the view controller subclass.**

**2. Give the outlet a name
and click Connect.**

3. An @IBOutlet is created.

Figure 4.16   Steps to create an outlet

3 A variable appears in your code. See figure 4.16 for clarification on the steps to
   create an outlet.

You should see a line of code appear in your code defining the outlet:

```
@IBOutlet weak var milesTextField: UITextField!
```

NOTE   An @ symbol indicates an attribute that provides more information to the compiler about a variable or type declaration. Attributes that begin with IB indicate a possible connection in Interface Builder.

You might notice several interesting aspects of this outlet property:

- @IBOutlet—This keyword lets Interface Builder know that this property is an outlet and can be connected to an object in the storyboard.
- weak—The weak keyword relates to memory management and is included to prevent strong reference cycles.

AUTOMATIC REFERENCE COUNTING   *Automatic Reference Counting* (ARC) is Apple's approach to automatically removing objects from memory that are no longer being referenced. All instance variables default to be strong. While at least one strong reference to an object exists, it won't be deallocated from memory. A weak reference to an object, on the other hand, won't prevent an object from being deallocated from memory. Why then, doesn't a weak IBOutlet variable get deallocated from memory? IBOutlet variables usually refer to a view in the view hierarchy, which are automatically strongly referenced in a view's subviews array. While the variable remains in the view hierarchy of a view controller in memory, it will not be deallocated from memory.

- *Implicitly unwrapped optional*—That exclamation mark at the end of the outlet declaration indicates that this is an implicitly unwrapped optional. As this outlet isn't defined in the init() method of the view controller, it needed to be an optional, and rather than unwrapping this property every time you use it, Apple made the decision that an implicitly unwrapped optional was most convenient for outlets.
- *A circle appears to the left of the declaration, in the line number column*—The filled-in circle within a circle indicates that this outlet is connected to an item in the storyboard. Hover over it to highlight the connected item in the storyboard.

EDIT OUTLET PROPERTIES

Now that you have an outlet for milesTextField, you can edit its properties, the way you did earlier when you created views in code.

1   In the viewDidLoad() method, set the text field's text property to the miles property of the distance object you set up earlier. As text is a String and miles is a Double, you'll need to use string interpolation to assign the value.

```
milesTextField.text = "\(distance.miles)"
```

2   Create an outlet for the kilometers text field as well, and this time set its text property to the km property of distance.

```
kmTextField.text = "\(distance.km)"
```

3 Run the app.

The value for miles that you used to instantiate your distance object will be converted to kilometers and displayed in the relevant text fields.

Congratulations, you can now make connections in code to views you set up in the storyboard!

✅ **CHECKPOINT**   If you'd like to compare your code with mine, you can check out the next branch at https://github.com/iOSAppDevelopmentwithSwiftinAction/DistanceConverter.git (2.ConvertDistanceFromCode).

In the next chapter, you'll make this distance conversion useful by including user interaction, using the special abilities of types of views called controls.

4.5   *Summary*

In this chapter, you learned the following:

- Manage your scene's root view and subviews with a subclass of `UIViewController`.
- Use outlets to connect views in the storyboard to variables in your code.
- Use the Assistant Editor to create outlets. Provide custom implementation to your `UIViewController` subclass by overriding methods that will be called at different moments during the view controller's lifetime. Here are several important `UIViewController` methods you can override:
  - `init()`: Initializer of view controller; view isn't yet available.
  - `viewDidLoad()`: Initial setup of view here.
  - `viewWillAppear()`: Updates view every time you navigate to this scene.
  - `viewDidAppear()`: Updates view every time you navigate to this scene. Use if processor intensive, for example, to start an animation or play a sound.
  - `viewWillDisappear()`: Cleans up before you navigate away from this scene, for example, to stop a sound file, animation, or store a state.
  - `viewDidDisappear()`: Cleans up after you navigate away from this scene.
  - `deinit()`: Tidies up when deallocating this view controller from memory.
  - `didReceiveMemoryWarning()`: Place to free up memory.

User interaction
5

This chapter covers

- Responding to simple touch events
- Responding to complicated touch gestures
- Using controls for user interaction

Apps would be static, linear, and boring if the user couldn't interact with them. In this chapter, we'll look at three different ways an app can respond to user interaction:

- *Controls* are special types of views that are built to receive user interaction. You've already seen one type of control in the distance converter app: the text field. In this chapter, you'll extend the distance converter app to convert kilometers or miles that the user enters in the text fields, by adding buttons and responding to changes in the text fields. Finally, we'll look at other available controls for receiving user interaction.
- Next, we'll look at receiving user interaction in a view via *touches*. Custom views can respond to touches by overriding relevant view methods. To explore this concept, you'll build an app with a custom view that changes color when you tap it.

- We'll then look at receiving user interaction via *gestures*. Using *gesture recognizers*, your app can detect much more complicated movements from touches such as pinching, rotating, long press, or swiping. In this chapter, you'll build a simple image viewer app that will respond to gestures.

5.1   Controls

A control is a special type of view that's designed for user interaction. Because controls come with UIKit and are available for everyone to use in their apps, they have a consistent and familiar look across different apps, making controls in your interface more intuitive for your users.

As with gestures, control events can trigger actions in your code. Let's look at several different types of controls, and how to receive notification of different control events.

5.1.1   Buttons

One of the most common controls in UIKit is the *button*. See figure 5.1 for default looks for several different button types.

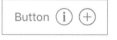

Figure 5.1   Button types

You'll use system buttons to make your distance converter app interactive. The user can convert the number of miles they've entered to kilometers or vice versa (see figure 5.2). Okay, we're not going to win any design awards, but we're focused on functionality for the moment.

✓ **CHECKPOINT**   Open the distance converter app where you left it at the end of the last chapter, or check it out at https://github.com/iOSApp-DevelopmentwithSwiftinAction/DistanceConverter.git.   (2.ConvertDistance-FromCode).

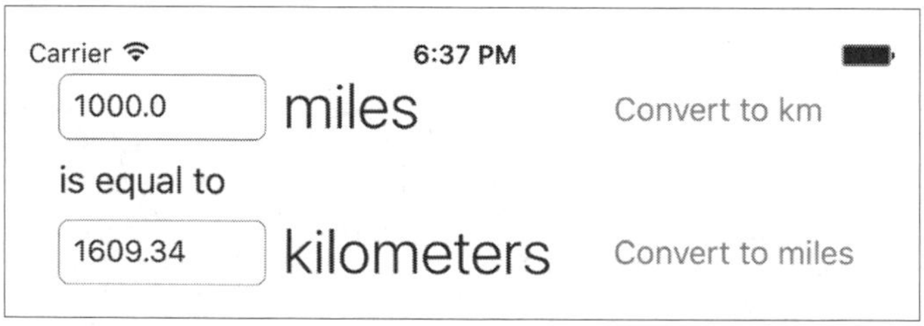

Carrier 📶	6:37 PM	🔋
1000.0	miles	Convert to km
is equal to		
1609.34	kilometers	Convert to miles

Figure 5.2   Distance converter interface

ADDING A BUTTON

Let's add the two convert buttons to the interface.

1 Open the main storyboard and drag on a Button from the Object Library beside the miles label.

2 Open the Attributes Inspector and take a moment to inspect the attributes available for buttons. Notice the State Config attribute. Buttons can have four different states, shown in table 5.1.

Table 5.1 Button states

State	Description
Default	The default state for the button
Highlighted	Active while the user is touching the button
Selected	Active if the button's `selected` property is set to `true`
Disabled	Active if the button's `enabled` property is set to `false`

One important thing to understand with buttons is that attributes below the State Config attribute only apply to the currently selected state. If you don't set specific attributes for a state, appropriate defaults for that state will be implemented.

For the default state, change the text of the button (called its *title*) to "Convert to km." While you're here, drag on a second button beside the kilometers label, and give it the title "Convert to miles."

Run it on the iPhone 6s Plus simulator. The interface should look something like figure 5.2.

CREATING CONTROL ACTIONS

Nothing happens yet when you tap the buttons. You're going to connect the convert buttons with methods in the view controller code that will perform the conversion and display the result.

To connect a method to a control event in Interface Builder, you'll need to define the method as an *action*. An action in simple terms is a method that will be triggered when something happens. In this case, you'll create an action method in your view controller code that will be triggered when a convert button is touched using the following steps:

1 As you did when creating an outlet in the previous chapter, open the Assistant Editor. Holding down the Control key, drag from a Convert-to-km button in Interface Builder to your view controller source code, below the `viewDidLoad` method.

TIP If you don't see the view controller source code, double-check you have the Automatic mode selected in the Assistant Editor jump bar.

2   This time, instead of creating an outlet, you'll create an action. Change the Connection type to Action. Give your action a Name—let's call it "`convert-ToKm`."

3   Notice the many event options available to you. Touch Down refers to a touch being detected on the button, while Touch Up Inside refers to a finger lifting off the button. The rest of the settings are fine left at their defaults. Select Connect, and an `@IBAction` will be generated in the view controller source. See figure 5.3 to clarify the steps.

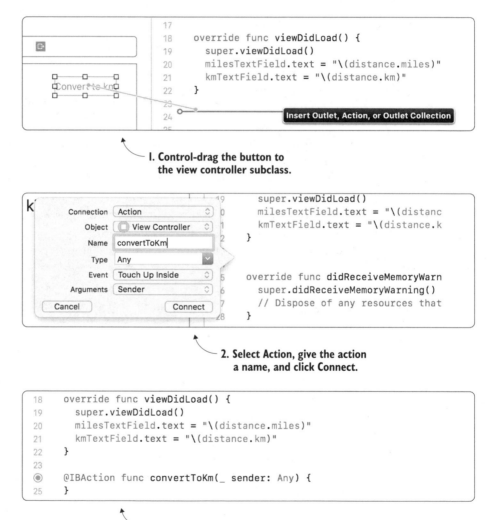

1. Control-drag the button to the view controller subclass.

2. Select Action, give the action a name, and click Connect.

3. An @IBAction is created.

Figure 5.3   Create control action

Now that you're receiving notification of the user tapping a convert button, you can perform the conversion.

Like outlets, action methods are tagged with a keyword that begins with `@IB`, which stands for Interface Builder. The `@IBAction` keyword indicates that this method can be connected to something in the storyboard and the filled-in circle next to the line number indicates that this action is indeed connected.

Connecting an event to a method (known as the action) in an object (known as the target) in this way is called the target-action pattern. Later, we'll explore setting up this connection in code.

4   First, you need to cast the `String` contents of the miles text field to a `Double` in the `convertToKm` method. As the result of this conversion is an optional, use optional binding:

```
if let miles = Double(milesTextField.text!) {
}
```

5   Reset the `distance` object's `miles` property, and the `distance` object will automatically convert the kilometers. Convert the km `Double` to an `Int` to remove the unnecessary decimal value, and display it in the kilometers text field:

```
distance.miles = miles
kmTextField.text = "\(Int(distance.km))"
```

CHALLENGE   Follow the same process to create a `convertToMiles()` method, triggered by the Convert to Miles button, that converts the value in the kilometers text field   to miles, and displays the result in the miles text field.

6   Run the app, and your distance converter app has become truly interactive, converting distances when you tap the conversion buttons.

✓   **CHECKPOINT**   Compare your solution with mine at https://github.com/ iOSAppDevelopmentwithSwiftinAction/DistanceConverter.git (3.ConvertDistanceWithButtons).

But wait—are the conversion buttons necessary? Maybe the conversion could happen automatically as the user types the distance into the text field.

As it happens, text fields are types of controls too, and can also trigger actions in your code. Let's take a look.

5.1.2   *Text field*

Text fields display one line of text that the user can edit using the pop-up software keyboard.

Select a text field now, and examine the attributes available in the Attributes Inspector.

- You can adjust how autocorrection works in Capitalization, Correction, and Spell Checking.
- With the return key attribute, you can change the look or text of the return key to a variety of predefined options.
- You can request that text entered be hidden (that is, Password field) by selecting Secure Text Entry.
- Under Keyboard Type, you can choose which type of keyboard you want to appear. Different types are relevant for different text field purposes.

KEYBOARD TYPES

There are three main categories of keyboards, with different variations, as explained in table 5.2.

Table 5.2   Keyboard categories

Category	Use
ASCII	Text, emails, URLs, and so on. The Numbers and Punctuation keyboard can be accessed if necessary.
Numbers and Punctuation	Numbers and punctuation, where the ASCII keyboard can be accessed if necessary.
Number Pad	For when numbers and relevant symbols are required, and the ASCII keyboard isn't required.

To make the different variations of keyboards, the bottom layer of keys in the ASCII keyboard is swapped out, and one of the Number Pad keys is swapped out. See figure 5.4 for all keyboard type variations.

That's not all the different keyboard types! Keyboard keys and layout vary depending on the language, the orientation of the device, and the device type itself!

Which type of keyboard is most appropriate for your miles and kilometers text fields? Choose an appropriate type and make the adjustment in the Attributes Inspector.

CONNECTING ACTIONS FROM INTERFACE BUILDER

You'll modify your distance converter app to automatically calculate the distance conversion as the user types it into the text field.

1. Open the Assistant Editor. Unlike earlier, where you created a new method, you'll connect an existing method, `convertToKm()`, to a text field event.
2. Holding down Control, drag from the miles text field to the `convertToKm()` method. The Connect Action text should appear (see figure 5.5).

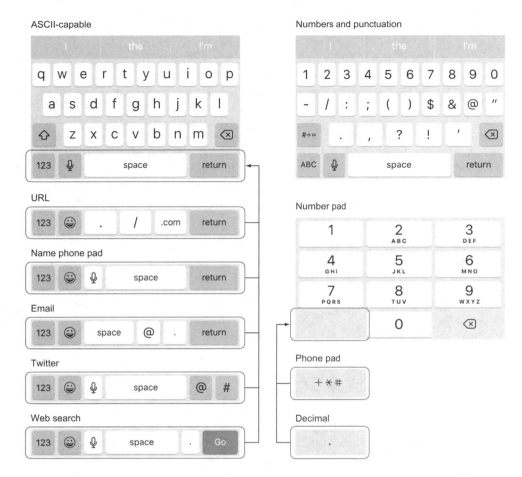

Figure 5.4   The three keyboard types

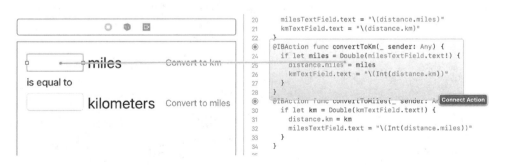

Figure 5.5   Connect Action from Interface Builder

3 Run the app, and make changes to the miles text field. Notice that the kilometers text *doesn't change.*

4 Inside your running app, tap in the kilometers text field. Notice that now the kilometers value *changes!* What's going on?

5 Back in Interface Builder, select the miles text field, and open the Connections Inspector to get a better idea of what's going on. You should see that the "Editing Did End" event is connected to the `convertToKm` method.

You may have noticed when you connected the action to the text field that you didn't have a choice of event. Connecting actions in this way assumes a control's default event. The Editing Did End event is the text field's default, which only triggers after a user *stops* editing a text field, for instance, by tapping on another text field.

DELETING CONNECTIONS

This isn't the event we're looking for, so delete the Editing Did End connection by selecting the X in the Connections Inspector (see figure 5.6).

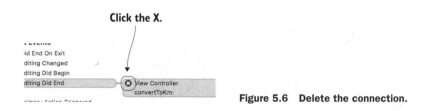

Figure 5.6   Delete the connection.

CONNECTING ACTIONS FROM THE CONNECTIONS INSPECTOR

The Editing Changed event triggers whenever the text in a text field is modified. This sounds more like it! Connect the Editing Changed event to the `convertToKm` method.

1 Drag from the Editing Changed circle in the Connections Inspector to the `convertToKm` method (see figure 5.7).

Figure 5.7   Connect Action from Connections Inspector

2   Run the app again. This time, as you make changes to the miles text field, you should see the kilometers text field converting automatically. Success!

CONNECTING ACTIONS FROM CODE

You could connect the Editing Changed event for the kilometers text field to the `convertToMiles()` method in the same way, but this time let's connect the action in code.

Use the `UIControl`'s `addTarget()` method to specify the target and the action. You'll also need to need to specify the control event itself that you're listening for (`editingChanged`). These steps show you how:

1   Add the following line to the view controller's `viewDidLoad` method:

```
kmTextField.addTarget(self, action: #selector(convertToMiles),
    for: .editingChanged)
```

In English, this line says, "When the `editingChanged` event is triggered, call the `convertToMiles()` action on `self` (that is, instance method of the view controller).

And that's all that's necessary to connect the action in code! Now that you've made the conversion happen automatically, you've made the buttons redundant!

2   Select and delete the buttons.

3   You could also remove the `@IBAction` keyword from the `convertToMiles()` method because this is called from code now, and isn't connected to an event in Interface Builder. If you forget to do this, don't worry; it's not strictly necessary.

4   Run the app again, and admire your work. You have completed a fully interactive distance conversion app!

✓   **CHECKPOINT**   If you want to check out my version of the app at this point, you can do that at https://github.com/iOSAppDevelopmentwith-SwiftinAction/DistanceConverter.git (4.ConvertDistanceWhenTextChanges).

5.1.3 Other controls

UIKit provides several controls for different purposes. We're not going to discuss all of them in detail now, but table 5.3 has a summary of what's available and what they're useful for.

Table 5.3   UIKit controls

Control	Default interface	Use	Example usage
Switch		Modify a Boolean value between an on or off state. Similar to a toggle button or checkbox.	Turn sound off or on.
Slider		Modify a numeric value between a continuous range of values, such as between 0 and 1.	Adjust the sound volume.
Stepper	− | +	Modify a numeric value by increasing or decreasing by a defined amount.	Select the quantity of a product in a shopping cart.
Picker	Mountain View Sunnyvale **Cupertino** Santa Clara San Jose	Select a value from a set of values. Similar to a drop-down or combo box, but allows for multiple selectors.	Select a language from a set of languages.
Date Picker	Tue Apr 26 4 45 Wed Apr 27 5 46 AM Today 6 47 PM Fri Apr 29 7 48 Sat Apr 30 8 49	Select a date and/or time.	Select a departure date in a travel app.
Segmented Control	First | Second	Select one value from a small set of values.	Select a travel class (Economy, Business) in a travel app.

NOTE   If we're being pedantic, Picker *isn't* a control, although Date Picker is! How could this be possible? While the `UIDatePicker` class subclasses `UIControl`, the `UIPickerView` class subclasses `UIView` directly, bypassing `UIControl`. Therefore, `UIPickerView` doesn't have access to connect events to action methods. Rather, it uses what's called the delegation pattern to be customized and receive user interaction (we'll look at the delegation pattern shortly). The user has no idea of the internal implementation of a view, so if it looks like a control and works like a control, it's a control! I've therefore included the Picker in this list of controls.

Controls are a useful high-level way to implement user interaction. But sometimes you don't need all the bells and whistles of controls—you might have a simple view, and you need to receive information on touch events.

5.2 *Touching views*

In this section, you'll create an app called Touch Views that displays simple views that change color when the user touches them. See figure 5.8 for the interface on the left, and the view hierarchy of the app on the right.

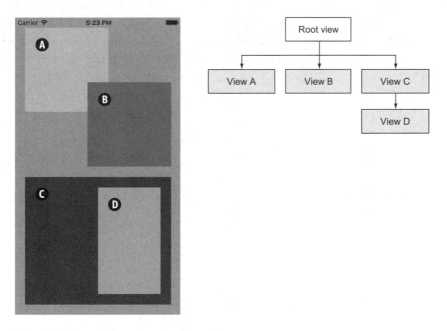

Figure 5.8   Touch Views app view hierarchy

✓ **CHECKPOINT**   To spare you the headache of setting up this interface, check out the TouchViews project repository at https://github.com/ iOSAppDevelopmentwithSwiftinAction/TouchViews.git (1.Initial Setup).

When you have the project open in Xcode, open the ViewController.swift file and examine how the views are constructed in code, passing in a `CGRect` structure to the `UIView` initializer, the way you did in the ViewsInCode project in the previous chapter.

To distinguish the views from each other, they each have a different random background color. The `random` property is already set up for you in a `UIColor` extension that you can find in the UIColorExtension.swift file.

Notice that while views A, B, and C are being added to the subviews of the root view, view D is added to the subviews of view C. Have another look at this view hierarchy in figure 5.8. Note that a view that is added after another view appears in front. This is why view B appears to be in front of view A.

5.2.1 *Hit testing*

Whenever an app receives a touch event, it first follows a path down the view hierarchy performing what is called *hit-testing* to determine the lowest-level view that was touched.

For example, if the user touches within the bounds of view D (see figure 5.9), iOS first checks the root views' subviews from front to back (that is, views C, B, and then A) until it finds a view that contains the touch. When it finds the touch in view C, it doesn't need to continue looking in views B and A. It then looks inside the subviews of view C and finds that view D contains the touch. As view D doesn't have any subviews, it determines view D is the lowest-level view that was touched.

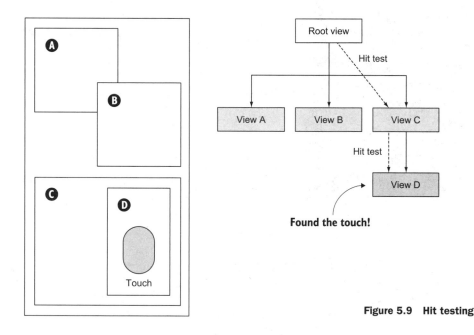

Figure 5.9   Hit testing

5.2.2 *Overriding touch methods*

After drilling down to view D, iOS will then call this view's `touchesBegan()` method, passing in a `Set` of touches. If you create a custom subclass of `UIView` and override this method, you can provide custom implementation for this view when it's touched.

1 Create a custom view class to receive and respond to this method. Select File > New > File > iOS > Source > Cocoa Touch Class. Subclass `UIView`, and name your custom view `ColoredView`.

2 Override the `touchesBegan()` method.

3 Call its super method.

4 Reset the background color of the view to another random color.

```
override func touchesBegan(_ touches: Set<UITouch>, with event:
UIEvent?) {
    super.touchesBegan(touches, with: event)
    self.backgroundColor = UIColor.random
}
```

Now, back in the `ViewController` class, instead of creating instances of `UIView`, create instances of your new view subclass, `ColoredView`.

5 Go through the `ViewController` class replacing all mentions of `UIView` with `ColoredView`.

6 Run the app again, touch the different views, and watch them change color.

Notice that when you touch view B where it *overlaps* view A, only view B changes color. iOS checks a view's subviews in the order that they're displayed, from front to back. When a view returns a successful hit test, iOS stops checking other views at this level. In the example, view B is closer to the front than view A because it was added last. Because it's the front view, when it returns a successful hit test, iOS stops there, and doesn't perform a hit test on view A.

Notice that when you touch view D, its superview, view C, also changes color. Why?

5.2.3 The responder chain

When a view receives an event such as a touch event, it passes this event up to its superclass, and so on. When the event arrives at the root view of a scene, it's passed to the scene's view controller. The view controller in turn passes the event on to the superview of its root view. In this example, the superview of the root view of the scene is the window of the app. The dotted line in figure 5.10 illustrates the path of the event in our app, called the *responder chain*.

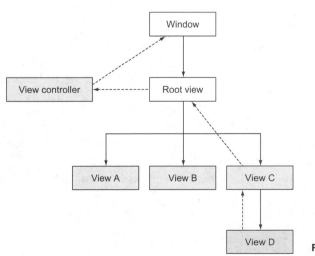

Figure 5.10   The responder chain

Every object that can receive these events is called a *responder* and every responder (that is, `UIView` and `UIViewController`) subclasses the `UIResponder` class. The `UIResponder` class is where you'll find the `touchesBegan()` method.

Let's demonstrate that the view controller is on the responder chain.

1   Add the same `touchesBegan()` method to the `ViewController` class. This time, change the background color of its root view.

```
override func touchesBegan(_ touches: Set<UITouch>, with event:
UIEvent?) {
    super.touchesBegan(touches, with: event)
    self.view.backgroundColor = UIColor.random
}
```

2   Run the app, and you should notice the background color of the root view changes on all touches.

Other `UIResponder` methods can be overridden to receive other touch events, as explained in table 5.4.

Table 5.4   `UIResponder` touch methods

Touch method	Trigger
`touchesBegan()`	One or more fingers touched down on a view.
`touchesMoved()`	One or more fingers moved within a view.
`touchesEnded()`	One or more fingers lifted off a view.
`touchesCancelled()`	A touch is interrupted by a system event.
`touchesEstimatedPropertiesUpdated()`	To ensure touch events are presented in a timely manner, sometimes touch attributes are estimated. These estimated values are later updated in this method.

CHALLENGE   Make the views also change color when the user lifts their finger off the view. You can check out the completed app at https://github.com/ iOSAppDevelopmentwithSwiftinAction/TouchViews.git (2.ColoredView).

With all these triggers for touches, you could easily respond to taps—but what if you want your view to also respond to double taps? Should you wait a short period before responding to the tap, in case it was going to be a double tap? How long would that short period of time be?

What if you want your app to pinch to zoom in and out on an image? Are you brushed up on your Pythagoras theorem?

Not to worry, Apple has you covered with another type of user interaction called *gesture recognizers*.

5.3 Gesture recognizers

Gesture recognizers go one step further than merely reporting touch information. Gesture recognizers *interpret* the touches and recognize the intention of the movement the way humans would. They can tell the difference between a swipe and a pan, a double tap and two single taps, or a pinch and a rotation.

Without needing to program or understand the complicated underlying code defining the gesture recognition algorithms, your app can detect and respond to all sorts of complex predefined gestures.

Having standardized gesture recognizers has the added benefit of consistency with other apps in the App Store, which should make your interface more intuitive for your users. Apple provides several gesture recognizers, each of which detects different types of gestures. See table 5.5 for different gestures, the relevant recognizer, and how this gesture can be used in your app.

Table 5.5 Gestures

Gesture	Recognizer	Example usage
Tap	`UITapGestureRecognizer`	Selecting a control or item.
Double tap	`UITapGestureRecognizer`	Zooming in (or out if already zoomed in).
Pinch	`UIPinchGestureRecognizer`	Zooming in/out.
Pan	`UIPanGestureRecognizer`	Dragging or panning content in any direction.
Flick	`UIPanGestureRecognizer`	Scrolling or panning content in any direction quickly.
Drag from edge of display	`UIScreenEdgePanGestureRecognizer`	Drag in additional content from off-screen.
Swipe (left, right, up, or down)	`UISwipeGestureRecognizer`	Returning to previous screen, revealing hidden view or button.
Two fingers circular movement	`UIRotationGestureRecognizer`	Rotating content.
Touch and hold	`UILongPressGestureRecognizer`	Positioning cursor in text fields.

You'll explore the possibilities with gestures by creating a simple image viewer app. In this app, you'll pan, zoom, and rotate an image, or tap to view the next image. The starter project is bare bones, with only an *image view* in the main scene ready for viewing.

✓ **CHECKPOINT** Check out a starter project for your image viewer app at https://github.com/iOSAppDevelopmentwithSwiftinAction/ImageViewer.git (1.InitialSetup).

Image views are straightforward—they're a special type of view that can display an image stored in your project.

If you open the project folder in Finder, you'll also find a folder called Images with three photos. Feel free to use these images or replace them with your own photos. Now let's add these files to your project!

1 Drag the Images folder into your ImageViewer project in the Project Navigator. A popup will appear with options when adding files.

2 Select Copy items, if needed, Create groups, and Add to ImageViewer target, and select Finish. A yellow group called Images should appear in the Project Navigator.

Options when adding files to your project

When you add files to your project, you have a few options to consider:

Destination: Copy items if needed. If you check this option, any files or folders you drag into your project will physically be copied into your project folder. You can theoretically include references in your project to files that aren't in your project folder. This could make sense, for example, if you're sharing resources with another project, though it's recommended to keep all relevant files within your project folder—it helps organize your resources into one place. The image folder is already in the project folder, so in this case checked or unchecked is irrelevant.

Added folders: Create groups/Create folder references. When you add a folder, you have the choice to add it as a reference to the folder, or a reference to each individual file bundled into a group. If you have a reference to a folder (blue icon), whenever you update the contents of the physical folder on disk, Xcode will automatically update its contents in the Project Navigator. A group, on the other hand (yellow icon), is no longer connected to the folder itself after being added to the project. Any files you add to the folder will not be reflected in the group, and any files you remove from the folder will be highlighted as missing files. Generally, it makes sense to go with groups, but cases exist where folder references can come in handy. For example, perhaps you're sharing a folder with a graphic designer and want the resources to update automatically.

Add to targets: Choose which *target* you would like to add the files to. Every resource and source file is explicitly included in the appropriate target. You can check this by selecting a file in the Project Navigator and noting the Target Membership section in the File Inspector. Generally, files are divided into their target groups in the Project Navigator, but files can also be shared between targets.

File categories

Xcode determines what to do with each file when building your app by categorizing files into *Compile Sources*, *Bundle Resources*, and *Frameworks and Libraries*.

Compile Sources—This category refers to all source files, such as Swift or Objective-C code. Source files are compiled into your app executable, called the *binary*.

Bundle Resources—This category refers to all sorts of resources and media you may want to include. Certain resource files such as images, audio files, or even PDF files are copied directly into your app bundle. Other resource files, such as the asset catalog or storyboards, are converted in different ways when copied into the app bundle.

Frameworks and Libraries—This category refers to frameworks that your app will link to. Distinct from third-party frameworks, frameworks from Apple are automatically linked with your project, and they don't need to be physically added. We'll look more at third-party frameworks and libraries in chapter 11.

You can examine the categories of the files in your app in the Build Phases tab of your project target settings. For more details about project settings, check appendix A.

3 Open the settings for the project target, select the Build Phases tab, and verify that the images have been added to the Copy Bundle Resources section.

4 Open the main storyboard, select the image view, and in the Attributes Inspector in the Image attribute, select one of the photos you've dragged into the project.

For a view to respond to a gesture, you need to add a gesture recognizer to the view. You can do this in code, or in Interface Builder. Let's start by adding a pan gesture recognizer to the image view in Interface Builder.

5.3.1 Pan gesture

Add a *pan gesture recognizer* to your image view to be able to pan the image around.

1 Find the Pan Gesture Recognizer in the Object Library, and drag it onto the image view.

You'll notice that the pan gesture recognizer appears in the document outline for the view controller and in the scene dock in the Interface Builder canvas. If you select the image view, you'll also find the pan gesture recognizer connected to the image view in the Connections Inspector (see figure 5.11).

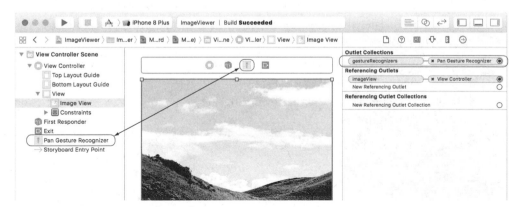

Figure 5.11   Pan gesture recognizer

Certain gesture recognizers can be customized. If you open the Attributes Inspector, you'll find attributes that you can use to customize the pan gesture recognizer. If you want your pan to only respond to only one- or two-finger pans, for example, you do that here.

2   In the Attributes Inspector for the pan gesture recognizer, adjust the maximum touches to 2. You're going to create an *action* to respond to the pan gesture.

3   Open the Assistant Editor.

4   Holding down the Control key, drag from the pan gesture recognizer in Interface Builder to your view controller source code below the `viewDidLoad` method.

5   Change the type of the connection to Action and name the action "handlePan."

6   Change the Type to "UIPanGestureRecognizer" so your method will explicitly receive the recognizer, correctly typed as a `UIPanGestureRecognizer`, in the function parameters. An action method should appear in your code.

See figure 5.12 for clarification on the steps to create an action for a gesture recognizer.

7   While you have the Assistant Editor open, the way you did in the last chapter, create an outlet for the image view and call it "imageView."

Now you have a method that's called whenever a pan gesture event is recognized. As gestures take place over a period of time, events could represent, for example, that a gesture began, changed, ended, or failed. The current state of the gesture is stored in the `state` property of the gesture recognizer that's passed into the method. The `state` property stores its current state as a `UIGestureRecognizerState` *enumeration*. Enumeration types store related values, such as states. We'll take a closer look at enumerations as well as create our own enumeration type in chapter 10.

The gesture recognizer also reports back important information about the gesture itself, measured from the moment the gesture began. The pan gesture recognizer reports a coordinate representing where the user has panned to, from the moment the gesture began. This information is perfect to use for moving the image.

You'll need to convert the pan movement to a coordinate value relative to the image view's superview. This type of conversion is called *translation*.

8   Translate the coordinate by calling the pan gesture recognizer's `translation` method, passing in the root view:

```
let translation = sender.translation(in: self.view)
```

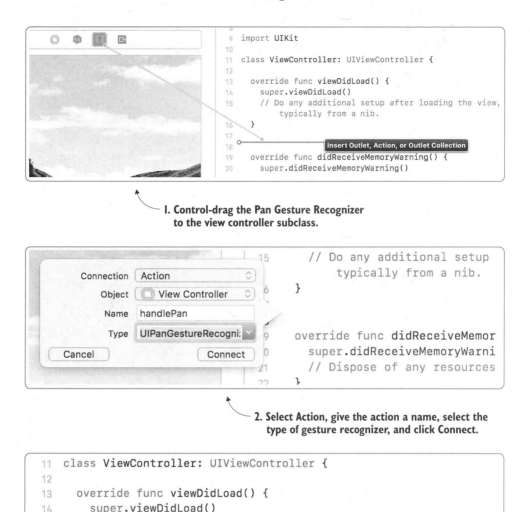

1. Control-drag the Pan Gesture Recognizer to the view controller subclass.

2. Select Action, give the action a name, select the type of gesture recognizer, and click Connect.

3. An @IBAction is created.

Figure 5.12   Create gesture recognizer action

9   You can add this x,y coordinate to the image view's current position to move the image. Use the `UIView`'s `center` property to set the image view's current position:

```
imageView.center = CGPoint(
    x: imageView.center.x + translation.x,
    y: imageView.center.y + translation.y)
```

Because gesture recognizers report on movement since the moment a gesture began, and the center property reports on the current location of the image view, if we continue adding the gesture movement to the image view location every time the gesture recognizer reports a movement, the image view will move exponentially.

To illustrate this, consider if the image view begins at (x:0, y:0). The first time the gesture recognizer is called, the translation may be a movement of (x:1, y:1), so the image view is moved to (x:1, y:1). The second time the gesture recognizer is called, the translation may have moved another 1 point in the x direction and 1 point in the y direction, so the translation (representing the movement from the moment the gesture began) will be (x:2, y:2). The new location of the image view should be (x:2, y:2) but following the code above, instead it will be (x:3, y:3). What can be done about this?

There are two possible solutions:

- You could use the gesture recognizer's `state` property to detect when the gesture begins, and at this point record the initial location of the view. You could then base all view movement calculations from this *initial* location rather than the view's *current* location.
- You could reset the gesture recognizer every time you respond to a gesture event, so that the gesture recognizer now reports on movement since the last pan gesture event.

Let's follow the second solution.

10   Reset the recognizer to zero:

```
sender.setTranslation(CGPoint.zero, in: self.view)
```

Your `handlePan` method should now look like the following code.

```
@IBAction func handlePan(_ sender:UIPanGestureRecognizer) {
    let translation = sender.translation(in: self.view)
    imageView.center = CGPoint(
        x: imageView.center.x + translation.x,
        y: imageView.center.y + translation.y)
    sender.setTranslation(CGPoint.zero, in: self.view)
}
```

Translates coordinate ⊳

Moves the image view

Resets the gesture recognizer ◁

Your pan gesture should be working!

11   Run the app and drag the image around.

5.3.2 Pinch gesture

A good image viewer can zoom in on the image as well.

Follow the same steps that you followed for the pan gesture recognizer, but with the *pinch gesture recognizer*:

1 Drag the pinch gesture recognizer from the Object Library onto the image view.
2 Open the Assistant Editor.
3 Control-drag the new pinch gesture recognizer to the view controller.
4 Set the Connection to Action, Name it "handlePinch," and make the Type explicitly UIPinchGestureRecognizer.

The pinch gesture recognizer has a property, `scale`, that estimates the degree that the user has pinched the view. You'll use this property to set the scale of the image view with a *view transformation*.

Transformations of a view, such as scale, are performed on a view's `transform` property. This property is a transformation matrix that can be manipulated to scale, rotate, translate, or skew an object (see figure 5.13).

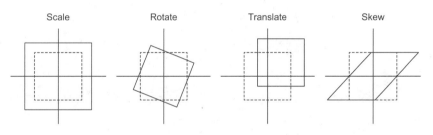

Figure 5.13 View transformations

Several helper methods exist that can take a transformation matrix and perform the calculations to generate a new transformation matrix based on the type of transformation you're looking for. For example, to adjust the scale of a view, you'd use the `scaledBy` method.

5 Scale the image view using the transformation matrix, passing in the recognizer's `scale` property:

```
imageView.transform = imageView.transform.scaledBy(
    x: sender.scale, y: sender.scale)
```

6 The way you did with the pan gesture recognizer, and to avoid the image view scaling up exponentially, you want to reset the recognizer's `scale` property. The default for scale is `1`:

```
sender.scale = 1
```

In the end, your `handlePinch` method should look like the following:

```
@IBAction func handlePinch(_ sender: UIPinchGestureRecognizer) {
    imageView.transform =
        imageView.transform.scaledBy(
            x: sender.scale, y: sender.scale)
    sender.scale = 1
}
```

Converts scale — (on `imageView.transform.scaledBy`)

Sets the transformation matrix — (on first line)

Resets the gesture recognizer — (on `sender.scale = 1`)

Run the app and confirm you can pinch the image to zoom.

> **NOTE** If you're running the app in the simulator, you can simulate two fingers if you hold down the Alt key.

Your image viewer app is coming along!

5.3.3 Rotate gesture

To round out your image viewer app, how about adding rotation to the mix?

> **CHALLENGE** After going through the process twice already, you should be familiar enough to try it yourself without following instructions. Add a rotate gesture recognizer to the image view. When you're done, compare your results with the code in listing 5.1 for the `handleRotate` method.

> **TIP** Use the `rotated` method to transform the rotation of the transformation matrix.

Listing 5.1 Rotate gesture action

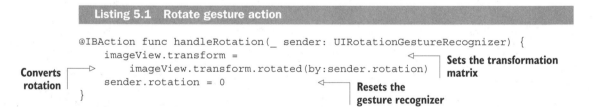

```
@IBAction func handleRotation(_ sender: UIRotationGestureRecognizer) {
    imageView.transform =
        imageView.transform.rotated(by:sender.rotation)
    sender.rotation = 0
}
```

Converts rotation — (on `imageView.transform.rotated`)

Sets the transformation matrix — (on first line)

Resets the gesture recognizer — (on `sender.rotation = 0`)

Run your app again, and you can rotate your view as well!

5.3.4 Simultaneous gesture recognizers

You may have noticed a limitation of the recognizers. By default, only one gesture can be performed at a time. If the system recognizes that you're pinching to zoom, for example, you can't rotate the image until you stop zooming by taking your fingers off the screen.

You can change this default behavior, however. You could be zooming and rotating and panning all at the same time! But to change this default behavior, you'll need to use the *delegation pattern*.

USING THE DELEGATION PATTERN

We've looked at the target-action pattern, where one object can call a method on another object. The delegation pattern is like the target-action pattern on steroids—in the delegation pattern, an object contains a property called the delegate, which contains a *list* of methods that the object can call. You can then implement this delegate object, providing custom responses to the methods the object calls.

An object can call methods on its delegate for various purposes:

- Notify the delegate that something is about to happen (usually prefixed with "will").
- Notify the delegate that something happened (usually prefixed with "did").
- Request permission from the delegate to do something (usually prefixed with "should").
- Request data. (In this case, the delegate is often called a data source. We'll explore data sources further in chapter 9.)

The list of methods in a delegate is defined by a protocol—in fact, all an object knows or cares about its delegate is that it can handle the methods in the delegate protocol. By convention, the delegate protocol has the suffix "Delegate."

You can create a delegate object that adopts the delegate protocol, and then set your object as the delegate property. Often, for simplicity, a view controller is used as a delegate object.

You'll find the delegation pattern is used frequently in the iOS SDK, including gesture recognizers!

All gesture recognizers have a property `delegate` with a list of methods defined by the `UIGestureRecognizerDelegate` protocol. This protocol contains methods such as

- `gestureRecognizerShouldBegin`—Requests permission from the delegate to begin recognizing gestures
- `gestureRecognizer(shouldRecognizeSimultaneouslyWith)`—Requests permission to recognize this gesture simultaneously with another gesture recognizer

Oh! That method sounds like exactly what you need to be able to zoom, rotate, and pan at the same time! How about using it?

To define your view controller as the delegate for a gesture recognizer, your view controller would need to

1 Set itself as the gesture recognizer's delegate.
2 Adopt the `UIGestureRecognizerDelegate` protocol.
3 Implement any required methods in the `UIGestureRecognizerDelegate` protocol.

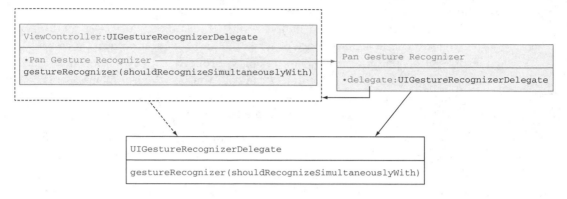

Figure 5.14   Gesture recognizer with a view controller as a delegate

See figure 5.14 for a visual representation of the relationships when a gesture recognizer uses a view controller as its delegate.

Implement the delegation pattern here by doing the following:

1 Set the view controller as the delegate of the three gesture recognizers. The gesture recognizers then know who to ask (the delegate, that is, the view controller) to find out if they should permit simultaneous recognition.

   This time, you'll set the delegate in Interface Builder.

2 Open Interface Builder, and from the Document Outline, Control-drag from the pan gesture recognizer to the view controller. Select Delegate (see figure 5.15).

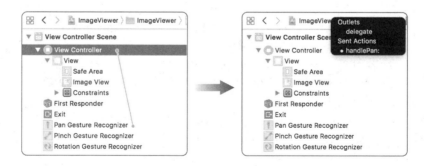

Figure 5.15   Set recognizer delegate

Do the same for each of the three gesture recognizers. When you're done, select the view controller and open the Connections Inspector. In the Referencing Outlets section, you should see that each of the three gesture recognizers is connected to the view controller as a delegate.

3 Adopt the `UIGestureRecognizerDelegate` protocol. You could directly adopt the protocol on the view controller class, but a useful convention is to adopt the protocol on an extension to the view controller. This helps keeps related code together.

Next, you need to implement any required methods on the protocol. The protocol contains the list of methods that a gesture recognizer can call on its delegate so that the recognizer knows how to behave. One of the methods determines whether it should allow other gesture recognizers to be recognized at the same time—and that's what you need!

Add the following to your view controller class.

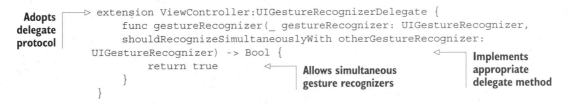

```
extension ViewController:UIGestureRecognizerDelegate {
    func gestureRecognizer(_ gestureRecognizer: UIGestureRecognizer,
    shouldRecognizeSimultaneouslyWith otherGestureRecognizer:
UIGestureRecognizer) -> Bool {
        return true
    }
}
```

Adopts delegate protocol

Allows simultaneous gesture recognizers

Implements appropriate delegate method

4 Run the app. You should be able to zoom, rotate, and pan at the same time!

5.3.5 Tap gesture in code

After implementing three gesture recognizers using Interface Builder, you could probably implement another gesture recognizer blindfolded! Let's explore an alternative approach to setting up a gesture recognizer: implementing it purely with code.

You're going to implement a single-finger double-tap gesture that will navigate to the next image.

1 Set up an array of the available images and a variable that keeps track of the current image number. If you've used your own images, make the necessary changes to this array:

```
let images = ["CradleMountain.JPG", "Laguna69.JPG", "PatagoniaSky.JPG"]
var imageNo = 0
```

2 Add a `handleTap()` action method that will be triggered when the user taps the image. The method increments the image number by 1 and returns it to 0 if it reaches the upper limit of elements in the images array. It then replaces the image in the image view with the next image in the array, as shown in the following code. (You could add a fancy transition here, but let's not complicate things too soon—all in good time!)

```
@objc func handleTap(_ sender: UITapGestureRecognizer) {
    imageNo += 1
    if imageNo == images.count {imageNo = 0}
    imageView.image = UIImage(named: images[imageNo])
}
```

NOTE   Unlike the other action methods, this action method doesn't begin with `@IBAction`. Because you're not going to trigger this method from Interface Builder, this attribute isn't necessary. Instead, this method will need to begin with the `@objc` keyword to make it available to Objective-C—more on that in a moment.

Now, to create the gesture recognizer itself. Every gesture recognizer is instantiated with two parameters, as shown in table 5.6.

Table 5.6   Gesture recognizer parameters

Parameter	Description
`target`	Specifies the object to receive any gesture events, which in this case will be `self`—the view controller.
`action`	Specifies the method to receive notification of the gesture event. You set up the `handleTap()` method to receive these notifications. The action is specified using a special expression called `#selector`. Use `#selector` to pass in the name of the method. Because the `#selector` expression uses the Objective-C runtime to connect to the associated method, the method will need to be exposed with the `@objc` keyword.

3   Add the instantiation of the tap gesture recognizer to your `viewDidLoad` method:

```
let tapGestureRecognizer =
    UITapGestureRecognizer(target: self, action: #selector(handleTap))
```

You can now customize the recognizer.

4   Holding down Command, click on `UITapGestureRecognizer` to explore the generated interface for the file. You'll find that this gesture recognizer has two forms of customization: `numberOfTapsRequired` and `numberOfTouches-Required`.

5   Return to your view controller code by pointing your mouse cursor at the editor area and swiping right with two fingers (see figure 5.16).

6   Use what you've learned about the tap gesture recognizer and customize yours to require a single-finger double-tap:

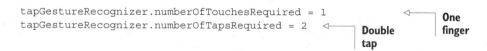

```
tapGestureRecognizer.numberOfTouchesRequired = 1
tapGestureRecognizer.numberOfTapsRequired = 2
```

Double tap

One finger

7   All that's left is to add this gesture recognizer to the image view:

```
imageView.addGestureRecognizer(tapGestureRecognizer)
```

8   Run your app again, and you should now be able to navigate to the next image!

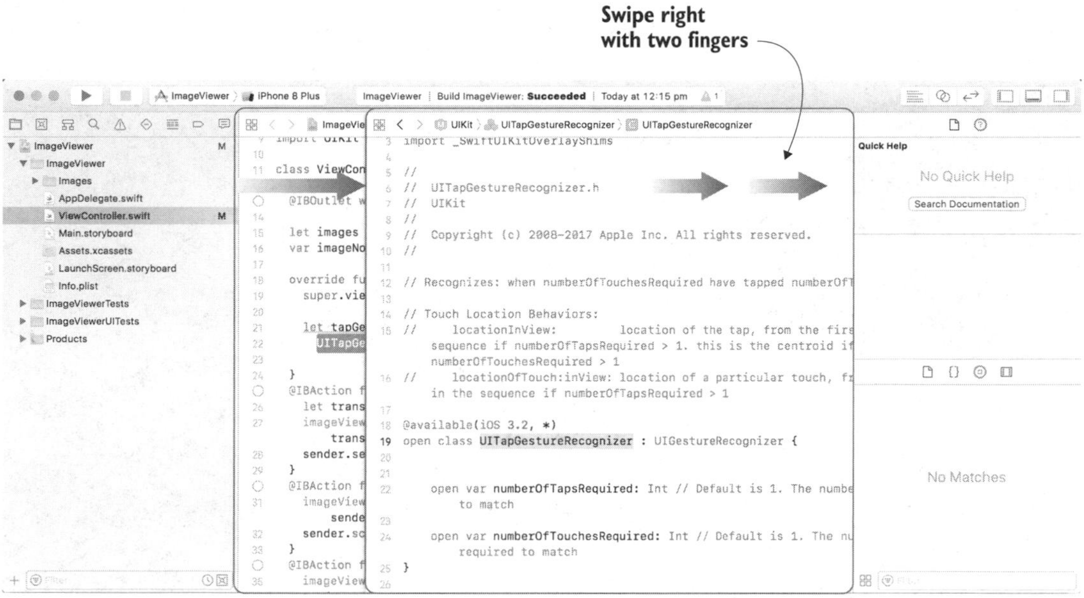

Figure 5.16 Shortcut to go back in the editor area

Well, you added double tapping to go to the next image, but how about double tapping with two fingers to go to the previous image? Because each tap recognizer only recognizes taps of a specific number of fingers and taps, you'll have to set up another tap gesture recognizer.

CHALLENGE Add a double-tap-with-two-fingers gesture recognizer to go to the previous image. If you want to peek at the answer, you can download the completed image viewer from https://github.com/iOSAppDevelopmentwithSwift-inAction/ImageViewer.git (2.ImageViewerComplete).

5.4 Summary

In this chapter, you learned the following:

- Use UIKit controls such as buttons, text fields, switches, and sliders to add an extra level of interaction to your app.
- When a view is touched, a touch event travels up the responder chain.
- Views or view controllers can respond to simple touches by overriding `UIResponder` touch methods.
- Use gesture recognizers to interpret touches as more-complex gestures such as pan, pinch, tap, and rotate.
- Controls and gesture recognizers can trigger actions that connect to methods in your code.
- Connect control events or gestures to methods via Interface Builder or in code.

Adaptive layout

From the iPhone 4S to the iPad Pro, vastly different device resolutions are available that your app needs to look good in. After adding landscape and portrait to the mix, plus all the different multitasking windows that your app can find itself in, it's a headache to think about designing different fixed app layouts for all the different combinations and permutations.

There must be an easier way. How can the interface of an app look great regardless of its environment?

Over the years, Apple has introduced several different approaches for setting up a layout that adapts to its environment. In this chapter, we'll look at various solutions and how to choose between them.

6.1   *The problems*

Before we look at the solutions, let's look closer at the problems we're facing.

DEVICE RESOLUTIONS

Once upon a time, there was one iPhone, and everyone was happy. Pixels were the same as points, and developers knew the resolution of the screen they were developing for. Fast-forward to today, and there are multiple devices on the market, let alone in people's hands, and multiple point resolutions that an app needs to look great on (see figure 6.1).

DEVICE ORIENTATION

Apps don't display *only* in portrait orientation. Apple recommends that apps display in both portrait and landscape orientation, where possible. Oops, that doubles the number of resolutions your app layout must accommodate (see figure 6.2).

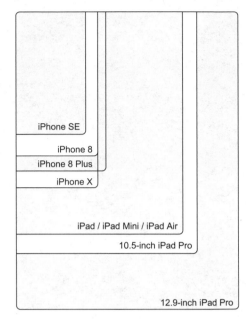

Figure 6.1   Device point resolutions

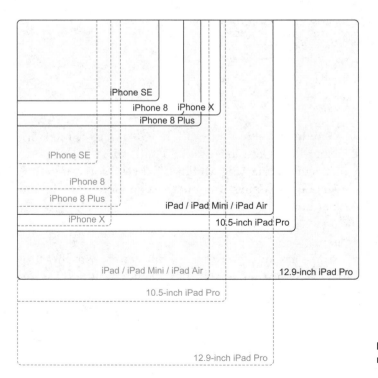

Figure 6.2   Device point resolutions with orientation

APP WINDOW SIZES

In iOS 9, Apple introduced different multitasking capabilities to iPads. *Slide Over*, available on most iPads, allows you to drag in a narrow version of an app. *Split View*, available on newer iPads, allows two apps to run side by side, at a width customizable by the user, giving iPads nearly infinite combinations of widths.

VIEW CONTROLLER SIZES

View controller root views don't always fill the screen. View controller views can take up a portion of a screen, for example, when presented as a popover or as part of a split view controller.

These factors—device resolutions, device orientations, app window sizes, and different view controller sizes—need to be considered when presenting a scene in your app.

CONTENT

And it doesn't stop there. Up to now, we've looked at how the layout of a scene's content must adapt to its environment. What if the content itself changes? A label could display dynamic text, for example, or your app could support different languages.

Whether the pressure is from external or internal forces, the layout of your app needs to adapt. But how?

6.2 *Auto layout*

Auto layout is a technique for describing interfaces using constraints. The Auto Layout engine uses these constraints to calculate how to lay out your app's interface.

In this book, you'll build a Bookcase app in which a user can keep track of books in their bookcase. The designer has sent through the interface in figure 6.3 for adding the details of a book. You're going to lay out this scene, exploring auto layout!

> ✔ **CHECKPOINT** Open the repo here, which contains the interface ready to lay out with auto layout from https://github.com/iOSAppDevelopment withSwiftinAction/Bookcase.git (Chapter6.1.Initial-Setup).

Figure 6.3 Add-a-book interface

In auto layout, views have a number of main layout constraints. Constraints are divided into size and *location*, which is divided further into horizontal (x-axis) and vertical (y-axis). See table 6.1.

Table 6.1   Constraint types

Categories	Attribute	Additional information
Location: Horizontal	Leading, Trailing	Constraints on the left (leading) and right (trailing) of a view. In right-to-left languages, their directions swap.
	Left, Right	It's usually preferable to use leading and trailing. See the note following the table for more information.
	Center X	
Location: Vertical	Top, Bottom	
	Center Y	
	Baseline, First Baseline	Text views such as labels contain a baseline representing the bottom of the first or last lines of text (excluding *descenders* that drop below the line in letters such as j, p, or q).
Size	Width, Height	Can be an absolute value, or relative to another view's size constraint.
	Aspect ratio (based on width and height)	To constrain a view's aspect ratio, constrain its width to its height.

NOTE   You may wonder, if *leading* and *trailing* are constraints on the left and right, wouldn't *left* and *right* attributes be redundant? Well, there's a difference. Although leading is on the left and trailing on the right if the device's current language is left-to-right (such as English), the two attributes switch sides if the current language is right-to-left (such as Arabic). Why would they do this? Whereas left-to-right language speakers expect to see their most important content on the left, right-to-left language speakers expect it on the right. It's recommended to use leading and trailing constraints over left and right, because they ensure the most important content is always in its correct place.

See figure 6.4 to help visualize these attributes.

Size constraints are the only constraints that can be a value in themselves, without relating to another view. All location constraints must (and size constraints *can*) specify the view that they relate to. It can make sense to say view A is 50 points high, but it doesn't make sense to say it's 50 points in the y direction … away from what? Fifty points away from its superview top? Fifty points away from another view's bottom?

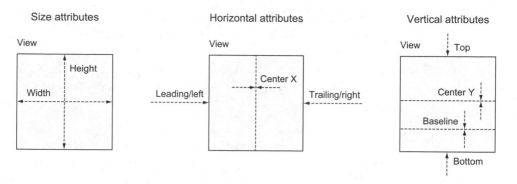

Figure 6.4   Constraint attributes

6.2.1 *Auto layout tips*

Auto layout can be a complicated topic at first, but with practice, the process of describing your layout using constraints will become easier.

After laying out the interface in the storyboard, it can help—especially while learning auto layout—to sketch out the constraints on paper, separating the horizontal and vertical constraints. Then ask yourself three questions:

- Is it possible to determine the size and position of every view based on these constraints?
- Do your constraints still make sense if the width or height of the scene's root view increases? Will a view stretch, for example?
- Do your constraints still make sense if the width or height of the scene's root view decreases? Will a view shrink, for example?

6.2.2 *Auto layout in Interface Builder*

Let's use auto layout in Interface Builder to describe the add-a-book form interface.

Open the main storyboard and select View As at the bottom left of the storyboard canvas. This opens the device configuration bar, where you can select to view the storyboard from the perspective of different devices or orientations (see figure 6.5).

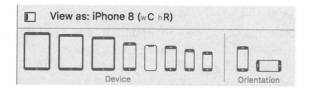

Figure 6.5   View as

You'll find the interface has been laid out nicely in the storyboard for when you're viewing it as iPhone 8, but because no adaptive layout has yet been implemented, it looks wrong viewed on other devices or orientations. Because views are merely positioned from the top left by default with absolute width and height point values, in different resolutions they can appear positioned incorrectly, or cut off (see figure 6.6).

Figure 6.6   Interface before auto layout

Let's implement auto layout constraints to rectify the situation.

Luckily, our helpful designer has sketched out how they want the design to look, separating the horizontal constraints (width and location) from the vertical constraints (height and location) and adding helpful comments. Take a moment to familiarize yourself with the horizontal constraints in figure 6.7. Confirm for yourself whether you could determine the x position and width of every view in the design based on these constraints, regardless of the width of the root view. (Don't worry if certain rules aren't clear yet; we'll look at each of them in turn.)

Before we look at the vertical constraints, how about adding a couple of horizontal constraints? Let's start with the horizontal constraints on the book view.

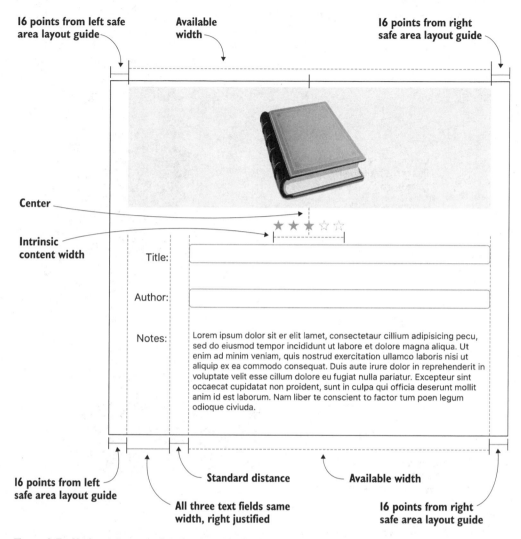

16 points from left safe area layout guide

Available width

16 points from right safe area layout guide

Center

Intrinsic content width

Title:

Author:

Notes:

Lorem ipsum dolor sit er elit lamet, consectetaur cillium adipisicing pecu, sed do eiusmod tempor incididunt ut labore et dolore magna aliqua. Ut enim ad minim veniam, quis nostrud exercitation ullamco laboris nisi ut aliquip ex ea commodo consequat. Duis aute irure dolor in reprehenderit in voluptate velit esse cillum dolore eu fugiat nulla pariatur. Excepteur sint occaecat cupidatat non proident, sunt in culpa qui officia deserunt mollit anim id est laborum. Nam liber te conscient to factor tum poen legum odioque civiuda.

16 points from left safe area layout guide

Standard distance

Available width

All three text fields same width, right justified

16 points from right safe area layout guide

Figure 6.7   Horizontal constraints for the add-a-book scene

If you select the book image and examine its attributes in the Attributes Inspector, you'll find that it's set to Aspect Fit mode. This means that it will *fit* the image inside its boundaries (represented in figure 6.7 by the shaded rectangle), but maintain its aspect ratio. This has been set to Aspect Fit mode, so that in the future, if this image is replaced by a wide and short image, it will fill out the available space. We'll look more at image views in chapter 13.

CREATING CONSTRAINTS IN THE CANVAS

Add your first constraint on the book image: 16 points from left safe area layout guide. Follow the steps in figure 6.8.

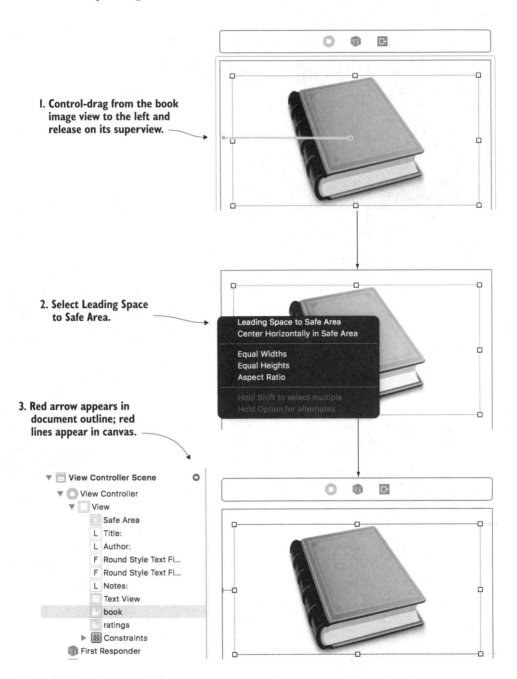

l. Control-drag from the book image view to the left and release on its superview.

2. Select Leading Space to Safe Area.

3. Red arrow appears in document outline; red lines appear in canvas.

Leading Space to Safe Area
Center Horizontally in Safe Area

Equal Widths
Equal Heights
Aspect Ratio

Hold Shift to select multiple
Hold Option for alternates

▼ View Controller Scene
  ▼ View Controller
    ▼ View
       Safe Area
       L Title:
       L Author:
       F Round Style Text Fi...
       F Round Style Text Fi...
       L Notes:
       Text View
       book
       ratings
    ▶ Constraints
   First Responder

Figure 6.8   Create a constraint.

When you create your first constraint, red *error* lines will appear in the canvas. Auto layout errors can indicate one of two types of errors, as explained in table 6.2.

Table 6.2 Auto layout errors

Error	Description
Unsatisfiable layout	Two or more constraints are in conflict.
Ambiguous layout	Your layout has two or more solutions, and the Auto Layout engine isn't clear which is preferable.

At this early stage, these error lines indicate that your layout is ambiguous because you have more constraints yet to define! You'll also see an error arrow at the top right of the document outline. Select this arrow to get more information about the problem. You'll find that the book view is missing a constraint for the y position. Not to worry, you'll get to that when you look at the vertical constraints!

> **Safe area layout guides**
>
> The root view of each scene automatically contains a safe area, bordered by what are called *safe area layout guides*. Pinning your view to safe area layout guides ensures that your view is not obscured by other interface elements such as status, navigation, and tab bars.

The book's width is represented with a dotted line in figure 6.7 because it's *implicitly* defined by other constraints. If the book view is pinned to the left and right of its superview, there's no option but for the width to fill the available space. If you were to specify an absolute width for the book, the layout may work for one resolution, but if the superview had a width of any other value, the layout rules would cause an unsatisfiable layout.

Similarly, the widths of the title text field, author text field, and notes text view are implicitly defined by the width of views to their left and right. If the root view is displayed on a wide device or orientation, these three views will merely grow to fill the available space.

Add the right constraint for the book:

1 This time, Control-drag to the *right*, releasing again on the book's superview.
2 Select Trailing Space to Safe Area. The book view is now pinned to the left and right safe area layout guides of the root view, and implicitly fills the available width.

3 You can confirm that the two constraints have been added correctly by opening the Size Inspector with the book view selected. See figure 6.9.

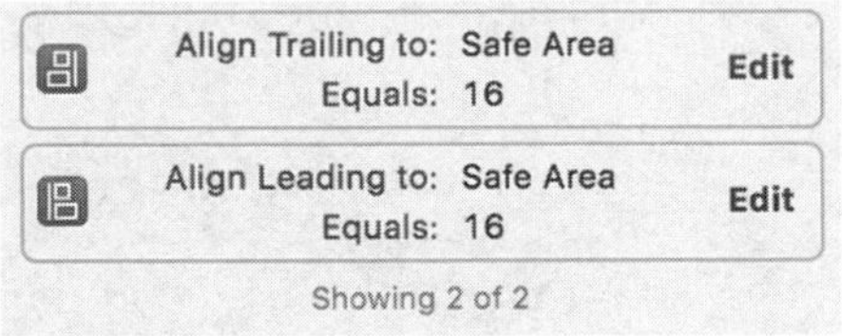

To finish off the book's constraints, in figure 6.10, look at the *vertical* constraints from the sketch of our friendly designer. Confirm for yourself again that these rules are sufficient for the Auto Layout engine to determine the y position and height of every view.

Figure 6.9   Constraints in the Size Inspector

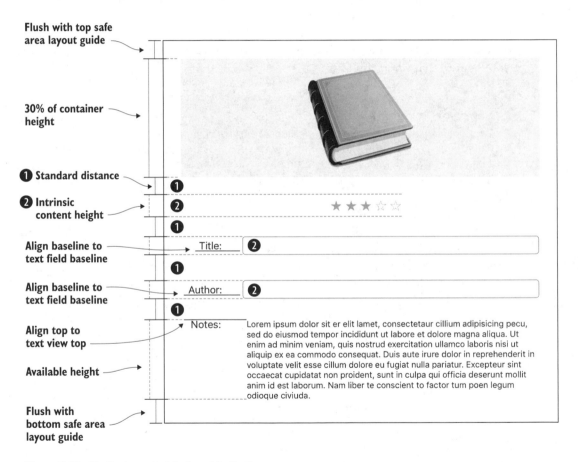

Figure 6.10   Vertical constraints for add-a-book scene

4 Pin the book to the top safe area layout guide by Control-dragging up from the book this time.

5 Select Top Space to Safe Area.

Notice that despite not defining the book's height yet, the red error lines are gone. The top, left, and right guidelines should be blue, indicating that these constraints are valid. However, there's a problem. The book image view has more than doubled in height. What's going on? Why would the Auto Layout engine do that?

Intrinsic content size

Certain types of views have an *intrinsic content size*. Labels and buttons, for example, have an intrinsic content size defined by their content, but text fields and switches have a default intrinsic content size. Image views, such as the book and the star-rating view in our example, have an intrinsic size defined by the size of the image.

If you don't specify a size for a view with an intrinsic content size, the Auto Layout engine will assume the intrinsic content size to determine the size of the view.

Intrinsic content size is why you won't need to specify height constraints for any of the labels or text fields in the example. Their intrinsic height works fine with the design.

Plain views don't have an intrinsic content size, so you have to define their size in auto layout. If you have created a subclass of `UIView`, for example, you can set its intrinsic content size in the code by overriding the `instrinsicContentSize` property.

The book image view has an intrinsic content size based on the size of the image it contains. Because you've specified that the book image view use auto layout to determine its size and position and you haven't added a height constraint for the view, the Auto Layout engine falls back to using the image view's intrinsic content size, which is based on the height of the image itself. However, in this case we don't want to use the book image view's intrinsic content size. The designer has requested that the book height be 30% the height of the root view.

6 Control-drag up from the book again, releasing when the root view is selected.

7 Select Equal Heights.

A height constraint will generate based on 100% of the root view in the canvas. That's not exactly what you were after, so you'll need to edit the additional constraint options.

EDITING CONSTRAINTS IN CONSTRAINT OPTIONS

Occasionally, you'll want to make more-detailed edits to a constraint. You can make these edits in the constraint options.

1 With the book selected, open the Size Inspector.
2 Find the Equal Height constraint you created, and select Edit. Here, you can formulate an equation to define the constraint.

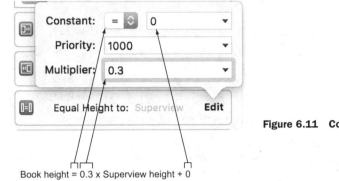

Figure 6.11   Constraint options

Book height = 0.3 x Superview height + 0

3 Modify the multiplier to 0.3 to base the book height on 30% of the root view's height (see figure 6.11).

IT'S ABOUT PRIORITIES

Notice in the options that constraints also have *priorities*. Priorities range from 1 to 1,000, clustering around 250 (low), 500 (medium), 750 (high), and 1,000 (required). You can use priorities to describe your preferences and help the Auto Layout engine understand how to resolve ambiguities. We'll come back to priorities shortly.

CREATING CONSTRAINTS IN THE ALIGN MENU

Now, to center the star-rating view. You *could* Control-drag from the star-rating view to its superview again (this time, dragging up). But for a change, you'll use the Align button. In the bottom, right-hand corner of the canvas, you'll find five curious buttons (see figure 6.12).

We'll come to each in turn, but first let's look at the Align menu: ▭. When you have two or more views selected, you can use the Align menu with two views selected to align

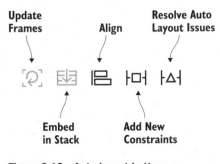

Figure 6.12   Auto layout buttons

their edges, centers, or baselines. When you only have one view selected, you can use the Align menu to center a view horizontally or vertically in its container.

1   Select the star-rating view and click Align.
2   Center the star-rating view in the root view by selecting Horizontally in Container.
3   Select Add 1 Constraint (see figure 6.13).

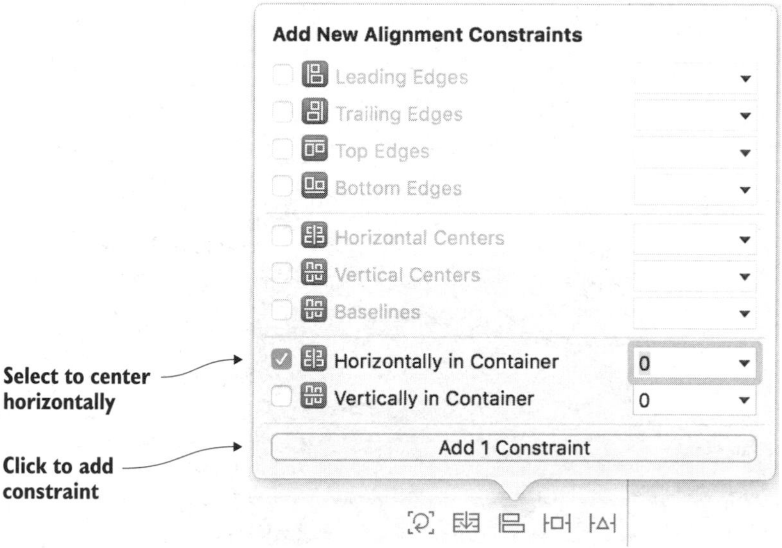

Figure 6.13   Add constraint in align menu

The star-rating view should now have an x position (center) and width and height (from intrinsic content size) and only needs a y position. The designer's brief suggests it should be a standard distance from the book view. A standard distance lets the Auto Layout engine choose the most appropriate value.

CREATING CONSTRAINTS IN THE ADD NEW CONSTRAINTS MENU

Now, you'll add a y position to the star-rating view, using the Add New Constraints menu: ├□┤.

1   With the star-rating view selected, click Add New Constraints.

The four spokes at the top of the menu can be used to pin an edge of the selected view to its nearest neighbor. The nearest neighbor could be another view, the edge of its container view, or a layout guide. You can specify a numeric value, the current distance between the views in the canvas, or a standard value. You'll use the standard value.

2   Select the drop-down on the top pin.
3   Select Use Standard Value.

TIP   In this menu, you can also see which view Interface Builder has detected that you're most likely intending to pin your view to. You can make a change to this here, if necessary, but your intention was to pin the star-rating view to the book view, Interface Builder has guessed correctly!

4   Select Add 1 Constraint to finalize your changes (see figure 6.14).

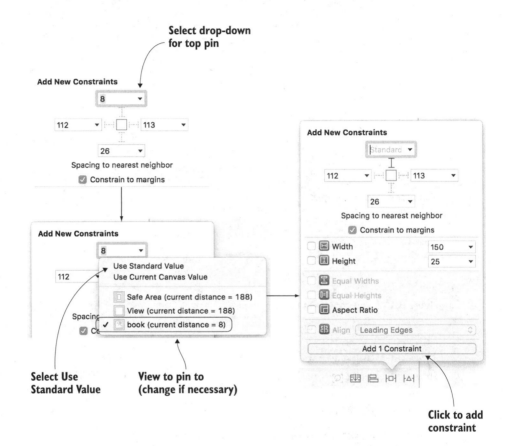

Figure 6.14   Add constraint in pin menu

CHALLENGE   Practice using the Add New Constraints menu, by adding constraints for the notes text view. Pin it a standard distance on the left, 0 points from the bottom safe area layout guide and 16 points to the right safe area layout guide. (At the time of writing, standard distance isn't available when pinning to the safe area layout guides.)

CREATING MULTIPLE CONSTRAINTS IN THE ADD NEW CONSTRAINTS MENU

You can also use the Add New Constraints menu to pin multiple views simultaneously.

The title text field, author text field, and notes text view all need to be separated by a standard distance, pinned to the right safe area layout guide, and a standard distance from their associated labels.

1   Select the title text field and the author text field.
2   Select the Add New Constraints button again.
3   Select a standard distance on the left, top, and bottom, and a value of 16 on the right.
4   Be sure that the red line connecting each of the four directions is active. If it's dim, you need to click on it to activate it.
5   Select the Add 7 Constraints button (see figure 6.15).

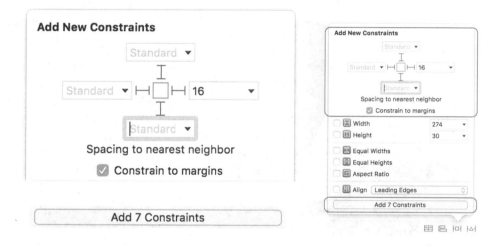

Figure 6.15   Adding multiple view constraints in the pin menu

Wait—why 7? You selected two views and gave each view four constraints. Two times four—doesn't that equal 8?

When you created a constraint pinning the bottom of the title field to the top of the author field, Xcode recognized it would be redundant to create a top constraint for the author field, reducing your constraints to 7.

You might notice your title and author text fields have shrunk and moved to the right of the scene. Strange! See figure 6.16.

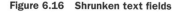

Figure 6.16   Shrunken text fields

Because you added constraints to the text fields, the Auto Layout engine takes over managing their position and size. Because these text fields are pinned to labels on their left that don't have auto layout positions yet, this is the Auto Layout engine's best guess as to your intention. The text fields have a width of 25 points, the default intrinsic content width of a text field that doesn't contain text.

Not to worry—this will all get sorted out when you add constraints to the labels.

The labels should already be set to right justified in the Attributes Inspector and pinned to their related text fields. As requested by the designer, let's make them the same width.

6 Select the three labels (Title, Author, and Notes).

7 Select Equal Widths in the Add New Constraints menu.

8 While you're in this menu, pin them flush to the left safe area layout guide as well, with a value of 16.

9 Don't forget to select the Add 5 Constraints button! The labels and text fields should return to their position on the left.

Why wouldn't you need to specify an absolute width for one of these three labels? You may have guessed it: the labels have an intrinsic content width based on their content. The only way for all three widths to be equal is for them to be equal to the widest option—otherwise, two labels would have to shrink smaller than their content width.

But as you've seen, text fields have an intrinsic content size too. If both labels and text fields have an intrinsic content size, how does the Auto Layout engine know which views to stretch and shrink to accommodate different resolutions?

HUGGING AND RESISTANCE

Imagine a hypothetical interface laid out with one view containing two labels. If the view width increases, the first label should stay the same width and the second label should stretch to fill the available space. If the view width decreases, again the first label should stay the same width and the second label should shrink to its available space (see figure 6.17).

How would you indicate this preferred behavior to the Auto Layout engine? Your first thought might be to specify a fixed width for the first label, but what happens one day when you decide to localize your app into different languages, and the word for "title" in another language is shorter—or worse, longer? Do you manually update the width of the title label for every language you've localized your app into? Or do you change the width value to the

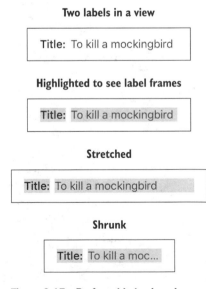

Figure 6.17   Preferred behavior when stretching and shrinking

longest possible version of the word "title"? A better approach is to allow the intrinsic content size of the label to do its job in defining the width of the label, and let the Auto Layout engine know which label you'd prefer to shrink and stretch if necessary. How? By setting the label's Content Hugging Priorities and Content Compression Resistance Priorities.

The higher the priority of Content Hugging, the more a view tries to hug its intrinsic content width and resists stretching. The higher the priority of Content Compression Resistance, the more a view resists compression of its content, or shrinking. See figure 6.18 to help grasp these concepts.

Figure 6.18 Compression resistance versus hugging

The default Content Hugging Priority for a label is 251 (low) and the default Content Compression Resistance Priority is 750 (high).

In the hypothetical interface of figure 6.17, to indicate that your preference is for the second label to shrink or stretch if necessary, you could give the second label *lower* priorities for horizontal hugging and compression in the Size Inspector (see figure 6.19).

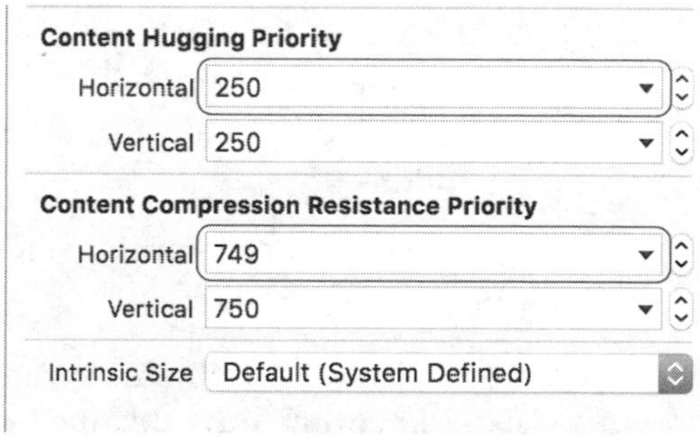

Conversely, you could also have given the first label *higher* horizontal hugging and compression priorities.

Great! But back to the add-a-book interface layout. Will you need to

Figure 6.19 Hugging and compression priorities

make changes to these priorities to indicate whether the title label and title text field should shrink or compress beyond their intrinsic content size? Well, no!

Because it's a common preference in a layout for a text field to grow or shrink while the label remains the same width as its content, defaults to accommodate this are baked into the system. Although the label hugging priority default is 251, the text field hugging priority default is 250. The text field will be the preferable view to stretch rather than using a label. Because the text field's intrinsic content width is a bare minimum width of 25 points, it's fine for the text field to continue to resist compression at the same priority level as other views.

CREATING BASELINE CONSTRAINTS

Now, all that's left is to give these three labels a y location.

1 Control-drag from the title label to the title text field.
2 Select Last Baseline to align the baselines of the two.
3 Repeat steps 1 and 2 for the author label. As the notes are taken in a scrollable multiline view, a baseline property doesn't make sense, so the designer has suggested the notes label could be aligned to the text view's top.
4 Control-drag between the notes label and the notes text view and select Top.

That's it—you've fully described the add-a-book form using auto layout constraints. Well done!

If you select all the views now by clicking on the storyboard and selecting Command-A, you should (hopefully) no longer be seeing any red error lines or arrows. You may, however, still see orange warning lines, most likely indicating several views are slightly misplaced on the canvas. Select the orange warning arrow at the top right of the document outline and skim over the issues.

RESOLVING AUTO LAYOUT ISSUES

Sometimes, you might have issues with your auto layout constraints, but two buttons can help you out:

- ⟳ *Update Frames* will automatically update the views in the canvas based on your constraints.
- ⊢△⊣ *Resolve Auto Layout Issues* can either update or create constraints based on the views' locations, or clear all constraints so you can start from scratch. Because Xcode can misinterpret your intention with your interface when defining your constraints for you in Resolve Auto Layout Issues, I generally avoid this option.

If you have any orange warning lines indicating a misplaced view, let's resolve the issue now by updating frames.

> **NOTE** If you don't have any orange warning lines, but you're interested in experimenting with updating frames, feel free to misplace a view by dragging it to where it shouldn't be!

1 Ensure that all views are still selected by clicking on the storyboard and selecting Command-A.

2 Say the magic word, and select *Update Frames*. Alakazam! The views in your scene should move into their perfect position, based on the constraints you set up. Orange error lines should be replaced with blue valid lines.

Regardless of the device you run your app on, the layout should adapt based on the rules you specified as constraints. See figure 6.20 for how your interface should look now on three different devices.

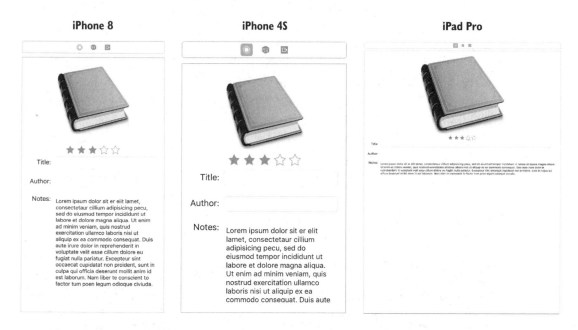

Figure 6.20   Interface after auto layout

Congratulations, you've laid out an interface using constraints and auto layout!

Run the app yourself to confirm that your design adapts to different device resolutions. You can rotate the simulator by holding down Command and the left-arrow (←) or right-arrow (→) buttons, and the interface will adapt to its new environment. Your app will even adapt to multitasking modes such as Slide Over or Split View!

> ✓ **CHECKPOINT**   If you'd like to compare your project with mine at this point, you can check mine out here: https://github.com/iOSApp-DevelopmentwithSwiftinAction/Bookcase.git (Chapter6.2.AutoLayout).

Upside-down orientation

If you're using an iPhone device or simulator, you may have discovered that the simulator doesn't want to rotate in one orientation. What's going on?

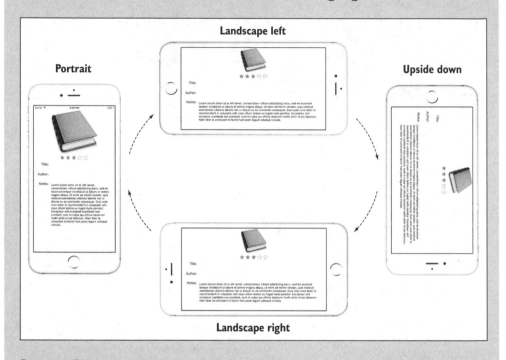

Because iPhone users are less likely than iPad users to want to use their handsets upside down, the default approach is to indicate to the user that the handset is upside down by not triggering a rotation for this orientation. This is set in the project's general target settings, under *Deployment Info*, where *Upside Down Device Orientation* is unchecked by default for Universal devices. (If you dig down and select iPad devices, you'll find that iPads override this universal behavior by allowing upside down device orientation.)

For more on project settings, see appendix A.

6.2.3 *Auto layout in code*

Because Interface Builder gives you the capacity to visualize your layout, and immediate feedback on errors and warnings, it's the best place to set up your constraints if possible. However, occasionally you may want your scene, or views within your scene, to change state, for example, after user interaction. This adjustment to your layout might need to be handled in code.

Luckily, it's possible to work with auto layout constraints in code. There are three main approaches you can use that are syntactic differences that, in the end, produce the same result: constraints that the Auto Layout engine can use to lay out a scene. You can set up your constraints with combinations of different approaches.

THREE APPROACHES

The following is a brief overview of the three different approaches to defining your constraints programmatically. Whichever approach you use, you'll generate an `NSLayoutConstraint` object. After generating the constraint, you then need to activate the constraint. (This is an easy step to forget.)

You can activate constraints in two ways:

- Set each constraint's active property to `true`:

  ```
  constraint.active = true
  ```

- Pass an array of constraints into `NSLayoutConstraint`'s `activate` method:

  ```
  NSLayoutConstraint.activate(constraints)
  ```

NSLAYOUTCONSTRAINT

`NSLayoutConstraint` is a powerful but verbose approach to defining individual constraints.

Back in figure 6.11, you saw that setting up the options that define a constraint is like formulating an equation. Using `NSLayoutConstraint`, you can create a constraint by passing in all the components of that equation and then activating the constraints (see figure 6.21).

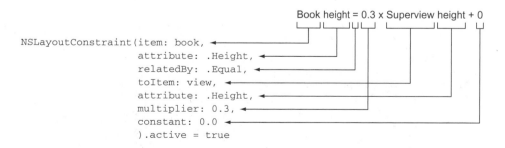

Figure 6.21 `NSLayoutConstraint` syntax

VISUAL FORMAT LANGUAGE

Visual Format Language (VFL) takes a different approach to defining constraints. In VFL, you can describe multiple constraints simultaneously.

Rather than setting up each individual constraint, you describe the horizontal and vertical sketches of your layout as strings in a *visual format*. Probably the easiest way to get grasp VFL is by looking at an example. Imagine you want to set up the horizontal constraints of a label and a text field, side by side, filling the available space.

First, set up a dictionary containing the elements:

```
let views = ["label": label, "textField": textField]
```

Then, you need to describe the horizontal layout, using VFL. See figure 6.22 for your first look at the VFL syntax.

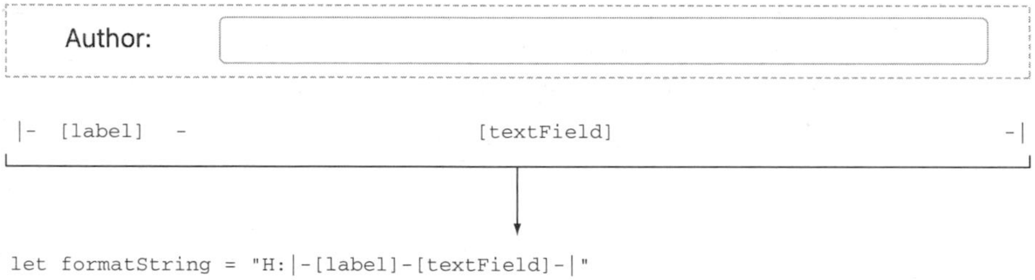

Figure 6.22   Visual Format Language syntax example

In English, this string says, "In the horizontal direction, place the label a standard distance from the left edge, place the text field a standard distance away, and then place the text field a standard distance away from the right edge."

This VFL string will automatically set up horizontal constraints for both the `label` and `textField`; not bad for a little string!

Once you define a VFL string, you can pass this and the dictionary of views into `NSLayoutConstraint`'s `constraintsWithVisualFormat` method, and then activate the constraints you generate, as shown in the following listing.

Listing 6.1   Create Visual Format Language constraints

```
let views = ["label": label, "textField": textField]
let formatString = "H:|-[label]-[textField]-|"
let constraints = NSLayoutConstraint.constraints (
        withVisualFormat: formatString,
        options: [],
        metrics: nil,
        views: views)
NSLayoutConstraint.activate(constraints)
```

VFL does have a limitation—it doesn't support multipliers. If multipliers are necessary, VFL needs to be used in combination with other techniques.

LAYOUT ANCHORS

NSLayoutAnchor creates individual constraints in a way similar to NSLayoutConstraint, but with a more succinct syntax. Every view and layout guide has *anchors* representing the 12 main constraint types (listed in table 6.1). You can constrain these anchors directly to each other to generate NSLayoutConstraints. Again, it's a matter of passing in the different components of the constraint equation, but in a different way (see figure 6.23).

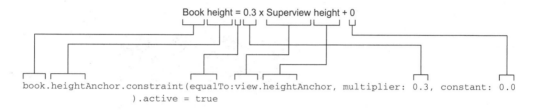

Figure 6.23 NSLayoutAnchor syntax

If the defaults for multiplier (1) and constant (0) are sufficient, these parameters can be left out of the call.

You'll practice using programmatic constraints by adding layout anchors to adapt views that were already created in code.

✓ **CHECKPOINT** Open the ViewsInCode project from chapter 4, or if you prefer, you can download it from https://github.com/iOSAppDevelopmentwithSwiftinAction/ViewsInCode.git (1.DisplayingViews branch).

Remind yourself of the project by running it on the simulator. In this project you added a red view that was the width and half the height of the root view. You then placed a label half-way down.

Great! These coordinates and dimensions were relative to the size of the root view, which was, by default, the same size as the app window. Regardless of whether you run this app on an iPhone 4S or on an iPad Pro, the calculation is correct.

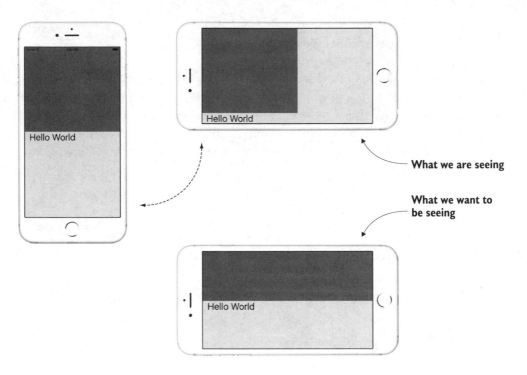

Figure 6.24   Rotating orientation

But wait, there's a problem. Rotate the simulator, and you'll see something like figure 6.24.

When the app window rotates to another orientation, the scene's root view automatically rotates, but any subviews don't automatically resize or reposition to the root view's new dimensions. What can we do about that?

Auto layout to the rescue!

1   After setting up the views programmatically in the `viewDidLoad` method, create the view's constraints, as shown in the code in this step.

First, pin the red view's top, and leading and trailing anchors to the root view, and set the red view's height to half the height of the root view.

Next, pin the label's leading anchor to the root view, and the top anchor of the label points from the bottom of the red view.

For simplicity, set up an array of `NSLayoutConstraints`, and then activate them all at once.

```
let constraints:[NSLayoutConstraint] = [
  //red view
  redView.topAnchor.constraint(equalTo: view.topAnchor),
  redView.leadingAnchor.constraint(equalTo: view.leadingAnchor),
  redView.trailingAnchor.constraint(equalTo: view.trailingAnchor),
```

```
     redView.heightAnchor.constraint(equalTo: view.heightAnchor,
       multiplier: 0.5),
     //label
     label.topAnchor.constraint(equalTo: redView.bottomAnchor, constant: 8),
     label.leadingAnchor.constraint(equalTo:
       view.layoutMarginsGuide.leadingAnchor)
   ]
   NSLayoutConstraint.activate(constraints)
```

2 Done. But wait! Run the app and rotate the simulator again. You'll find that not only are your new constraints being ignored, but there are a bunch of messages in the console that Xcode was "Unable to simultaneously satisfy constraints." What's going on?

AUTOMATIC AUTORESIZING CONSTRAINTS

Each view has a `translatesAutoresizingMaskIntoConstraints` property, which, if `true`, will automatically convert your *autoresizing masks* into auto layout constraints. We'll look at autoresizing masks in a moment, but for the moment it's sufficient to understand that these additional, automatically generated constraints are conflicting with the constraints you're manually creating.

The `translatesAutoresizingMaskIntoConstraints` property defaults to `true`, but will automatically swap to `false` if you add auto layout constraints to a view in Interface Builder. If you plan to add your views programmatically using auto layout as you're doing now, you must set this property on each view in code to `false`, or these automatically generated constraints may conflict with yours.

1 Set this property to false for the `redView`.

```
   redView.translatesAutoresizingMaskIntoConstraints = false
```

2 Do the same for the label.

```
   label.translatesAutoresizingMaskIntoConstraints = false
```

That's it! You've set up sufficient constraints for the red view and label to know how to display, regardless of the device or orientation they're displayed in.

3 Run the app in different device simulators and rotate the simulators to confirm that the app is displaying correctly.

6.3 *Autoresizing*

Before auto layout, Apple's first attempt at solving the problem of adaptive layout was called *autoresizing*, known also as springs and struts. As you'll see, autoresizing does have limitations compared to auto layout, but can still be a useful tool for quickly building simple interfaces, and the more powerful auto layout can be implemented for more-complex layouts.

As you've seen, views by default maintain the absolute position (x-y) and size (width-height) that they're instantiated with. If a view's superview (such as a scene's root view) changes size (perhaps due to a rotation), its subviews by default won't adjust accordingly. Autoresizing aims to correct this by adding certain rules that determine how a view resizes when its superview resizes.

The four outer margin attributes (top, left, right, and bottom) and the two size attributes (width and height) can be set to flexible (the springs) or fixed (the struts). See figure 6.25 to see how springs and struts define a view's relationship with its superview.

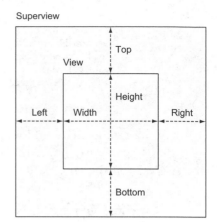

6.3.1 Autoresizing in code

We're going to explore how autoresizing works in code by looking again at the ViewsInCode project.

Figure 6.25   Autoresizing attributes

✅ **CHECKPOINT** You could remove (by selecting Source Control > Discard all Changes) or *comment out* any adjustments you made to the layout earlier, or if you prefer, you can check it out at https://github.com/iOSApp-DevelopmentwithSwiftinAction/ViewsInCode.git (1.DisplayingViews branch).

NOTE   You can comment out code by surrounding it with forward slash + asterisk (/*), and asterisk + forward slash (*/); for example: /* Comment */.

Let's consider how autoresizing could be used to automatically resize the red view and the label of the ViewsInCode project. Take another look at figure 6.24 to remind yourself of what the intention of the interface is, and then look at a written description of that intention for the red view in table 6.3.

Table 6.3   Red view

Attribute	Description
Left margin	0
Width	The width of the superview
Right margin	0
Top margin	0
Height	Half the height of the superview
Bottom margin	Half the height of the superview

Describing the interface this way helps make it clear which attributes are *relative* to the size of the superview (and therefore springs), and which are *absolute* values (and therefore struts).

When setting up the autoresizing rules for a view, rather than specifying all six attributes, only relative or flexible measurements (springs) are specified, and all unmentioned attributes are assumed to be absolute or inflexible (struts).

The width, height, and bottom margin are all relative to the superview, so you'll set them to be springs. Use the UIView's `autoresizingMask` property, and pass in an array containing the three flexible attributes.

1 Add the following line where you set up the `redView` in the `viewDidLoad` method:

```
redView.autoresizingMask = [.flexibleHeight, .flexibleWidth,
    .flexibleBottomMargin]
```

Follow the same process for the label described in table 6.4.

Table 6.4 Label

Attribute	Description
Left margin	20
Width	Fixed width
Right margin	Width of superview (minus) width (minus) left margin
Top margin	Half the height of the superview
Height	Fixed height
Bottom margin	Superview height (minus) height (minus) top margin

In the label's case, the right margin, top margin, and bottom margin are all relative to the superview, so you should set them to springs.

2 Add the following line after instantiating the label:

```
label.autoresizingMask = [.flexibleTopMargin, .flexibleBottomMargin,
    .flexibleRightMargin]
```

3 Run the app and rotate the simulator to check how the views resize on rotation (see figure 6.26). (I've given the label a background color to highlight the difference more clearly.)

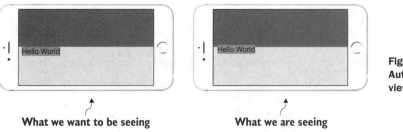

Figure 6.26
Autoresizing
views in code

What we want to be seeing   What we are seeing

Close, but not perfect! The red view resized great, but the label is slightly off. The simple calculation that Xcode performs to determine the top and bottom margins of the label aren't sufficient to place it precisely where you'd like it. This is a case where a more precise method such as auto layout will be necessary to perfect the layout.

6.3.2   *Autoresizing in Interface Builder*

You can perform autoresizing in Interface Builder as well. After laying out your views, you go to the Size Inspector for each view, where you'll find an autoresizing section with the six autoresizing attributes that you saw in figure 6.5.

Click on the six attributes to turn them on and off. Margins attributes are represented by struts (lines with flat ends), and size attributes are represented by springs (lines with arrowheads). The default attributes are represented by the Top-Left margin struts turned on and the Left-Bottom struts and Width-Height springs turned off (see figure 6.27). Notice the image to the right of the autoresizing attributes gives you a visual indication of the expected result with this combination of springs and struts.

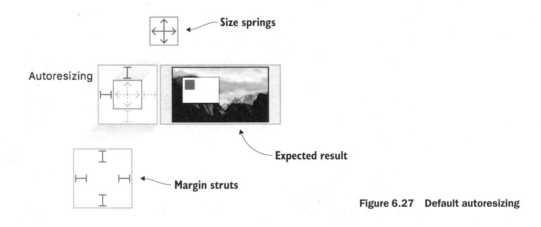

Figure 6.27   Default autoresizing

For example, to replicate the red view's attributes from table 6.3, you'd turn on the Width-Height springs, and the right margin strut (see figure 6.28).

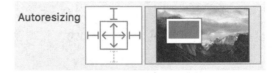

Figure 6.28   Red view autoresizing

6.3.3   *Autoresizing considerations*

You probably already have noticed some limitations of autoresizing:

- Each measurement needs to be defined as either absolute or relative, but sometimes you want a combination of both. For example, you might want a label to be positioned at a relative y position (half the height of its superview) *plus* an absolute position (a margin). This sort of combination isn't possible with autoresizing only.

- In autoresizing, the only relationship a view has is with its container. In real-life interfaces, views can have relationships with other views at the same level.

- Autoresizing doesn't take into consideration the possibility that the content of a view could change, requiring layout adjustments.

How does Xcode know to use autoresizing or auto layout to lay out your interface? When you drag a view onto Interface Builder, it will by default begin with top and left struts defined in autoresizing. As soon as a view contains at least one constraint, Interface Builder assumes you're planning to use auto layout constraints on this view rather than autoresizing, and the autoresizing attributes disappear from the Size Inspector.

Using autoresizing in a scene doesn't prevent you from using auto layout on *other views* in the same scene. It's possible to lay out a scene using the simpler autoresizing and then incrementally adopt the more powerful and complex system of auto layout on views where it's needed.

6.4 Manual adaptive layout

Auto layout (along with size classes discussed in the next chapter) will be sufficient for most interfaces, but occasionally you may need to implement adaption and transitions of your interface manually in code.

To explore manual adaptive layout, you'll work on the same ViewsInCode project from the previous section, but from its initial state.

✓ **CHECKPOINT** Again, discard or comment out changes, or check out the repo again from https://github.com/iOSAppDevelopmentwithSwift-inAction/ViewsInCode.git (1.DisplayingViews branch).

6.4.1 Receiving transition events

Whenever the root view of a view controller changes size (such as when the app rotates), a `UIViewController` event called `viewWillTransition()` triggers. This method passes in an argument containing the new size of the root view.

Override this method, and use this `size` parameter to resize the red view and reposition the label, as shown in the following listing.

Listing 6.2 Reposition/Resize views when view size transitions

```
override func viewWillTransition(to size: CGSize,
    with coordinator: UIViewControllerTransitionCoordinator) {
    super.viewWillTransition(to: size, with: coordinator)
    self.redView.frame.size = CGSize(width: size.width,
        height: size.height / 2)
    self.label.frame.origin.y = size.height / 2
}
```

Overrides method ⟶ (points to `override func viewWillTransition`)

Calls super method ⟵ (points to `super.viewWillTransition(to: size, with: coordinator)`)

Resizes red view (points to `self.redView.frame.size = CGSize(...)`)

Repositions label ⟵ (points to `self.label.frame.origin.y = size.height / 2`)

Run the app again, and rotate the simulator to test your repositioning code. The end result of the rotations is great, but the rotation transition doesn't look quite right and it's hard to tell exactly what's happening with the speed of the transition. Slow down the transition to get a better look at it by selecting Debug > Slow Animations.

Remember the yellow view is the root view of the scene, and is resized automatically by UIKit. On the other hand, the red view, a subview of the yellow view, is controlled by you.

When the animations are slowed down, notice that the yellow view's rotation, width, and height transition over the duration of the rotation transition. Meanwhile, at the moment the rotation is triggered, the red view's width and height change to their new values without transitioning. How can you make the red view's resizing transition over time like the yellow view's?

There's an argument in the `viewWillTransition` method that's the key to performing this transition: the *transition coordinator.*

The transition coordinator is generated when a scene transition begins, and handles animations of views during the transition. You can tell the transition coordinator to animate your views for you too, using the `animate` method.

The `animateAlongsideTransition` method accepts two arguments that are both closures, as explained in table 6.5.

Table 6.5 `animateAlongsideTransition` **arguments**

Argument	Description
animation	Any changes to properties within this closure will automatically animate for the duration of the transition.
completion	This closure will be called after the animation is complete, and can be used for any cleanups, such as removing subviews.

In general, the structure of a `viewWillTransition` method should look like the following listing.

Listing 6.3 `viewWillTransition` method structure

```
override func viewWillTransition(to size: CGSize,
        with coordinator: UIViewControllerTransitionCoordinator) {    Setup prior
    super.viewWillTransition(to: size, with: coordinator)        ◁──┘ to transition

    coordinator.animate (alongsideTransition: { (context) in    ◁──┐ Properties
                                                                    │ to animate
    }) { (context) in              ◁──┐ Cleanup after
                                       │ transition
    }
}
```

For our ViewsInCode example, you could resize the red view and reposition the label within the animation block, as shown in the following listing.

Listing 6.4   Animate reposition/resize views

```
override func viewWillTransition(to size: CGSize,
      with coordinator: UIViewControllerTransitionCoordinator) {        No setup
   super.viewWillTransition(to: size, with: coordinator)            ◁─┘ necessary

   coordinator.animate (alongsideTransition: { (context) in
      self.redView.frame.size = CGSize(width: size.width,
         height: size.height / 2)                              ◁──┐ Animate property
      self.label.frame.origin.y = size.height / 2                 │ changes
   }) { (context) in             ◁──┐ No cleanup
                                     │ necessary
   }
}
```

Run the app again with animations slowed down, and notice that this time the red view and the label animate smoothly to their new positions and dimensions.

6.4.2   Receiving layout events

Rather than programmatically adjusting the size and position of views in a scene at the moment a view transitions, developers may prefer to adjust them at the moment the scene's root view's layout is being updated.

WHEN IS A VIEW'S LAYOUT UPDATED?

Every view contains a flag that indicates that it requires updates to its layout. If this flag is set to `true`, it will be updated at the next appropriate moment in the run cycle. A view could be *flagged* as needing layout several times in the same cycle, but the actual layout *process* is only performed once.

   The system can set this flag to `true`. When does the system flag that the root view's layout needs updating? Here are common times:

- When the view appears
- When the view is resized (for example, after an orientation change)
- When the view's subviews change (that is, a subview is added to the view, or a subview is removed from the view

You can also set the flag to `true` by calling the view's `setNeedsLayout` method. If you do need to manually request the layout process to be performed immediately, this is possible as well, by calling the `layoutIfNeeded` method.

UPDATING VIEW LAYOUT

When the appropriate time arrives in the run cycle to update a view, and it's flagged to require updates, three methods are called to lay out a view's subviews (see figure 6.29).

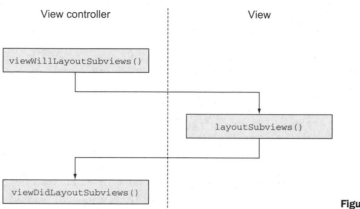

View controller   View

```
viewWillLayoutSubviews()
```

```
layoutSubviews()
```

```
viewDidLayoutSubviews()
```

Figure 6.29   Layout subviews

The view controller first registers that it *will* lay out the subviews, then the view *does* the layout of subviews, and finally the view controller registers that it *did* lay out the subviews. You can override any of these methods to manually resize and reposition subviews. If the trigger to lay out involves a transition such as resizing a view, the transition coordinator will animate any changes made in these three methods as well.

To explore this alternative approach, you'll use the `viewWillLayoutSubviews` method to update the position and size of the `redView` and label.

First, remove or comment out the `viewWillTransition` method from the previous section.

Override the `viewWillLayoutSubviews` method, and call its super method. Resize the red view and reposition the label. To see when this method is called, print a message to the console, as shown in the following listing.

Listing 6.5   Reposition/Resize views when view is laid out

```
override func viewWillLayoutSubviews() {              ◁── Override method
    super.viewWillLayoutSubviews()
    self.redView.frame.size = CGSize(width: view.frame.width,
        height: view.frame.height / 2)                    Resizes red view
    self.label.frame.origin.y = view.frame.height / 2
    print("View will layout subviews")              ◁── Prints to
}                                                        console
```

Calls super method → `super.viewWillLayoutSubviews()`

Repositions label → `self.label.frame.origin.y = view.frame.height / 2`

Run the app on the simulator again, and rotate the app. You should see the red view resizing and the label repositioning, animated the way it was before.

CONSIDERATIONS

The approach you decide to go with is up to you and the specifics of your app, but advantages do exist for repositioning and resizing when the layout updates:

- The layoutSubviews method will be called when a view appears, *and* when the view resizes (such as a rotation). You can take advantage of this to perform repositioning and resizing that will be consistent initially and on rotation.
- You can take advantage of the call setNeedsLayout to manually request that the layout updates.
- By overriding the layoutSubviews method in a UIView subclass, you can pass on the responsibility of managing a view's layout to the view itself, something that can make sense in many cases.

Certain disadvantages to this approach are these:

- You probably noticed in the console that the viewWillLayoutSubviews method was called twice when the view appeared. Despite the use of a flag to avoid redundant layout updates, it's still possible for this method to be called on multiple run cycles. You should consider this possibility. Avoid processor-intensive work in these methods and ensure that any one-off work is only performed once.
- Repositioning and resizing views manually in a simple interface with a view and a label isn't too bad, but what happens when the interface contains dozens of different types of views? What if you want the interface to look different on an iPad and an iPhone, or portrait and landscape? Setting up an interface entirely in code can get complex quickly.

Although certain developers prefer to adapt views programmatically, most iOS developers use programmatic repositioning and resizing of views as a last resort, useful for certain circumstances where auto layout isn't sufficient, such as dynamic interfaces or customized animations.

6.5   *Choosing an approach*

In this chapter, you've looked at several approaches to building an adaptive layout:

- Manually
  - Responding to transition events
  - Responding to layout events
- Automatically
  - Using autoresizing
    - In Interface Builder
    - Setting autoresizing mask in code
  - Using auto layout
    - In Interface Builder
    - In code

- Using layout constraints
- Using layout anchors
- Using visual format language

Wow, that's a long list of alternatives! How do you know which to use?

We covered some of the pros and cons of each. Beyond those, it comes down to personal preferences. Some users may prefer the granular control of making changes manually. Others may prefer the relative simplicity of autoresizing. Another group may prefer to have everything in code, whereas others like to work visually.

I generally lean toward auto layout. It can be complicated at first, but the time investment in getting familiar with it is worth it, and with practice the process of describing your layout using constraints will become easier. I also prefer to use Interface Builder where possible to visualize the interface, and more quickly recognize issues with my constraints.

That said, auto layout isn't like working in a vacuum, and it's a good idea to be familiar with other adaptive layout options. Different combinations of techniques can be used where appropriate. Dynamic designs, for example, are great candidates for working with adaptive layout in code.

We're not done with adaptive layout yet! We'll explore more ways to adapt interfaces in the next chapter. Though our layouts have adapted, they've still been similar on different devices and rotations. In the next chapter, you'll make your apps adapt even more to their environment!

6.6   *Summary*

In this chapter, you learned the following:

- The position and size of the views in your layout should adapt to their environment—regardless of the device resolution, orientation, or if they're presented in a multitasking mode or split view controller.
- You can manually adapt views in code when the scene's view loads and transitions, or when the scene's view is laid out.
- You can adapt views using autoresizing, which can be sufficient on simpler layouts.
- Constraints are the rules that describe a layout in auto layout, and can be defined in Interface Builder or in code.
- Auto layout allows more-complicated relationships between views.
- A view in Interface Builder by default is positioned with autoresizing, until it's given an auto layout constraint.
- A layout can use a combination of methods to adapt its views.

More adaptive layout 7

This chapter covers

- Adapting layouts for size classes
- Adapting layouts with stack views

In this chapter, we'll look at a useful feature for manipulating layouts in different environments, called *size classes*. We'll use size classes to adjust layouts programmatically and from within Interface Builder.

We'll then explore stack views—a feature introduced in iOS 9 that speeds up the process of setting up an adaptive layout (in most cases).

7.1 Size classes

Auto layout is great for adjusting a layout based on constraints, but sometimes a layout requires more-significant adjustments based on the device type, screen size, or orientation.

For example, you may want

- A bigger font size in the huge iPad Pro screen than on the tiny iPhone 4S.
- A view laid out differently on iPhones when in landscape or portrait mode.

- To provide additional buttons in the iPad version of your app.
- To lay out content differently when your app is in slide-over or split-view mode.

How can you make these sorts of adjustments to a layout?

In older versions of Xcode, you may have had multiple storyboards for iPads and iPhones. Or perhaps you used the device orientation or window size to determine the environment for laying out a scene. Along with increasing numbers of devices, split view controllers (introduced in iOS 8), and slide-over and split-view multitasking modes (introduced in iOS 9), adjusting a layout to its environment became more complex.

To simplify things, Apple recommends a new paradigm. Rather than considering your layout in terms of the many device types, resolutions, multitasking modes, and device orientation, you should focus instead on adjusting your layout to two types of widths (called *compact* and *regular)* and two types of heights (also *compact* and *regular)*. These distinctions are called size classes. You can then use these size classes to define or adjust your layout.

Size classes reduce all the different potential horizontal and vertical configurations to just two types: compact for constrained space and regular for more expansive space. An iPhone portrait orientation, for example, is considered to have a compact width and a regular height. See figure 7.1 for a comprehensive breakdown of how the size classes correspond to devices and device orientations.

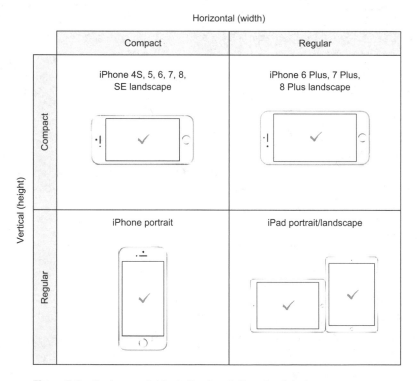

Figure 7.1   Devices and orientation in relations to size classes

In defining the size classes, Apple made interesting decisions worth noting:

- When in landscape orientation, iPhones (other than the Plus range) are still considered to have compact widths.
- All iPads in portrait or landscape mode are considered to have regular widths and regular heights, so a change in orientation on an iPad doesn't trigger a change in size class.

Size classes don't describe only device types and orientation. Size classes also describe an app's environment when the app is presented inside iPad multitasking modes—such as Slide Over, Split View, and Side by Side (see figure 7.2). Note that although the horizontal size class may change for certain iPad multitasking modes, the vertical size class remains regular. In fact, a compact vertical size class is sufficient to imply that we're working with an iPhone in landscape mode.

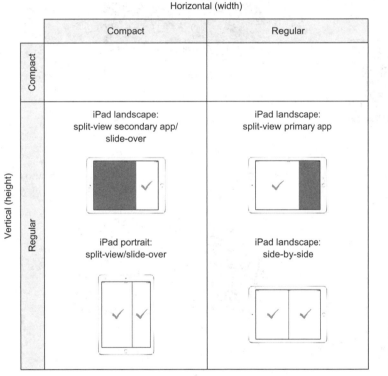

Figure 7.2
Multitasking
modes in relation
to size classes

WHAT CAN YOU DO WITH SIZE CLASSES?

Size classes aren't an alternative to constraints and auto layout; rather, they work in tandem. You can make many changes to a layout with size classes, such as

- Constraints can be activated or deactivated (called *installed* and *uninstalled*).
- Views can be resized or repositioned.

- Views can be added or removed (called *installed* and *uninstalled*).
- Colors and fonts can be changed.

In fact, programmatically, you could make *any* change based on a size class.

7.1.1   *Size classes in code*

Let's take another look at the ViewsInCode app you added constraints to in the previous chapter. With the layout anchor constraints you added, the layout adjusts when the device rotates, but perhaps the layout could be made even *more* appropriate for its space. The designer has decided the iPhone layout could be improved when the user rotates the app to landscape orientation. Instead of the red rectangle squishing to the top half of the view, it should move to the left of the scene (see figure 7.3).

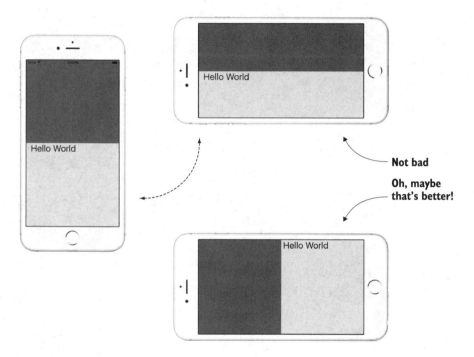

Figure 7.3   New adaptive layout for ViewsInCode

Great, everyone agrees that this improves the layout in landscape on the iPhone, but implementing this requires a different array of constraints. You can no longer define, for example, the red rectangle's height as half the height of the root view, because this isn't always the case.

You're going to need two arrays of constraints—one array that you've already defined and another array to define the new layout in landscape.

NOTE Certain constraints will essentially be the same and can be reused in the two arrays, but the savings obtained by reusing constraints is generally minimal. Depending on the complexity of the change, it can be cleaner and simpler to create new constraints in both arrays. Knowing that all constraints in an array are unique also makes it easier to confirm if an array of constraints is active.

✓ **CHECKPOINT** Open the ViewsInCode app where you left it after adding layout anchor constraints in the previous chapter, or check out the repo from https://github.com/iOSAppDevelopmentwithSwiftinAction/ViewsIn-Code.git (2.LayoutAnchorConstraints branch).

CHALLENGE Create a new array of layout anchor constraints matching the new landscape layout in figure 7.3 below the `constraints` variable in `view-DidLoad`. Call this new array `landscapeConstraints`.

Now you should have two arrays of constraints ready to use: `constraints` and `land-scapeConstraints`. If you'd like to check your `landscapeConstraints` against mine, they're shown in the following listing.

Listing 7.1 Landscape constraints

```
let landscapeConstraints:[NSLayoutConstraint] = [
//red view
redView.topAnchor.constraint(equalTo: view.topAnchor),
redView.leadingAnchor.constraint(equalTo: view.leadingAnchor),
redView.bottomAnchor.constraint(equalTo: view.bottomAnchor),
redView.widthAnchor.constraint(equalTo: view.widthAnchor,
  multiplier: 0.5),
//label
label.topAnchor.constraint(equalTo: view.topAnchor),
label.leadingAnchor.constraint(equalTo: redView.trailingAnchor,
  constant: 8)
]
```

DISPLAY LAYOUT FOR SIZE CLASS

To apply the appropriate array of constraints *in code* using size classes, you need to do two things:

1 Set up the correct layout for the current size class when first laying out your views.

2 Update the layout when the size class changes (for example, when the user rotates the device).

Let's start by activating the correct array of constraints for the current size class. But how can you get access to the current horizontal and vertical size classes?

The current size classes are defined in the *trait collection*.

TRAIT COLLECTION

`UIView` and `UIViewController` both adopt the `UITraitEnvironment` protocol, giving them a property called `traitCollection` that describes its environment. You can use the information in the trait collection to make decisions about how to build or adjust the layout of your app.

Trait collections contain information on several important *traits*, as shown in table 7.1.

Table 7.1 Trait collection information

Trait information	Description
`displayScale`	Indicates the scale of the screen. iPhone 8 Plus has a display scale of 3.0, other Retina devices have a display scale of 2.0, and older non-Retina devices (such as the iPad 2) have a display scale of 1.0.
`userInterfaceIdiom`	Indicates the type of device, such as `Pad` for iPads, or `Phone` for iPhones. (Apple recommends you ignore idioms where possible and instead use size classes.)
`forceTouchCapability`	Indicates whether 3D touch is available on this device.
`horizontalSizeClass`	Indicates if the horizontal size class is `Compact` or `Regular`.
`verticalSizeClass`	Indicates if the vertical size class is `Compact` or `Regular`.

By examining the horizontal and vertical size classes inside the `traitCollection`, you can determine which set of constraints to install.

SET UP LAYOUT FOR SIZE CLASS

You may have noticed that if the vertical size class is compact, you can assume an iPhone in landscape orientation. This means you can check the vertical size class in the `traitCollection` to determine the appropriate array of constraints to activate.

1 Activate the correct set of constraints in the `viewDidLoad` method:

```
if traitCollection.verticalSizeClass == .compact {      ◁—— Determines the
    NSLayoutConstraint.activate(landscapeConstraints)         vertical size class
} else {
    NSLayoutConstraint.activate(constraints)      ◁—— Activates the nonlandscape
}                                                        constraints
```

Activates the landscape constraints (annotation for the first `NSLayoutConstraint.activate(landscapeConstraints)` line)

2 Run the app in an iPhone simulator (or an actual iPhone!). The layout of the app should depend on the initial orientation of the simulator.

Great, you have the correct initial layout set up, but now you'll need to change layout when the size class changes (that is, a change in orientation).

UPDATE LAYOUT ON CHANGES IN SIZE CLASS

To update the layout when the size class changes, you'll need to listen for changes to the `traitCollection`. You can do this by overriding `UIViewController`'s `traitCollectionDidChange` method.

In the `traitCollectionDidChange` method, you can check the new vertical size class and make any changes to constraints if necessary by deactivating the current array of constraints and activating the appropriate array of constraints.

But before you can do this, you'll need to upgrade your two arrays of constraints to instance properties, so you can access them outside the `viewDidLoad` method.

1   Move your two arrays of constraints out of the `viewDidLoad` method to instance properties of the `ViewController` class now.

Whoops! When you defined your constraints as instance properties, you encountered a compiler error: "…property initializers run before 'self' is available."

You can't initialize one instance property from another property of the same instance. Why? Well, a property is initialized in the initialization phase—other properties can't be guaranteed to be initialized until this initialization phase is complete. How can you initialize a property whose initial state depends on another property?

You might wonder if this is a job for a *computed property*. One thing to consider with computed properties is that the property is calculated *every time* it's requested. Because you only want *one* instance of the array of constraints so that you can deactivate the same instance later, computed properties won't help you here, unfortunately.

Your next thought might be to initialize the arrays of constraints *after* the initialization process. This means your arrays of constraints either need to be initialized temporarily as something else (such as an empty array) or made optional. A working solution, but not as elegant as *lazy stored properties*.

Lazy stored property

A lazy stored property is a property that isn't generated until it's first used. Lazy stored properties are useful for two main situations:

- The initial value of a property depends on the initial value of another property.
- The property requires a large amount either of computation or memory, and would be better left for when it's needed rather than instantiated during the initialization process.

Consider an alphabet class that merely stores two strings: the alphabet, and the alphabet in uppercase computed from the alphabet string:

```
class Alphabet {
    let letters = "abcdefghijklmnopqrstuvwxyz"          Error
    let lettersUpper= letters.uppercased()          ⬅
}
```

You have an error! The `lettersUpper` property can't be initialized, because it depends on the initial value of another property. Not to worry, this can be resolved by making this property *lazy* with the `lazy` keyword:

```
lazy var lettersUpper:String = self.letters.uppercased()
```

(continued)

Phew! Now this property can be based on the initial value of another property. Notice four additional factors:

- Lazy stored properties must be variables rather than constants.
- Lazy stored properties based on other instance properties or methods need to specify the `self` keyword first.
- To assist the compiler to infer the type of lazy stored properties based on other instance properties, you'll need to explicitly type the variable.
- Because you can use an instance method to initialize your property, you could also initialize your lazy stored property with a closure:

```
lazy var lettersUpper:String = {
    return self.letters.uppercased()
}()
```

---

2   Define the two constraints arrays as the lazy stored properties shown here:

```
lazy var constraints:[NSLayoutConstraint] = [          ⟵  Now lazy stored
    self.redView.topAnchor.constraint(equalTo:              property
        self.view.topAnchor),
    self.redView.leadingAnchor.constraint(equalTo:
        self.view.leadingAnchor),
    self.redView.trailingAnchor.constraint(equalTo:
        self.view.trailingAnchor),                     Add references
    self.redView.heightAnchor.constraint(equalTo:      to self
        self.view.heightAnchor, multiplier: 0.5),
    self.label.topAnchor.constraint(equalTo:
        self.redView.bottomAnchor, constant: 8),
    self.label.leadingAnchor.constraint(equalTo:
        self.view.layoutMarginsGuide.leadingAnchor)
]
lazy var landscapeConstraints:[NSLayoutConstraint] = [ ⟵  Now lazy stored
    self.redView.topAnchor.constraint(equalTo:              property
        self.view.topAnchor),
    self.redView.leadingAnchor.constraint(equalTo:
        self.view.leadingAnchor),
    self.redView.bottomAnchor.constraint(equalTo:
        self.view.bottomAnchor),                       Add references
    self.redView.widthAnchor.constraint(equalTo:       to self
        self.view.widthAnchor, multiplier: 0.5),
    self.label.topAnchor.constraint(equalTo:
        self.view.topAnchor),
    self.label.leadingAnchor.constraint(equalTo:
        self.redView.trailingAnchor, constant: 8)
]
```

Now that you have instance properties for your constraints, let's get back to your `traitCollectionDidChange` method. See figure 7.4 for a look at an old-fashioned flow chart that explains what we intend to do.

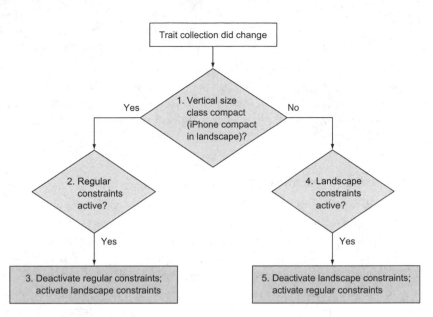

Figure 7.4   **Update constraints when the trait collection changes**

After (1) examining the new vertical size class, check to see whether the incorrect constraints are currently active (2 and 4). If they are, deactivate them and activate the correct constraints (3 and 5).

3 Let's see how this would look in code. Add the following `traitCollection-DidChange` method to your `ViewController` class:

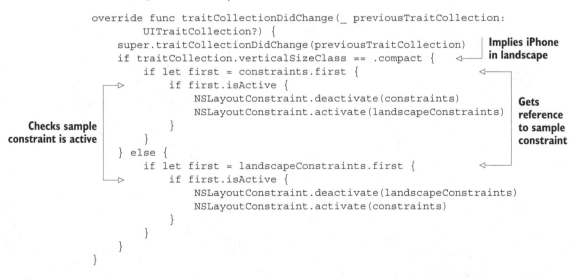

```
override func traitCollectionDidChange(_ previousTraitCollection:
        UITraitCollection?) {
    super.traitCollectionDidChange(previousTraitCollection)
    if traitCollection.verticalSizeClass == .compact {          Implies iPhone
        if let first = constraints.first {                      in landscape
            if first.isActive {
                NSLayoutConstraint.deactivate(constraints)
                NSLayoutConstraint.activate(landscapeConstraints)   Gets
            }                                                       reference
        }                                                           to sample
    } else {                                                        constraint
        if let first = landscapeConstraints.first {
            if first.isActive {
                NSLayoutConstraint.deactivate(landscapeConstraints)
                NSLayoutConstraint.activate(constraints)
            }
        }
    }
}
```

Checks sample constraint is active

4 Run the app on an iPhone simulator. The layout should (fingers crossed!) adapt in a more significant way to its new environment as you rotate the device.

If you rotate an iPhone to landscape, the red view moves from the top to the left, and the label moves from halfway down the view, to halfway across.

✓ **CHECKPOINT**   If you've run into problems on the way, not to worry! You can look at the project at this point, by checking it out from https://github.com/iOSAppDevelopmentwithSwiftinAction/ViewsInCode.git (3.SizeClasses).

7.1.2   *Size classes in Interface Builder*

Adapting your layout to size classes isn't limited to code. You can also assign your layouts and constraints to specific size classes in Interface Builder, and your layout will update automatically when the size class changes—without writing a line of code!

You're going to explore adding customizations for different size classes in Interface Builder in an app with a simple layout that displays an article with a title and body text.

You'll first build the iPhone interface, which contains the title in a *label* and the body text in a *text view* (see the iPhone layout on the left of figure 7.5). This layout, however, doesn't look great on the iPad (layout in the center of figure 7.5) To resolve this, you'll use size classes to adapt the interface (layout on the right of figure 7.5). Note the subtle and not so subtle differences between the layouts—because the iPad has more space, you'll adjust font and margin sizes, and add a subtitle label.

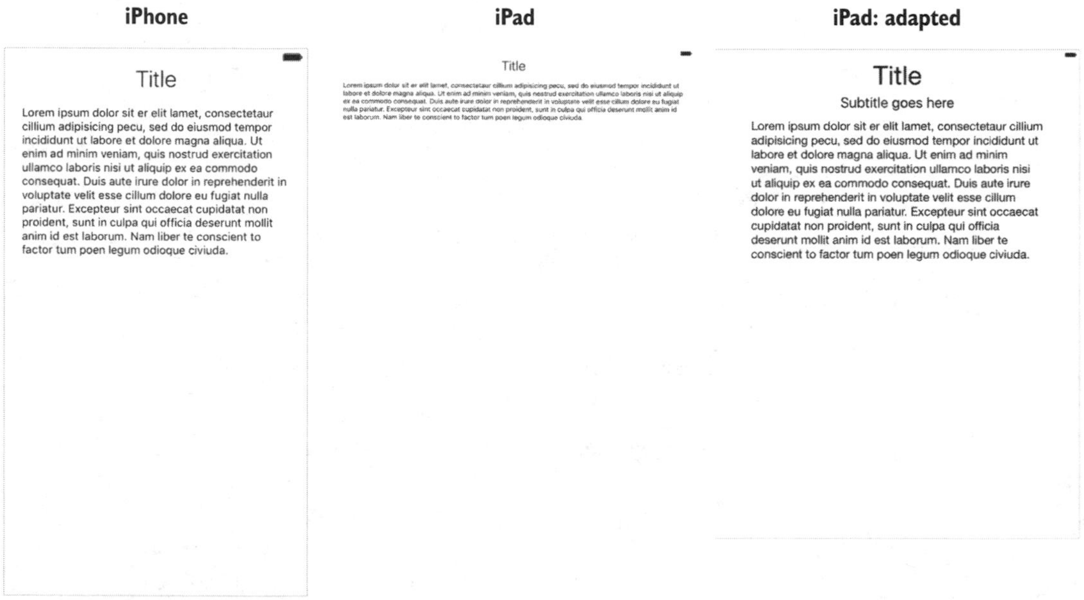

Figure 7.5   Spot the difference!

Let's start by setting up the basic interface and constraints.

1 Create a simple Single View Application and call it *SimpleSizeClasses*.
2 Select the File Inspector for the main storyboard. Note that the storyboard automatically has Use Auto Layout and Use Trait Variations selected (see figure 7.6.) This indicates that this storyboard is ready for adaptive layout with constraints and size classes.

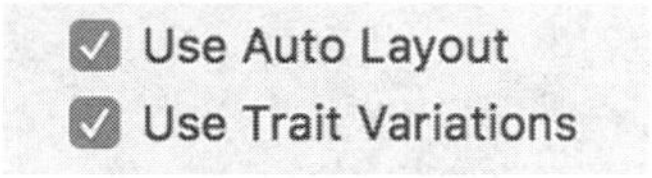

✓ **Use Auto Layout**
✓ **Use Trait Variations**

Figure 7.6 Adaptive storyboard checkboxes

NOTE An app that uses auto layout and size classes is not only ready for adaptive layout but can take advantage of iOS multitasking environments. If you want users to use Slide Over or Split View with your app, make sure you don't deselect these options!

Now to set up the basic interface. (If you're feeling lazy, feel free to skip to the checkpoint, where the basic interface is ready to go!)

3 Drag a label onto the main storyboard.
4 Replace the label's text with Title.
5 Use constraints in Interface Builder to center the label.
6 Pin the label to the top safe area layout guide.
7 Choose the Title 1 font type.
8 Drag on a text view below the label, filling the available space.
9 Pin the text view to the title label, the bottom safe area layout guide, and the left and right safe area layout guides.

✓ **CHECKPOINT** You can compare your app at this point with mine at https://github.com/iOSAppDevelopmentwithSwiftinAction/Simple-SizeClasses.git (1.InitialSetup branch).

SPECIFYING LAYOUTS FOR SIZE CLASSES

Now that you've set up the basic interface of the article app, let's look at how to specify different layouts for different size classes in Interface Builder. Two main approaches are available that you can use in tandem:

1 Add customizations to an attribute.
2 Vary for traits.

You'll use both approaches to customize your simple layout for different size classes. Let's look at each in turn.

ADDING CUSTOMIZATIONS TO AN ATTRIBUTE

You can add customizations for a size class directly to an attribute. Let's explore this feature by modifying font sizes and margin sizes for different size classes in your sample application.

View the storyboard in the device configuration bar as an iPad Pro, and zoom out to see the whole scene. Notice how tiny the text is on the expansive iPad screen. (You can also see this in the center image of figure 7.5.) Let's increase the font size for larger size classes.

1 Select the title label and open the Attributes Inspector. Notice the grey plus (+) symbol to the left of the font attribute. Selecting the plus symbol gives you the opportunity to add a customized value for a size class.

2 Select the plus symbol to the left of the font attribute now. Here, you can select the size class you're interested in, from Width, Height, and Gamut (a display type). The current size class is suggested as a default.

3 Select Regular Width, Regular Height to add a customized value for iPads. A customized value appears for the font attribute, for the specified size class. The cryptic wR hR to the left of the new attribute stands for width Regular, height Regular.

NOTE If you're not interested in adding a customization for a certain size class, you can set it to Any. Because we're not interested in customizing for Gamut, leave it as Any.

4 You can now modify the new value for this size class. Make it a *System* font of 55 points (see figure 7.7).

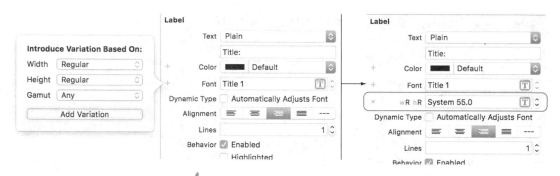

Figure 7.7   Add customized value for size class

5 Go through the same process to modify the font size for the text view as well—how about a System font of 25 points?

6 Check the layout in different devices, orientations and adaptations. You should find that the font attributes adjust appropriately for the different size classes.

You can easily add more attributes for other size classes by going through the process again. Removing a customized attribute is straightforward too—select the X to the left of the attribute.

What other attributes can you customize? Explore the Attributes and Size Inspectors for the label. Any attribute with a plus sign can be customized. For the label, for example, this includes color attributes in the Attributes Inspector (see figure 7.8) and margin attributes in the Size Inspector.

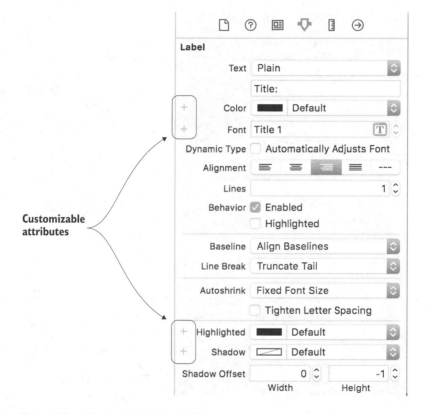

Figure 7.8 Label customizable attributes

ADDING CUSTOMIZATIONS TO A CONSTRAINT

Importantly, you can also customize the values of a constraint for a size class. Let's increase the leading and trailing margins of the text view to make it narrower on the iPad.

1 Select the text view and the Size Inspector and find the Leading space constraint.

2   Instead of selecting Edit, double click on the constraint in the Size Inspector to open a more detailed edit view for the constraint. Notice that the constraint's Constant value has a plus sign.

3   Add a variation for iPads (Regular Width, Regular Height).

4   Give the Constant a customized value of 50 (see figure 7.9).

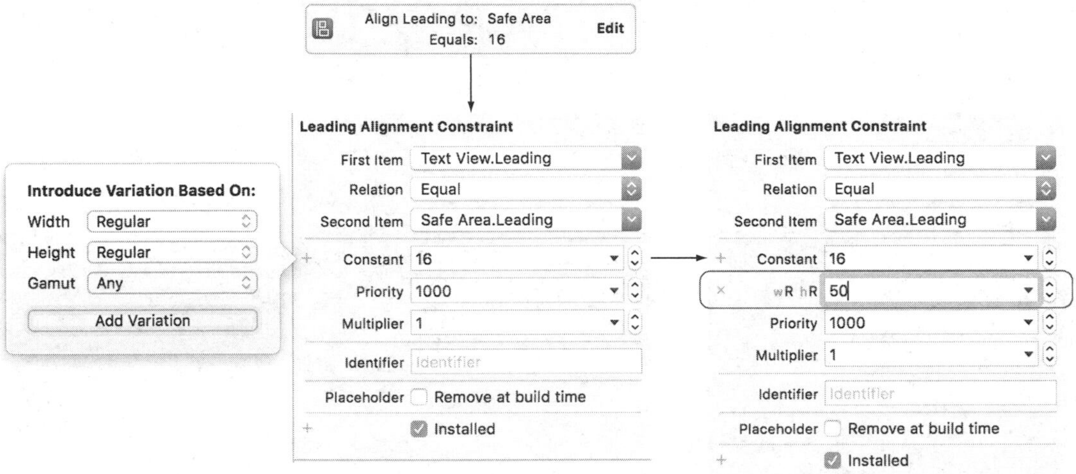

Figure 7.9   Add customization to a constraint

5   Do the same for the text view's trailing constraint (you'll need to select the text view again to be able to choose a different constraint).

TIP   If the text view goes offscreen after setting up the trailing constraint, you need to reverse the first and second items. Select the drop-down for either the first or second item and select Reverse the First and Second Item. Now modify the constant again to 50, and the constraint should be set up correctly.

Note the effects of the changes you've made to the layout in different configurations. If all's gone well, the text view should have a wider margin on the iPad.

ADDING CUSTOMIZATION TO THE INSTALLED ATTRIBUTE

Now, to make some more-significant changes to the iPad layout. You'll add a subtitle label for iPad users. But first, you need to remove the constraint between the title and the text view to make room for the subtitle view.

You may have noticed another customizable attribute in both the Constraint Inspector and the Attribute Inspector for the view: Installed. Views and constraints can be installed or uninstalled for specific size classes. Let's use this attribute to remove the constraint.

1 Double-click the text view Top Space constraint.
2 Select the plus symbol next to the Installed attribute to add a customization.
3 Deselect the checkbox for wR hR (see figure 7.10).

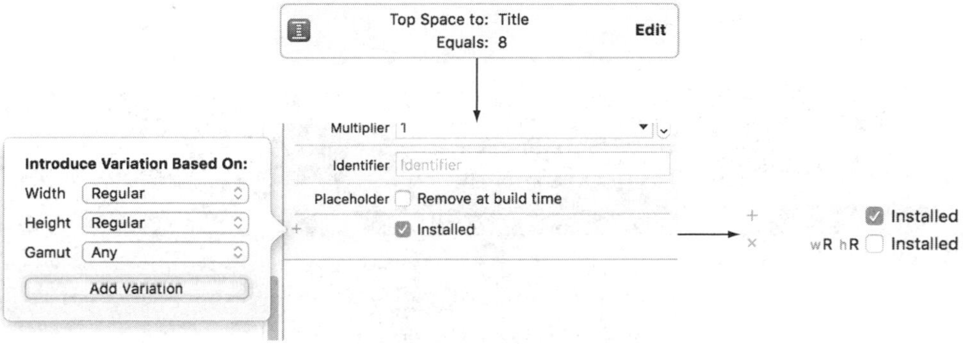

Figure 7.10   Uninstall constraint

NOTE   Don't panic if the text view disappears—it's temporarily confused about where to go; you'll resolve this shortly.

Now to add the subtitle view. Let's add it by *varying for traits*.

VARYING FOR TRAITS

Varying for traits is great for making more-significant changes to a layout for a size class. Let's explore varying for traits by adding a view and a constraint for different size classes in the sample application.

You may have noticed the Vary for Traits button at the right of the device configuration bar, and wondered what that button was for. Well, wonder no more! You can use the Vary for Traits button to start varying a layout just for specific size classes.

1 With an iPad device selected in the device configuration bar, select Vary for Traits. You'll be given the option to vary for the width size class (wR), height size class (hR) or both (wR hR).
2 Select both width and height. When you make your selection, the device configuration bar will turn blue, and you'll see visually which devices, orientations,

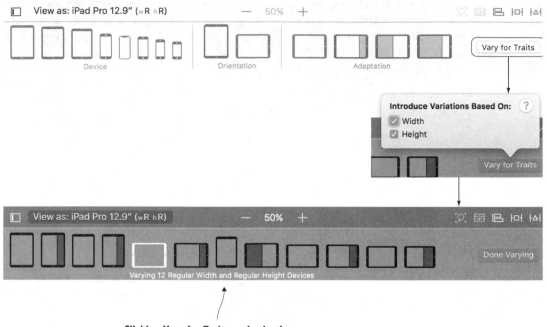

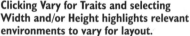

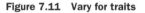

Clicking Vary for Traits and selecting Width and/or Height highlights relevant environments to vary for layout.

Figure 7.11 Vary for traits

and adaptations (multitasking environments) you'll vary the layout for (see figure 7.11).

As you can see, the wR hR size class isn't relevant only to iPads, but also certain adaptations. You can now go ahead and vary the layout for this size class.

3 Add a subtitle label below the title.

4 Give it sample text, such as "Subtitle goes here."

5 Give it a System font size of 30.

6 Pin the subtitle label to the title and align it horizontally.

7 Pin the text view to the subtitle label. (if you don't see the text view in the storyboard, you can find it in the Document Outline)

8 Modify the constraint constant to 8 points. The text view should slide in nicely underneath the new subtitle label. You're done varying the layout!

9 Select Done Varying in the device configuration bar.

Again, select different devices or orientations in the device configuration bar to admire the results of your work. The subtitle should appear for iPads and disappear for other size classes. Note that different views and constraints are installed or uninstalled in different size classes. Faded symbols in the document outline represent uninstalled views and constraints (see figure 7.12).

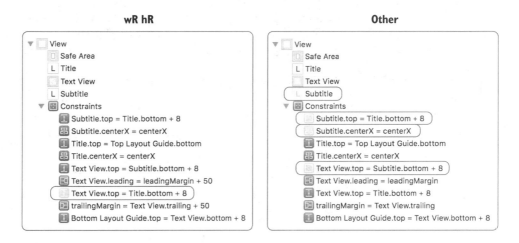

Figure 7.12 Uninstalled views and constraints

✅ **CHECKPOINT** If you'd like to compare your project with mine at this point, you can check mine out at https://github.com/iOSAppDevelopmentwithSwiftinAction/SimpleSizeClasses.git (2.iPadLayout branch).

Automatic adaption

Up to now, we've been looking at creating your own customizations for different size classes, but UIKit provides its own customizations based on size classes for you automatically:

- Split view controllers manage the display of two related views. The current size class automatically determines whether the user can see both views of the split view controller at once, or one view at a time with navigation between the two.
- Different types of popovers are automatically presented differently in different size classes. We'll look more at popovers in chapter 9.
- The correct assets (such as images) in asset catalogs can be automatically chosen for the appropriate size class. We'll look more at asset catalogs in chapter 13.

VARYING THE BOOKCASE LAYOUT

Well, varying a simple layout was fairly straightforward, but what about a more significant change between size classes?

✔ **CHECKPOINT**   Open the Bookcase app where we left it in the previous chapter. You can find it at https://github.com/iOSAppDevelopment-withSwiftinAction/Bookcase.git (Chapter6.2.AutoLayout branch).

It's looking great on iPhone in portrait, but maybe a two-column approach instead of laying out all the elements from top to bottom would be a more attractive layout in landscape on the iPhone (see figure 7.13).

Previous layout

Proposed new layout

Figure 7.13   Proposed layout for iPhone landscape

1   View the storyboard as an iPhone 8 in landscape, and select Vary for Traits. Notice if you select to vary for height, you're left with all iPhones in landscape. That makes sense, if you go back to the size classes chart in figure 7.1. If you

also select to vary for width, notice that this deselects the larger screen of the iPhone 8.

2 Because you want to adjust the layout for all iPhones, you can vary just for height.

Rather than determining which constraints to add, which to keep, and which to uninstall, sometimes when a new layout is significantly different, it can be simpler to uninstall all constraints for a size class and start over.

3 With the device configuration bar blue for varying for compact-height devices, ensure that the view controller is selected, and select the Resolve Auto Layout Issues button, at the right of the five auto layout buttons.

4 In the All Views in View Controller section, select Clear Constraints.

Now it's a matter of laying out the views according to the new layout in figure 7.11, and setting up the new constraints. This could be a good opportunity to practice your auto layout skills from chapter 6!

CHALLENGE Lay out the views for compact-height devices and add the appropriate constraints. If you run into problems, select the red or orange error indicator in the Document outline and resolve any pending issues. Good luck!

5 When you're done laying out the new design, select Done Varying.

6 Compare the portrait and landscape orientations. If all's gone well, you should see the original layout in portrait, and the layout you've set up in landscape. Well done! You've set up a truly adaptive layout without writing a line of code.

✅ **CHECKPOINT** If you'd like to compare your project with mine at this point, you can check mine out at https://github.com/iOSAppDevelopmentwithSwiftinAction/Bookcase.git (Chapter7.1.SizeClasses branch).

7.2 Stack views

Stack views are container views that can contain multiple views in a specific arrangement, applying the appropriate constraints automatically. Let's look at the problem they solve.

7.2.1 The problem with auto layout

Let's be honest, auto layout and constraints can be a pain to deal with sometimes. Setting up rules to describe the frame of each element in the app can be time consuming, and making a small change to a layout can be frustrating.

Imagine that you need to make a small change to the Bookcase app scene you were working in earlier. You want to make a simple change, inserting a field for ISBN between the author and notes fields (see figure 7.14).

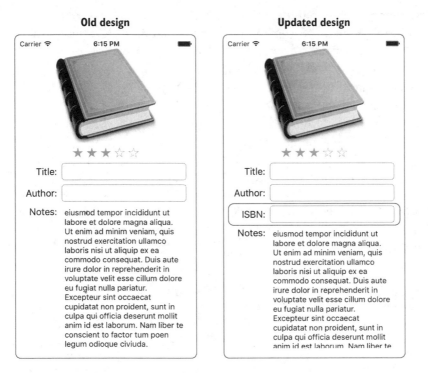

Figure 7.14   Update to bookcase design

What would you need to do to make that change? There are a few tasks you would have to do, so quickly skim over the steps:

1   Delete the constraint between the notes and author fields.
2   Move the notes title and field down to make room for the new field.
3   Drag in the label and text field for ISBN.
4   Reposition the notes title and field to the correct position.
5   Add four constraints to the ISBN label (leading, trailing, baseline alignment, and make it equal width to another title label).
6   Add three constraints to the ISBN text field (trailing, and pin it to the author and notes fields).

Wow, that's quite a bit to do—and it doesn't take into consideration the complications with multiple layouts for different size classes!

And what if you wanted to make these sorts of changes to a layout at runtime? You'd have to perform similar steps, but in code!

Let's take a step back for a second. One of the golden rules of interface design is *consistency* of layout. You most likely want the distribution, alignment, and spacing between each view to be consistent.

Wouldn't it save time and make the app less prone to error if you could declare these consistent rules for a *group* of views rather than for each individual view? This would make life so much easier when you're adding or removing views to a preexisting layout.

Well, that's basically the idea behind *stack views*.

We'll come back to converting the Bookcase app to use a stack view shortly, but first let's learn a bit more about stack views by implementing one in a simpler example.

7.2.2 *Stack view properties*

While constraints take a more granular approach by defining rules (constraints) for each view, stack views allow you to take a broader approach by defining rules (properties) for a *stack* of views.

For example, while auto layout requires you to specify the vertical constraints between *each* view, stack views allow you to specify one property representing vertical spacing for *all* views arranged in the stack view. In the article app iPad layout (see figure 7.15), you defined one constraint for the vertical space between the title and the subtitle, and a second constraint for the vertical space between the subtitle and the text view. If the three views are arranged in a vertical stack view, you only need to specify the vertical spacing once, and it's applied to all views in the stack.

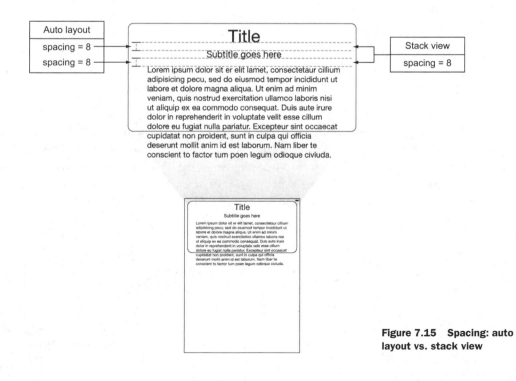

Figure 7.15 Spacing: auto layout vs. stack view

What other properties are necessary to define the arrangement of views in a stack view? Figure 7.16 demonstrates how the four main properties of a stack view describe the article layout in the SimpleSizeClasses app.

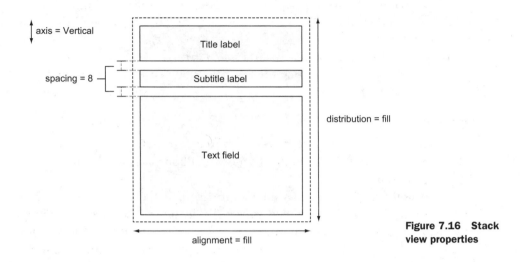

Figure 7.16   Stack view properties

We'll convert the simple article layout to use a stack view in a moment, but first, let's look closer at the four properties shown in figure 7.16: axis, spacing, alignment, and distribution.

AXIS
All stack views lay out their views in either a *horizontal* or *vertical* direction.

SPACING
Spacing is a point value defining the space between the views.

ALIGNMENT
The alignment property specifies how to arrange the views in the direction contrary to the axis. For example, if the views of a stack view are arranged in a vertical axis as in our example, alignment refers to how the views will be aligned horizontally. See figure 7.17 for horizontal alignment properties. They probably look familiar enough—they're similar to text justification styles you'll find in Microsoft Word.

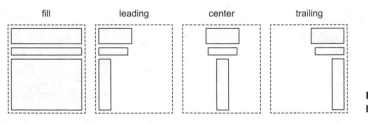

Figure 7.17   Stack view horizontal alignment

The only alignment property that affects the size of the views is *fill* alignment. All other alignment alternatives only affect the position of the view, and the view defaults to its intrinsic content size. This is fine for buttons or labels, for example, because their intrinsic content size defaults to the size of their content. But certain views such as plain views or scrolling text views don't have an intrinsic content size. You need to give the Auto Layout engine enough information to define the frame for views with no intrinsic content size.

Vertical alignments are relatively predictable: fill, top, center, and bottom. However, the vertical axis has two additional alignments: firstBaseline for aligning with the baseline of the first line of a text view, and lastBaseline for the last line.

DISTRIBUTION

The distribution property specifies how to distribute the views in the direction of the axis to fill the stack view's available space.

See figure 7.18 for an example of how distribution properties affect a vertical stack view containing arranged views with hypothetical intrinsic content sizes.

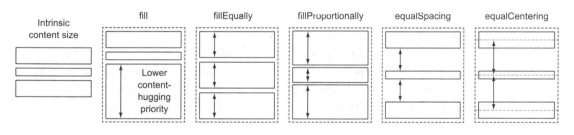

Figure 7.18   Stack view vertical distribution

The *fill* distribution looks for one view to stretch or shrink. The Auto Layout engine stretches the view with the lowest content-hugging priority (or shrinks the view with the lowest content-compression resistance priority). Because labels automatically have higher content-hugging priority, the text view in the SimpleSizeClasses layout would automatically stretch. If all of them had the same priority, the engine would stretch or shrink the first view.

The fillEqually distribution ignores the intrinsic content size, and simply resizes views to have an equal size. The fillProportionally distribution resizes views maintaining the proportions of the view sizes, based on intrinsic content size. The equalSpacing distribution arranges views adding equal space between the views. The equalCentering distribution arranges views so that their centers are at equal distances.

7.2.3   *Simple stack view in Interface Builder*

Now that you know about the four properties of stack views, let's convert a simple layout to use a stack view.

Duplicate your SimpleSizeClasses project folder in Finder, and call the new folder SimpleStackViews. If you need to, you can check out the SimpleSizeClasses project at https://github.com/iOSAppDevelopmentwithSwiftinAction/SimpleSizeClasses.git (2.iPadLayout branch).

1 Open the main storyboard and select View as iPad.
2 Select the title, subtitle, and text view.
3 Embed these views in a stack view. You can do this the long way by selecting Editor > Embed In > Stack View or the short way by selecting the Embed in Stack button, that you'll find with the five auto layout buttons (see figure 7.19).

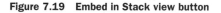
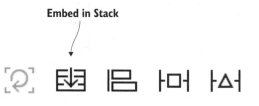

Figure 7.19   Embed in Stack view button

The three views automatically lose any existing constraints because their constraints are now going to be automatically generated by the stack view. You'll see a red error indicator in the document outline. The stack view itself needs to be given auto layout constraints.

4 Select the stack view. This can be a little tricky to select in the canvas because it contains other views. You could select it in the document outline, but another trick is to bring up a view hierarchy in the canvas, by Control-Shift-clicking on the stack view (or Shift-right-clicking). Select the stack view in the context menu that appears (see figure 7.20).

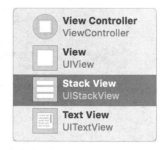

Figure 7.20   Context menu

5 Pin the stack view to the safe area layout guides of the root view. Great! The red error symbol should go away.
6 Now focus on the attributes of the stack view in the Attributes Inspector, and modify them to look like figure 7.21.

Figure 7.21   Stack view attributes

A distribution of fill for the stack view makes the most sense. Because the text view automatically has a lower content-hugging priority than the two labels, it will automatically fill the available space. Spacing the distribution by 8 points will give the views a little breathing space.

Because the text view has no intrinsic content size, fill makes the most sense for alignment as well, so that it fills the available width. This means the title and subtitle labels will need to be center-aligned.

7 Select the title and subtitle labels, and select center-alignment in the Attributes Inspector.

The layout should work perfectly now on an iPad, but check what's happening with the iPhone layout. You'll encounter a couple of problems. First, the stack view's leading and trailing margins need to be adjusted for the iPhone.

8 Select the two constraints and add a customization for the constraint constants for wR hR (iPads).

9 Set the default constant to 0 and the wR hR constant to 50. Because the views lost any existing constraints when they were embedded in a stack view, the subtitle is appearing again in the iPhone. This is easy enough to remove.

10 Add a customization for the subtitle's Installed attribute for wR hR. Deselect the default Installed checkbox and select Installed for wR hR.

Notice how easy it is once a stack view is set up to add and remove views that follow the same rules. Drag another label into the stack view and notice how the layout adjusts accordingly. Remove the label by selecting it and pressing Delete or by deselecting Installed, and again, the layout adjusts automatically. Too easy!

✓ **CHECKPOINT** If you would like to compare your code with mine, you can check out my project at this point at https://github.com/iOSApp-DevelopmentwithSwiftinAction/SimpleSizeClasses.git (3.SimpleStackViews branch).

7.2.4 *Nested stack views in Interface Builder*

Each stack view can only work with a horizontal or vertical layout. Layouts are often a little more complicated. How do stack views help with more-complicated layouts? The simple answer is that stack views can be *nested*.

Let's go back to our more complicated add-a-book layout from the Bookcase app, and convert it to use nested stack views.

✓ **CHECKPOINT** Duplicate the project folder in the Finder if you like and call the new folder BookcaseStackview. If you need it, you can find the Bookcase project where we left it at https://github.com/iOSAppDevelopment-withSwiftinAction/Bookcase.git (Chapter7.1.SizeClasses branch).

The Bookcase app layout can be described as several horizontal stack views and other views, nested inside a vertical stack view (see figure 7.22). Notice how much simpler this description of the layout is than the constraints version in the previous chapter.

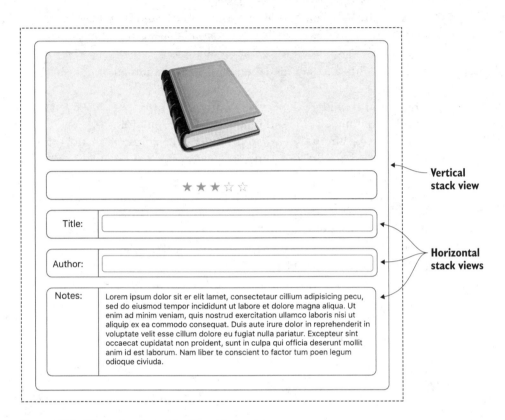

Vertical stack view

Horizontal stack views

Figure 7.22   Stack view layout for the add-a-book scene

The easiest approach for defining the stack views is to work from the inside out.

1 Select the title label and text field and embed them in a stack view. Xcode should automatically detect that you want a horizontal stack view.

2 Do the same with the author label and text field, and then the notes label and text view. You should now have the book image view, the star-rating view, and three horizontal stack views.

3 Select them all and embed them in a stack view. Again, Xcode should automatically detect that you want a vertical stack view. Now you have tidying up to do.

4 Pin your outer vertical stack view to the safe area layout guides of the root view as you did earlier.

As you saw earlier, when you embed your views in stack views, they lose their constraints. But you still want the title, author, and notes fields to be constrained to an equal width.

5 Reinstate the equal width constraints on these three fields. They may or may not be cut off in Interface Builder, but not to worry—they should look fine in the simulator.

TIP You might find that Interface Builder occasionally has difficulty displaying stack view interfaces accurately. While Apple continues to iron out these bugs, it's always best to test your interface on various simulators for a true test of how your interface will appear.

6 Because the text view has an intrinsic content height of its contents, you need to manually constrain it to the height of the stack view it is embedded in.

7 Now you need to tweak the stack view properties. They're fairly straightforward, as shown in table 7.2.

Table 7.2 Stack view properties

Stack view	Axis	Alignment	Distribution	Spacing
Outer	Vertical	Fill	Fill	8
Title	Horizontal	Fill	Fill	8
Author	Horizontal	Fill	Fill	8
Notes	Horizontal	Top	Fill	8

The notes stack view should be aligned to top so that the top of the Notes label is aligned with the top of the text view.

That's it! You've successfully converted a layout to use stack views. You could even add customizations to any of the four main stack view properties to tweak the layout for other size classes.

But what of the original problem: how can you add another field for ISBN?

8 Select the author stack view, and select Edit > Copy and then Edit > Paste.

9 Add an Equal Widths constraint between the author label and one of the other three labels.

10 Replace the author label's text property with *ISBN:*.

That's all! Another line has been inserted into the layout, and you didn't have to worry about breaking the original layout apart to squeeze it in; the other fields adjusted themselves automatically.

7.2.5   *Adding or removing views from a stack view*

Not everyone is interested in seeing the book's ISBN. How could you set up the Book-case app to just display the ISBN when the user taps on a special *info* button? Here are two solutions:

- After instantiating the ISBN view in code, you could add it to the outer stack view with either the `addArrangedSubview` method (which adds the view to the stack view's arranged views) or the `insertArrangedSubview` method (which inserts the view into a specific location in the stack view's arranged views).
- Create the ISBN view in Interface Builder, and set its `isHidden` attribute to hide or unhide the view when required.

You'll use the second option, taking advantage of Interface Builder and the fact that you've already created the ISBN view. You'll use the `isHidden` attribute to hide it until the user taps an info button.

1 First, create outlets for the book cover and the ISBN stack view. I've called mine `bookCover` and `isbnStackView`.

2 Set the ISBN stack view to Hidden in the Attributes Inspector.

   You're going to add the info button as a subview to the book cover image view. Because image views are, after all, special types of views, you can add subviews to them too.

3 Be sure that the book cover is set to User Interaction Enabled in the Attributes Inspector, so that the user can interact with the button it contains.

4 Add the info button in the `viewDidLoad` method of `BookViewController`:

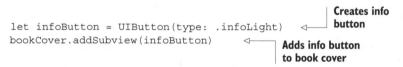

```
let infoButton = UIButton(type: .infoLight)     ⊲──┐ Creates info
                                                    │ button
bookCover.addSubview(infoButton)     ⊲──┐
                                         Adds info button
                                         to book cover
```

5 Add an action to the button for the `touchUpInside` event that calls a `toggleISBN` method:

```
infoButton.addTarget(self,
    action: #selector(toggleISBN),       Call toggleISBN
    for: .touchUpInside)                 on touch button
```

6 Now, add the `toggleISBN` method that will be called when the user touches the info button.

   All this method will need to do is toggle the `isbnStackView`'s `isHidden` prop-erty, and the Auto Layout engine takes care of the rest, expanding and contract-ing the outer stack view's space to accommodate the ISBN stack view when necessary:

```
                                                    Toggles ISBN
                                                    visibility
@objc func toggleISBN() {
    self.isbnStackView.isHidden = !self.isbnStackView.isHidden     ⊲──
}
```

As you saw in chapter 5, for a method to be visible to the `#selector` keyword, it must be prefixed with the `@objc` keyword.

You could even easily animate this change.

7   Move the setting of the `isHidden` property in the `toggleISBN` method into an animations closure of a call to the `animate` method of `UIView`:

```
                                                          Calls animate on UIView
UIView.animate(withDuration: 0.5, animations: {  ◄┘
    self.isbnStackView.isHidden = !self.isbnStackView.isHidden  ◄── Sets
})                                                                  isHidden
```

8   Run the app, tap on the info button, and you should see the ISBN field smoothly animate into view.

9   Tap the info button again and it should smoothly animate away. Too easy!

We'll look more at animation of views in chapter 8.

✔ **CHECKPOINT** The project at this point can be found at https://github.com/iOSAppDevelopmentwithSwiftinAction/Bookcase.git (Chapter7.2.StackViews).

CHALLENGE   Combine what you learned about stack views and size classes to adapt the layout of the stack view for iPhones in landscape (compact height) with the book and star-rating view on the left, just as you did in figure 7.13 using pure auto layout.

HINT   You'll probably want to create two new vertical stack views. One stack view will contain the book and star-rating view, and the other will contain all the horizontal stack views containing the labels and text fields. The axis of the outer stack view could then be adapted for size views—a horizontal axis for compact height and a vertical axis otherwise.

We're going to leave the Bookcase app there for now.

✔ **CHECKPOINT**   If you would like to compare your solution with mine, you can check out my project at this point at https://github.com/iOSAppDevelopmentwithSwiftinAction/Bookcase.git (Chapter7.3.StackViews-SizeClasses).

7.2.6   *Stack views in code*

Stack views are easiest to set up in Interface Builder, but you can set them up completely in code if you want to.

All you need to do is instantiate the stack view, passing in an array of views you want the stack view to arrange. For example, the following listing instantiates a stack view with three arranged views.

Listing 7.2   Instantiate stack view

```
let stackView = UIStackView(arrangedSubviews: [
    titleLabel, subtitleLabel, greenView
    ])
```

You can then set the four main stack view properties directly in code, as shown in the following listing.

Listing 7.3   Set stack view properties

```
stackView.axis = .vertical
stackView.alignment = .fill
stackView.distribution = .fill
stackView.spacing = 8
```

Don't forget to give the stack view auto layout constraints when adding it to the root view, as shown in the following listing.

Listing 7.4   Add stack view and constraints

```
view.addSubview(stackView)
//stack view constraints
stackView.translatesAutoresizingMaskIntoConstraints = false
let constraints = [
    stackView.topAnchor.constraint(equalTo:
        self.topLayoutGuide.bottomAnchor),
    stackView.leadingAnchor.constraint(equalTo:
        self.view.layoutMarginsGuide.leadingAnchor),
    stackView.trailingAnchor.constraint(equalTo:
        self.view.layoutMarginsGuide.trailingAnchor),
    stackView.bottomAnchor.constraint(equalTo: self.view.bottomAnchor)
]
NSLayoutConstraint.activate(constraints)
```

CHALLENGE   Practice what you've learned in this chapter. Recreate the simple stack view article layout you created earlier in Interface Builder, but this time build it in code! For extra points, have the layout adapt for iPads and use lazy stored properties.

✓   **CHECKPOINT**   When you're done, you can compare your answer with mine at https://github.com/iOSAppDevelopmentwithSwiftinAction/ SimpleStackViewsInCode.git.

7.3 Summary

In this chapter, you learned the following:

- Rather than designing layouts for specific devices or orientations, try to think more in terms of size classes.
- Use size classes to add more-significant variations in your layout to accommodate for different environments.
- Use lazy stored properties when a property's initial value depends on the initial value of another property, or when the property requires more computation or memory and may not be needed.
- Use stack views instead of auto layout where possible—you'll work faster, your layouts will be easier to maintain, and you'll have better consistency across views.

Keyboard notifications, animation, and scrolling

This chapter covers

- Getting notifications of system events
- Dismissing the keyboard
- Animating views
- Implementing scrolling

In this chapter, you'll solve a real-world problem: what do you do when the user taps on an editable text field and the keyboard pops up over the text field, obscuring from view what the user's typing? How can you recognize when the user taps on the text field and move it so that the user can see what they're typing?

Along the way, we'll encounter several important iOS concepts:

- *First responders*—The first responder is the first view in a scene to receive system events.
- *Notifications*—Use notifications to listen to messages being broadcast from elsewhere in your app or from other iOS SDK frameworks.
- *View animation*—Animate any views in the UIKit framework.
- *Scroll view*—Use the scroll view to animate content.

8.1   *The problem with the keyboard*

Imagine that you've published what you think is a brilliant app for users to keep records of all the books they own. Great! You submit it to the App Store, and then you start getting comments back . . .

> *"Unusable!"*
> *"The keyboard covers up the text fields!"*
> *"The keyboard won't go away!"*

Oh no, what's going on? You open the app on an iPhone SE simulator and immediately see the problem (see figure 8.1).

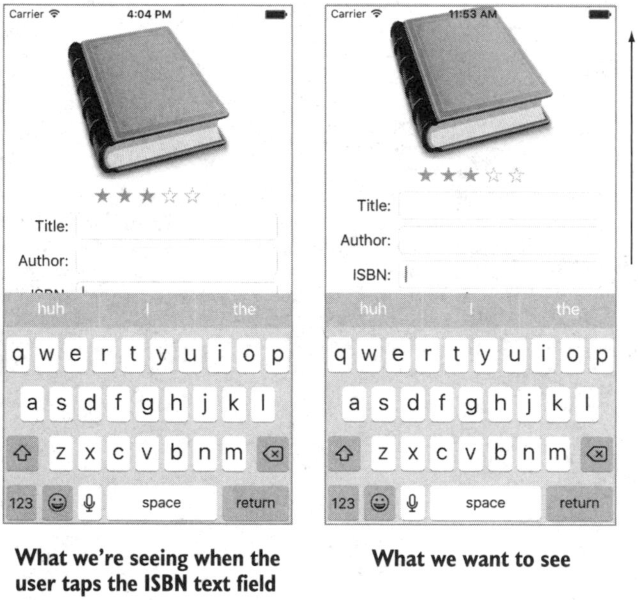

What we're seeing when the   **What we want to see**
user taps the ISBN text field

Figure 8.1   The problem with the keyboard

When the user taps on text entry fields—depending on the device—the keyboard opens right over the top of the field, obscuring the field the user's typing into! To top things off, tapping Return doesn't make the keyboard go away! Oh no, what a disaster!

You did all your testing on your iPad Pro, where there was so much screen real estate this wasn't an issue. "I knew I should have done beta testing!" you think to yourself. (Not to worry, we'll get to beta testing later in the book!)

After getting over the embarrassment, you think about how to solve the problem. You decide that the best approach is probably to move the text fields up when the keyboard animates on. Good plan! "I'd better get to fixing this straight away!" you decide. "But how?"

Let's break the problem into its components, and then we'll look at each of the parts in turn.

- First, you need to ensure there's a way for the user to dismiss the keyboard. You'll do this by detecting when the user taps the Return key or outside the keyboard, and then by *resigning the first responder.*
- Then, you need to detect *when* the keyboard shows and hides. You'll do this by observing *keyboard notifications.*
- When the keyboard is showing, you want to move the editable field to above the keyboard so that it can be seen. You'll do this by *animating the view,* and then later you'll explore how this could also be done with *scroll views.*

✔️ **CHECKPOINT**   Open the Bookcase project where you left it in the previous chapter. Alternatively, you can check it out at https://github.com/iOSAppDevelopmentwithSwiftinAction/Bookcase.git (Chapter7.3.StackViews-SizeClasses).

Let's start by ensuring the user has a way to dismiss the keyboard.

8.2   *Dismissing the keyboard*

As you saw in chapter 5, the keyboard can look different depending on the device type and orientation. While a special button exists on some keyboards to close the keyboard, the keyboard on iPhones in portrait mode doesn't have such a button (see figure 8.2). You need to provide a way for the user to close the keyboard in every configuration. A common approach is to manually close the keyboard when the user taps the Return key.

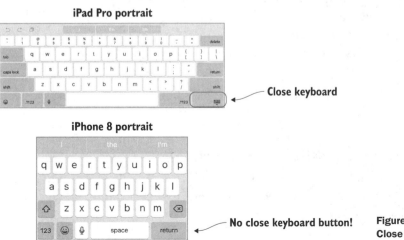

Figure 8.2
Close keyboard

To manually close the keyboard when the user taps the Return key, you need to

1 Detect when the user taps the Return key or outside the keyboard.
2 Manually dismiss the keyboard.

We'll explore detecting *when* the user taps the Return key shortly, but first, how do you manually dismiss the keyboard?

To manually dismiss the keyboard, you need to resign the first responder. What's the first responder?

8.2.1 *Dismissing the keyboard by resigning the first responder*

When I explained touch events in chapter 5, you discovered that an object that receives events is known as a *responder*. The event travels up the view hierarchy from the responder that first receives the event in what is called the *responder chain*.

As you saw in chapter 5, touch events use *hit testing* to determine the lowest-level view that was touched and therefore which responder should first receive the event.

Other UIKit objects also make use of the responder chain, including

- *Motion events* to detect shakes
- *Remote control events* to detect commands from a remote control
- *Editing-menu messages* to handle operations such as cut, copy, and paste
- *Text editing* to handle text entry on an editable text field

The view that will be first to respond to these objects has a special name: the *first responder*. In general, you tell UIKit which view you want to be the first responder by calling its `becomeFirstResponder` method. But text fields and text views have a special power—as soon as they're tapped, they automatically set themselves as the window's first responder.

When a text field or text view becomes first responder, the keyboard automatically appears. Conversely, when they're no longer the first responder, the keyboard automatically disappears. How do you make a view stop being the first responder? Call its `resignFirstResponder` method.

If you want to dismiss the keyboard, you need the relevant text field or text view to no longer be first responder, and you can do that by calling their `resignFirstResponder` method:

```
textField.resignFirstResponder()
```

Now that you know *how* to hide the keyboard, you need to determine *when*!

8.2.2 *Detecting when to dismiss the keyboard*

The user would reasonably expect the keyboard to disappear when they tap the Return key for the three text fields. You need to detect this moment, so you can manually dismiss the keyboard.

DETECTING THE RETURN KEY TAP TO DISMISS THE KEYBOARD

You can detect that the Return key was tapped on a text field by using the delegation pattern. The text field's delegate has a `textFieldShouldReturn` method that's called when the Return key is tapped, that has a reference to the text field itself. Follow the three steps for the delegation pattern:

1 Set the view controller as the delegate for the title text field. Control-drag from the text field to the view controller.

2 Select Delegate in the Outlets section of the context-sensitive menu that pops up, just as you did with gesture recognizers in chapter 5 (see figure 8.3).

3 Repeat steps 1 and 2 for the author text field, notes text view, and ISBN text field.

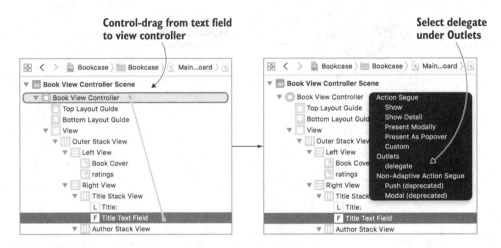

Figure 8.3 Set text field delegate

4 Adopt the `UITextFieldDelegate` protocol on an extension of the `ViewController`.

5 Implement any required methods on the protocol.

6 You want to implement the `textFieldShouldReturn` method:

```
extension BookViewController: UITextFieldDelegate {
    func textFieldShouldReturn(_ textField: UITextField) -> Bool {
        textField.resignFirstResponder()        ◁──┐
        return true                                 │  Hides the keyboard
    }
}
```

Run the app, tap on a text field, and tap the Return key. The keyboard should animate away. That works great for the three text fields. But what about the notes text view?

Because text views such as notes are multiline, the Return key has another meaning—it represents a new line within the text view. Therefore, the Return key on a text view shouldn't be used to hide the keyboard. To bring that point home, the text view delegate doesn't even provide a way to recognize that the Return key was tapped!

How can the user indicate that they'd like to dismiss the keyboard when editing the text view? Well, how about tapping outside the keyboard and outside the text fields (see figure 8.4)?

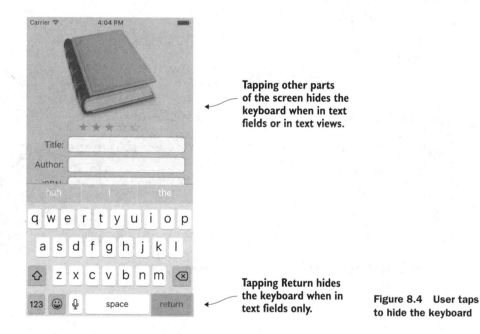

Tapping other parts of the screen hides the keyboard when in text fields or in text views.

Tapping Return hides the keyboard when in text fields only.

Figure 8.4   User taps to hide the keyboard

DETECTING TOUCHES TO DISMISS THE KEYBOARD

As you saw in chapter 5, you can detect touches using the `touchesEnded` method. You can use this method to dismiss the keyboard when the user touches anywhere on the screen.

Perfect for your intentions, controls such as text fields trap touches, preventing them from continuing up the responder chain to the view controller. Similarly, the keyboard appears in a different window that prevents touches from being recognized in the main application window. Because of this, you can know that when the `touchesEnded` method is called, the user hasn't touched the keyboard or the text fields.

Only problem: the `touchesEnded` method doesn't know which text field the user is currently editing to choose which first responder to resign, and UIKit doesn't provide an easy way to get a reference to the current first responder. (We'll explore a way to do this later.)

To resign the first responder, instead of calling `resignFirstResponder` directly on the view, you can also use the more generic method `endEditing` on the root view of the scene. The `endEditing` method goes on a hunt through its subview hierarchy until it finds the first responder, and then it asks it politely to resign. If its `force` parameter is set to `true`, it's slightly less polite with the first responder, forcing it to resign.

1 Add the `endEditing` method to a `touchesEnded` method:

```
override func touchesEnded(_ touches: Set<UITouch>, with event: UIEvent?) {
    super.touchesEnded(touches, with: event)
    view.endEditing(true)
}
```

2 Run the app again, and you should find that the keyboard dismisses either when you tap the Return key or when you tap elsewhere on the screen.

That's the first problem solved!

8.3 Observing keyboard notifications

Next, you need to move the editable field so that it's visible when the keyboard shows. You need to detect *when* the keyboard shows, and you need to know the size of the keyboard to move the text fields accordingly. To do that, you need to listen for a special keyboard notification. When the keyboard notification is broadcast, a selector method you write will be notified, along with information about the keyboard, such as its size.

8.3.1 What is a notification?

Notifications are a way of posting and receiving messages. One object in your app (the *publisher*) can *broadcast* notifications, while other objects in your app (*observers*) listen for the notification.

The UIKit's `UIWindow` class broadcasts notifications when the keyboard is about to be shown or hidden, or when its frame changes, and your app can listen for those broadcasts. It's a perfect time to make adjustments to your scene's interface to accommodate the keyboard!

> **TIP** Did you know that keyboards can change size? iPad keyboards, for example, can be split in two, triggering a keyboard frame change notification. Because all *keyboard shows* notifications and *keyboard hides* notifications trigger *keyboard frame change* notifications, but all *keyboard frame changes* don't necessarily trigger *keyboard show* or *hide* notifications, `UIKeyboardWillChangeFrame` is the best notification to listen for.

Each app has its own default Notification Center that is the middleman between the observers and publishers. Your `ViewController` class can register as an *Observer* with the Notification Center for *keyboard change notifications*, and when the UIWindow class broadcasts the *keyboard frame change* notification to the Notification Center, any registered observers of that notification (your ViewController class, in this case) will be notified (see figure 8.5).

Figure 8.5   The Notification Center

In using the Notification Center as a middleman, the publisher and observers are *decoupled*—the publisher doesn't know who's listening, and the observer doesn't necessarily know who posted the notification. The decoupling of the publisher and the observer is especially useful with frameworks, such as the frameworks of the iOS SDK. Frameworks know nothing about how your app is structured, but your app still needs a mechanism for receiving important messages from frameworks.

NOTE   To make things super confusing, be aware of an unrelated iOS concept called remote and local notifications. These notifications refer to apps notifying the user of important information with banners, sounds, and badges on the app icon. To add to the confusion, missed notifications can be found in your device's "Notification Center," also an unrelated concept to the Notification Center we're discussing!

8.3.2   *Observing a keyboard frame change notification*

Next, you'll make your view controller become an observer of the keyboard frame change notification.

1   Set up a method in BookViewController.swift to be called when the notification is observed that the keyboard's frame changes. This method should receive the notification as an argument.

```
@objc func keyboardFrameChanges(notification:Notification) {
    print("Keyboard frame changes")
}
```

You can now register this method to be called on a specific notification, by calling the default notification center's addObserver method. The addObserver method expects four parameters:

- The *observer* to be notified (usually self)
- The *selector* to be notified (a method in the observer class)

- The notification *name* you want to observe
- The *object* to optionally only observe notifications from a specific sender (we've left this parameter as `nil` to ignore the sender)

2 Connect this observer method to the keyboard notification in the `viewDidAppear` method:

```
override func viewDidAppear(_ animated: Bool) {
    super.viewDidAppear(animated)
    NotificationCenter.default.addObserver(self,
        selector: #selector(keyboardFrameChanges),
        name: NSNotification.Name.UIKeyboardWillChangeFrame,
        object: nil)
}
```

3 Run the app on the simulator and tap on a text field. As the keyboard appears, you should see "Keyboard frame changes" in the console.

4 Tap the Return key. The keyboard should disappear, and the text "Keyboard frame changes" should again print to the console.

Other notifications

Many objects in iOS SDK frameworks broadcast notifications. Here are several examples of notifications you could listen for in your app.

Class	Examples of notifications
`UIApplication`	Application became active, entered the background, finished launching, and is about to terminate.
`UIDevice`	Orientation changed, battery level changed.
`UIWindow`	Window became visible, keyboard shows, keyboard hides, and keyboard's frame changes.

8.3.3 *Unregistering a notification*

Don't forget that when this scene is no longer active, you want this view controller to stop receiving keyboard notifications. You can unregister an observer for specific notifications, but to be safe, it can be easiest to remove all notifications for this observer in one swoop.

Remove all observers in the `viewDidDisappear` method:

```
override func viewDidDisappear(_ animated: Bool) {
    super.viewDidDisappear(animated)
    NotificationCenter.default.removeObserver(self)
}
```

Broadcasting notifications

The power to broadcast notifications isn't limited to the iOS SDK. An object in your app can broadcast notifications too, and observe notifications from elsewhere in your app.

To broadcast a notification, first create a notification name. To help organize your code, it's probably a good idea to define all your notification names in the same struct. Use the `Notification.Name` method to generate your notification.

```
struct Notifications {
    static let TimeOutNotification = Notification.Name("TimeOut")
}
```

Your publisher then broadcasts the notification with the default Notification Center's `post` method:

```
NotificationCenter.default.post(
    name:Notifications.TimeOutNotification object: nil)
```

You can use the `object` parameter to optionally pass a reference to the sender of the notification along with the notification. We've left it as `nil` here.

You can also pass in an optional `userInfo` parameter with any additional information you'd like to pass with the notification.

Now you've detected when the keyboard frame changes, but how can you get the y position of the keyboard, to determine the extent to which it's currently overlapping the main view?

8.3.4   *Extracting keyboard information from the notification*

When a keyboard notification is posted, information about the keyboard is included in the notification's `userInfo` parameter:

- *Keyboard frame*—`UIKeyboardFrameEndUserInfoKey`
- *Keyboard animation duration*—`UIKeyboardAnimationDurationUserInfoKey`
- *Keyboard animation curve*—`UIKeyboardAnimationCurveUserInfoKey`

With a bit of work, you can extract this information out of the `userInfo` dictionary. It's useful information to have as you coordinate your views to animate with the keyboard!

Let's start by getting the y position of the keyboard.

1   After unwrapping the `userInfo` dictionary, extract the keyboard frame. This is passed as a generic `NSValue` from which a `CGRect` can be extracted. Add the following to the `keyboardFrameChanges` method:

```
//get keyboard height                                          Unwraps userInfo
guard let userInfo = notification.userInfo,
    var keyboardFrame = (userInfo[UIKeyboardFrameEndUserInfoKey]
        as? NSValue)?.cgRectValue()
    else { return }                                            Casts to NSValue
                                                               and extracts CGRect
```

Unwraps keyboard frame

Returns if above unsuccessful

2 To make things more complicated, you need to then convert this value to accommodate for any rotation factors, using the `convert` method.

Converts keyboard frame

```
keyboardFrame = self.view.convert(keyboardFrame, from: nil)   ⟵
```

3 Finally, you can extract the keyboard's y position from the `CGRect`'s `origin` property.

```
let keyboardY = keyboardFrame.origin.y   ⟵
```
Gets y position from frame origin

While you're here, why not get other details on the animation that's available in the `userInfo` parameter?

4 Extracting the animation *duration* and *curve* is relatively straightforward. (The animation curve refers to any easing applied to the animation.)

Unwraps duration

```
guard let duration = userInfo[UIKeyboardAnimationDurationUserInfoKey]   ⟵
           as? Double,
       curve = userInfo[UIKeyboardAnimationCurveUserInfoKey]   ⟵
           as? UInt   ⟵
       else { return }   ⟵
```
Casts to Double

Unwraps curve

Returns if above unsuccessful **Casts to UInt**

Great, you have the y position of the keyboard and some other animation properties, but how do you know how far up to animate the layout? You'll need to get the y position of the text field or text view that the user is editing. You saw earlier that this view is called the first responder.

8.3.5 Getting a reference to the first responder

Frustratingly, you have no simple way to get a reference to the current first responder. Every `UIView` does, however, have an `isFirstResponder` property, so without too much effort, it's possible to recursively iterate through a view's subviews to find the first responder. This could even be appropriate to add as a property in an extension to the `UIView` class for easy reuse.

1 Add this extension to the Bookcase project now. Create a Swift file called UIViewExtension.swift, and add the following code:

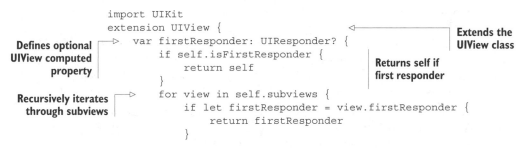

```
import UIKit
extension UIView {                        ⟵
    var firstResponder: UIResponder? {
        if self.isFirstResponder {
            return self
        }
        for view in self.subviews {
            if let firstResponder = view.firstResponder {
                return firstResponder
            }
```
Extends the UIView class

Defines optional UIView computed property

Returns self if first responder

Recursively iterates through subviews

```
        }
        return nil                    ◁────┐  Returns nil if no first
    }                                       │  responder found
}
```

2   For convenience, you could add an additional `firstResponder` property in an
    extension to the `UIViewController` class.

```
extension UIViewController {
    var firstResponder: UIView? {
        return view.firstResponder
    }
}
```

You can now always get a reference to the first responder!

8.3.6   *Calculating the offset to animate*

Now that you can get a reference to the first responder, you can use it to calculate how
far to animate the layout to accommodate the keyboard.

1   Unwrap the `firstResponder` property from the `UIViewController` exten-
    sion you created. If no first responder exists, you can safely assume that the user
    isn't editing a field, and the offset of the view should be zero.

```
var offset: CGFloat = 0                          ◁────────────┐  Creates offset
if let firstResponder = firstResponder {                      │  variable of 0
                                      ◁────────────┐
}                                                  │ Defines offset here
```

**Unwraps first
responder**

Now that you have the first responder, you can calculate the offset to animate
the view.

2   Get the first responder's frame in the view with the `convert` method. (We'll
    come back to the `convert` method in a moment.)

```
let frFrame = view.convert(firstResponder.frame,       │ Gets first responder
    from: firstResponder.superview)            ◁───────┘ frame in view
```

3   Next, get a reference to the lowest point that it reaches in the view with the
    `maxY` property, taking into consideration the top constraint and adding in a
    five-point margin.

```
                                                               │ Gets maxY of
let frMaxY = frFrame.maxY - topConstraint.constant + 5  ◁──────┘ first responder
```

4   You can now compare this lowest point with where the keyboard frame begins,
    to determine the offset to animate the view.

```
                                                    │ If keyboard covers
if frMaxY > keyboardFrame.origin.y {        ◁───────┘ first responder
    offset = frMaxY - keyboardFrame.origin.y  ◁──────┐  Calculates offset
}                                                    │  to animate
```

Converting frames and points

You can use the convert method to convert a *rect* or *point* from one coordinate system to another.

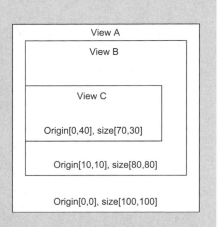

Imagine you have three views. View C is a subview of view B, which is, in turn, a subview of view A.

Each view has an origin (position) relative to the coordinate system of their superview. For this reason, view C's position in the x direction is 0. If you want to know the position of view C within view A, use the convert method of UIView:

```
let point = viewA.convert(viewC.frame.origin, from: viewB)
//point = [10,50]
```

The first parameter is the point or frame that you want to convert. In the from parameter, you need to pass in the coordinate system in which that point or frame currently resides. In this example, viewC currently resides in viewB, so that's the from parameter.

Finally, you're all set to animate the layout!

✓ **CHECKPOINT** If you want to compare your project with mine at this point, you can check it out at https://github.com/iOSAppDevelopment-withSwiftinAction/Bookcase.git (Chapter8.1.KeyboardNotification).

8.4 *Animating views*

Now that you've detected when the keyboard moves on, you want to move the text field up so the user can see where they're editing. Rather than the interface jumping into place, animating it smoothly is a much better idea. Animation in an app can be the difference between a boring, static app and a slick, interesting, energetic experience. But animation isn't only pretty; it can also be practical. You can use animation to indicate elements you want the user to interact with; you can animate elements the user interacts with to give the user the illusion of a more tactile experience; and you can animate elements to help illustrate instructions or results.

TIP If you want to create a visually rich app such as a game with frequent animations and transitions, you might want to look at the SpriteKit framework. SpriteKit provides a straightforward approach to working with graphics in 2D. SceneKit literally takes it to another dimension, giving developers a useful framework for working with 3D graphics.

8.4.1 *Animating the view from under the keyboard*

So far, you've extracted the keyboard frame, animation duration, and animation curve from the keyboard notification, and determined the offset to animate the view by comparing the keyboard frame with the first responder frame.

Now, you're ready to animate the outer stack view.

1 Create outlets for the top and bottom constraints of the outer stack view. You'll modify the constants of these constraints to move the view up. Call the outlets `topConstraint` and `bottomConstraint`.

2 Create a `UIViewAnimationOptions` object from the easing curve of the keyboard:

```
let options = UIViewAnimationOptions(rawValue: curve)
```

3 Call the `animate` method on `UIView` to animate the constraint constants. The `animate` method can be passed several parameters to customize the animation:

- `withDuration` to specify the duration of the animation.
- `delay` to specify a delay before the animation begins.
- `options` to customize a range of details, such as the easing curve, whether the animation should reverse and whether the animation should repeat. You'll use it to pass in the easing curve of the keyboard.
- `animations` to pass in a closure of properties to animate.
- `completion` is another closure where you can perform any tasks after the animation has completed.

```
UIView.animate(                                       ◁──── Initiates
    withDuration: duration,                                 animation
    delay: 0,
    options: options,          ◁──── Passes in
    animations: {                     curve option
        self.topConstraint.constant = -offset
        self.bottomConstraint.constant = offset       │ Moves view up by offset
        self.view.layoutIfNeeded()     ◁──── Requests update
    },                                      to layout
    completion: nil            ◁──── No completion
)                                          closure necessary
```

4 Run the app on the iPhone SE simulator with its smaller screen. Tap on a text field or text view, and if it's covered by the keyboard, the whole view should move up the appropriate amount. Hooray!

✔ **CHECKPOINT** If you want to compare your project with mine at this point, you can check it out at https://github.com/iOSAppDevelopment-withSwiftinAction/Bookcase.git (Chapter8.2.AnimateView).

8.4.2 *Diving deeper into animating views with a sample bar chart*

You may wonder—why did you animate the *constraints* rather than the *location* of the view? And why did you call `layoutIfNeeded` in the animations block? For the answers to these questions and to explore view animation deeper, let's explore the basics on a simple fresh project.

Imagine your task is to animate a basic horizontal bar chart with the results of a vote of whether to eat Chinese or Thai food tonight. As you can see, the results are close! When the user taps the View button, the two bars of the bar chart should animate from the left while changing color. The titles for the bars should then appear over the top (see figure 8.6).

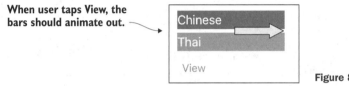

When user taps View, the bars should animate out.

Figure 8.6   Animate bar chart

Let's get started!

1   Create a new project called AnimatingViews.
2   Add two simple 25 x 25 views to the main view, one above the other.
3   Add `IBOutlet`s for the two views called `bar1` and `bar2`.
4   Add a button below the two bars and give it the title View.
5   Add an `IBAction` for the view button and call it `touchViewButton`.

See figure 8.7. I've colored the two views so you can see them.

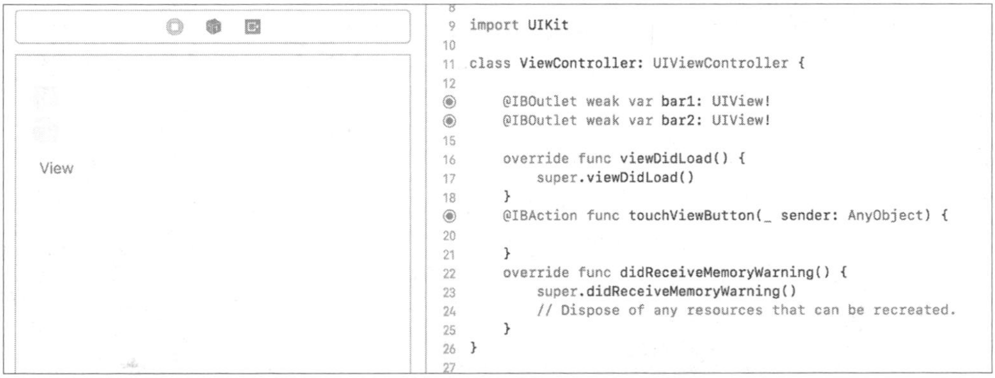

```
 8
 9  import UIKit
10
11 class ViewController: UIViewController {
12
       @IBOutlet weak var bar1: UIView!
       @IBOutlet weak var bar2: UIView!
15
16     override func viewDidLoad() {
17         super.viewDidLoad()
18     }
       @IBAction func touchViewButton(_ sender: AnyObject) {
20
21     }
22     override func didReceiveMemoryWarning() {
23         super.didReceiveMemoryWarning()
24         // Dispose of any resources that can be recreated.
25     }
26 }
27
```

View

Figure 8.7   Initial project setup

> ✓ **CHECKPOINT** If you prefer, you can check out my project at this point at https://github.com/iOSAppDevelopmentwithSwiftinAction/ AnimatingViews.git (1.InitialSetup).

ANIMATING VIEW PROPERTIES IN THE BAR CHART

We've already explored adding animations to coordinators of scene transitions called *transition coordinators*. In chapter 6, you passed a closure to a transition coordinator object containing changes to properties of a view that you want to animate during a size change. You can also pass a closure of animations to the transition coordinator during transitions between trait collections (size classes), or transitions between scenes, called *segues*. We'll come back to animation during segues in chapter 9.

You can also initiate a closure of animations by passing them into a type method on the `UIView` class called `animate`. You'll use this method now to animate basic properties on a view.

Most properties that affect how a view appears can be passed into the closure of animations. These properties include those shown in table 8.1.

Table 8.1 Animatable properties

Type of animation	View properties
Size	`frame.size` or `bounds.size`
Location	`frame.origin` or `center`
Transparency	`alpha`
Background color	`backgroundColor`
Rotation, scale, skew, translate	`transform`

1   Add the following to the `touchViewButton` method to trigger when the user taps the View button. Pass in the two required parameters of the `animate` method, `withDuration` and `animations`:

```
self.bar1.frame.size.width = 0          Sets up prior to animation
self.bar2.frame.size.width = 0
UIView.animate(withDuration: 1,
    animations: {
        self.bar1.backgroundColor = UIColor.red
        self.bar1.frame.size.width = 150
        self.bar2.backgroundColor = UIColor.orange        Closure of properties
        self.bar2.frame.size.width = 150                  to animate
    }
)
```

Initializes the property → points to `UIView.animate(withDuration: 1,`

2   Play the app on the simulator to see the results of your animation.

It's not looking bad, but with both bars animating simultaneously, it looks a little boring.

NESTING ANIMATIONS

How about animating the two bars in sequence?

1 Nest the animations on the two views by animating the second bar in the `completion` closure. Replace your `animate` method with the following:

```
UIView.animate(withDuration: 1,
    animations: {
    self.bar1.backgroundColor = UIColor.red
    self.bar1.frame.size.width = 150
    }, completion: { finished in
        UIView.animate(withDuration: 1, animations: {
            self.bar2.backgroundColor = UIColor.orange
            self.bar2.frame.size.width = 150
        })
    }
)
```

Completion closure

Nested animation

2 Run your app again to check that your bars animate in sequence now. Great! It's time you added the labels.

3 Add a completion closure to the second `animate` method, instantiate labels for the two bars and add them to your scene's view:

```
}, completion: { finished in
    let label1 = UILabel(frame: self.bar1.frame)
    label1.textColor = UIColor.white
    label1.text = "Chinese"
    self.view.addSubview(label1)
    let label2 = UILabel(frame: self.bar2.frame)
    label2.textColor = UIColor.white
    label2.text = "Thai"
    self.view.addSubview(label2)
}
```

4 Run your app again, and this time after animating, labels should appear for both bars in your chart. Smooth!

ANIMATING THE BAR CHART WITH CONSTRAINTS

This all looks great, but you've spent two chapters looking at adaptive layout. What happens to the animations when you add constraints to your views?

1 Add constraints for the two bars to the top, leading, width, and height.

2 Run your app again to see how your animations act now.

✓ **CHECKPOINT** If you prefer, you can check out my project at https://github.com/iOSAppDevelopmentwithSwiftinAction/AnimatingViews.git (2.AnimationsConstraints).

Ouch! What happened? The size and colors of the bars animate, but as soon as you add the labels, the bars snap back to their size as defined by their constraints (see figure 8.8).

Adding the labels set the flag that the layout needs updating, which triggers auto layout to calculate the size and position of views based on their constraints.

Figure 8.8   Bars return to their constraints

You haven't made any changes to the constraints of the two bars, so in calculating their size, auto layout arrives at the same figure it did prior to the animation.

How can you make changes to the constraints? The first things you need are outlets for the relevant constraints.

3   Select one of the bars in the storyboard, and you'll see its four constraints represented by blue lines.

4   Find the width constraint. (You can also find it in the Document Outline on the left.) See figure 8.9.

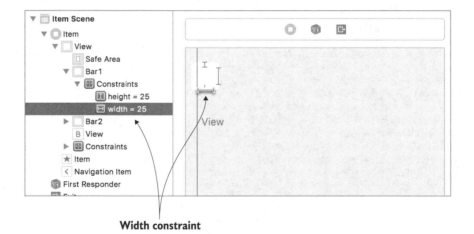

Width constraint

Figure 8.9   Width constraint

5   Create an `NSLayoutConstraint` `IBOutlet` for the width constraint by Control-dragging from the constraint to the view controller Swift file, and call it `bar1width`.

6   Do the same for the second bar, and you guessed it, call it `bar2width`.

ANIMATING CHANGES TO CONSTRAINTS BY UPDATING CONSTRAINTS IN COMPLETION
Great, now that your constraints have outlets, we can look at a couple of solutions to animating views with constraints.

One solution is to update the layout's constraints to represent its new layout after the animation is complete. In this case, as in the new layout, the two bars should be 150 points wide; you could pass `150` to the constants of the two width constraints.

1 Add the following to the second completion closure:

```
self.bar1width.constant = 150
self.bar2width.constant = 150
```

2 Run the app, and you should find that when the layout updates now, auto layout correctly calculates the new width of the two bars.

Updating the constraints of the layout in the completion handler is one solution, but another, perhaps more elegant approach, exists.

ANIMATING CHANGES TO CONSTRAINTS WITH LAYOUTIFNEEDED IN ANIMATIONS CLOSURE

Rather than modifying the size and position properties on the view directly, you're going to make modifications to the constraints of the view.

1 To start with, instead of setting the initial width of the bars, set the constant value of the two bar width constraints to `0`.

```
self.bar1width.constant = 0          Update constraint constants
self.bar2width.constant = 0
```

2 Next, call `layoutIfNeeded` to request the Auto Layout engine to immediately make any necessary adjustments to the layout.

```
self.view.layoutIfNeeded()     ◁     Immediately
                                     update layout
```

Because there have been changes to the constraints, the Auto Layout engine recalculates the new sizes and positions of the views based on the constraints.

Next up is animating based on updates to the constraints. Constraints themselves can't be animated; they're purely variables in the formula that the Auto Layout engine uses to calculate the sizes and positions of each view.

3 To confirm this, replace the update to the width of the bars in the animation closures with updates to the width constraints of the bars:

```
self.bar1.frame.size.width = 150
self.bar1width.constant = 150
...
self.bar2.frame.size.width = 150
self.bar2width.constant = 150
```

What you notice when you run the app is that these updates to the constraints seem to register immediately. The properties of the constraints themselves aren't animated, so when the `animations` closure completes, the Auto Layout engine notices that the layout is flagged to need updating, and handles it in the next update cycle (almost immediately!).

What *can* be animated are these size and position properties that the Auto Layout engine calculates from your constraints. You can take advantage of this.

4   After updating constraints in the `animations` closure, you should call `layoutIfNeeded`. Here's the complete first `animations` closure:

```
animations: {
        self.bar1.backgroundColor = UIColor.red
        self.bar1width.constant = 150
        self.view.layoutIfNeeded()        ◁─────┐ Requests update
    }                                            │ to layout
```

You'll need to add this call to `layoutIfNeeded` to both animations closures. This call requests the Auto Layout engine to immediately update the size and position properties. These size and position properties will then animate.

5   Run the app again, and this time you should see the bars animate out, and stay there. Hooray!

✅   **CHECKPOINT**   If you like, you can check out my project at this point at https://github.com/iOSAppDevelopmentwithSwiftinAction/Animating-Views.git (3.AnimationLayoutUpdate).

8.5   Scroll views

The Bookcase app looks good, but it could be even better if the user could scroll around the form when the keyboard appears and the space available for the form is reduced. You can add scrolling by embedding the bookcase form in a *scroll view*. What's a scroll view?

Sometimes, the content that you want on a view doesn't fit in the view, such as when the keyboard appears over the top of the bookcase form. Scroll views make it possible for the user to scroll around a view to explore its content.

8.5.1   Scroll view with form content and keyboard

Using scroll views for form content can make sense, because giving the user more freedom to scroll where they like makes it possible to build up a form or form field that could go beyond the height of the app window. Embedding the form in a scroll view allows unlimited space to add fields in the future.

Scroll views have other advantages related to managing the keyboard:

1   They have a built-in mechanism for dismissing the keyboard.
2   Scroll views automatically move their content so that a text field currently being edited is visible.
3   You can call the scroll view instance method `scrollRectToVisible` to request that a specific area of content be visible.

Let's embed the bookcase form in a scroll view.

> ✔ **CHECKPOINT** If you want to download the starting point of the project at this point, you can check it out at https://github.com/iOSApp-DevelopmentwithSwiftinAction/Bookcase.git (Chapter8.2.AnimateView).

Follow the steps to set up the form to use scroll views:

1 Select the Outer Stack View in the storyboard, and select Editor > Embed in > ScrollView. Unfortunately, the book will lose its constraints, so you need to add them back.

2 Set the book height to 0.3x the height of the root view and uninstall the constraint for the compact height size class.

3 Pin the four edges of the scroll view to the root view. This defines the area of the scroll view.

4 Pin the four edges of the outer stack view to the scroll view. This defines the edges of the scrollable content.

Next, you'll need to define the width and height of the scroll view's scrollable content. Because the width and height of the scrollable content will be the width and height of the scroll view, you should indicate this in constraints.

5 Set the width and height of the outer stack view (the scroll view's scrollable content) equal to the width and height of the scroll view. Now the interface will be tightly flush on the edges.

6 Give the outer stack view fixed margins by selecting Fixed in the Layout Margins section of the Size Inspector, with margins of 16 all round.

The stack view should now be nicely framed in the scroll view (see figure 8.10).

Figure 8.10   Fixed margins

You can take advantage of the scroll view's ability to dismiss the keyboard.

7 Select the scroll view, and open the Attributes Inspector. In the Keyboard property, select Dismiss Interactively.

You'll find two alternative approaches for dismissing the keyboard, which are really two means to the same end with slightly different effects. Dismiss on Drag will dismiss the keyboard as soon as the user starts scrolling the scroll view. Dismiss Interactively will begin to dismiss the keyboard when the user scrolls into the area of the keyboard, from which the keyboard then follows the user's movement.

Because the scroll view will be managing scrolling to the current text field, you'll no longer be animating the constraints, so you can remove any code related to this.

8   Remove the constraint outlets and everything in the `keyboardFrameChanges` method that follows calculating the `keyboardFrame`.

If you run your app now, you'll notice that the form still doesn't scroll, even if you select a text field, causing the keyboard to appear. Because the scrollable content is the same size as the scroll view, scrolling isn't necessary, and the keyboard showing doesn't automatically make any adjustments to the scrollable area—you need to do this part manually.

The best approach to make this adjustment is to create a bottom margin for the scrollable content with the scroll view's `contentInset` property (see figure 8.11).

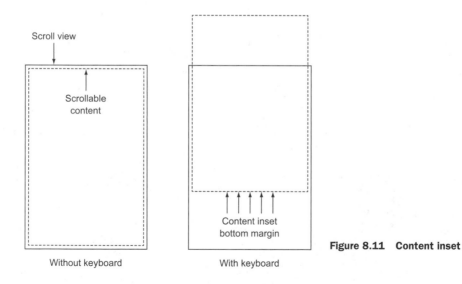

Figure 8.11   Content inset

You'll need to determine the amount to offset the scrollable content. The keyboard height itself doesn't change as it shows, so you'll need to calculate this by subtracting the keyboard y position from the height of the root view.

9   Add the following to the `keyboardFrameChanges` method after calculating the `keyboardFrame`:

```
let offset = self.view.frame.height - keyboardFrame.origin.y
```

10 Create an outlet for the scroll view and call it `scrollView`.

11 You can now set the `contentInset` property on the scroll view:

```
scrollView.contentInset.bottom = offset
```

12 Run the app, tap on a text field, and you should find that your form is now scrollable! One thing will appear a little strange though—the scroll indicator on the right isn't right. Set a bottom margin for the scroll indicator as well to resolve this:

```
scrollView.scrollIndicatorInsets.bottom = offset
```

13 Run the app again on the iPhone SE simulator, and the scroll indicator should work as you expect.

14 Check that your tap gesture recognizer is working by tapping on the info button. The ISBN field should appear. Tap on the ISBN field, and as the keyboard covers it up slightly, the scroll view should automagically scroll so that the field is visible—no programming required!

15 Tap on the notes text view, and get ready for disappointment. Because the text view is itself a type of scroll view, the scroll view doesn't automatically scroll for it. Not to stress, it's quite straight forward to set this up manually.

16 Add an outlet for the outer stack view, and call it `outerStackView`. You'll use this to calculate the location of the text view in the scrollable content with the `convert` method.

17 Still in the `keyboardFrameChanges` method, get a reference to the current first responder if it's a text view, and a reference to its superview for the convert method.

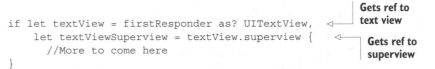

```
if let textView = firstResponder as? UITextView,
    let textViewSuperview = textView.superview {
        //More to come here
}
```
Gets ref to text view
Gets ref to superview

18 Convert a frame for the text view within the scrollable content (the outer stack view), and manually request the scroll view to make this frame visible:

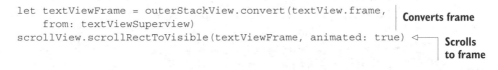

```
let textViewFrame = outerStackView.convert(textView.frame,
    from: textViewSuperview)
scrollView.scrollRectToVisible(textViewFrame, animated: true)
```
Converts frame
Scrolls to frame

19 Run your app on the simulator, and edit the notes text view. This time, when the keyboard appears, the scroller should scroll to ensure your text view is visible.

Congratulations, the bookcase form is embedded neatly in a scroll view, and text fields and text views are visible when the keyboard appears. You could probably submit it to the App Store again now—but maybe beta test it this time!

✅ **CHECKPOINT**   If you'd like to compare projects, you can check mine out at https://github.com/iOSAppDevelopmentwithSwiftinAction/Book-case.git (Chapter8.3.ScrollView).

8.5.2   *Diving deeper into scroll views with image content*

Scroll views can also make it easier to zoom in and out on content. Let's explore scroll views with a simple image viewer with zoom functionality.

In chapter 5, you used gesture recognizers to create an image viewer app. Let's update this app to use a scroll view. Check out the starter branch for the image viewer app at https://github.com/iOSAppDevelopmentwithSwiftinAction/ImageViewer.git (1.InitialSetup).

1 Open the storyboard, where you'll find an image view has already been added to the view controller. This image view will be the scrollable content of your scroll view.

2 Select the image view, and embed it in a scroll view by selecting Editor > Embed in > Scroll View.

3 Pin the scroll view to the root view with 0 points on all four sides. This defines the scroll view to have the same frame as the root view (see figure 8.12).

You want to pin the image view to the scroll view, but first be sure you're starting from scratch by clearing any existing constraints.

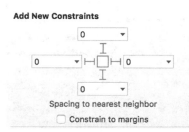

Figure 8.12   Pin all sides

4 Clear constraints on the image view by selecting the image view, and then selecting Clear Constraints in the Resolve Auto Layout Issues menu.

5 Pin the image view to the scroll view, also with 0 points on all four sides. This defines the edges of the scroll view, but unlike a normal view, this doesn't define its width and height to the same as the view it's pinned to. The size of scrollable content is defined only by its *content size.* You need to either specify content that has an intrinsic content size, or use constraints to define the size of the content. Because you haven't specified an image for the image view yet, the image view doesn't have an intrinsic content size. The scroll view doesn't yet know the size of its scrollable content, and you'll see a red layout error in the document outline.

6 Just as you did in chapter 5, drag the Images folder into the Project Navigator.

7 Select the image view in the storyboard. Under Image in the Attributes Inspector, select one of the images you dragged into the project, and the red layout error will go away. If you can still see a yellow layout warning, select the Update Frames button.

8 Run the app, and believe it or not, that was all that was necessary to set up an image that scrolls! It even has a fancy bounce animation if you stray past the boundaries of the image.

But how about zoom? Well, that's a little more work, but still mostly painless!

1 Select the scroll view, and in the Attributes Inspector, find the zoom properties.

2 Select a minimum zoom of 0.5 and a maximum zoom of 2. You might think this would be it, but wait—don't run the app yet! You have to tell the scroll view which view you want it to zoom.

3 First, create an outlet in the `ViewController` class to get a reference for the image view, and call it `imageView`.

4 Make the view controller the delegate for the scroll view by Control-dragging from the scroll view to the view controller in the document outline, and selecting delegate in the context menu.

5 Now, add an extension to the view controller that adopts the `UIScrollView-Delegate` and implements the `viewForZooming` method to let the scroll view know which view you would like to zoom.

```
extension ViewController: UIScrollViewDelegate {
    func viewForZooming(in scrollView: UIScrollView) -> UIView? {
        return imageView
    }
}
```

6 Run the app, and zoom the image. Remember, if you're running in the simulator, you can simulate pinching by holding down the Alt key.

✓ **CHECKPOINT** If you would like to compare your project with mine, you can check it out at https://github.com/iOSAppDevelopmentwithSwift-inAction/ImageViewer.git (3.ImageViewerScrollView).

As you can see, the scroll view is a convenient approach for setting up scrollable content. In addition to its built-in scroll and zoom behaviors that require little coding, it provides neat scroll indicators while scrolling and nice bounce animations for when you go beyond the bounds of the content.

8.6 *Summary*

In this chapter, you learned the following:

- Resign the first responder to dismiss the keyboard.
- Use the `UIKeyboardWillChangeFrame` notification to listen for keyboard events.
- Get information on the keyboard frame and animation from the `userInfo` property in keyboard notifications.

- To animate views with constraints, call `layoutIfNeeded` in the animations closure in the `animate` method of `UIView`.
- Animate the showing or hiding of an arranged view in a stack view by setting its `isHidden` property in an animations closure.
- Unlike other types of views, scrollable content does not imply its size from the size of its superview.
- Use `contentInset` and `scrollIndicatorInsets` to give margins to the content and scroll indicator in a scroll view.

Part 3

Building your app

This part examines various common techniques and technologies used in iOS app development that can transform your app from just looking pretty to doing something cool or useful.

In chapters 9 and 10, you'll look at laying out data in your app using tables and collections. You'll also look at navigation between different scenes using segues and tab bars, and searching and sorting data.

Various techniques for persisting data locally are reviewed in chapter 11.

Chapter 12 demystifies persisting data in iCloud.

In chapter 13, you'll look at various topics related to graphics and media—adding icons and images, drawing graphics, taking photos, selecting photos from the photo library, detecting barcodes, and playing sound.

Chapter 14 focuses on requesting data and downloading from a web service. You'll also look at parsing JSON and using a dependency manager.

In chapter 15, you'll explore debugging tools and techniques available in Xcode. You'll also try out different types of testing.

In these chapters, you'll explore these various concepts while building up the Bookcase app from a simple interface to a complex and useful tool. Working through challenges with the Bookcase app will help you to see a way forward for developing your own great idea!

Tables and navigation

9

This chapter covers

- Displaying data in single-column tables
- Adding, editing, and deleting rows
- Adding navigation to other scenes
- Passing data between scenes

Most useful apps display dynamic information in one form or another. If you have a list of items to display, Apple provides a convenient object for you to use called a *table view*.

In this chapter, you'll create the first scene of the Bookcase app you've been working on. This scene will show a list of all the books the user enters into the app. When the user adds or edits a book record, they'll navigate to the bookcase form you've worked on in previous chapters.

In this chapter, you'll explore

- *Table views* and *table view controllers*—Table views manage a list of data and display it in a simple one-column table. Table view controllers are view controllers that contain a table and handle part of the boilerplate setup for you.

- *Navigation controllers* and *navigation bars*—You'll use navigation controllers to navigate between scenes. By default, navigation controllers provide a navigation bar that indicates where you are in the app, gives you a back button for returning to the previous scene, and can be used for additional controls.
- *Segues*—The transition between two scenes is also known as a segue. You'll use different kinds of segues to display view controllers in different ways.

9.1   Displaying data in table views

When you think of tables, you probably think of multicolumn spreadsheets or perhaps HTML tables. Well, table views in the world of iOS display a list of data in *one* column. Each row or item in the list is displayed in what's called a *cell*.

You probably see tables in apps more than you realize. See figure 9.1 for types of tables you could encounter in standard Apple apps.

Figure 9.1   Tables in Apple apps

Tables are mighty useful for presenting a scrollable list of information. They're also useful for allowing the user to select items in the list. Selections can toggle a checkmark in the cell or enable navigating to another scene.

Notice the variations available in table views. Table views can be grouped into sections (such as the Settings and Calendar apps in figure 9.1) or can display an index such as letters on the right of the table (such as the Contacts app in figure 9.1). We'll focus on a plain table view (such as the Reminders app in figure 9.1) in this chapter.

Apple provides several different styles of default table view cells, which we'll look at shortly. You could also create your own completely customized look for table view cells. We'll look at customized cells in the next chapter.

You're going to add a table view to the Bookcase app, which will display a list of books in your bookcase. Then you'll add tapping on a book in the list to edit the book in the form you've been working on. Let's not get ahead of ourselves, though! For now, let's focus on adding the table view to the app (see figure 9.2).

You have two main ways to set up a table view using Interface Builder:

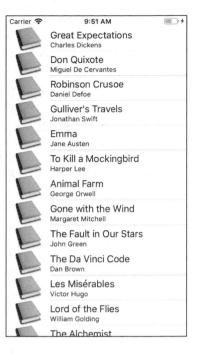

Figure 9.2   Books table

- You could drag a table view object onto your scene's root view. You'd then need to connect the view controller to the table view—you'd make your scene's view controller the *delegate* and *data source* for the table view and implement any required delegate methods. More on the delegate and data source of the table view shortly.

- You can drag a special type of view controller called a *table view controller* onto the storyboard. The table view controller comes with a table view ready to go and connected to the table view. All you need to focus on is customizing the table view to display your data.

9.1.1 Setting up a table view controller in the storyboard

You're going to use the table view controller to display a list of books in your app.

> ✅ **CHECKPOINT**   Open the Bookcase app where you left off in the previous chapter. Alternatively, you can check out my project at the same point at https://github.com/iOSAppDevelopmentwithSwiftinAction/Bookcase.git (Chapter8.3.ScrollView).

1 Open the main storyboard. Move the book detail view controller scene you've been working on to the right for the moment. We'll come back to this later in the chapter, but for now, you'll set up a table view controller.

2   Find the Table view controller in the Object Library and drag it onto the storyboard. A table view controller will appear in the storyboard with a table view already loaded as the root view of the scene (see figure 9.3).

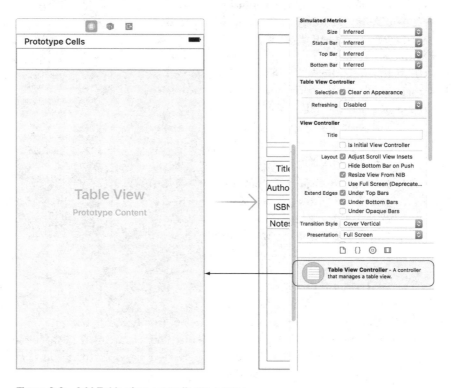

Figure 9.3   Add Table view controller to canvas

3   Drag the arrow indicating the initial view controller from the book detail view controller to the new table view controller (see figure 9.4).

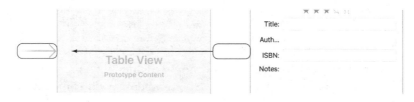

Figure 9.4   Move initial view controller arrow.

4 Select the table view in the Document Outline. Notice in the Attributes Inspector that the content of the table view is using Dynamic Prototypes by default (see figure 9.5).

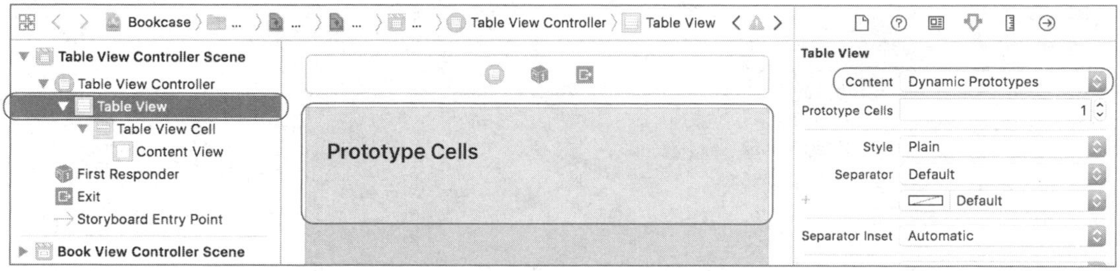

Figure 9.5 Dynamic prototypes table view

Table views can use one of two types of cells:

- *Static cells*—Use table views with static cells to build up a static design using a table. The number of rows in a table with static cells is set at design time, and each cell has its own unique design. A list of customizable settings in an app could be a good candidate for a table using static cells.
- *Dynamic prototypes*—Use table views with dynamic prototypes to build a table with content that can change at runtime and/or where cells have the same layout. A table view set to dynamic prototypes will automatically give you a *prototype cell* to customize the look of the cells in the table.

Because the books in the Bookcase app will eventually change over time, and each cell will have the same layout, a table view with dynamic prototypes is ideal for our example.

5 Select the white rectangle at the top of the table view, underneath the title Prototype Cells. This special table view cell is like a template that cells in your table will emulate.

6 Find Style in the Attributes Inspector for the cell and select Subtitle.

Table view cell styles

Apple gives you four simple table view cell styles to work with.

Each style uses different combinations of three main elements:

- *imageView* for displaying an image
- *textLabel* for displaying a primary text label
- *detailTextLabel* for displaying a secondary text label

Not all styles contain every element—the *basic* style doesn't contain a detail text label, and the *left detail* style doesn't provide for an image view. If you don't use an element such as the image view, for example, the other elements will grow to fill the space.

If none of these cell styles suits your data, you can create your own custom table view cell by subclassing the UITableViewCell class. We'll look at custom cells in the next chapter, but for now, the *subtitle* style looks great for displaying books, so let's go with that!

7   Find Identifier in the Attributes Inspector for the cell. Give the table view cell a reuse identifier—let's call it bookCell. You'll use this to identify the cell template when you generate cells.

8   Notice the Accessory attribute in the Attributes Inspector—you're going to leave this set to None.

Table view cell accessory views

Table view cells can contain an optional *accessory view* as well, for helping to indicate what will happen when the user selects a cell.

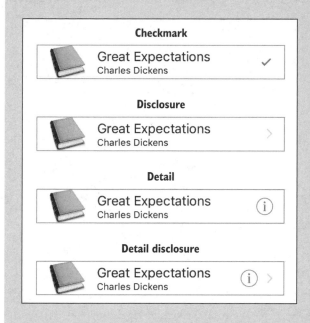

Checkmark can be used to indicate when a cell is selected.

Disclosure can be used to indicate that selecting a cell goes to another table view, such as in Apple's Settings app.

Detail displays additional information about the selected cell when the user selects the accessory view itself.

Detail disclosure displays additional information about the selected cell in another view when the user selects the accessory view itself.

9.1.2   *Displaying data in the table view*

Now that you have the table view controller set up in the storyboard, you'll need to customize the table view in code. Select the table view controller and open the Identity Inspector. Note that the view controller's base class is `UITableViewController` (see figure 9.6).

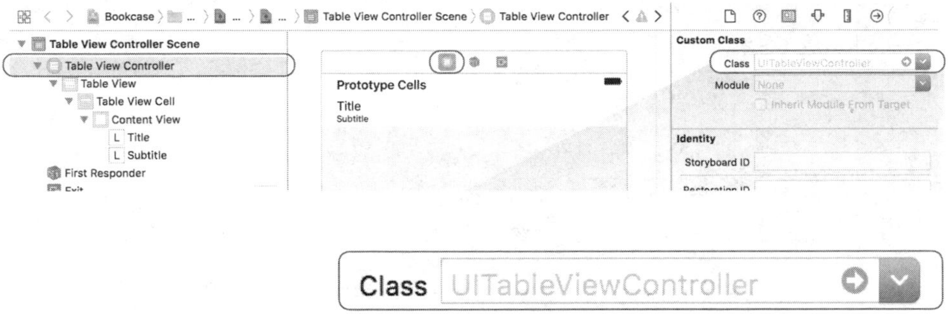

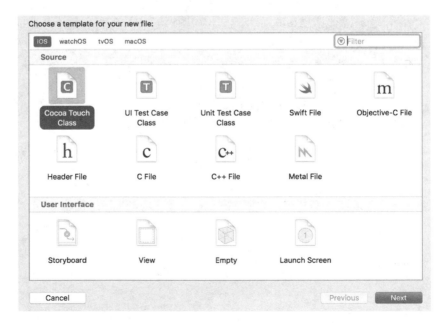

Figure 9.6   Table view controller identity

You're going to subclass `UITableViewController` to manage its table view.

1   Select File > New > File. A selection of templates will appear. In the iOS > Source category, select Cocoa Touch Class (see figure 9.7).

Figure 9.7   Select Cocoa Touch Class template

2 Give your class a name, and specify which class you want it to subclass. You want to subclass `UITableViewController`, and you could call your class `Books-TableViewController`.

TIP A common convention when defining the name of your class is to suffix it with the name of the iOS class you're subclassing. You can type the word `Books` in the `Class` field, and when you specify the subclass, Xcode will automatically fill in the rest for you.

3 Leave XIB file unchecked.

4 Choose the language as Swift and select Next (see figure 9.8).

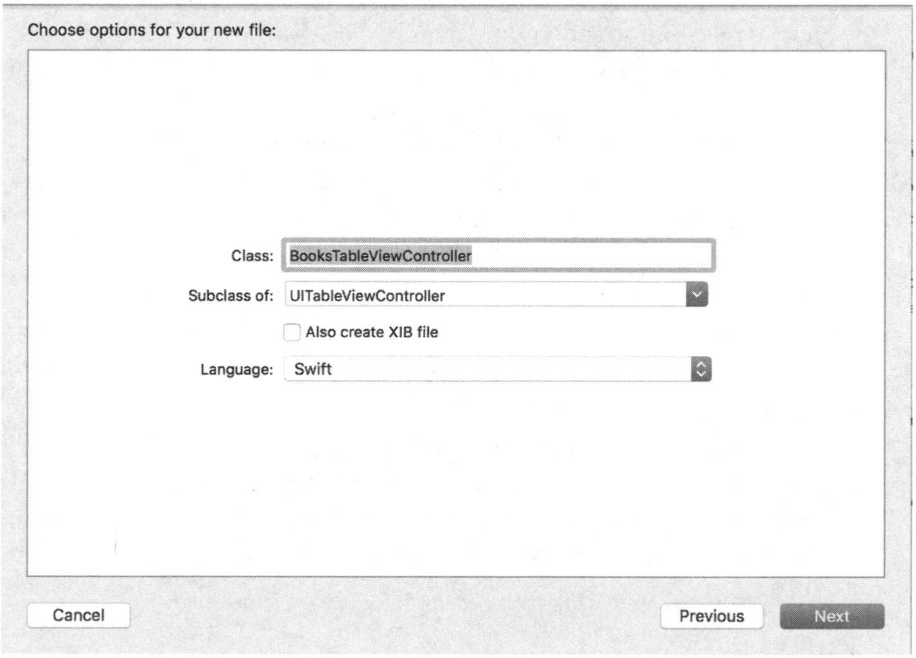

Choose options for your new file:

Class:	BooksTableViewController
Subclass of:	UITableViewController
	☐ Also create XIB file
Language:	Swift

Cancel   Previous   Next

Figure 9.8   Create file options

5 Save your file in the default folder for your project. Xcode will automatically open your new `UITableViewController` subclass generated from a template, with additional methods ready to use.

You need to connect the table view controller in the storyboard with the subclass you created.

6 Open the main storyboard again, and select your table view controller.

7 Under Custom Class, replace the base class with your subclass (see figure 9.9).

DATA SOURCE AND DELEGATE

In certain UIKit views, your view controller can directly request a view to display data. For example, you could tell a `UILabel` to display "Hello World" by the following:

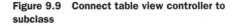

Custom Class

Class `BooksTableViewController`

Module `Bookcase`

☑ Inherit Module From Target

Figure 9.9   Connect table view controller to subclass

```
label.text = "Hello world"
```

Table views work a little differently. Instead of passing the table's data directly into the table and letting the table view manage its data, table views use the delegation pattern, and request information on demand. This way ensures separation of the view (table view in this case) and the model (the table view's data), and maintains a good MVC structure.

Table views divide their delegation responsibilities in two:

- The data source provides the table view with all the information necessary to display the data in the table. For example, when a table view needs to know how many rows it should display in the table, it asks its data source. When it needs to display a cell for a specific row, it asks the data source for it.
- The delegate handles additional responsibilities such as selecting and deleting rows or specifying the height of a specific row. The table view will also notify the delegate of certain events, such as when the user selects or edits a row.

If you drag a table view object into a regular view controller in the storyboard, you have to configure the data source and delegate yourself. However, because you're using a table view controller, the `UITableViewController` class comes automatically preconfigured to be both the table view's delegate and data source (see figure 9.10).

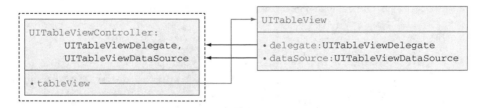

Figure 9.10   Table view controller relationships

Stubs for delegate and data source methods are also already implemented in the `UITable-ViewController` class. To customize your subclass, you'll need to *override* any delegate or data source methods you wish to implement. In fact, if you're subclassing `UITableView-Controller`, it doesn't really matter whether you override a method from the data source or the delegate—the main takeaway here is that you have several methods to override to manage your table view.

The suggested methods in the template will get you off to a great start. Before you implement the Bookcase table, let's create a basic implementation of a table to get an idea of how this is going to work (see figure 9.11).

You'll implement three methods in `Books-TableViewController` that will answer three important data source questions that the table view needs to know to display the table. Here are the three questions and your answers in plain English:

Carrier 🛜	10:30 AM	🔋⚡
Row # 0		
Row # 1		
Row # 2		
Row # 3		
Row # 4		
Row # 5		
Row # 6		
Row # 7		
Row # 8		
Row # 9		

Figure 9.11   Basic table

- *How many sections are there in the table?* Just the one.
- *How many rows are there in this section of the table?* I'll say ten!
- *What cell goes in this row?* I'd like cells based on the bookCell reuse identifier I set up earlier, and I want to display the text "Row #" with the row number.

Now, let's see how this looks in code.

1   Replace the following methods in your `BooksTableViewController` class:

```
                          override func numberOfSections(
How many                      in tableView: UITableView) -> Int {        Returns number
sections                      return 1                                    of sections
in the table?             }
                          override func tableView(_ tableView: UITableView,
How many rows                 numberOfRowsInSection section: Int) -> Int {   Returns number
in each section?              return 10                                      of rows
                          }
                          override func tableView(_ tableView: UITableView,
                              cellForRowAt indexPath: IndexPath
                              ) -> UITableViewCell {
What cell goes                let cell = tableView.dequeueReusableCell(       Gets table view cell
in this row?                      withIdentifier: "bookCell", for: indexPath)
                              cell.textLabel?.text = "Row # \(indexPath.row)"  Customizes table
                              return cell                                       view cell
                          }                                Returns table
                                                           view cell
```

The first two methods are straightforward. The number of sections in the table or rows in each section is returned from the methods. If multiple sections exist, you can check the section number the table view was asking about before returning the number of rows. (Because your table only has one section, it's unnecessary to check the section number.)

The third method is interesting. It receives an `IndexPath` parameter, which contains the number of the section and the row of the cell it's interested in. It then gets a table view cell for this index path, based on the reuse identifier you defined earlier in Interface Builder.

You can then customize the table view cell how you like. The index path is generally useful here to know what data to inject into the cell.

The interesting thing about this method is where it gets its cell from. Imagine if you had a million rows in your table. It would start to be a major *memory* issue if the table view kept a million cells in memory. On the flip side, imagine if the app removed cells from memory as soon as they were scrolled offscreen and created new cells every time they scrolled onscreen. This strategy could be a *performance* issue, especially if the cells were graphically intensive.

Apple's shrewd solution is to keep a cache or *queue* of table view cells. When you call the `dequeueReusableCell` method, it first checks for any cells with the requested reuse identifier in the cache, and if none are found, it creates a new cell. When a cell is scrolled offscreen, rather than removing the cell from memory, it's sent to the cache to be reused.

2   Run the app, and you should see 10 cells appear in the simulator.

Now that you know the basics of table views, you'll set up the table view controller to display books for the Bookcase app. But first, you'll need to set up a model class to hold the properties of a book.

SET UP THE MODEL

To display books in the table view controller for the Bookcase app, you'll first need a way to store data for each book. You'll set up a simple `Book` structure based on the data the user can enter for each book. Remind yourself of the book properties with another look at the bookcase form in figure 9.12.

1   Select File > New File > Swift File.

2   This time, in the iOS > Source category, select Swift File.

3   Call it Book and select Create.

Figure 9.12   Bookcase form

4 In this Book.swift file, create a `Book` type that stores the book properties with an initializer that sets their initial values:

```
import UIKit                                                    ←——————————  UIKit necessary
struct Book {                                                                for UIImage
    static let defaultCover = UIImage(named: "book.jpg")!
    var title: String
    var author: String
    var rating: Double
    var isbn: String
    var notes: String
    var cover: UIImage {
        get {
            return image ?? Book.defaultCover
        }                                              Computed property
        set {
            image = newValue
        }
    }
    private var image: UIImage?                    ←——  Optional UIImage
                                                        property
    init(title: String, author: String,
            rating: Double, isbn: String,
            notes: String,
            cover: UIImage? = nil) {               ←——  Cover defaults
        self.title = title                              to nil
        self.author = author
        self.rating = rating
        self.isbn = isbn
        self.notes = notes
        self.image = cover
    }
}
```

A few notes about the code listing:

- Because `UIImage` comes in the UIKit framework, you need to import the UIKit framework!
- As this type does not need to subclass, and the value of the properties defines a book's identity, define the `Book` type as a structure rather than a class.
- Later in the book, we'll look at allowing the user to add an image for the book cover; you can store this image in a `UIImage` object. Because entering a cover image for the book isn't required, leave the `image` variable as an optional defaulting to `nil`, and set up a default cover image. Set up a computed property `cover` that returns the `image` if it exists, and the default cover otherwise.

Access control

Observant readers will notice the `private` keyword defining the `image` property. Other classes should access the `cover` property, which provides a default image if the `image` property is `nil`. To prevent other classes from accessing the `image` property by mistake, you define it as `private`, restricting access to this property from other files.

There are five access levels in Swift. Here they are, from most to least restrictive:

Private—Access is restricted to the *entity* (for example, structure or class) it's declared in.

File-private—Access is restricted to the *file* it's declared in.

Internal—Access is restricted to the *module* it's declared in. A module is a unit of code distribution, such as an application, framework, or build target. The default access level is `internal`.

Public—Access is *unrestricted*, but classes marked as public can't be subclassed from another module.

Open—Access is *unrestricted*. (The open keyword only applies to classes.)

Great, you can now use this `Book` class to create an array of `Book` objects that eventually will be used to fill the table.

CREATING A BOOKS MANAGER

You could create this array directly in your `BooksTableViewController` class, but to keep responsibilities of the controller and the model separate, maintaining a good MVC structure, it's a good idea to manage the books data in a model class. In our Bookcase app, this model class is basically going to be your friendly librarian! It will store books; give books to the user; manage adding, updating, and removing books; and eventually it will handle sorting and searching the books.

Call your friendly librarian class the `BooksManager`. The `BooksManager` will lazily load an array of books that's preloaded with sample data.

1 Create a `BooksManager` Swift file preconfigured with a computed property for returning the number of books (`bookCount`), a method returning a specific book (`getBook`), and a lazy property (the `books` array) that preloads with sample data.

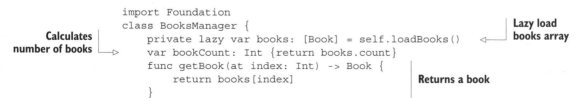

```
import Foundation
class BooksManager {
    private lazy var books: [Book] = self.loadBooks()      ← Lazy load books array
    var bookCount: Int {return books.count}      ← Calculates number of books
    func getBook(at index: Int) -> Book {
        return books[index]      ← Returns a book
    }
}
```

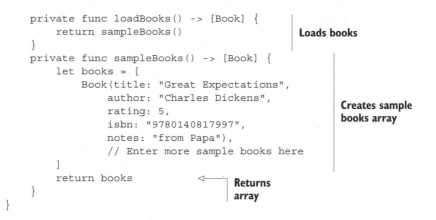

```
private func loadBooks() -> [Book] {
    return sampleBooks()                          Loads books
}
private func sampleBooks() -> [Book] {
    let books = [
        Book(title: "Great Expectations",
            author: "Charles Dickens",
            rating: 5,                             Creates sample
            isbn: "9780140817997",                 books array
            notes: "from Papa"),
            // Enter more sample books here
    ]
    return books                  ←┐  Returns
}                                   │  array
}
```

2 You can now define an instance variable of the books manager in your `Books-TableViewController` class:

```
var booksManager: BooksManager = BooksManager()
```

Now that your books table view controller has an array of books, you can update your answers to the three important data source questions. There's still going to be only one section, so the answer to the number of sections won't need updating from before. The number of rows has changed though, so it should reflect the number of books in the array.

3 Update your code:

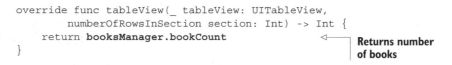

```
override func tableView(_ tableView: UITableView,
        numberOfRowsInSection section: Int) -> Int {
    return booksManager.bookCount          ←┐  Returns number
}                                            │  of books
```

Next, you'll need to update your answer to "What cell goes in this row?"

4 First, get a reference to the relevant book from the `books` array for this row. Then, you can update the elements of the cell with the data from the book object.

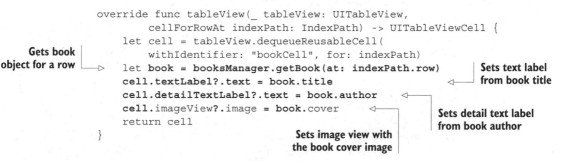

```
override func tableView(_ tableView: UITableView,
        cellForRowAt indexPath: IndexPath) -> UITableViewCell {
    let cell = tableView.dequeueReusableCell(
        withIdentifier: "bookCell", for: indexPath)
    let book = booksManager.getBook(at: indexPath.row)
    cell.textLabel?.text = book.title
    cell.detailTextLabel?.text = book.author
    cell.imageView?.image = book.cover
    return cell
}
```

Gets book object for a row

Sets text label from book title

Sets detail text label from book author

Sets image view with the book cover image

5 Run the app, and you should find that your sample books appear in the table. Success!

9.2   *Adding a row*

It's time for your users to add a book to the books table.

To add the data for a book, you want your users to tap an add button (plus), and then navigate from the books table to the bookcase form to fill in the details for the new book (see figure 9.13).

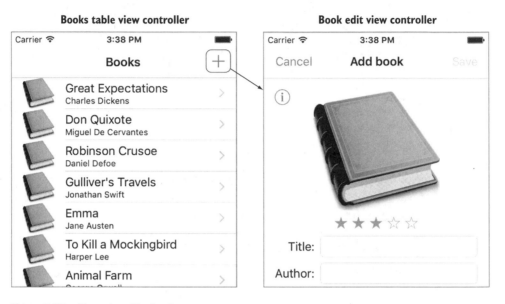

Figure 9.13   Tap + to add a book.

One useful approach for managing navigation between view controllers is to embed your view controller in a *navigation controller*.

> ### Container view controllers
>
> Until now, we've only looked at *content* view controllers with limited navigation, but another category of view controllers exists called *container* view controllers. Container view controllers manage the content from multiple view controllers, and each have their own approach to view hierarchies. Certain container view controllers that you may encounter include
>
> *Tab bar controllers*—Adds a tab bar at the bottom of the interface to navigate between view controllers
>
> *Split view controllers*—Shows two content view controllers simultaneously in certain devices and orientations and navigates between the two in other devices or orientations
>
> *Navigation controllers*—Manages navigation between content view controllers

9.2.1 *Embedding a navigation controller*

A navigation controller manages navigation going forward and back through a hierarchy of content view controllers. The navigation controller is usually used in conjunction with a *navigation bar*. The navigation bar can be helpful to orient the user with a title for the scene and a back button to return to the previous scene. The navigation bar can also be a useful location for additional buttons—a great place for the add button!

The navigation controller manages its view controllers in a navigation stack, which is an array of view controllers. The navigation controller's root view controller will be the first view controller in the navigation stack. When the navigation controller navigates to a new scene, the new view controller is added to the stack. When the user selects the *back* button, the current view controller is removed from the stack.

The iPhone Settings app is an example of a navigation controller. The Settings scene is the navigation controller's root view controller. After navigating down to the Speak Selection scene, it becomes the fourth view controller in the navigation stack (see figure 9.14 to see the current state of the navigation stack in each scene in the navigation hierarchy).

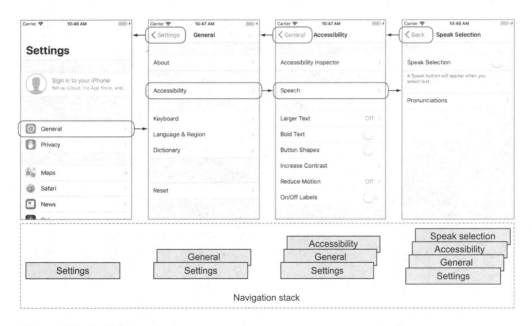

Figure 9.14 Navigation controller

You're going to set up a navigation controller for navigating to the book detail view controller, to add a book to the books table.

1. With the books table view controller selected, select Editor > Embed In > Navigation Controller.

The navigation controller will appear to the left of the books table view controller, with a symbol and arrow between, indicating the relationship. The initial view controller indicator arrow moves to the navigation controller, and a navigation bar appears at the top of your books table view controller (see figure 9.15).

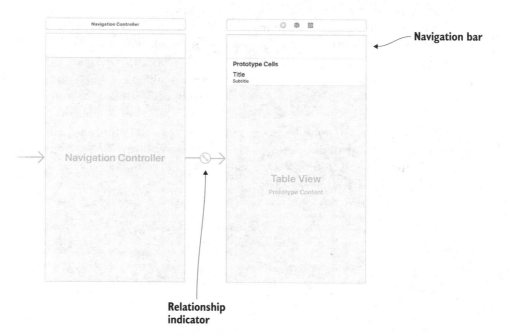

Figure 9.15   Navigation controller

2   Add a title for the scene in the navigation bar. Double-click in the middle of the navigation bar to open the edit title field and give it the title *Books.*

Navigation bars accept special kinds of buttons called *bar button items*. When you use the navigation controller to navigate to another view controller, a special back button automatically appears in the left of the navigation bar with the name of the previous view controller.

3   You can add your own bar button item to the navigation bar, too. Find Navigation Bar Item in the Object Library and drag it to the right side of the navigation bar. The bar button item will say Item by default, but you want an add button.

4   Select the bar button item and open the Attributes Inspector. Examine the options in the System Item attribute. Apple has several different preconfigured button styles.

5   Select Add, and a + symbol will appear.

9.2.2 Creating a segue

When the user taps the add button, you'll transition to the book detail view controller. A transition from one scene to another is called a segue.

1. Create a segue for when the user taps the add button, by Control-dragging from the add button to the book detail view controller.
2. We'll explore different types of segues shortly, but for now select *Show*. A symbol appears between the two scenes representing the type of segue you created (see figure 9.16).

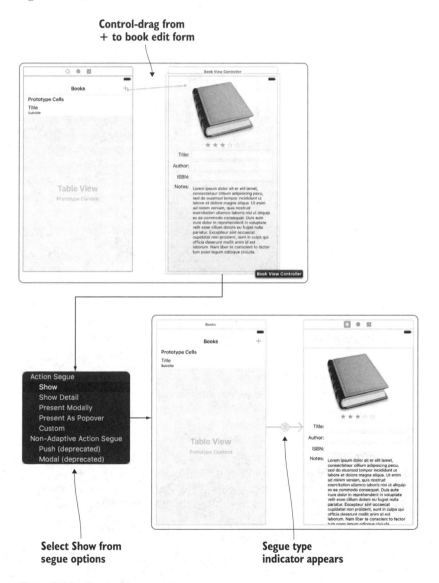

Figure 9.16   Create Show segue

3 Run the app to see your show segue in operation!

4 Tap the plus button in the navigation bar. The book detail view controller should slide in from the right, with a back button on the left of the navigation bar (see figure 9.17).

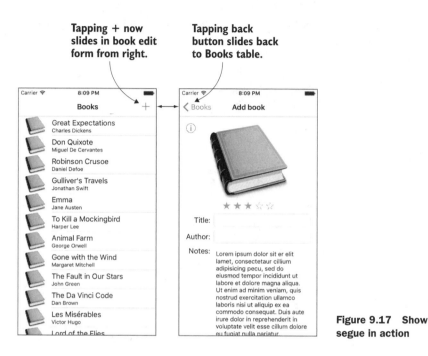

Figure 9.17   Show segue in action

The show segue is most appropriate for content that provides more details about the user's selection. When *adding* content, a *modal* segue is more appropriate. Rather than adding the new view controller to the navigation stack, a modal segue replaces the current view controller, displaying the new view controller over the top.

5 Select the segue, open the Attribute Inspector, and change the kind of segue to Present Modally.

Kinds of segues

There are four main kinds of segues, each with its own unique approach and attributes, and which act differently depending on the size class they're in, or whether they're embedded in a navigation controller or a split view controller.

Show Detail—This segue is most useful for *split view controllers*. Split view controllers support dividing an interface into a master view and a detail view when in landscape orientation in a regular size class environment. If a detail view is available, the show detail segue will *replace* the current detail view.

Show—This segue really shines if the presenting view controller is in a navigation controller or a split view controller. The presented view controller is added or *pushed* onto the navigation stack of view controllers (in the split view controller's detail view if available), and a back button automatically appears in the navigation bar. If no navigation controller is available, it acts the same as a modal segue.

Modal—A modal window presents over the top of the presenting view controller and must be closed before returning to the presenting view controller. Modal segues can be customized using two attributes:

- *Presentation*—Modal windows are always full-screen in a compact-width size class environment, but in regular-width size class environments, the presented view controller can appear in different presentation styles, such as *form sheet*, which displays as a centered window. The default presentation is *full-screen*.
- *Transition*—By default, the modal window transitions from below (*cover vertical*), but you can also use fancy flips, dissolves, and curls.

Popover—Popovers appear as a bubble with an arrow pointing to an anchor view in your presenting view. Popovers only look like bubbles in regular-width size class environments—in compact-width, popover segues appear as full-screen modal segues.

Here's what the four kinds of segues look like in landscape orientation on an iPad.

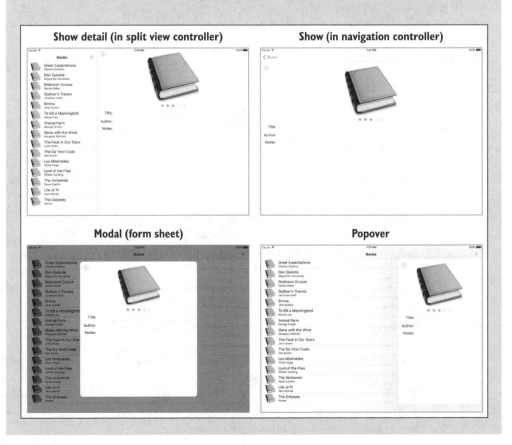

Notice that when you change the navigation to a modal segue, the second view controller loses its navigation bar because it's no longer added to the navigation controller's stack. The user has no way of exiting this scene!

9.2.3 *Embedding second navigation controller*

A Cancel button and a Save button would be perfect for exiting the book detail view controller, and the best place for these buttons is on a navigation bar (see figure 9.18).

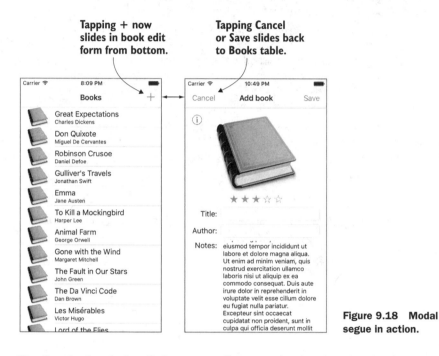

Tapping + now slides in book edit form from bottom.

Tapping Cancel or Save slides back to Books table.

Figure 9.18   Modal segue in action.

To give the book detail view controller a navigation bar for the Save and Cancel buttons, embed it in its own navigation controller.

1 Select the book detail view controller and select Editor > Embed In > Navigation Controller.

2 Select the navigation bar in the book detail view controller, and in the attributes inspector give it the title *Add book*.

3 Drag in a bar button item on the left of the navigation bar. In the Attributes Inspector and under System Item select Cancel.

4 Drag in another bar button item on the right of the navigation bar, and select a System Item of Save.

5 Run the app again to see your changes. Notice that the default transition for modal transition slides up rather than across.

   The Save and Cancel buttons don't *do* anything yet. You need to hook them up to return to the books table. If the user taps the Save button, you need to pass the book data back to add to the books array.

6 With the Assistant Editor open, Control-drag from the Cancel button to the `BookViewController` class, to create an `IBAction`. Call the method `touchCancel`.

7 Do the same with the Save button, creating a `touchSave` method.

8 From both methods, you can now call a `dismissMe` method where you can dismiss the view controller. A view controller can request itself to be dismissed with the `dismiss` method.

```
@IBAction func touchCancel(_ sender: AnyObject) {
    dismissMe()
}
@IBAction func touchSave(_ sender: AnyObject) {
    //need to save data here
    dismissMe()
}
func dismissMe() {
    dismiss(animated: true, completion: nil)
}
```

9 Run the app, and you should find that tapping the Cancel or Save button now closes the book detail view controller. But if you select Save, your book is still not being added to the books table!

When the user selects Save, your book detail view controller needs to pass the new book data back to the books scene for it to then add the data to the `books` array and display the new book in the table. You'll facilitate this communication with the *delegation pattern* that we looked at in chapter 5.

9.2.4 *Communicating with the books scene using your own delegate*

To use the delegation pattern, you'll need to set up a delegate protocol that defines a list of all the methods that the delegate should implement. In this case, the protocol will only need one method that will pass a book object to the delegate ready for saving. The table view controller would then adopt the protocol and define itself as the book detail view controller's delegate. See figure 9.19 for a visual representation of the relationships.

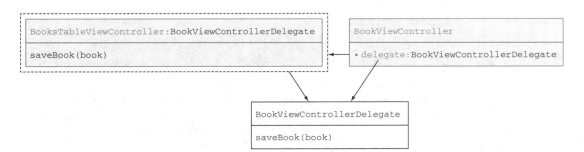

Figure 9.19   Delegate to save book

1   Create the delegate protocol. The naming convention for the delegate of a class is to use the same name of the class with the suffix `Delegate`. Add the BookViewControllerDelegate protocol to the BookViewController.swift file.

```
protocol BookViewControllerDelegate {
    func saveBook(_ book: Book)
}
```

2   Add a reference to the delegate in `BookViewController`, and make it an optional.

```
var delegate: BookViewControllerDelegate?
```

Now, to extract the data that the user has entered for the book, you'll need to create outlets for each of the elements in the form.

3   In the Assistant Editor, Control-drag from each text field and text view in the form to the `BookViewController` class. (You probably already have a reference to the book cover.)

```
@IBOutlet weak var titleTextField: UITextField!
@IBOutlet weak var authorTextField: UITextField!
@IBOutlet weak var isbnTextField: UITextField!
@IBOutlet weak var notesTextView: UITextView!
```

4   In the `touchSave` method before calling the `dismissMe` method, create a book object from the fields in the book edit form, and pass it into the delegate method:

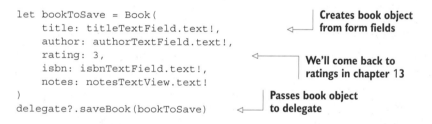

```
let bookToSave = Book(                          Creates book object
    title: titleTextField.text!,                from form fields
    author: authorTextField.text!,
    rating: 3,                                  We'll come back to
    isbn: isbnTextField.text!,                  ratings in chapter 13
    notes: notesTextView.text!
)                                               Passes book object
delegate?.saveBook(bookToSave)                  to delegate
```

USING YOUR DELEGATE PROTOCOL

As you saw in chapter 5, for a class to use a delegate protocol, it needs to follow three steps:

- Set itself as the delegate.
- Adopt the delegate protocol.
- Implement any required methods in the protocol.

Let's follow these steps to set up the `BooksTableViewController` class to implement the `BookViewControllerDelegate` protocol you created.

First, during the segue, the `BooksTableViewController` class needs to tell the `BookViewController` that it is the `BookViewController`'s delegate. The problem is that because the segue was created in Interface Builder, the instantiation of the new view controller is managed automatically.

Fortunately, view controllers contain a prepareForSegue method that's called after any new view controllers are instantiated but before the segue is performed.

1 Override this method so that you can get a reference to the destination view controller using the segue parameter's destinationViewController property, ready to perform any additional customization.

```
override func prepare(for segue: UIStoryboardSegue, sender: Any?) {
```

Because the BookViewController is embedded in a navigation controller, the segue's destinationViewController will be a navigation controller. The destinationViewController property is a UIViewController type, so you'll need to downcast it to a UINavigationController.

2 Use optional binding to get a reference to the destinationViewController as a navigation controller.

```
if let navController = segue.destination
    as? UINavigationController {
```

3 Now that you have a reference to the navigation controller, you can get a reference to its root view controller. You can get a navigation controller's root view controller with the topViewController property. Because this returns a UIViewController object, you'll need to downcast it to a BookView-Controller.

```
if let bookViewController = navController.topViewController
    as? BookViewController {
```

4 Now you have a reference to the bookViewController, and the Books-TableViewController can set itself as its delegate.

The following code shows the whole prepareForSegue method.

```
override func prepare(for segue: UIStoryboardSegue,      │ Override prepareForSegue
        sender: Any?) {
    if let navController = segue.destination             │ Get reference to navigation controller
            as? UINavigationController {
        if let bookViewController = navController.topViewController
                as? BookViewController {
            bookViewController.delegate = self           ◄─┐ Set delegate
        }                                                  │ as self
    }
}
```

Get reference to book view controller

You'll notice that an error appears on the delegate line, indicating that the BooksTableViewController class isn't the correct type to be the BookView-Controller's delegate. To resolve this, the BooksTableViewController class needs to adopt the protocol.

5   Adopt the `BookViewControllerDelegate` protocol in an extension to `BooksTableViewController`:

```
extension BooksTableViewController: BookViewControllerDelegate {

}
```

While this resolves the type error, another error will appear indicating that the `BooksTableViewController` doesn't conform to the `BookViewController Delegate` protocol.

6   Ensure that `BooksTableViewController` conforms to the protocol by implementing any required methods in the `BookViewControllerDelegate` protocol:

```
extension BooksTableViewController: BookViewControllerDelegate {
    func saveBook(_ book: Book) {
        // save book here
    }
}
```

9.2.5   *Adding data to the table*

Let's recap where we are—the user has tapped the + symbol to add a book and then entered details for the book (such as a title and author) into the book edit form. They then selected Save or Cancel to dismiss the form. If they selected Save, the book detail view controller passed the data back to the books table view controller via a delegate, and requested it to be saved.

Now that the books table view controller has received a book object representing the data entered into the book edit form, it's ready to add the data to the data source.

1   First, add a method to the `BooksManager` to handle adding a book to the books array:

```
func addBook(_ book: Book) {
    books.append(book)
}
```

2   Now, you can request `BooksManager` to add a book from the `saveBook` method in the `BooksTableViewController` extension:

```
booksManager.addBook(book)
```

In general, when updating a table's data, you have two choices:

- Perform a requested operation (for example *insert*, *delete*, or *move* rows) on the table.
- Reload the table data. This will rebuild the table with the updated data.

Where an animation of the update to the table is possible, you should specifically request the appropriate operation, such as add or delete row (and only after making the same change to the data source, or a runtime error will occur!). In this case, an animation won't be necessary because the table won't be onscreen when the update is performed, so you'll call a simple `reloadData`.

3 Add a call to reload data in the `saveBook` method:

```
func saveBook(_ book: Book) {
    booksManager.addBook(book)          ⟵   Adds book to
    tableView.reloadData()                   data source

}                                       ⟵   Reloads
                                            table data
```

4 Run the app to see your hard work in action!

Tap the + symbol to add a book to the table. Add a title for the book, and tap Save. You should see your new book appear in the table. Tap the + symbol again, and this time tap Cancel. There should be no change in the table.

> **CHALLENGE**   You may notice that it's possible to save an empty book at this stage. Because a book without a title doesn't make sense, you should probably require at least the title for each book. Check that the title field contains text when the text in the title text field changes (the way you did in chapter 5), and adjust the Save button's `isEnabled` property appropriately. While you're tidying up loose ends, open the main storyboard and remove the placeholder text that text views add by default from the notes text view.

> ✓ **CHECKPOINT**   If you'd like to compare your project with mine at this point, you can check mine out at https://github.com/iOSAppDevelopmentwithSwiftinAction/Bookcase.git (Chapter9.1.TableViewController).

Passing data back to the presenting view controller

There are often many ways to achieve the same goal in iOS development, and the same goes with how data entry view controllers (also called *detail* view controllers) return and pass data back to their presenting view controller. We've looked at one solution for doing this using the delegation pattern, but alternative approaches are often used. Let's look at a couple—perhaps you might find one or another more attractive than the delegate protocol approach you used.

Pass in a closure

This alternative has similarities to the delegation pattern, but focuses on one closure rather than a list of methods in a protocol. The presenting view controller simply passes in a closure to the detail view controller that the detail view controller can then call before resigning itself.

Closures can be stored as variables to be called later. The following sets up an optional closure declaration in the detail view controller class that could receive a `Book` object and doesn't return anything:

```
var saveBook: ((Book) -> Void)?
```

(continued)

In the `prepareForSegue` method, the presenting view controller would then pass the complete `saveBook` method into the detail view controller as a closure:

```
bookViewController.saveBook = { (_ book: Book) in
    self.booksManager.addBook(book)
//etc
}
```

Alternatively, the `saveBook` method itself could be passed in:

```
bookViewController.saveBook = saveBook
```

The detail view controller can now directly call the `saveBook` method. Because closures *capture* variables from their original scope, when the detail view controller calls the `saveBook` method, it will automatically have access to variables it refers to in the presenting view controller's scope. Because the closure is declared as an optional, it must be unwrapped when called:

```
saveBook?(bookToSave)
```

Now, when the user taps the Save button in the detail view controller, before resigning itself, it will call a closure scoped to the presenting view controller that performs any necessary operations, such as saving data.

Unwind segue

Similar to the way a transition from a presenting view controller to another view controller is called a segue, transitioning back to the presenting view controller is called an *unwind* segue. You can trigger an unwind segue from a button in a detail view controller by following two magical and mysterious steps.

1 Create a function in the presenting view controller with an @IBAction keyword that accepts a `UIStoryboardSegue` object. You can name this function whatever you like!

```
@IBAction func unwind(_ sender: UIStoryboardSegue) {
    //will be called after unwinding
}
```

2 Now comes the magical part! From the button in the presented view controller from which you want to trigger the unwind segue, control-drag to the Exit button in the scene dock, and select the `unwind` function you created.

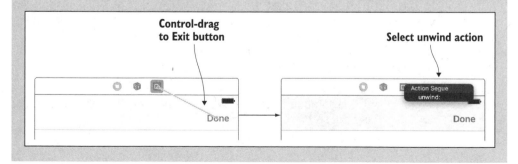

When the user selects the button in the presented view controller, the unwind method you set up will be called and an unwind segue will trigger back to the presenting view controller. If your detail view controller needs to do something before the unwind segue, such as store data, you can use the `prepareForSegue` method, the way you did with normal segues.

9.3 Editing a row

Now that you've implemented adding a row, editing the data for a book when the user taps on one of the rows in the table won't be too difficult (see figure 9.20).

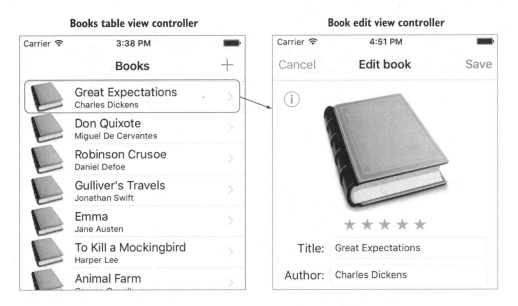

Figure 9.20 Tap a cell to edit the book.

You'll need to

1 Create a segue from the prototype cell to the book detail view controller.
2 Pass in the book object to edit to update the book edit form's initial state.
3 Remove the view controller correctly when the user selects Save or Cancel.
4 Update the appropriate book object in the table when the user selects Save.

Let's start by creating a segue for editing a row.

9.3.1 Creating a segue from a row

You want the app to navigate to the book detail view controller when the user selects a row in the books table. Because the book detail view controller will present more information about the user's selection, a show segue will be most appropriate. The show segue maintains the navigation bar from the presenting navigation controller, so the additional navigation controller that you needed with the `Modal` segue for adding a book won't be necessary.

1 Control-drag directly from the prototype cell in the table view controller to the book view controller, and select Show.
2 Move the navigation controller out of the way to see the show segue you created (see figure 9.21).

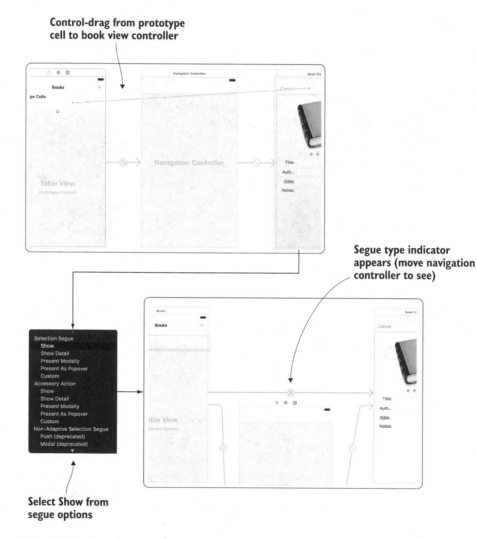

Control-drag from prototype cell to book view controller

Segue type indicator appears (move navigation controller to see)

Select Show from segue options

Figure 9.21   Creating a segue

9.3.2 *Passing in the book object to edit*

If the user selects a book from the table, they'll expect the book form to automatically fill with the current contents of that book. The presenting view controller should pass in the book object to edit to the book edit view controller.

1 Define an optional book object in the `BookViewController` class:

```
var book: Book?
```

2 In the `viewDidLoad` method, the `BookViewController` should check if the book object exists, and if it does, prefill the fields. If a book object exists, you know that you're *editing* rather than *creating* a book. Take the opportunity to adjust the navigation bar's title accordingly. Be sure to fill the fields before checking if the Save button should be enabled.

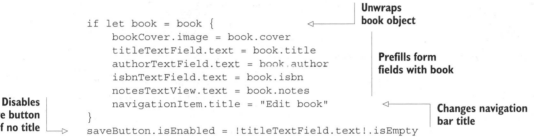

```
if let book = book {                              ◁────  Unwraps book object
    bookCover.image = book.cover
    titleTextField.text = book.title
    authorTextField.text = book.author            Prefills form fields with book
    isbnTextField.text = book.isbn
    notesTextView.text = book.notes
    navigationItem.title = "Edit book"            ◁────  Changes navigation bar title
}
saveButton.isEnabled = !titleTextField.text!.isEmpty
```

Disables Save button if no title

3 Now, the book view controller is ready to receive a book object and the books table view controller needs to pass it in when the user is editing a book. If the user has selected a row, you know the user is editing a book. In the `prepare-ForSegue` method of the `BooksTableViewController` class, check that there is a value in the table view's `indexPathForSelectedRow` property:

```
if let selectedIndexPath = tableView.indexPathForSelectedRow {
            //Editing
```

4 You need to unwrap a reference to the destination view controller. Because you've created the segue directly to the book view controller, it will be the destination view controller:

```
if let bookViewController = segue.destination
    as? BookViewController {
```

5 This time, as well as setting itself as the delegate, the table view controller will pass in the book to edit:

```
bookViewController.book = booksManager.getBook(at: selectedIndexPath.row)
bookViewController.delegate = self
```

After merging the `if` statements together, the full `prepareForSegue` method to pass the delegate and book data to the detail view controller will now look like this:

```
override func prepare(for segue: UIStoryboardSegue, sender: Any?) {
    if let selectedIndexPath = tableView.indexPathForSelectedRow,
        let bookViewController = segue.destination
            as? BookViewController {
        //Editing
        bookViewController.book =
            booksManager.getBook(at: selectedIndexPath.row)
        bookViewController.delegate = self
    } else if let navController = segue.destination
            as? UINavigationController,
        let bookViewController = navController.topViewController
            as? BookViewController {
        //Adding
        bookViewController.delegate = self
    }
}
```

9.3.3 *Removing the view controller*

If you run the app now, you'll find that the Cancel and Save buttons no longer dismiss the view controller. The `dismiss` method is appropriate for when a view controller has been presented, such as via a modal segue. The show segue *pushes* the view controller onto the navigation stack. When a view controller in a navigation stack wants to be removed, it needs to request this from the navigation controller, using the `popViewController` method.

You need to update the `dismissMe` method to check how the view controller was displayed to determine the appropriate method it should use to dismiss itself.

If the view controller was presented via a modal segue, the view controller's `presentingViewController` property will contain a value. If the view controller was pushed via a show segue, `presentingViewController` will be `nil`.

1   Check the `presentingViewController` property and dismiss the view controller appropriately:

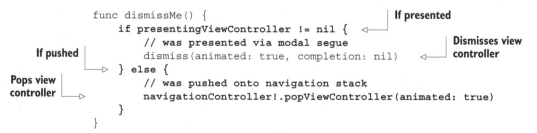

Similar to the way you can remove view controllers in code, they can also be displayed in code, rather than using storyboard segues. Table 9.1 shows the segues and their related methods.

Table 9.1 Displaying and removing a view controller

Managed by	Equivalent segue	Method to display	Method to remove
Navigation controller	Show	`pushViewController`	`popViewController`
View controller	Modal/Popover	`present`	`dismiss`

2 Run the app, tap a row, and then tap Save or Cancel.

The detail view controller should close. However, the Save button will add the book you're editing to the `books` array—not exactly what you're after!

9.3.4 *Updating the book object*

If the user is editing a book, you want to *update* the data for the book in the data source and the table, rather than add it.

1 Add a method to update a book to the `BooksManager` class:

```
func updateBook(at index: Int, with book: Book) {
    books[index] = book
}
```

Next, in the `saveBook` method in the `BooksTableViewController` extension, you want to check if the user is editing or adding a book before performing the relevant operation. You know if a row of the table is selected, the user is editing a book.

2 Unwrap this index path to determine which book in the array needs updating, and then reload the appropriate row in the table. Here's the updated `saveBook` method:

```
func saveBook(_ book: Book) {
    if let selectedIndexPath = tableView.indexPathForSelectedRow {
        // Update book
        booksManager.updateBook(at: selectedIndexPath.row, with: book)
    } else {
        // Add book
        booksManager.addBook(book)
    }
    tableView.reloadData()
}
```

3 Run the app, and you should now be able to edit a book!

9.4 *Using large titles*

The observant amongst you may have noticed that the title first navigation controller in the settings app back in figure 9.14 was in a large font. Since iOS 11, Apple has introduced large titles in navigation bars, and recommends that you use them, especially in the first scene in a navigation stack.

Add a large title to your Books Table View Controller.

1   Select the navigation bar of the Books Table View Controller's navigation controller, and select Prefers Large Titles in the attributes inspector.

This will set up large titles for this navigation controller's root view controller, and for each subsequent view controller in the navigation stack. As you're using a show segue to push the book detail view controller onto the navigation stack when the user edits a book, it will also by default use a large font. For a detail view controller however, the smaller title font is more appropriate.

2   Select the navigation bar and look for the Large Title attribute in the attributes inspector.

By default, it's set to Automatic, inheriting its font style.

3   Select Never to display the title of the book detail view controller in a smaller font.

9.5   Deleting a row

You can't let the user add rows without letting them delete! It's surprisingly straightforward to implement row deletion in tables with a fancy swipe mechanism (see figure 9.22).

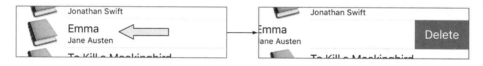

Figure 9.22   Swipe to delete row

The user swipes left to request a delete, and then continues swiping left or taps the Delete button to confirm (or taps the cell again to cancel).

1   First, add a `removeBook` method to the `BooksManager` to handle removing a book from the `books` array:

```
func removeBook(at index: Int) {
    books.remove(at: index)
}
```

Swiping left to delete is already built into table views in UIKit—when the user confirms they'd like to delete a row, a data source method will be called. All you need to do is override this method in `BooksTableViewController` and double-check that the user is requesting to delete a row.

2   You can now make the appropriate change to update both the data and the table, identifying the row to delete with the index path parameter. Request the

booksManager to remove the book from the books array, and the tableView to delete the row:

Checks user requested deletion

Removes book from table

Overrides table view method

Removes book from array

```
override func tableView(_ tableView: UITableView,
    commit editingStyle: UITableViewCellEditingStyle,
    forRowAt indexPath: IndexPath) {
    if editingStyle == .delete {
        booksManager.removeBook(at: indexPath.row)
        tableView.deleteRows(at: [indexPath], with: .fade)
    }
}
```

NOTE Surprisingly, overriding this method is all that's required for swiping to delete functionality to be enabled. This method will also be called if the user tries to move a row, if reordering of rows is enabled via the data source method canMoveRowAt.

3 Run the app and swipe left on a row.

4 Tap the Delete button that appears, and the row should disappear from the table.

Swiping row custom actions

Swiping rows isn't limited to just delete actions, nor just swiping to the left. Since iOS 11, you can implement all sorts of custom actions, swiping left or right, and with one or more actions available per swipe.

To implement custom actions on swipe, instantiate one or more UIContextual-Action objects, use these to instantiate a UISwipeActionsConfiguration object, and then return this object from data source methods for trailing and/or leading swipe actions. Swipe action buttons can be customized with images and different colors.

Our delete action, for example, could be rewritten as a custom swipe action:

Overrides table view method for trailing swipe

Creates UIContextualAction

Removes book from array

Calls completion handler indicating success

Returns UISwipeActionsConfiguration object

Removes book from table

```
override func tableView(_ tableView: UITableView,
    trailingSwipeActionsConfigurationForRowAt indexPath: IndexPath)
    -> UISwipeActionsConfiguration? {
  let deleteAction = UIContextualAction(style: .destructive,
    title: "Delete") {
      (contextAction: UIContextualAction,
      sourceView: UIView,
      completionHandler: (Bool) -> Void) in
    self.booksManager.removeBook(at: indexPath.row)
    self.tableView.deleteRows(at: [indexPath], with: .left)

    completionHandler(true)
  }
  return UISwipeActionsConfiguration(actions: [deleteAction])
}
```

✓ **CHECKPOINT**   If you'd like to compare your project with mine at this point, you can check mine out at https://github.com/iOSApp-DevelopmentwithSwiftinAction/Bookcase.git (Chapter9.2.EditDeleteBook).

9.6   *Summary*

In this chapter, you learned the following:

- To display data in a table view. At a minimum you need to answer three data source questions: how many sections are in the table, how many rows are in each section, and what cell goes in each row?
- Embed a view controller in a navigation controller to push a view controller onto the navigation stack. A navigation controller has the additional advantage of a navigation bar, where you can display a back button, additional controls, and information about the current view controller.
- Use show (push) segues to navigate to a scene that presents more information about the user's selection. Use a present (modal) segue to perform a self-contained operation.
- Use access control keywords *private* (restricted to file) and *public* (unrestricted) to change the access control from the default internal (restricted to module).
- Use `prepareForSegue` to pass data to a presented view controller. Pass data back to the presenting view controller with a delegate, via a closure, or with an unwind segue.

Collections, searching, sorting, and tab bars

10

This chapter covers
- Sorting and filtering data
- Displaying data in more-customizable layouts
- Using a tab bar to navigate between scenes

It's one thing to simply display and edit your data; it's another to *do* something with it—sort it, search it, or display it in a more visually interesting way.

In this chapter, you'll extend your Bookcase app. You'll add the ability to sort and search the books data, and you'll display the books in a more customized grid layout. You'll add a tab bar to navigate between the table view of books and your new grid view of books.

Specifically, we'll explore

- *Sorting the data*—You'll explore sorting your data and giving the user the ability to select the sort order with a *segmented control*.
- *Search controllers*—You'll use a search controller to add a search bar to a scene, filtering your data and displaying search results.

- *Collection views* and *collection view controllers*—*Collection views* manage a collection of data and display it in a customizable layout, such as a grid. Similar to table view controllers, *collection view controllers* handle part of the boilerplate setup for you.
- *Tab bar controllers*—*Tab bar controllers* are useful for managing the navigation between different sections of your app.

10.1   *Sorting the data*

Imagine when the Bookcase app takes off and people start adding hundreds of books to their collection. With all that data in the table, it's going to be impossible for the user to find the book they're looking for. You need to implement strategies to make it easier for the user to explore the books data.

You'll achieve this in two ways:

- Keep the data sorted.
- Add search capability.

We're going to first examine how to keep the data nicely sorted by title, and then we'll implement search by adding a search bar to the books scene.

✓   **CHECKPOINT**   Open the Bookcase project where you left it at the end of chapter 9, or check it out at https://github.com/iOSAppDevelopment-withSwiftinAction/Bookcase.git (Chapter9.2.EditDeleteBook).

Believe it or not, you're only going to have to make changes to the `BooksManager` class to keep the data nicely sorted.

10.1.1   *Creating a sort method to sort the books array*

Back in chapter 2, we looked at the `sorted` higher order function, which sorts an array and returns the result. This time, you'll use the `sort` function, which sorts an array directly. To indicate that you're going to modify the `books` array within the function, you should tag the parameter with the special `inout` keyword.

1   Add a sort method to the `BooksManager` class to sort the array.

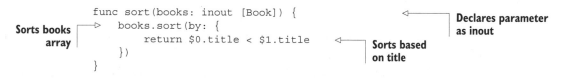

```
func sort(books: inout [Book]) {            ◁———  Declares parameter
    books.sort(by: {                              as inout
        return $0.title < $1.title      ◁——  Sorts based
    })                                       on title
}
```

Sorts books array

But what if two books have the same title? How can you also sort based on author as a secondary field? A solution for sorting two fields is to use a little tuple magic! Rather than comparing strings, you can compare tuples containing two strings.

```
return ($0.title, $0.author) < ($1.title, $1.author)
```

Another problem remains with this sort, however. Uppercase and lowercase characters are by default treated differently in comparisons, meaning that if the user enters a title beginning with a lowercase character, it will appear after all the other books. Furthermore, different locales have their own rules for sorting that must be considered. Fortunately, strings have a `localizedLowercase` property that's a more appropriate version for comparisons.

2 Add this property to the return call:

```
return ($0.title.localizedLowercase, $0.author.localizedLowercase) <
    ($1.title.localizedLowercase, $1.author.localizedLowercase)
```

Great, you have a way to sort the `books` array. Now the only question is, where in the `BooksManager` class do you need to call this method? The array must be sorted every time that it could be out of order. The array could be out of order in three places:

- After loading the sample data. Use the `sampleBooks` method in `BooksManager`.
- After adding a book. Use the `addBook` method in `BooksManager`.
- After updating a book. Use the `updateBook` method in `BooksManager`.

3 Call the sort method in each of these three methods, passing in the `books` array. To indicate that you're aware that the `inout` variable can be modified, you need to mark the argument with an ampersand (`&`):

```
sort(books: &books)
```

If you run your app now, you should find that the data stays nicely in order, even after you add a book or edit a book's title. But what if the user also wants to sort the table view by *author*?

10.1.2 Changing sort order

Because tables in iOS are single column, there's no built-in mechanism for changing the sort order. If you want your user to change the sort order, you'll have to implement this yourself.

ADDING A SEGMENTED CONTROL

The segmented control allows the user to choose between two or more options. Let's add a segmented control to enable the user to choose between title and author to sort the table (see figure 10.1).

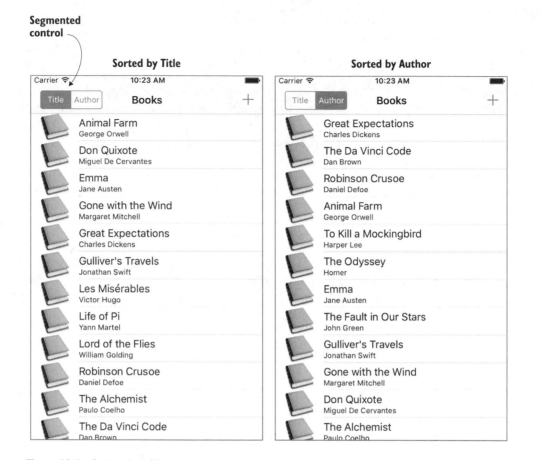

Figure 10.1   Sort order with segmented control

1   In the storyboard, find the segmented control in the Objects Inspector, and drop the segmented control directly into the table view controller's navigation bar on the left.

This will automatically embed the segmented control inside a *bar button item*. For a strange reason, the default style that Interface Builder gives the bar button item may produce a warning.

2   Change the bar button item's style to Bordered and the warning should go away. The segmented control will by default contain two segments.

3   Select the segmented control and open the Attributes Inspector. (Remember the Control-Shift-click trick to select the segmented control and not the bar button item.) The Segment attribute indicates which segment the other attributes relate to (see figure 10.2).

4 Select Segment 0, and give it the title "Title."

5 Select Segment 1, and give it the title "Author."

Figure 10.2 Segment attributes

Because the segmented control is a *control*, you can register a target action method to be called when the user changes a value.

6 With the storyboard open in the Assistant Editor, Control-drag from the segmented control to the `BooksTableViewController`, and create an action. Call it `changedSegment`. Be sure to change the type from the generic `Any` to `UISegmentedControl`. You should see this:

```
@IBAction func changedSegment(_ sender: UISegmentedControl) {
    // change sort order here
}
```

This method now needs to let the `BooksManager` know that you want the sort order changed, and to update the table.

UPDATING THE SORT ORDER

Let's update the `BooksManager` first to deal with changes in the sort order.

The sort order currently is by *title* (then *author*). You want to add a second sort order of *author* (then *title*). Who knows? Maybe at some point in the future, you might also like to add another sort order—perhaps sorting by *ISBN* or *rating*.

You need to set up a property in the `BooksManager` to record the current sort order. Swift has a useful data type you can take advantage of here called an *enumeration*.

Enumerations

An enumeration defines a group of related values. Perhaps you might want to store references to days of the week or monsters in your game. Storing values in an enumeration ensures type safety and prevents bugs such as spelling mistakes.

Enumerations are declared with the `enum` keyword, and each identifier in an enumeration is called a `case`. Cases don't need to store values. Here's an example of an enumeration of a `Monster`:

```
enum Monster {
    case blinky
    case pinky
    case inky
}
```

A variable can then be declared based on one of the cases of this enumeration:

```
let monster = Monster.blinky
```

Cases can be referred to with a dot prefix. For example:

```
if monster == .blinky {
    print("Color is red")
}
```

If an enumeration is declared to be a data type such as `String` or `Int`, each case will store a raw value. If no values are provided, Swift can imply the raw values. With `String` enumerations, cases are implied to store their name. With `Int` enumerations, cases are implied to store an incrementing value.

For example, here's an enumeration to store the sort order of your books:

```
enum SortOrder: Int {
    case title
    case author
}
```

The `title` case is implied to store a raw value of `0`, and the `author` case is implied to be `1`.

You can declare an enumeration with a type using the *raw value* of the case. Because this type of request could fail, an optional will be returned that will need unwrapping.

For example, the following would declare a `SortOrder` with the `title` case.

```
guard let sortOrder = SortOrder(rawValue: 0) else {return}
```

The power of enumerations is evident in `switch` statements. Because the enumeration type defines the exhaustive list of options for a group, Swift can ensure that `switch` statements are also exhaustive, without the need for a `default` case.

Here's a `switch` statement for the `sortOrder` property:

```
switch sortOrder {
case .title:
    print("sort titles first")
case .author:
    print("sort authors first")
}
```

1   Add the `SortOrder` enumeration to the BooksManager.swift file, but before the `BooksManager` class.

2   Add a `sortOrder` property to the `BooksManager` class that defaults to `.title` initially.

```
var sortOrder = SortOrder.title
```

3   You can now adjust the `sort` method to sort appropriately based on the current `sortOrder`:

```
switch sortOrder {
case .title:                          Sorts by title, then author
    books.sort(by: {
        return
            ($0.title.localizedLowercase,$0.author.localizedLowercase) <
            ($1.title.localizedLowercase,$1.author.localizedLowercase)
    })
case .author:                         Sorts by author, then title
    books.sort(by: {
        return
            ($0.author.localizedLowercase,$0.title.localizedLowercase) <
            ($1.author.localizedLowercase,$1.title.localizedLowercase)
    })
}
```

4   Back in the `BooksTableViewController` class, you can now set the `sortOrder` in the `changedSegment` method when the segmented control value changes. The indices of the segments coincide with the indices of the enumeration, so you can instantiate a `SortOrder` enumeration directly from the segmented control's selected index. You can then pass this straight into the `booksManager`, and request the table to reload.

```
guard let sortOrder = SortOrder(rawValue: sender.selectedSegmentIndex)
    else {return}
booksManager.sortOrder = sortOrder
tableView.reloadData()
```

If you ran your app now, selecting a different sort order wouldn't trigger the data to be sorted. The BooksManager has to call the `sort` method whenever the `sortOrder` changes. There's a trick in Swift for detecting when a property changes, called a *property observer*. (More on property observers in the sidebar "Property observers.")

5   You want the data to be sorted every time the `sortOrder` property is changed. Add the `didSet` property observer to the `sortOrder` property:

```
var sortOrder: SortOrder = .title {
    didSet {
        sort(books:&books)
    }
}
```

6   Run the app now and tap Author in the segmented control. The table should automatically be ordered by author. Done!

Property observers

You can use *property observers* to perform an action every time the value of a property is set. You have a choice of two property observers:

- `didSet` is called immediately after a property is set.
- `willSet` is called immediately before a property is set.

CHECKPOINT   If you'd like to compare your project with mine at this point, you can check mine out at https://github.com/iOSAppDevelopment-withSwiftinAction/Bookcase.git (Chapter10.1.Sort).

10.2   Searching the data

Let's now add search capability to the app. You'll add a search bar between the table view and the navigation bar. When the user taps on the search bar to enter text, the search bar will transition up to replace the navigation bar, and text entered into the search bar will filter the rows (see figure 10.3).

**Figure 10.3
Search bar**

10.2.1 *Creating a search controller*

To build up this search capability, you'll need a UISearchController. This class works hard for you: it instantiates a search bar for displaying, handles interactions with the search bar, transitions movements of the search bar, optionally displays a second view controller where you can display search results, and notifies you via a delegate every time the search text changes. What the UISearchController class *doesn't* do, however, is search your data for you—this is something you'll need to do for yourself.

NOTE In iOS 8, Apple deprecated the UISearchDisplayController class and replaced it with a shiny new UISearchController class. That's fine, but at the time of writing, the shiny new search controller hasn't yet been updated in the Interface Builder object library. To use the updated class, you'll need to do it in code.

1 In your BooksTableViewController class, instantiate a new UISearch-Controller. Pass it nil for searchResultsController to indicate that you don't want it to navigate to another view controller to display the results—you're going to show the results in the same view controller.

```
let searchController = UISearchController(searchResultsController: nil)
```

Now, you need to configure how the search controller works. By default, when the user taps in the search bar, the table view is grayed out, but you want the user to still select and delete rows while they're searching.

2 Turn this feature off in the viewDidLoad method:

```
searchController.obscuresBackgroundDuringPresentation = false
```

By default, the search bar will remain in the navigation bar when the user navigates to a new scene.

3 Turn this off, too:

```
searchController.definesPresentationContext = true
```

4 Great, now you can set the BooksTableViewController as the search controller's delegate, called searchResultsUpdater.

```
searchController.searchResultsUpdater = self
```

5 As usual, the class needs to adopt the delegate protocol and implement any required methods in the protocol.

```
extension BooksTableViewController: UISearchResultsUpdating {
    func updateSearchResults(for searchController: UISearchController)
    {
        // filter data here
    }
}
```

The `updateSearchResults` method is called every time the text in the search bar changes.

10.2.2 *Adding the search controller to the view controller*

Now that you've created your search controller, you have two options for adding it to a table view controller:

- Table views have optional header and footer views available for additional content. One approach is to add the search controller's search bar to the table view's header view.

  ```
  tableView.tableHeaderView = searchController.searchBar
  ```

- A second, newer approach is to embed the search controller into the navigation bar.

  ```
  navigationItem.searchController = searchController
  ```

See figure 10.4 to compare the two. The search controller in the navigation bar looks more tightly integrated into the interface, but is only available from iOS 11, meaning that your app would be unavailable to devices on earlier versions of iOS.

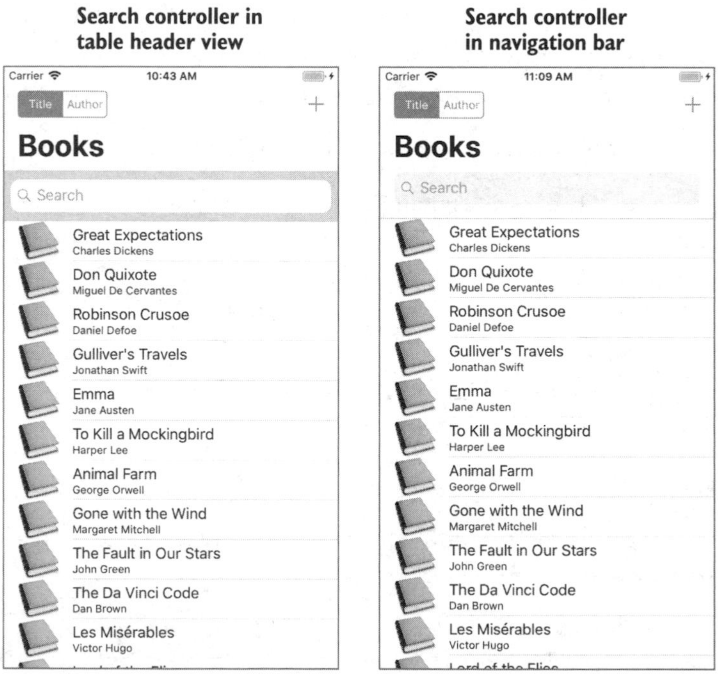

Figure 10.4   Search controller alternative approaches

> ### ◢ Checking if an API is available
>
> Should you dive into the new API or use the old API to support older versions of iOS? You have three main options here:
>
> - Only support versions of iOS from where the new API was introduced by changing the deployment target in your project's General settings. The disadvantage of this alternative is that users who haven't updated iOS can't download your app. Apple's App Store page gives you the percentage of devices with different versions of iOS installed to help you make an informed decision on your minimum deployment target.
> - Continue to use the older API until you decide that a sufficient percentage of users are using the version of iOS that the new API requires.
> - Use the special keyword #available to specify that a section of code is only to be used for a specific version of iOS.

Let's use the #available keyword to specify that if the user has iOS 11, the search-Controller will be added to the navigationBar, using the newer API. If the user is still running a version of iOS lower than 11, the search controller would be added to the table view's header view.

1   Add the search controller to the table view controller, using the #available keyword to match the appropriate API with the user's iOS version.

2   Run your app.

You should see the search bar working perfectly—well, except for one little detail: when you enter text in the search bar, the data in the table view doesn't change! Let's do something about that.

10.2.3 *Filtering the data*

Now that the search controller is set up and you're receiving a notification every time the search text changes, you can filter the data in the table view.

To maintain the model and the controller as separate as possible, let's filter the data in the BooksManager class. First, the BooksManager will need to know what you're searching on.

1   Add a variable to the `BooksManager` class that will receive the current search string. When this variable is set, the `BooksManager` uses it to filter the data. You'll create the `filter` method next.

```
var searchFilter = "" {                        When variable is set
    didSet {
        filter()
    }                              Filter the data
}
```

2   You can now use the higher order filter function to filter the `books` array based on the search text. You only want books to appear in the `filteredBooks` array if their `title` or `author` properties contain the search text.

Use the `localizedLowercase` string property again to ensure that case or other local considerations such as accents don't affect the search.

```
func filter() {                                              Higher-order
    filteredBooks = books.filter { book in                  filter function
        return book.title.localizedLowercase.contains(
            searchFilter.localizedLowercase) ||
            book.author.localizedLowercase.contains(        Checks author
                searchFilter.localizedLowercase)            contains searchFilter
    }
}
```

Checks title contains searchFilter

3   The `updateSearchResults` method in the `UISearchResultsUpdating` extension of `BooksTableViewController` can now pass in the new search filter text to the `BooksManager`. After passing in this text, the `BooksManager` should freshly filter the data, so the table view can reload here.

```
guard let searchText =                                  Unwraps search
    searchController.searchBar.text else { return }     text from search bar
booksManager.searchFilter = searchText            Passes search text
tableView.reloadData()                            to BooksManager

        Reloads table view
```

That's all you need to do in the `BooksTableViewController`. Now, you need to ensure that the `BooksManager` deals with filtered data when the `searchFilter` variable contains text.

4   Add a second array in the `BooksManager` that holds an array of filtered books:

```
var filteredBooks: [Book] = []
```

You now need to adjust how the `BooksManager` reports on the number of books the table should display and the data in each row. If text appears in the search filter, the `BooksManager` should get this information from the `filteredBooks` array. Otherwise, if the user *isn't* currently searching, the `BooksManager` should return this information from the full `books` array.

5 Make the appropriate adjustments:

```
var bookCount: Int {
    return searchFilter.isEmpty ? books.count : filteredBooks.count
}
func getBook(at index: Int) -> Book {
    return searchFilter.isEmpty ? books[index] : filteredBooks[index]
}
```

10.2.4 Removing and updating rows with filtered data

If you run the app now and enter text in the search bar, the table should update with only books whose titles or authors contain the search text. However, if you try to edit or delete a row, things will start to go badly—in fact, the app may even crash! See figure 10.5. What's going on?

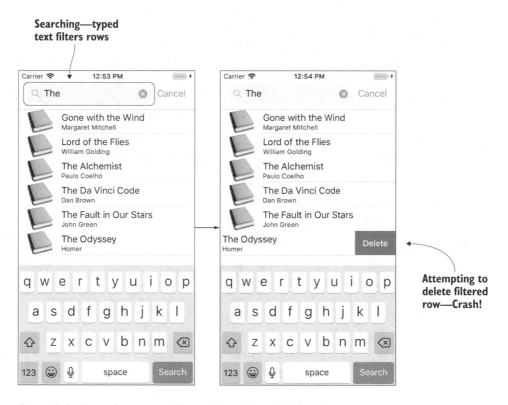

Figure 10.5   Removing a row while searching can crash the app!

If the `searchFilter` isn't empty, the table view is updated from the `filteredBooks` array. The index then being passed to the `removeBook` and `updateBook` methods relates to the index in the `filteredBooks` array; but currently the `BooksManager` is using this index to update or delete a row in the `books` array, and that's not right!

REMOVING A ROW WITH FILTERED DATA

When the user searches the table and selects to remove a row, you need to remove this item from the `filteredBooks` array and then determine the correct item to remove in the `books` array.

1 First, update the `removeBook` method in the `BooksManager` to check if the `searchFilter` is empty and remove the book from the correct array.

```
func removeBook(at index: Int) {
    if searchFilter.isEmpty {
        books.remove(at: index)
    } else {
        filteredBooks.remove(at: index) //incomplete
    }
}
```

You're not done, however. Even if the user is currently searching, you still need to remove the book from the `books` array. The `remove` method from an `Array` returns the object being removed.

2 Use the book object returned from the `remove` method to find the returned book in the `books` array and remove it from there, too:

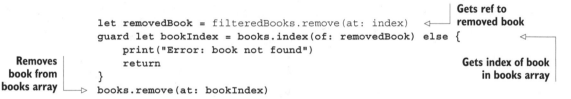

```
let removedBook = filteredBooks.remove(at: index)       ◁──── Gets ref to removed book
guard let bookIndex = books.index(of: removedBook) else {       ◁────
    print("Error: book not found")
    return                                              Gets index of book
}                                                        in books array
books.remove(at: bookIndex)
```

Removes book from books array

MAKING AN OBJECT EQUATABLE

You'll find a compiler error appear on the `guard` statement: Cannot invoke 'index' with an argument list of type '(of: Book)'.

This tells you that Swift doesn't know how to determine if two books are equal or how to find a book's index in an array of books. For example, if two books have the same properties, are they equal? Or perhaps they need to point to the same memory address (in the case of reference types)?

To tell Swift how to determine the index of an object in an array, you need to do two things:

1 Overload the `==` operator for the object type to explain how to determine if two objects are equal. Because two books are equal if all their properties are equal, compare each property in the overloaded `==` operator for `Book`. Add the following to the Book.swift file, but outside the class:

```
func ==(lhs: Book, rhs: Book) -> Bool {
    return (
        lhs.title == rhs.title &&
        lhs.author == rhs.author &&
        lhs.rating == rhs.rating &&
        lhs.isbn == rhs.isbn &&
        lhs.notes == rhs.notes &&
        lhs.cover == rhs.cover
    )
}
```

2 The object must adopt the `Equatable` protocol. That's easy enough! All you
   need to do is add an extension to the `Book` structure:

```
extension Book: Equatable {}
```

The only requirement that the `Equatable` protocol has is an implementation of the
`==` operator for the class or struct that implements it, and you've done that!

UPDATING A ROW WITH FILTERED DATA

If you ran your app now and typed text into the search bar, you could remove a book,
but if you tried to update a book, you would probably find you've updated the wrong
book!

   If the user is currently searching the table (the search filter isn't empty), you need
to find the index of the book to update in the `books` array.

   Update the `updateBook` method in your `BooksManager` class.

```
func updateBook(at index: Int, with book: Book) {
    if searchFilter.isEmpty {
        books[index] = book
        sort(books: &books)                              ◁──── Gets ref to book
    } else {                                                    to update
        let bookToUpdate = filteredBooks[index]    ◁──
        guard let bookIndex = books.index(of: bookToUpdate) else {
            print("Error: book not found")
            return
        }
        books[bookIndex] = book        ◁──── Updates book
        sort(books: &books)                  in books array
        filter()
    }

}
```

Gets index of book in books array — points to the `guard let bookIndex` line

Notice that after sorting the `books` array, you'll want to refilter the `filteredBooks`
array, because the order may have changed.

> **NOTE** *Adding* a row doesn't need any adjustments after adding search to the
> app! Because the search bar moves to the navigation bar when the user is
> searching, it's only possible to add a row when you're not searching.

Run the app and, with fingers crossed, you should find that search is fully operational within your app. Play around with adding, updating, and deleting rows to confirm.

✓ **CHECKPOINT** If you'd like to compare your project with mine at this point, you can check mine out at https://github.com/iOSAppDevelopment-withSwiftinAction/Bookcase.git (Chapter10.2.SearchSort).

The table of books is certainly a practical view for exploring the data, but when the user starts adding cover images, wouldn't a more visual approach also be appropriate?

10.3 *Displaying data in collection views*

You're going to add a secondary scene for the Bookcase app that displays the book cover images in a grid format. If a book cover isn't available for a book, a gray default cover will appear with the title of the book (see figure 10.6).

You can display a customizable layout, such as a grid, using a *collection view.* After working with table views, you'll find that collection views feel familiar:

- A *collection view controller* can be used to handle part of the boilerplate setup of a collection view.
- You need to implement data source methods to determine the number of sections and number of items in each section, and return a cell for each item.
- You need to *dequeue* cells. You can do this by setting up a reusable cell in the storyboard and giving it a reuse identifier.

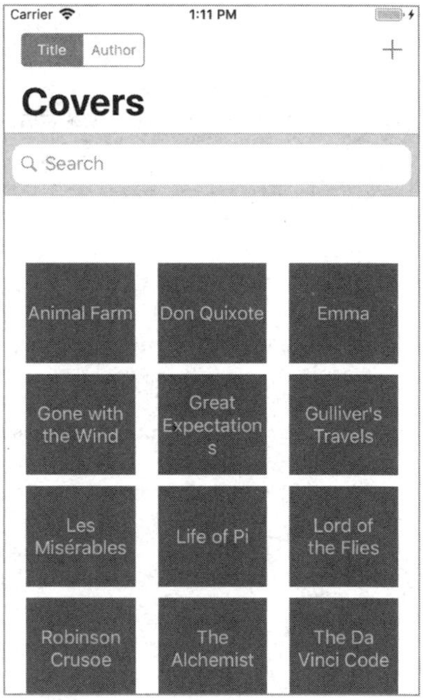

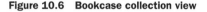

Figure 10.6   Bookcase collection view

CHALLENGE Using what you've learned about table view controllers, set up a basic collection view controller that will show as many cells as books. Follow the steps to guide you through the process. You should end up with something like figure 10.7.

1 Add a collection view controller to the storyboard, and set it as the initial view controller. Xcode will warn you that your navigation controller is unreachable now, but don't worry, you'll resolve this shortly.
2 Give the collection view a white background, and give the prototype cell a dark gray background, and the reuse identifier bookCollectionCell.

3 In the Size Inspector for the collection view, give the cells a width and height of 80. Inset the content from the margins by setting the section insets to 20 in all four directions.

4 Create a subclass of `UICollection-ViewController` called `Books-CollectionViewController`, and connect it up to the collection view controller in the Identity Inspector in the storyboard.

5 In the class you set up, comment out the call to the `register` method in the `viewDidLoad` method.

In both the table view controller and collection view controllers, the `register` method is used to register a class to use for a specific reuse identifier. Because you're defining your prototype cell in the storyboard, this step isn't necessary and, in fact, will quietly remove the connection to the storyboard prototype cell.

Figure 10.7 Basic collection view

Next, you need to customize the three data source methods.

6 The number of sections is simple—as with the table view controller, you'll use one section, so you can return 1. To customize the remaining two data source methods, you need a `booksManager` property.

7 Instantiate a `booksManager` in your `BooksCollectionViewController` class.

8 Use the `bookCount` property of the `booksManager` you set up to determine the number of items in the collection to complete the `numberOfItemsIn-Section` delegate method.

9 Make sure to use the `reuseIdentifier` bookCollectionCell in the `cell-ForItemAt` method. (Feel free to modify the `reuseIdentifier` constant that this template uses). Don't worry about configuring these cells; we'll come back to that in a moment.

10 Run the app, and you should see the layout in figure 10.7.

✔ **CHECKPOINT** If you'd like to compare your project with mine at this point, you can check mine out at https://github.com/iOSApp-DevelopmentwithSwiftinAction/Bookcase.git (Chapter10.3.CollectionView-InitialSetup).

Obviously, the cells need customization—gray rectangles won't do!

Not much customization is possible on the collection view prototype cell. Unlike table view prototype cells, no labels or images are ready to use in the cell. You have to create your own custom cell.

10.3.1 *Creating custom collection cells*

You're going to create a custom cell that will display the image cover in an image view. If there isn't a cover image for the book, it will instead display the book title in a label inside a gray default cover.

1 In the storyboard, drag the image view to the collection view prototype cell.
2 Pin each of the four sides to the cell in the Add New Constraints menu (see figure 10.8).

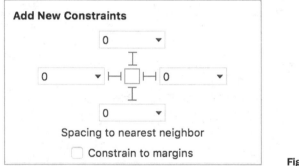

Figure 10.8   Pin sides

3 Drag in a label, too, and pin each of its sides to the edges of the cell.
4 Adjust the attributes for the label in the Attribute Inspector. Give the label a light gray color, center the text, remove the default text "Label," and for the Lines attribute, specify 0.

NOTE   Zero lines isn't as silly as it sounds—it's telling the label to use as many lines as required.

Now you need to create a custom class for the cell.

5 Create a Cocoa Touch class called BookCollectionViewCell, based on UICollectionViewCell.
6 Back in the storyboard, connect the prototype cell to the class you created in the Identity Inspector. To update the text in the label or the image in the image view, you need to set up outlets in the BookCollectionViewCell class.
7 Create outlets called imageView and titleLabel.

TIP   When you open the Assistant Editor and select either the image view or the title label in the document outline, the BookCollectionViewCell class should become available as a secondary automatic class in the jump bar. If the class doesn't appear in the automatic options, you can always drill down to it using the manual option (see figure 10.9).

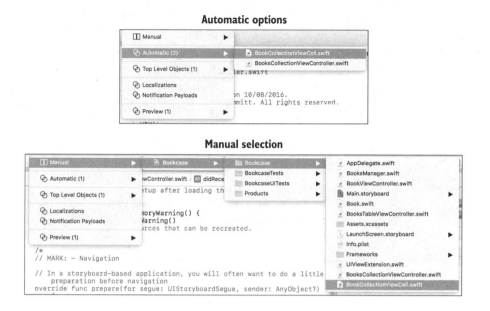

Figure 10.9   Jump bar automatic versus manual file selection

You now have a custom collection view cell ready to use in your collection view controller!

10.3.2 *Displaying data in a custom collection view cell*

Let's see if your custom cell is working.

1   Open the `BooksCollectionViewController` class, and locate the "Configure the Cell" section. Because you've defined the prototype cell in the storyboard to subclass your `BookCollectionViewCell` class, you know that the cell you dequeue with a `bookCollectionCell` reuse identifier is going to be your custom cell class.

2   Force downcast the cell:

```
let cell = collectionView.dequeueReusableCell(withReuseIdentifier:
    reuseIdentifier, for: indexPath) as! BookCollectionViewCell
```

3   The same way you did in the related section in the `BooksTableView-Controller` class, get a reference to the relevant book object for this cell based on the index path:

```
let book = booksManager.getBook(at: indexPath.row)
```

4   Now, you can pass the book cover image into the image view you set up in your custom cell:

```
cell.imageView.image = book.cover
```

If you run the app now, you should see that the gray rectangles have been replaced by cover images for each of the books (see figure 10.10).

None of the books have a cover image yet, so you only see default blank cover images, which doesn't give any indication which book is which! When a book doesn't have a cover image, let's display its title instead.

5   First, add a property to the `Book` structure to be able to check if it has a cover image:

```
var hasCoverImage: Bool {
    return image != nil
}
```

6   Now, back in the collection view controller, you can check this property to determine whether to display text in the label and hide the image view:

```
cell.titleLabel.text = book.hasCoverImage ? "" : book.title
cell.imageView.isHidden = !book.hasCoverImage
```

Run the app, and you should see, as in figure 10.11, titles displayed for all books that don't have cover images (all of them!). When you add cover images to books in chapter 13, this screen will look much prettier!

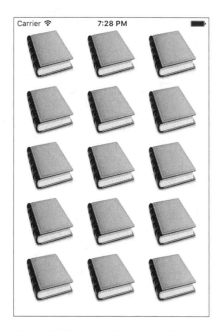

Figure 10.10   Collection view with custom cells

Figure 10.11   Collection view with custom cells

10.3.3 *Implementing a flow layout*

Collection views have a `Layout` attribute that defines how the items are to be laid out. You can select the custom layout to define your own layout style, providing endless possibilities to customize the collection view. A preconfigured layout style called *Flow* is available that allows you to build up your items in a grid. Collection views with Flow layout have the option to scroll horizontally or vertically.

If you open the Attribute Inspector for the collection view, you'll notice that by default your collection is already set to a Flow layout with vertical scrolling (see figure 10.12).

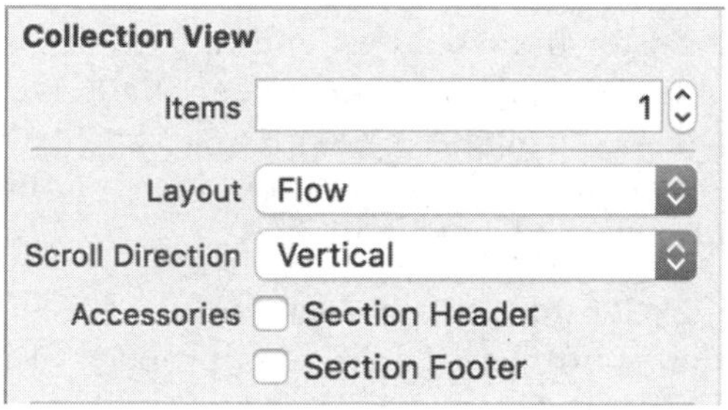

Figure 10.12   Collection view attributes

10.3.4 *Adding a search bar to the collection view*

As you saw when searching the table view controller, you either add the search controller to the navigation bar for iOS 11, or use a search bar as the table header view for prior to iOS 11. Unfortunately, at the time of writing, the iOS 11 technique of adding a search controller to the navigation bar in a collection view doesn't seem to be working, and collection views don't have an equivalent to the table header view. There is a workaround, however! Collection views with the Flow layout style do have optional *section* header views. If you only have one section, this works fine as a header view for the whole collection view that can be used to hold the search bar.

Notice in the Attribute Inspector for the collection view that your section doesn't have a section header.

1 Check the Section Header to add a search bar. When you check Section Header, you should notice a header appear in the collection table view. (If you don't, select Editor > Refresh All Views.) Like cells, this header has a reuse identifier.

2 Select the header, and in the Attributes Inspector, give it an identifier of collectionHeader.

   Section headers work differently than the `tableHeaderView`. Rather than implementing the header by replacing a collection view property, you need to implement another data source method that returns a dequeued view (similar to the table and collection view cells).

3 Add the following method to your `BooksCollectionViewController` class:

```
// MARK: Header
override func collectionView(_ collectionView: UICollectionView,
        viewForSupplementaryElementOfKind kind: String,
        at indexPath: IndexPath) -> UICollectionReusableView {
    let reusableView =
        collectionView.dequeueReusableSupplementaryView(ofKind: kind,
        withReuseIdentifier: "collectionHeader", for: indexPath)
    // Customize reusable view here
    return reusableView
}
```

A blank header view should now appear ready to display a search bar.

CHALLENGE   The same way you did for the table view controller, instantiate and configure the search controller. Adopt the `UISearchResultsUpdating` protocol to receive and respond to the `updateSearchResults` method. Don't worry about adding the search bar yet because this is done a little differently in a collection view controller; we'll look at that next.

NOTE   The collection view controller has an optional `collectionView` property, but unlike the table view controller's `tableView` property, it isn't implicitly unwrapped. You need to use optional chaining to reload the collection view: `collectionView?.reloadData()`.

4 Now that you have a search controller, you can add its search bar to the reusable view as a subview, before returning the reusable view.

```
reusableView.addSubview(searchController.searchBar)
```

5 Run the app, and you should find that a search bar appears in the header view.

✓   **CHECKPOINT**   If you'd like to compare your project with mine at this point, you can check mine out here: https://github.com/iOSApp-DevelopmentwithSwiftinAction/Bookcase.git (Chapter10.4.CollectionViewSearchBarInitial).

But Houston, there's a problem. Notice that when you tap the search bar once, the keyboard appears and disappears. Tapping it again will make the keyboard appear, but after you've typed two letters, the keyboard disappears again. What's going on?

The `reloadData` method (which is triggered whenever the search bar becomes first responder or the user edits the search text) doesn't just reload the data—unfortunately, it *also* reloads supplementary views for the section, reloading the header. When the header is reloaded, the search controller gets resigned as first responder, and the keyboard is dismissed.

This is one of those moments where, as an iOS developer, you may need to be creative to get around a limitation of the UIKit framework.

10.3.5 *Creating a second section*

The `reloadData` method isn't the only way to reload the data in your collection. The `reloadSections` method will load only the data in a section. To avoid having your section header reload, you could move your book data to a second section, and then only reload that section:

1 To begin with, your `numberOfSections` method should now return 2:

```
override func numberOfSections(in collectionView: UICollectionView) -> Int
{
  return 2
}
```

2 Your `numberOfItemsInSection` should also specify the correct amount depending on the section number:

```
override func collectionView(_ collectionView: UICollectionView,
    numberOfItemsInSection section: Int) -> Int {
  return section == 0 ? 0 : booksManager.bookCount
}
```

Because the `numberOfItemsInSection` method returns 0 for the first section, the `cellForItemAt` method will never be called for the first section, so you won't need to make any modifications to that method.

Now, you want to only add the search bar to the section header view for the first section.

3 Add the following condition in the `viewForSupplementaryElementOfKind` method:

```
if indexPath.section == 0 {
  reusableView.addSubview(searchController.searchBar)
}
```

Now that you've moved your data to the collection view's second section, you'll need to ensure that only the second section is reloaded when the search results are updated.

4 Replace your `reloadData` method with `reloadSections`:

```
collectionView?.reloadSections(NSIndexSet(index: 1) as IndexSet)
```

Run your app again, and this time your search bar should work great! However, because the collection view thinks it needs to make room for two section headers, the content begins a little way down the screen.

How can you tweak these sorts of details in this flow layout?

10.3.6 *Implementing the flow layout delegate*

You can further customize how your collection view flow layout looks by implementing methods in the flow layout delegate.

1 Add an extension to your `BooksCollectionViewController` class that adopts the flow layout delegate:

```
extension BooksCollectionViewController:
➡ UICollectionViewDelegateFlowLayout
{
}
```

2 Specify the size of the header for both sections in the `referenceSizeFor-HeaderInSection` method:

Implements delegate method
```
func collectionView(_ collectionView: UICollectionView, layout
    collectionViewLayout: UICollectionViewLayout,
    referenceSizeForHeaderInSection section: Int) -> CGSize {
  if section == 0 {
    return searchController.searchBar.bounds.size      ◁—— Returns search |
  } else {                                                     section 0
    return CGSize.zero        ◁—— Returns zero size
  }                                   for section I
}
```

While you're working in the flow layout delegate, let's adjust the sizes of the book cover images. Ideally, each item in your collection will have the same proportions as the book cover image.

3 Implement a delegate method to adjust the size of each book cover image individually:

Implements delegate method
Sets standard height
Derives width from cover image
```
func collectionView(_ collectionView: UICollectionView,
        layout collectionViewLayout: UICollectionViewLayout,
        sizeForItemAt indexPath: IndexPath) -> CGSize {
    let book = booksManager.getBook(at: indexPath.row)     ◁——  Gets book for
    let itemHeight:CGFloat = 90                                    index path
    let itemWidth = (book.cover.size.width /
      book.cover.size.height) * itemHeight
    return CGSize(width: itemWidth, height: itemHeight)    ◁—— Returns item size
  }
}
```

✓ **CHECKPOINT** If you'd like to compare your project with mine at this point, you can check mine out at https://github.com/iOSApp-DevelopmentwithSwiftinAction/Bookcase.git (Chapter10.5.CollectionView-SearchBar).

NAVIGATION CHALLENGE   Your collection view controller is looking good, but it's not yet hooked up to the detail view controller! The same way you did with the table view controller, embed the collection view controller in a navigation controller and create segues to add or edit a book. You'll need to implement the *prepare for segue* method and adopt your `BookViewControllerDelegate` to save books.

SORT CHALLENGE   Now that your collection view controller has a navigation controller, add the segmented control to the navigation bar to adjust the sort order of books, the way you did earlier for the table view controller. You'll need to add an action to respond to user interaction on the segmented control.

Organize your project

It's a great idea to keep your project clear and tidy by organizing your classes in the Project Navigator sorted into *Model, View,* or *Controller* categories. The way you did in chapter 1, select the three view controller classes in the Project Navigator, right-click, select *New Group from Selection*, and call the group "Controller." The Book.swift and BooksManager.swift files could go into the Model group and the UIViewExtension.swift and BookCollectionViewCell.swift files would qualify for the View group. As you progress through the book, try to keep new files categorized into one of these groups. This will also help you be clear about the role and responsibilities of each class.

Ah, that's better! Your Project Navigator should now look much more organized.

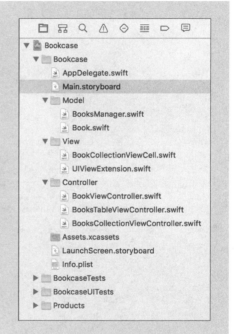

✓ **CHECKPOINT**   If you'd like to compare your project with mine at this point, you can check mine out at https://github.com/iOSApp-DevelopmentwithSwiftinAction/Bookcase.git (Chapter10.6.CollectionView).

The books collection scene is working great, but hmm ... something's wrong.

The storyboard of your app should be looking something like figure 10.13. Note that you currently have no way to navigate to the books table scene! In fact, Xcode will warn you that several view controllers have no "entry points." What can you do about this? A useful way to switch between different sections of your app is called the *tab bar controller.*

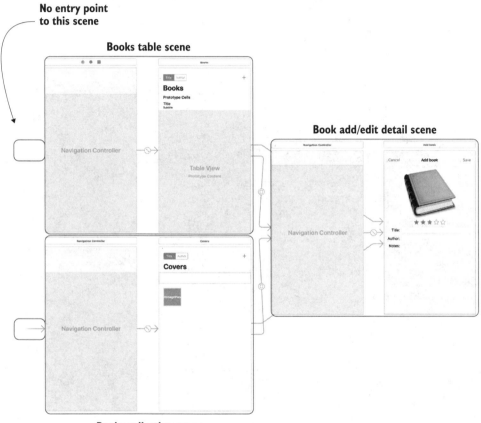

No entry point to this scene

Books table scene

Book add/edit detail scene

Books collection scene

Figure 10.13   App storyboard

10.4   *Creating sections with a tab bar controller*

A tab bar is displayed at the bottom of the app window and is typically used to navigate between different sections of your app. Tab bars contain a series of *tab bar items* with titles and images that change color when the tab is selected. Like a segmented control, only one tab can be selected at a time. See figure 10.14 for a few example tab bars in Apple iOS apps.

The most convenient way to implement a tab bar is via a *tab bar controller*. A tab bar controller is a container view controller that manages navigation between multiple content view controllers when different tabs are selected in the tab bar.

Figure 10.14 Tab bars in Apple apps

You'll implement a tab bar controller in the Bookcase app to navigate between the books table scene and the book covers collection scene (see figure 10.15).

Implementing a tab bar controller is simple:

1 Select the navigation controller for the table view controller and select Editor > Embed in > Tab bar controller. Everything should move over, and a tab bar controller will appear to the left of the navigation controller.

   Now, you'll need to edit the title and image for the tab bar item. The content view controller provides the tab bar item to the tab bar controller, so you'll need to edit the attributes of the tab bar item by selecting it in the navigation controller. Apple provides several standard tab bar items that you can explore in the *System Item* attribute, but you're going to create a *Custom* tab bar item.

2 Select the tab bar item, and type "Books" for the title. You'll leave the tab bar item images blank for now (represented in the storyboard by a blue square), and come back to them when we look at graphics in chapter 12.

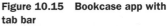

Tab bar

Figure 10.15 Bookcase app with tab bar

Next, you'll embed the navigation controller for the collection view controller in the same tab bar controller.

3 Hold down Control and drag from anywhere on the tab bar controller to the navigation controller. A segue menu will pop up.

4 Select a *Relationship Segue* by selecting view controllers. A second tab bar item should appear in the tab bar controller.

5 Select the tab bar item in the second navigation controller, and name it "Covers."

6 Select the tab bar controller as the initial view controller for the storyboard.

Note the change to the flow of the app in the storyboard in figure 10.16. (I've rearranged my storyboard to make the flow clearer.) It's clear the user can now navigate to either books scene.

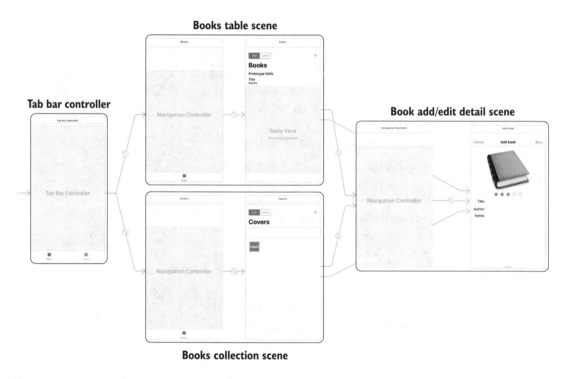

Figure 10.16   Storyboard with tab bar controller

Run the app, and you should see a tab bar appear at the bottom of the window, which you can use to navigate between the two books scenes.

10.4.1 Sharing data between tabs

Notice that if you edit a book in one tab and then go to the other tab, your edits seem to have disappeared. Each tab is currently creating its own books manager and therefore its own set of data—producing two books arrays, or one for each tab. How can you ensure that both tabs use the same set of data?

Sharing data between view controllers is a theme that often pops up in iOS development. We've already looked at strategies for passing data when navigating with segues, but tab bars are a different beast altogether. As you've seen, they have *relationship* segues with their scenes, which don't trigger the prepareForSegue method.

Several alternative solutions exist for sharing data between tabs, each with their own pros and cons:

- Global variables
- Singletons
- Dependency injection

Figure 10.17 demonstrates the difference between the different relationships in each alternative.

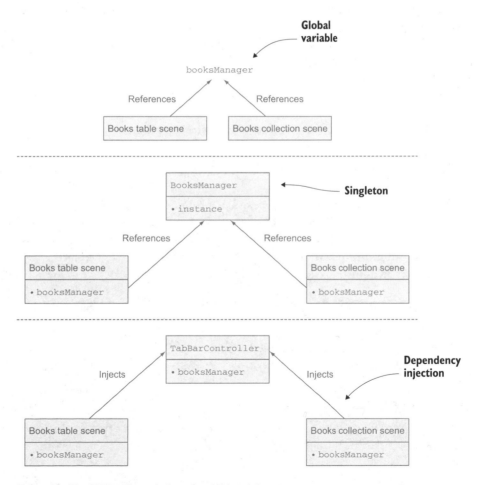

Figure 10.17 Alternative solutions for sharing data

You'll implement *dependency injection* in your app, but first let's have a quick look at the alternatives.

GLOBAL VARIABLES

If you create a variable outside of a class or struct, it's automatically defined in the global scope, available from anywhere in your project.

All that's required to implement this solution is to remove the instantiation of the `booksManager` from both the `BooksTableViewController` and `Books-CollectionViewController` classes, and instead instantiate it in the global scope. You could, for example, create a GlobalVars.swift file, that contains

```
var booksManager = BooksManager()
```

The books view controllers would then automatically reference the `booksManager` property in the global scope.

When the user navigates away from a tab, the related view controller will remain in memory. If the data is edited while the user is on a different tab, this change in data won't be represented when the user returns. To ensure the table or collection is up to date when the user returns, you'll probably want to request them to reload in the `viewDidAppear` method.

Plenty has been written over the years about the dangers of global variables: they create possible conflicts, make unit testing difficult, and make code more difficult to understand and harder to maintain. It's good to know the possibilities, but use global variables with care and look for alternatives where possible!

SINGLETONS

Singletons enforce that an object has been instantiated once and only once by maintaining its own instance internally.

It's straightforward to convert a class to a singleton in Swift. All a class requires is a type property containing a reference to an instance of the class. You could make the singleton's initializer private to ensure it can only be referenced from this instance property and not reinstantiated.

The following listing demonstrates how to convert `BooksManager` to a singleton.

Listing 10.1   Convert `BooksManager` to singleton

```
class BooksManager {
    static let instance = BooksManager()          ◁──────  Create shared
    private init() {}                             ◁──             instance
    lazy var books: [Book] = self.loadBooks()
    // etc                                        Prevent reinstantiation
}
```

The `BooksTableViewController` and `BooksCollectionViewController` classes no longer instantiate a `BooksManager`; rather, they access it via the `instance` property:

```
var booksManager = BooksManager.instance
```

Like the global variables solution, in this solution, view controllers won't receive notification when the user updates data in another tab, and you'll want to reload the table or collection views in the `viewDidAppear` method.

Plenty has been written about the dangers of singletons, too. Connections between different parts of your app can be obscured, making your app difficult to maintain and test. Future scenarios where perhaps multiple users require multiple libraries of books will consequently require significant refactoring.

Whatever your opinion on singletons, there's no question that they're ubiquitous in iOS. The iOS notification center, the file manager, the compass, the screen—even the application itself contains a singleton. I suggest that singletons can be useful depending on the scale of a project, but use with caution, being aware of their drawbacks.

DEPENDENCY INJECTION

With dependency injection, an object can *inject* a dependency such as data or a service into another object.

Let's use dependency injection to inject the `booksManager` into the two books scenes. Because the tab bar controller controls both books scenes, it makes sense to instantiate the `booksManager` in a subclass of the `UITabBarController` and then inject it into the scenes when required.

1 Remove the instantiation of the books manager in the `BooksTableView-Controller` and `BooksCollectionViewController` classes, and replace with an implicitly unwrapped optional:

```
var booksManager:BooksManager!
```

Yes, you should be extra cautious using implicitly unwrapped optionals, but in this case, you'll inject them into the view controller as soon as they're instantiated.

2 Create a class that subclasses `UITabBarController`, and call it `TabBar-Controller`.

3 Set `TabBarController` as the class of the tab bar controller in the Identity Inspector in the storyboard.

4 Instantiate the books manager in your new class:

```
var booksManager = BooksManager()
```

To inject the books manager into both view controllers, you'll set up an `Injectable` protocol that both view controllers will adopt. Create the `Injectable` protocol in the TabBarController.swift file, with an `inject` method ready to pass in the books manager.

```
protocol Injectable {
    func inject(data: BooksManager)
}
```

5 In the table view controller, adopt the `Injectable` protocol:

```
class BooksTableViewController: UITableViewController, Injectable {
```

6   Implement the `inject` method:

```
func inject(data: BooksManager) {
    self.booksManager = data
}
```

After setting the instance variable, this is a good time to reload the table view. Use optional binding in case the `tableView` implicitly unwrapped optional hasn't yet been instantiated.

7   Ensure the table view is up to date whenever the view appears:

```
override func viewDidAppear(_ animated: Bool) {
    tableView?.reloadData()
}
```

8   Do steps 5 through 7 again, but for the collection view controller. The books view controllers are now ready to be *injected*!

Back in the `TabBarController` class, you'll inject both view controllers with the data in the `viewDidLoad` method. `UITabBarController` has a `view-Controllers` array that stores a reference to the navigation controllers containing the view controllers for each tab.

9   Loop through the `viewControllers` array, getting a reference to the navigation controllers, from which you can then get a reference to its root view controller to inject your data!

```
for navController in viewControllers! {          ⟵──┐ Loops through tab
    if let navController = navController             │ bar view controllers
            as? UINavigationController,
        let viewController = navController.viewControllers.first   Gets ref to navigation controller
            as? Injectable {
        viewController.inject(data: booksManager)    ⟵──┐ Injects
    }                                                    │ data
}
```

Gets ref to nav controller's root view controller

It does take more work to implement the dependency injection pattern, but it can be worth it. Dependency injection avoids global states, and connections between objects are explicit and clearer, making testing and maintenance easier. On the other hand, if in the future changes are made to the flow of the app, the approach for the injection of data will need to be revised, whereas the singleton solution could potentially be fine without any modification.

In the end, the solution you choose for such coding dilemmas is up to you! In the next chapter, you'll use more iOS singletons when you take your app data to the next level—*saving* the data!

✓   **CHECKPOINT**   If you'd like to compare your project with mine at this point, you can check mine out at https://github.com/iOSAppDevelopment-withSwiftinAction/Bookcase.git (Chapter10.7.TabBarController).

10.5 Summary

In this chapter, you learned the following:

- When comparing strings for sorting, use their `localizedLowercase` property to ignore case and follow local sorting rules. Use tuples to compare multiple strings.
- Use a search controller to manage searching data in your app.
- Use enumerations to define a group of related values.
- Use property observers `willSet` and `didSet` to perform an action before or after a property is set.
- Make a custom object *equatable* to find its index in an array.
- Use singletons or dependency injection to share data between view controllers at the same level, such as those contained in a tab bar controller.

Local data persistence

This chapter covers

- Storing app state on the device
- Storing user preferences on the device
- Using different techniques for storing data on the device

In this chapter, we'll take a lightning tour of several options for persisting data locally on the device. We can't comprehensively cover all features of all alternatives in one chapter, but we'll explore the basics of the different options and the differences in approaches, so you can choose for yourself which option you prefer or which is more appropriate for a project.

Specifically, we'll explore storing data using

- *State preservation and restoration*—Your app remembers where you left it.
- *User defaults*—Your app remembers your preferences.
- *Property lists*—Serialize your model objects into a type of structured data often used by Apple.
- *XML*—Serialize your model objects into an XML format.

- *JSON*—Encode your model objects into the JSON format.
- *Archiving objects*—Store model objects directly to the device by making them encodable.
- *SQLite*—Use SQLite operations to store data in a local database.
- *Core data*—Store data using object-oriented code built over a relational database.

Along the way, we'll also explore

- *App delegate*—Responding to app-level events in your app's delegate.
- *Error handling*—Dealing with errors that may occur during your app's execution.
- *Using Objective-C in a Swift project*—Creating a *bridging header* to import Objective-C classes in your Swift project.

As you can see, we have much to get through, so let's get started!

11.1 *Preserving user preferences and state*

Have you ever modified an app with your preferences—perhaps you turned sound off or you navigated to the scene you're most interested in—only to find the next time you open the app that everything is back to its defaults? Frustrating!

Your app can use several techniques to remember where the user was and what they prefer. Let's look at state preservation.

11.1.1 *Preserving and restoring state*

Your app can remember where the user last navigated to and return them to the same place when they reopen the app. What's more, it's super easy to set this up!

When the user opens the Bookcase app, they always go directly to the books table view. What if the user prefers the more visual books collection view?

Let's explore the steps involved in preserving and restoring state by setting up the Bookcase app to remember the user's scene preference.

✔ **CHECKPOINT**   Open the Bookcase project where you left it at the end of chapter 10, or check it out at https://github.com/iOSAppDevelopmentwithSwiftinAction/Bookcase.git (Chapter10.7.TabBarController).

The first thing to do is inform UIKit that you want to opt in to preserving and restoring state. You do this in the app delegate.

App delegate

You've probably seen the AppDelegate.swift file in the Project Navigator and wondered what it's for. Perhaps you've also wondered, could it be related to the *delegation pattern*?

Well, if you wondered that, you'd be right! The app delegate is your app's customizable *delegate*, and is the best place to customize how your app responds to important app-level events.

Explore the app delegate file that Xcode automatically generates for each project. Several `UIApplicationDelegate` methods are already implemented for you, ready for customization.

You can customize app delegate methods such as

- App launch
- App state changes (for example, app enters background/foreground)
- App receives remote or local notifications
- Manage preserving and restoring app state

1 Add the following methods to the app delegate to request the system to save and restore the app's state:

```
func application(_ application: UIApplication,
        shouldSaveApplicationState coder: NSCoder) -> Bool {
    return true
}
func application(_ application: UIApplication,
        shouldRestoreApplicationState coder: NSCoder) -> Bool {
    return true
}
```

Now that these methods exist in the app delegate and return `true`, the system will walk down the view controller hierarchy from the root view controller, looking for view controllers with a restoration identifier. (When the system reaches a view controller *without* a restoration identifier, it won't examine its children.) Those view controllers with a restoration identifier will have their state preserved when the app moves to a background state and restored when the app launches.

2 Open the storyboard, select the tab bar controller, and open the Identity Inspector.

3 Enter a string in the Restoration ID property—it doesn't really matter what the ID is, as long as it's unique.

4 Do the same for the two navigation controllers the tab bar controller displays in its tabs. That's it! The app should now remember the user's last tab preference.

5 Run the app and switch to the books collection tab.

6 Send the app to the background by clicking the simulator's Home button.

7 Now run the app again, and it should launch straight to the collection scene!

In addition to tab bar controllers and view controllers, you can also use state preservation and restoration to preserve the state of

- Navigation controllers
- Table views and collection views
- Scroll views
- Text fields and text views
- Image views

NOTE   View controllers with restore identifiers can also encode and decode additional state data by overriding the `encodeRestorableStateWith-Coder` and `decodeRestorableStateWithCoder` methods. We'll look more at encoding and decoding data using `Codable` shortly.

11.1.2 *Preserving user preferences on the device*

Sometimes you may want to set a *preference* that will be preserved for future launches of the app. Perhaps you want to preserve a user's name, whether the user has turned off sound or music, or the color scheme the user prefers.

User defaults are the perfect place for preserving small, discrete pieces of data such as these. See figure 11.1 for sample preferences screens in various apps that could be stored in user defaults.

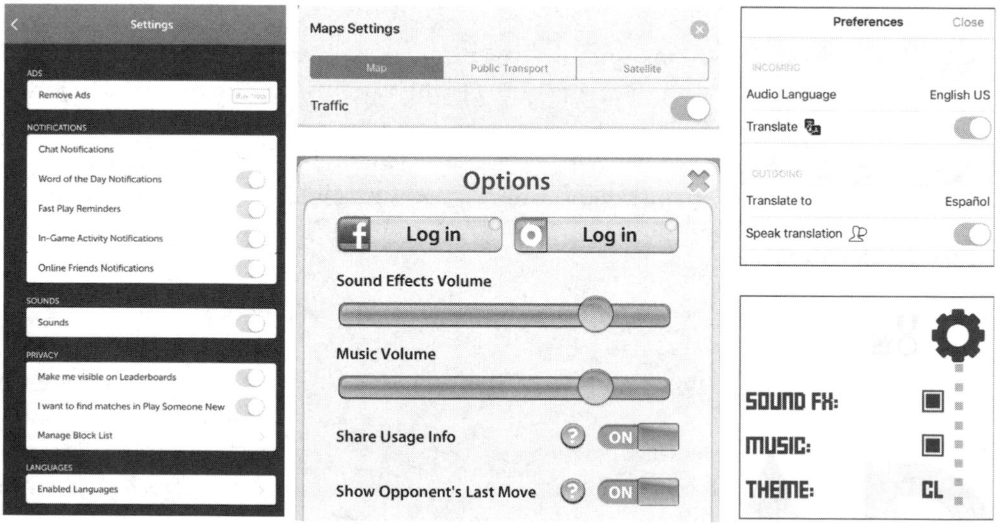

Figure 11.1   In-app settings are often stored in User Defaults.

You'll use user defaults in your Bookcase app to keep track of whether the user prefers to see the optional ISBN field in the book detail scene. All that's necessary is to set the user default for the ISBN field when the user hides or shows the field. When the book detail scene loads, you can get this value from the user defaults and show or hide the field accordingly.

1 First, you'll need a *key* for the ISBN user default. The key is a string that's used to reference this preference when you store and retrieve its value. In the Book-ViewController.swift file (external to the `BookViewController` class), create a private global variable for the key.

```
private let isbnKey = "ISBN"
```

2 In the `toggleISBN` method, store the new user default using this key. Get a reference to the standard defaults with the `standard` singleton, and call its `set` method.

```
UserDefaults.standard.set(isbnStackView.isHidden, forKey: isbnKey)
```

3 Now, all that's left is to retrieve this user default and use it to show or hide the field. To retrieve user defaults, you can use convenience methods that specify the data type you expect. As the `isHidden` property you stored was a Boolean type, retrieve it using the `bool` method. Add the following to the `viewDidLoad` method:

```
isbnStackView.isHidden = UserDefaults.standard.bool(forKey: isbnKey)
```

Now, test if the ISBN preference is persisting in user defaults.

4 Run the app, select to add a book, and select the Info button to show the ISBN field.

5 Run the app again, select to add a book again, and you should discover that your preference for seeing the ISBN field has been preserved.

User defaults can store all sorts of Core Data types: `Bool`, `String`, `Int`, `Float`, `NSURL`, `NSData` (binary data), and even arrays or dictionaries of any of the above. User defaults, however, are most useful for small chunks of data. If there's any sort of complexity to the data, you're better off looking at the features of alternative approaches, starting with `NSKeyedArchiver`, which we'll be looking at shortly.

CHALLENGE Using user defaults, record the user's choice of sort order in the segmented controls in the books table and books collection scenes.

CHECKPOINT If you'd like to compare your project with mine at this point, you can check mine out at https://github.com/iOSApp-DevelopmentwithSwiftinAction/Bookcase.git (Chapter11.1.UserPreferences).

11.2   *Storing data locally*

Adding, deleting, and updating items in a table are pointless if your changes don't stick around for the next time you launch the app! User preferences are great for small, bite-sized pieces of data, but for complex data, you'll need a more robust solution.

You have many options for storing data locally on your device, including those shown in table 11.1.

Table 11.1   Local storage alternatives

Alternative	Description	Pros	Cons
Structured data files	Parse structured data such as XML or property lists to/from a file.	Simple; output is human readable.	Storing/retrieving data in its entirety (called *atomic stores*); can have higher memory requirements and be slower due to higher disk access.
Archiving objects	Archive and unarchive objects in your code directly to/from a file.	Simple, object-oriented approach.	
SQLite	Perform database operations on a database file.	Powerful and fast; can define relationships between entities; sophisticated queries with familiar and portable syntax.	Overkill for smaller amounts of data. Native SQLite syntax can be unwieldy, but third-party alternatives can resolve this. (See third-party alternative cons.)
Core Data	Manage model objects, including data persistence.	Powerful and fast; can define relationships between entities; sophisticated queries; track changes; caching; validation.	Can be overkill for smaller amounts of data. High learning curve, boilerplate setup.
Third-party alternatives	Plenty of third-party solutions can be worth exploring, such as FMDB to help with SQLite or Realm for mobile databases.	Can be useful for automating boilerplate code or common tasks.	Can go out of date or favor; no guarantees of updates.

Like tools in a toolbox, there isn't one alternative local storage solution that will be perfect for every project and scenario. The alternative you choose depends on the requirements and complexity of your project, along with your own personal preferences.

Before you choose the right tool for the job, it's a good idea to understand each alternative.

In the rest of this chapter, we'll look at several of these alternatives by exploring how they could be used to store books data locally for the Bookcase app.

11.2.1   *Storage setup*

Before we get into comparing alternatives, let's perform additional setup to the Bookcase app that will be useful for different options.

DETERMINING STORAGE LOCATION

Every iOS app has its own little space on the device for storing files. This space is called its *sandbox*, as access by other apps is generally prohibited. Similarly, your app generally doesn't have access to the sandboxed file system of other apps.

By default, every app's sandbox contains several standard directories, including those shown in table 11.2.

Table 11.2 Useful iOS directories

Directory	Description
App bundle	This read-only directory contains the app itself and all resources bundled with it.
Documents	Files generated by the user that may be accessible to the user directly through file sharing.
Application support	Files your app can generate to support itself that will be invisible to the user.
Temporary files	Store files here temporarily while you work with them.
Caches	Store files here temporarily for possibly improving download speed.

You're going to add local storage of the user's books to your Bookcase app.

It makes sense to store the data in the *application support* folder, so let's get a reference to its path.

You can use the `FileManager` class to handle regular file system activities such as creating, copying, and moving files and directories. You can also use the `FileManager` class to return a path for one of the iOS directories.

Use the `FileManager`'s `urls` method to get an array of `URL` objects for the *application support* directory. Because you only want the first item in the array, use its `first` property.

Unlike the documents folder, the application support folder isn't generated for your app automatically, so before returning the URL, check if the folder exists, and if not, create it.

1 Define the `appSupportDirectory` private global variable in the BooksManager.swift file (outside the `BooksManager` class).

```
private let appSupportDirectory: URL = {
    let url = FileManager().urls(
        for: .applicationSupportDirectory,              Gets URL to application
        in: .userDomainMask).first!                     support directory
    if !FileManager().fileExists(atPath: url.path) {    Checks that
        do {                                            directory exists
            try FileManager().createDirectory(at: url,         do-catch
                withIntermediateDirectories: false)            statement
        } catch {                                       Creates directory if necessary
            print("\(error.localizedDescription)")
        }
    }
```

```
        }
        return url
    }()
```

Returns url

Because the `createDirectory` method can throw an error, you'll need to surround it in a `do-catch` statement. (See sidebar "Error handling.")

2 Once you have a path to the application support directory, generate a path to a directory to store the books data, using the `URL` object's `appendingPathComponent` method.

```
private let booksFile =
    appSupportDirectory.appendingPathComponent("Books")
```

Gets URL to Books file

Error handling

If a method can cause an error, it's marked with the keyword `throws`, and then at a point it may throw an error. Errors are defined by an enum that adopts the `Error` protocol. The following example defines an error, and a method that can throw it:

```
enum HyperdriveError: Error {
    case broken
    case missing
}
class Spaceship {
    var hyperdriveOperational: Bool = false
    func goHyperspace() throws {
        if !hyperdriveOperational {
            throw HyperdriveError.broken
        }
    }
}
```

To call a method that can throw an error, surround it in a `do-catch` block, identifying the call with a `try` keyword. Use the `do` block to `try` code that could throw errors, and then catch any errors in the `catch` block. The following would catch an error in the `goHyperspace` method. The `localizedDescription` property offers an explanation of the error.

```
var spaceship = Spaceship()
do {
    try spaceship.goHyperspace()
} catch {
    print("\(error.localizedDescription)")
}
```

Alternatively, you can choose to catch specific errors.

```
do {
    try spaceship.goHyperspace()
} catch HyperdriveError.broken {
    print("It's broken!")
} catch HyperdriveError.missing {
    print("It's missing!")
}
```

PREPARING FOR STORING AND RETRIEVING DATA

In many of the local storage alternatives you'll explore, you'll store and retrieve data from disk in its entirety, also known as an *atomic* store. This process is fairly simple and can make sense for small amounts of data. When you start working with thousands of records, or are modeling relationships and filtering data, alternatives that update the data using database operations can be more appropriate (such as SQLite or Core Data).

For now, let's prepare the Bookcase app to store and retrieve data in its entirety.

1 Create stubs for a `storeBooks` method and a `retrieveBooks` method in the BooksManager, ready to fill in later with appropriate serializing and parsing methods.

```
// MARK: Local storage
func storeBooks() {
    // Store books array to disk here
}
func retrieveBooks() -> [Book]? {
    // Retrieve books array from disk here
    return nil
}
```

Notice that the `retrieveBooks` method returns an optional array of `Book`. Obviously, at first there won't be any books data to retrieve, so the first time the app runs, this method will return `nil`.

Now that you have a method set up to store books, you can call it whenever changes are made to the `books` array, such as when a book is added, updated, or removed.

2 Add a call to the `storeBooks` method at the end of each of the `addBook`, `removeBook`, and `updateBook` methods.

```
storeBooks()
```

3 Now that you have a method set up to retrieve books, request them from the `loadBooks` method. If no books are stored, resort to the sample books.

```
func loadBooks() -> [Book] {
    return retrieveBooks() ?? sampleBooks()
}
```

Generally, when serializing data, each property will require a name to identify it.

4 To avoid typos, set up a private `struct` in the Book.swift file (but outside the Book structure) that defines keys for each property in the Book structure.

```
internal struct Key {
    static let title = "title"
    static let author = "author"
    static let rating = "rating"
    static let isbn = "isbn"
    static let notes = "notes"
}
```

> ✅ **CHECKPOINT** If you'd like to follow along from my project, we'll explore each local storage alternative beginning from the same starting point at https://github.com/iOSAppDevelopmentwithSwiftinAction/Book-case.git (Chapter11.2.StoreDataStart).

Now that you have stubs and a `struct` of Keys, you're ready to explore various alternatives for storing data.

11.2.2 Structured data files

In this section, you'll *serialize* your model objects into a specific structure, such as JSON, XML, or property lists, that can be written to disk in a file. Later, you can read the file back in and *deserialize* or *parse* it back into your model object (see figure 11.2).

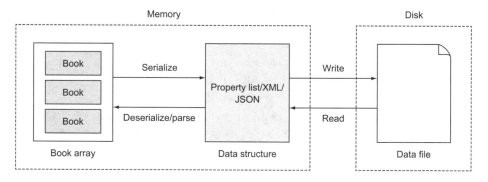

Figure 11.2   Data persistence with structured data files

If you have a good parser, the specific syntax of the format you're encoding the data into doesn't matter too much, and the code you write to encode and decode the data will be fairly similar.

You're probably already familiar with common text-based formats for encoding data, such as JSON or XML. You may not be as familiar with property lists, also known as plists.

PROPERTY LISTS

Property lists are another way of structuring data, common in iOS. When you create a new project, for example, Xcode automatically generates an Info.plist file containing additional preferences for your project. If you select the Info.plist file in the Project Navigator, you'll examine the contents of the .plist file in the property list editor by default. To see the underlying structure of the plist, right-click on it and select Open As > Source Code.

Property list editor

Bundle versions string, short	⬍	String	1.0
Bundle creator OS Type code	⬍	String	????
Bundle version	⬍	String	1
Application requires iPhone enviro...	⬍	Boolean	YES
Launch screen interface file base...	⬍	String	LaunchScreen
Main storyboard file base name	⬍	String	Main

Source code editor

```
<key>CFBundleShortVersionString</key>
<string>1.0</string>
<key>CFBundleSignature</key>
<string>????</string>
<key>CFBundleVersion</key>
<string>1</string>
<key>LSRequiresIPhoneOS</key>
<true/>
<key>UILaunchStoryboardName</key>
<string>LaunchScreen</string>
<key>UIMainStoryboardFile</key>
<string>Main</string>
```

Figure 11.3 Info property list edited two ways

You'll find that under the hood, the .plist file is actually a special type of XML. Each property in the plist is represented by a key followed by a value (see figure 11.3).

You already created a property list earlier in this chapter! Behind the scenes, user defaults are represented by property lists. You can also store an `Array` or `Dictionary` to disk as a property list, as long as they contain foundation data types that can be stored in property lists such as `String`, `Data`, or other arrays and dictionaries.

You're going to convert your array of `Book` objects to an array of dictionaries of strings that can be stored on the device as a property list. You'll then retrieve the property list and convert it back into an array of `Book` objects.

1 Add a `dictionary` computed property to the `Book` structure that returns a representation of the `Book` object as a dictionary of strings.

```
var dictionary: [String: String] {
  return [
    Key.title: title,
    Key.author: author,
    Key.rating: String(rating),
    Key.isbn: isbn,
    Key.notes: notes
  ]
}
```

Now, you can use this property and the `map` higher-order function to generate an array of dictionaries, from an array of `Book` objects.

```
books.map( { $0.dictionary })
```

The Objective-C `NSArray` data type contains methods for writing and reading to the device that don't exist in the Swift `Array` data type. Before writing to disk, you'll need to cast your array of book dictionaries to an `NSArray`.

TIP Many core Swift data types are *bridged* with their Objective-C counter-parts, meaning that the two types can be used interchangeably. But in certain cases, Objective-C functionality may be missing in the Swift implementation, and you'll need to *cast* your variable to the Objective-C implementation (usually beginning with *NS*) for access to additional Objective-C methods and properties.

2 Add the following to the `storeBooks` method in your `BooksManager` class:

```
func storeBooks() {
    (books.map( { $0.dictionary }) as NSArray).write(
        to: booksFile, atomically: true)
}
```

Storing files *atomically* has more safeguards to ensure that the file being written to isn't corrupted if a crash occurs.

That's it for storing the property list. Now you can retrieve it! Because you stored each book as a dictionary of strings, when you retrieve your `books` array, you'll need to regenerate `Book` objects from this data.

3 Give the `Book` structure an initializer that generates a new `Book` based on a dictionary. Unwrap the dictionary string values (casting them to the appropriate data type where necessary, such as the rating `Double` property), and then instantiate the new Book by calling the designated initializer.

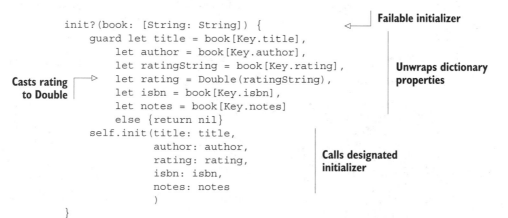

```
init?(book: [String: String]) {                              ⟵⎯ Failable initializer
    guard let title = book[Key.title],
        let author = book[Key.author],
        let ratingString = book[Key.rating],                        Unwraps dictionary
        let rating = Double(ratingString),                          properties
        let isbn = book[Key.isbn],
        let notes = book[Key.notes]
        else {return nil}
    self.init(title: title,
            author: author,
            rating: rating,                    Calls designated
            isbn: isbn,                        initializer
            notes: notes
            )
}
```

Casts rating to Double

NOTE　The question mark following the `init` method indicates that this is a *failable* initializer, meaning that it can return `nil`. If you're instantiating an object via a failable initializer, you need to unwrap the object that's returned.

Next, you retrieve your `books` array from file in the `retrieveBooks` method in the `BooksManager`. The `NSArray` class can be instantiated directly from a file.

```
NSArray(contentsOf: booksFile)
```

4 You need to cast this `NSArray` as a Swift array of dictionaries of strings.

```
guard let array = NSArray(contentsOf: booksFile)
    as? [[String: String]] else {return nil}
```

You can then use `map` to regenerate an array of `Book`, using the initializer you just created.

```
array.map( { Book(book: $0) } )
```

5 Because the initializer is failable, it returns an array of optional `Book`, so you'll need to unwrap it.

```
guard let books = array.map( { Book(book: $0) } )
  as? [Book] else {return nil}
```

6 Return the `books` property. Your finished `retrieveBooks` method in the BooksManager class should look like this:

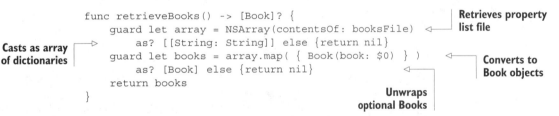

Casts as array of dictionaries

Retrieves property list file

Converts to Book objects

Unwraps optional Books

```
func retrieveBooks() -> [Book]? {
    guard let array = NSArray(contentsOf: booksFile)
        as? [[String: String]] else {return nil}
    guard let books = array.map( { Book(book: $0) } )
        as? [Book] else {return nil}
    return books
}
```

7 Run the app; add, delete, or update a book.

8 Run the app again, and you should find that your changes have persisted as property lists!

TIP　If you're using the simulator, you can see the file that your app output! Print the value of `booksFile` to the console, paste the path into a Spotlight search, and as simple as that, the property list your app output should open in Xcode.

✓　**CHECKPOINT**　If you'd like to compare your project with mine at this point, you can check mine out at https://github.com/iOSAppDevelopmentwithSwiftinAction/Bookcase.git (Chapter11.3.StoreDataPropertyList).

You may want to keep a version of your project working with property list files before we move on to exploring alternatives.

XML

In this section, we'll explore storing and retrieving data locally as XML.

✓ **CHECKPOINT**   We're going to start fresh from the same starting point as earlier: https://github.com/iOSAppDevelopmentwithSwiftinAction/ Bookcase.git (Chapter11.2.StoreDataStart).

---

iOS comes with a low-level XML parser. Rather than converting the XML to a format that can be more easily manipulated, the XML parser in iOS explores the XML hierarchy, dispatching events to its delegate as it discovers the various elements and attributes contained.

It can be more convenient to use a higher-level XML parser that converts the XML structure to objects that can then be more easily converted to your customized model objects. Because this functionality doesn't come packaged with the iOS SDK (curiously, it does come with the macOS SDK), I built an XML parser that you can use in your projects. You can check out the parser here (https://github.com/craiggrummitt/SwiftXML.git) and drag the XML.swift file into the Project Navigator.

Now that you have an XML parser in your project, you'll explore how to use it by serializing the `books` array to an XML structure that can be stored on the device in a text file. You'll then retrieve the XML structure, and parse it back into your `books` array.

1   Add an `xml` computed property to the `Book` structure that returns a representation of the `Book` object as an XML node.

```
var xml: XMLNode {
    let bookNode = XMLNode(name: "book")
    bookNode.addChild(name: Key.title, value: self.title)
    bookNode.addChild(name: Key.author, value: self.author)
    bookNode.addChild(name: Key.rating, value: String(self.rating))
    bookNode.addChild(name: Key.isbn, value: self.isbn)
    bookNode.addChild(name: Key.notes, value: self.notes)
    return bookNode
}
```

Now that you have the structure for each book node, you could serialize a books array into an entire XML structure.

```
let booksXML = XMLNode()
for book in books {
    booksXML.addChild(book.xml)
}
```

You're going to access a String representation of the XML document using the XMLNode's `description` property. Once you have a String, you can use its write method to write it to disk. As this request can fail, you'll need to encapsulate it in a do-catch statement.

2 Add the following to the storeBooks method in your BooksManager class:

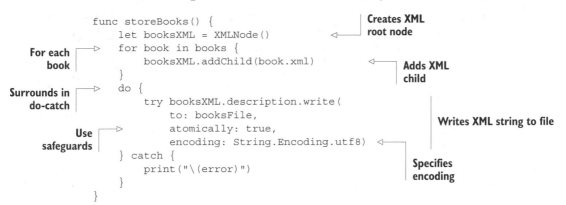

```
func storeBooks() {
    let booksXML = XMLNode()          ◁───┘ Creates XML
    for book in books {                      root node
        booksXML.addChild(book.xml)   ◁──── Adds XML
    }                                        child
    do {
        try booksXML.description.write(
            to: booksFile,
            atomically: true,                        Writes XML string to file
            encoding: String.Encoding.utf8)  ◁────
    } catch {                                Specifies
        print("\(error)")                    encoding
    }
}
```

Creates XML root node

For each book

Adds XML child

Surrounds in do-catch

Use safeguards

Writes XML string to file

Specifies encoding

3 Give the Book structure an initializer that generates a new Book object based on an XML node. Unwrap the XML node text values, and instantiate a new Book. This code is similar to the property list code in the previous section.

```
init?(book: XMLNode) {
    guard let title = book[Key.title]?.text,
        let author = book[Key.author]?.text,
        let ratingString = book[Key.rating]?.text,
        let rating = Double(ratingString),
        let isbn = book[Key.isbn]?.text,
        let notes = book[Key.notes]?.text
        else {return nil}
    self.init(title: title,
              author: author,
              rating: rating,
              isbn: isbn,
              notes: notes
              )
}
```

Failable initializer

Casts rating to Double

Unwraps dictionary properties

Calls designated initializer

The BooksManager can now retrieve the XML structure from file using the XML class. The root element of the XML will contain a series of children nodes that represent book data.

4 You can use the initializer you set up in the Book structure to parse each book node and, finally, generate an array of Book objects:

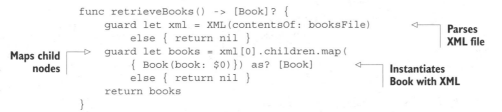

```
func retrieveBooks() -> [Book]? {
    guard let xml = XML(contentsOf: booksFile)    ◁──┐ Parses
        else { return nil }                            XML file
    guard let books = xml[0].children.map(
        { Book(book: $0)}) as? [Book]      ◁──── Instantiates
        else { return nil }                      Book with XML
    return books
}
```

Maps child nodes

Parses XML file

Instantiates Book with XML

Again, if you run the app, make modifications to books, and run the app again, you should find that your changes have persisted locally, this time as an XML file.

> ✓ **CHECKPOINT**   If you'd like to compare your project with mine at this point, you can check mine out at https://github.com/iOSAppDevelopmentwithSwiftinAction/Bookcase.git (Chapter11.4.StoreDataXML).

You should notice several similarities between property lists and XML structures. The code involved in writing and reading a structure of data to disk doesn't change too much depending on the type of structure. After going through this process twice, you already have an idea of what the process would be to read and write your data as JSON! (We'll look more at JSON in the next chapter.)

You might want to keep a version of your project working with XML, because we'll move on to a different alternative next.

11.2.3 *Archiving objects*

In this section, we'll explore storing model types in your project directly to a local file.

> ✓ **CHECKPOINT**   We'll start fresh again from the same starting point as earlier: https://github.com/iOSAppDevelopmentwithSwiftinAction/Bookcase.git (Chapter11.2.StoreDataStart).

This approach has similarities to storing data as structured data files. You'll still encode (the equivalent of serializing) model types into a different data format, store and retrieve data from disk, and decode (the equivalent of parsing) data back into model types (see figure 11.4). One important difference is that data is stored as binary files rather than text files, resulting in more-compact files.

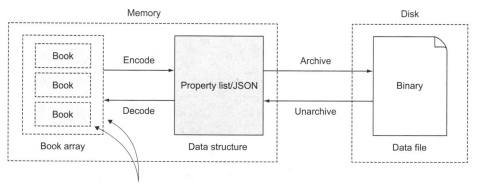

Figure 11.4   Data persistence: archiving objects

Your model types can be made encodable into another format by adopting the `Encodable` protocol. At the time of writing, Apple provides two encoders: a JSON encoder and a property list encoder.

Once your model object has been encoded, it can then be *archived* to a format that can be written to disk. To unarchive and decode your data, you'll need to adopt the `Decodable` protocol to make your model types decodable. For your convenience, you can make types both encodable and decodable by adopting the `Codable` protocol.

You're going to persist books data in your Bookcase app by archiving the `books` array.

ADOPTING CODABLE PROTOCOL

Let's start by making the `Book` structure codable.

1 Indicate that your model object can be encoded and decoded by adopting the `Codable` protocol.

```
class Book: Codable {
```

Believe it or not, in many cases that's all you'll need to do for the encoder to understand the structure of your model object! As long as every property of your model object is also codable—and many standard types such as `String`, `Int`, `Double`, `Bool`, and `Array` already are—then your model type is ready to be automatically encoded.

However, the `Book` structure contains a `UIImage` property that unfortunately doesn't adopt the `Codable` protocol. In chapter 13, we'll take a closer look at this problem, but for now, the app isn't yet receiving custom images for books from the user, so let's tell the compiler to omit this property from encoding and decoding. But how can you omit a property?

When you adopt the `Codable` property, the compiler automatically generates three things in your model object:

- An enumerator called `CodingKeys` that lists of all the properties in the object.
- An `init` method that generates your model object from data using the `Decoder`.
- An encode method that encodes your model object's data using the `Encoder`.

You can implement your own version of any or all these to replace the automatically generated version. In implementing your own `CodingKeys` enumerator, you can omit properties or modify names of properties from the encoded version.

2 Implement your own version of the `CodingKeys` enumerator in the `Book` structure. This is identical to the `CodingKeys` enumerator that would have been automatically generated, but by defining it yourself, you can omit the `image` property.

```
enum CodingKeys: String, CodingKey {
  case title
```

```
        case author
        case rating
        case isbn
        case notes
    }
```

ENCODING AND ARCHIVING DATA

Now that your `Book` structure adopts the `Codable` protocol, you can encode and archive the array of books to disk. You have a choice of two encoders: `JSONEncoder` or `PropertyListEncoder`. Either will work fine. Let's use the `PropertyList-Encoder`.

In the `storeBooks` method in the `BooksManager` class, get a reference to the `PropertyListEncoder`, and use it to encode the `books` array. As encoding can fail, you'll need to encapsulate it in a `do-catch` statement.

1　Update the method in the `BooksManager` to archive the array of books.

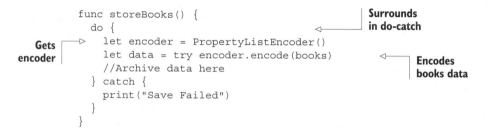

```
func storeBooks() {                                    Surrounds
  do {                                                 in do-catch
    let encoder = PropertyListEncoder()
    let data = try encoder.encode(books)              Encodes
    //Archive data here                               books data
  } catch {
    print("Save Failed")
  }
}
```

Gets encoder

Now that you have the data encoded as a property list, you can archive it with the `NSKeyedArchiver` class, calling the `archiveRootObject` method, passing in the object and the file path. This method will return a `Bool` that indicates whether the data was written successfully.

2　Add the following after encoding the books array:

```
let success = NSKeyedArchiver.archiveRootObject(      Archives encoded books data
  data, toFile: booksFile.path)
print(success ? "Successful save" : "Save Failed")    Prints result
                                                      to console
```

Next, you need to unarchive an object when you want to retrieve it from disk. For unarchiving, you'll use the `NSKeyedUnarchiver` class, calling the `unarchiveObject` method and passing in the file path. You can unwrap the value returned as a `Data` object.

3　Update the method in the `BooksManager` to retrieve archived data.

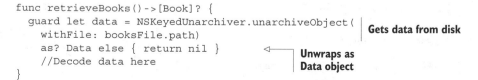

```
func retrieveBooks()->[Book]? {
  guard let data = NSKeyedUnarchiver.unarchiveObject(   Gets data from disk
    withFile: booksFile.path)
    as? Data else { return nil }                        Unwraps as
    //Decode data here                                  Data object
}
```

Now that you have the data that was archived as a property list, you can decode it back to a `books` array using the `PropertyListDecoder`. Tell the `decode` method what type you're expecting this data to decode to (in this case, an array of `Book`), and magically, your `books` array should reappear! Of course, the decode could fail, so again, you'll need to surround it in a `do-catch` statement.

4 Decode the unarchived data in the `retrieveBooks` method.

```
do {                                           ← Surrounds in do-catch
    let decoder = PropertyListDecoder()    ← Gets decoder
    let books = try decoder.decode([Book].self, from: data)    ← Decodes as array of Book
    return books
} catch {
    print("Retrieve Failed")
    return nil
}
```

5 Run the app, make changes to your data, and run the app again. If all has gone well, the changes you made should persist!

✔ **CHECKPOINT**   If you'd like to compare your project with mine at this point, you can check mine out at https://github.com/iOSApp-DevelopmentwithSwiftinAction/Bookcase.git (Chapter11.5.StoreData-Archiving). Again, you might like to keep a version of the project storing data locally by archiving objects before we move on.

11.2.4 *SQLite*

If all the other techniques we've looked at for storing data locally have been hammers and screwdrivers, SQLite is the power drill of local storage options!

✔ **CHECKPOINT**   Open up the same starting point: https://github.com/iOSAppDevelopmentwithSwiftinAction/Bookcase.git (Chapter11.2.StoreDataStart).

Your iOS app comes ready to implement a relational database using a SQLite3 library. If your app has a lot of data, contains complex relationships between model objects, or will need to perform many queries (such as filtering, searching, and so on), you might want to consider using the power of SQLite to manage your data.

SQLite is fast—operations using SQLite3 can even perform better than equivalent operations on Core Data types. Rather than storing the whole database in memory or encoding the entire model using *atomic* storage, SQLite3 operations only make specific changes to the database such as adding, deleting, or updating rows. To get data out of your database, you'd *query* the database with an SQLite `SELECT` statement, and

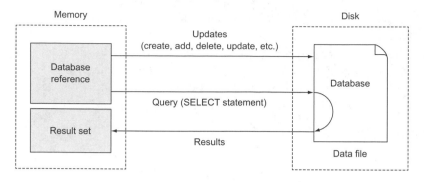

Figure 11.5   Data persistence: archiving objects.

receive a dataset in response. This type of data store is called a *transactional* store (see figure 11.5).

SQLite3 syntax is standard, so if you're already familiar with working with databases, applying this knowledge to iOS shouldn't be too much of a learning curve, especially compared to the far more involved Core Data. I don't intend to go into detail on SQLite3 syntax here, but if you need to brush up, https://sqlite.org contains more information.

You're going to explore using SQLite3 to store and retrieve data for the Bookcase app. The first job to do is to create the database itself.

SET UP THE SQLITE3 DATABASE FILE
You have two choices to set up the database:

- You could build the database in code if it doesn't yet exist.
- You could build the database in an SQLite3 database management program, and include the database file with your app in the app bundle directory.

The latter has the advantage of being able to easily include data in the database before adding it to your project. Because supplying data to a project via the database can sometimes be an additional motivation for using databases, you'll focus on adding a database file to your app bundle.

I use the free SQLiteBrowser (http://sqlitebrowser.org) to generate and edit databases, but if you have a preferred program, feel free to use that.

You'll want to create a Books database containing a Book table recreating the data structure of the `Book` structure.

1 Feel free to create the Books database yourself, or you can download a version of the database that I've set up here: http://mng.bz/t9IF. Once you've generated a database file, add it to your project.
2 Drag the database file into your bookcase project's Project Navigator. Be sure to check the Bookcase target.

This introduces the database file into your app bundle directory. An important thing to note is that the app bundle is *read-only*. The first time the app runs, it will need to copy this file into the application support directory to make changes to it.

3 Update your `booksFile` property to ensure the file exists before returning the path.

```
private var booksFile: URL = {
    let filePath = appSupportDirectory.appendingPathComponent(
        "Books").appendingPathExtension("db")
    if !FileManager().fileExists(atPath: filePath.path) {
        if let bundleFilePath =
            Bundle().resourceURL?.appendingPathComponent(
            "Books").appendingPathExtension("db") {
            do {
                try FileManager().copyItem(
                    at: bundleFilePath, to: filePath)
            } catch let error as NSError {
                //fingers crossed
            }
        }
    }
    return filePath
}()
```

Gets db path in App Support

Gets db path in Bundle

Copies db to App Support

If db doesn't exist

do-catch statement

NOTE To preserve system resources, global variables and constants are lazy by default, without the need for the `lazy` modifier. Once the system determines if the books database exists in the application support directory and copies it over if not, this process won't be repeated.

Now that you have the database set up, you can start performing operations on it using the SQLite3 framework. SQLite3 is written in the C programming language, which contains quite a laborious and un-Swift-like API. Most who use SQLite prefer to use a wrapper that simplifies the code you need to write to perform operations on your database.

SET UP SQLITE WRAPPER

You'll include SQLite3 in your project and set up a library of code that will act as a wrapper to the SQLite3 framework, making interactions with the database more straightforward.

You're going to use a popular SQLite wrapper library in your project called FMDB. The only problem with this library is that it's written in Objective-C. Not to worry, it's not too difficult to incorporate Objective-C in a Swift project.

Using Objective-C in a Swift project

To use Objective-C in a Swift project, you'll need to set up what's called a *bridging header*, which explicitly imports the Objective-C classes you want access to from Swift.

(continued)

The quickest way to set up a bridging header is to create an Objective-C file (with extension .m), or drag a .m file into a project that doesn't yet contain one. Xcode will automatically offer to configure a bridging header for you.

Would you like to configure an Objective-C bridging header?

Adding these files to Bookcase will create a mixed Swift and Objective-C target. Would you like Xcode to automatically configure a bridging header to enable classes to be accessed by both languages?

Cancel   Don't Create   Create Bridging Header

After selecting Create Bridging Header, you'll see a bridging header file appear in your Project Navigator. Xcode also automatically adds a path to this header file in the Objective-C Bridging Header setting in the target's build settings.

Once your bridging header is set up, import the headers for any Objective-C classes you wish to use.

Let's go through the steps in setting up the FMDB framework.

You first need to request that Apple's SQLite framework be included in the Bookcase project.

1 Open the General tab for the Bookcase target.

2 Select the plus (+) symbol under Linked Frameworks and Libraries.

3 Select libsqlite3.tbd and tap the Add button. The SQLite framework is ready to go, and you're ready to install the FMDB wrapper!

4 In the Project Navigator for your Bookcase app, create an fmdb group in the Bookcase project, ready to contain the wrapper.

5 Download the FMDB framework from here: https://github.com/ccgus/fmdb.git.

6 Locate the fmdb group inside the Source group. Notice that it contains .m and .h files; these are Objective-C *implementation* files and *header* files, respectively. Select the .m and .h files and drag them into the fmdb group in the Project Navigator.

   As FMDB is written in Objective-C, you'll need to create a bridging header.

7 Xcode will offer to configure the bridging header for you. Select Create Bridging Header.

8 Import the header for FMDB in the Bookcase-Bridging-Header.h file that was automatically generated by Xcode when you dragged in the FMDB classes.

```
#import "FMDB.h"
```

The *FMDB.h* file, in turn, will import headers for all the FMDB classes.

That's it—the FMDB wrapper should be ready to use. To double-check, build your project and then, somewhere inside a method, start typing FMDB. If all is well, code completion should suggest one of the several FMDB classes you imported.

RETRIEVING BOOKS FROM THE DATABASE

Let's kick off by retrieving books from your Books database.

First, you'll need to use the FMDB wrapper to get a reference to the database. Before performing any queries on a database you'll also need to open it.

1   Set up a method in the BooksManager class that performs these frequent tasks.

```
func getOpenDB() -> FMDatabase? {
    guard let db = FMDatabase(path: booksFile.path) else {
        print("unable to create database")
        return nil
    }
    guard db.open() else {
        print("Unable to open database")
        return nil
    }
    return db
}
```

NOTE   After opening a database and performing any necessary queries, be sure to close it again to free up any system resources.

Once you have a reference to an open database, you can perform a SELECT query on it to extract data from a database. For example, the following will query all data in the books table:

```
let rs = db.executeQuery("select * from books", values: nil)
```

Because a database query can throw an error, it must be surrounded in a do-catch statement.

Queries return a special FMDB data type called a result set. Result sets contain the results of a query. In this case, it will contain the data for each row of the books table, beginning with the first row. You can iterate through a result set by calling its next method.

2   Set up an initializer in the Book structure to instantiate a new book based on a row in a result set.

```
init?(rs: FMResultSet) {
    let rating = rs.double(forColumn: Key.rating)
    guard let title = rs.string(forColumn: Key.title),
        let author = rs.string(forColumn: Key.author),
        let isbn = rs.string(forColumn: Key.isbn),
        let notes = rs.string(forColumn: Key.notes)
        else { return nil }
    self.init(title: title,
              author: author,
              rating: rating,
```

```
                    isbn: isbn,
                    notes: notes
        )
    }
```

With this initializer set up, you can now retrieve book data from the database table and parse it into an array of `Book` objects.

3 Set this up in the `retrieveBooks` method in the `BooksManager`.

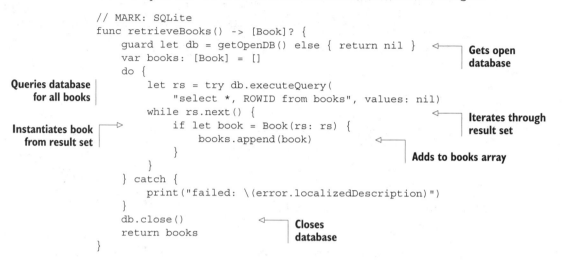

```
// MARK: SQLite
func retrieveBooks() -> [Book]? {
    guard let db = getOpenDB() else { return nil }    ⊲──┐ Gets open
    var books: [Book] = []                                 database
    do {
        let rs = try db.executeQuery(
            "select *, ROWID from books", values: nil)
        while rs.next() {                             ⊲──┐ Iterates through
            if let book = Book(rs: rs) {                    result set
                books.append(book)                    ⊲──┐
            }                                              Adds to books array
        }
    } catch {
        print("failed: \(error.localizedDescription)")
    }
    db.close()                       ⊲──┐ Closes
    return books                          database
}
```

Queries database for all books

Instantiates book from result set

4 The way you did in the structured data files and archiving sections, you'll want to call this `retrieveBooks` method in the `loadBooks` method. Because you could supply sample books in the database itself if you want, remove the `sampleBooks` method. If you have any problems retrieving books, revert to a blank array.

```
func loadBooks() -> [Book] {
    return retrieveBooks() ?? []
}
```

ADDING, UPDATING, AND REMOVING BOOKS

Rather than storing the entire database when an update occurs, it makes sense to take advantage of the power of SQLite and perform the specific operations required, such as adding, updating, or removing books.

To facilitate performing operations on specific rows, SQLite stores a unique primary key on each row called `ROWID`. It's a good idea to keep track of these primary keys in your model class to identify each row for updating or deleting books.

1 Add an `id Int` property to the Book structure.
2 Update the initializers to update the property also. Give the `id` a temporary value of `-1`. Don't worry, as soon as the user adds a new book, the database will return its ID ready to update this value.

To perform an add/update/remove operation, you need to call the database's `executeUpdate` method, using question marks to bind values. As this method can throw errors, you need to surround it in a do-catch statement.

After adding a book to the database, the `lastInsertRowId` method of your database will contain the new ROWID of the book you added. Use this to provide your Book object with an ID.

3   Create a `SQLAddBook` method in your `BookManager` class that receives a book object and updates this in the database. Because you're updating the book object's ID, you'll need to tag the parameter as `inout`.

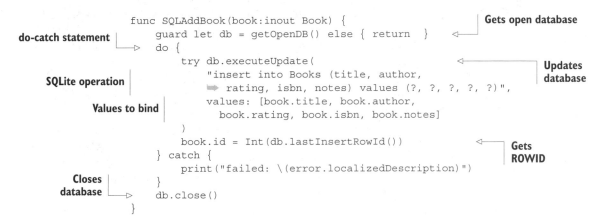

```
func SQLAddBook(book:inout Book) {              Gets open database
    guard let db = getOpenDB() else { return  }
    do {
        try db.executeUpdate(                   Updates database
            "insert into Books (title, author,
            rating, isbn, notes) values (?, ?, ?, ?, ?)",
            values: [book.title, book.author,
                book.rating, book.isbn, book.notes]
        )
        book.id = Int(db.lastInsertRowId())     Gets ROWID
    } catch {
        print("failed: \(error.localizedDescription)")
    }
    db.close()
}
```

do-catch statement · SQLite operation · Values to bind · Closes database

4   You can now call this new method at the beginning of the addBook method in your BookManager class. As the book object is updated with the ID, you'll need to mark the argument with an ampersand. To make this parameter mutable, you'll need to reassign it as a variable.

```
var book = book
SQLAddBook(book: &book)
```

The methods for deleting and updating books will be similar, except the SQLite operation will change and you won't need to get the ROWID (a book's ID won't change when updated, and you no longer need a book's ID after deleting it).

The following listing shows the contents of the executeUpdate methods for deleting and updating a book.

Listing 11.1   Delete and update book

```
try db.executeUpdate(
    "delete from Books where ROWID = ?",
    values: [book.id]

try db.executeUpdate(
    "update Books SET title = ?, author = ?,
    rating = ?, isbn = ?, notes = ? WHERE ROWID = ?",
```

```
values: [book.title, book.author, book.rating,
    book.isbn, book.notes, book.id]
```

CHALLENGE   Fill out the `SQLUpdateBook` and `SQLRemoveBook` methods, based on the `executeUpdate` statements in the section "Adopting `Codable` protocol," calling these methods at the appropriate times.

Run your app to test what you've done. You can add, delete, and remove books. If you run the app again, the data should persist.

✓ **CHECKPOINT**   If you'd like to compare your project with mine at this point, you can check mine out at https://github.com/iOSAppDevelopment-withSwiftinAction/Bookcase.git (Chapter11.6.StoreDataSQL).

Again, you might want to store a version of the project at this point using SQLite3 before moving on.

11.2.5 *Core Data*

If SQLite is the power drill to manage your app's local data, Core Data is the jack hammer! Using Core Data, you can create a relational diagram of your model objects visually in Xcode, and then create and update your data in an object-oriented manner, with Core Data managing the underlying database implementation behind the scenes. The way you can with SQLite, you can fetch data from Core Data performing queries using search criteria.

Core Data isn't only about storing relational data—it also offers additional features such as these:

- Tracking changes, and implementing undo or redo
- Caching or lazy loading of your objects
- Minimizing the number of objects in memory
- Validation of property values

Core Data is fast, powerful, and feature-rich, and if you're planning a data-intensive app and are interested in these sorts of additional features, it's worth looking into. On the other hand, Core Data can be overkill for many apps. No point getting the jackhammer out if all you're interested in is hammering a nail!

Core Data does have a reputation for being a challenging framework to learn, but don't be discouraged—recent improvements have made it easier to use.

We're going to explore using Core Data to store and retrieve data for the Bookcase app.

✓ **CHECKPOINT**   Though we're going to tweak it a little, you can open at the same starting point at https://github.com/iOSAppDevelopment-withSwiftinAction/Bookcase.git (Chapter11.2.StoreDataStart).

CREATING A DATA MODEL

The first thing to do is create a data model describing the entities of your app (such as database tables), the properties they contain, and any relationships between entities. Core Data will then manage these entities for you.

The only entity you have in the bookcase is the Book object.

1 Delete the Book.swift file; Core Data will generate the Book structure for you.

2 Create a data model file. Select File > New > File > Data Model (in the Core Data section) > Next. The default name "Model" will be fine. Change the group to *Model* to neatly store the data model in an appropriate group (see figure 11.6).

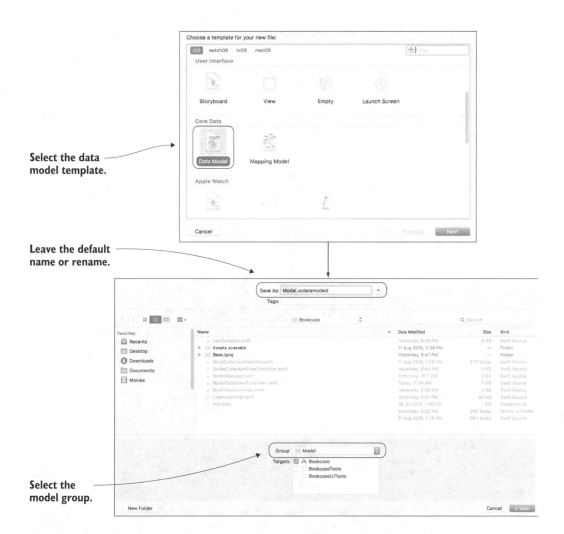

Select the data
model template.

Leave the default
name or rename.

Select the
model group.

Figure 11.6   Create data model file

Now it's time to edit your data model.

3 Find the Model file you created in the Project Navigator, and select it. The data model editor will appear.

4 Add your first entity with the Add Entity button, and call it "Book" (see figure 11.7). Notice that you can add three types of things to your new entity:

- *Attributes*—Similar to object properties.
- *Relationships*—Connections with other entities. Relationships can be to-one or to-many.
- *Fetched properties*—Similar to lazy computed properties.

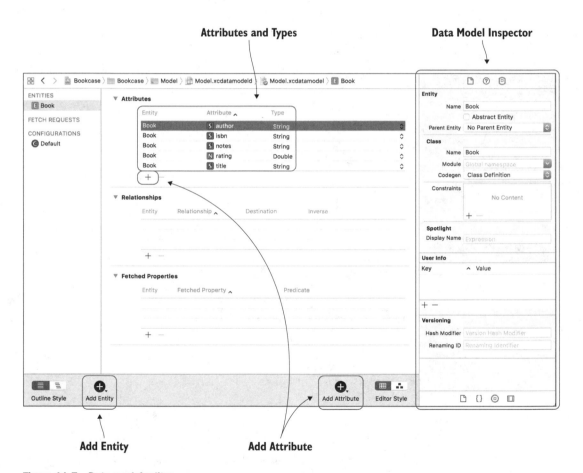

Figure 11.7   Data model editor

5 Add *attributes* to the `Book` entity with the Add Attribute button, and assign *types* to each attribute:

- `title`—String
- `author`—String
- `rating`—Double
- `isbn`—String
- `notes`—String

6 Select one of the attributes you've added. Notice that you have a new inspector in the Inspectors panel called the *Data Model Inspector*. Here, you can change the attribute type, add validation specifications, give the attribute a default value, or make the property optional—or not! Uncheck Optional for all the attributes in the `Book` entity so you won't have to unwrap your book properties.

Each entity will be represented in code by an `NSManagedObject` class, but Xcode can generate a neat subclass of `NSManagedObject` for each entity you create in the data model that contains the attributes you specified. By default, you need to manually request this subclass to be generated, but you can request for this to be done for you automatically.

7 Turn on automatic subclass generation: select the `Book` entity, and open the Data Model Inspector. Find the `Codegen` attribute, and instead of Manual/None, select Class Definition.

That's it: your data model is ready to go! Before you start using the data model for persisting data to disk, I want to cover a few setup details.

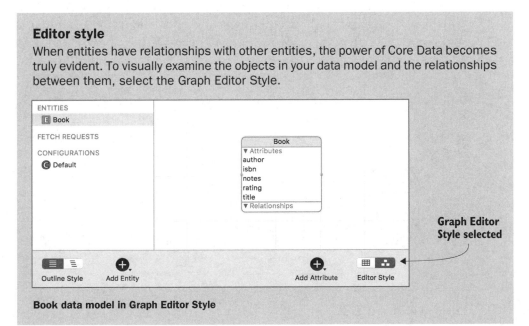

Editor style

When entities have relationships with other entities, the power of Core Data becomes truly evident. To visually examine the objects in your data model and the relationships between them, select the Graph Editor Style.

Book data model in Graph Editor Style

INITIAL SETUP

When you first create a project, you have the option to use Core Data. Selecting this option automatically creates the data model file you edited and generates boilerplate code that's necessary for using Core Data. In this section, you'll build up this boilerplate code manually and explore exactly what's involved.

Core Data requires objects to manage your data. These objects are called the *Core Data stack*, and include the objects shown in table 11.3.

Table 11.3   Core Data stack

Object	Description
Managed object context	Responsible for managing the data model in the memory. The managed object context is the object in the Core Data stack that you will interact with most directly.
Persistent store coordinator	Persists to and retrieves data from the *persistent object store*.
Persistent object store	Maps between the objects in the persistent store and the objects defined in the managed object model of your application.
Persistent store data file	The data file itself stored on disk. The underlying data file can be stored as different formats: SQLite (the default), XML, or binary data.
Managed object model	Describes the data model in your application.

See figure 11.8 for how they all fit together.

That's a lot of objects to keep track of—what a headache! Not to worry; since iOS 10, Apple has greatly simplified creating and accessing the objects in this stack with the `NSPersistentContainer` class. By instantiating the persistent container and requesting it to load persistent stores, it will create the Core Data stack for you.

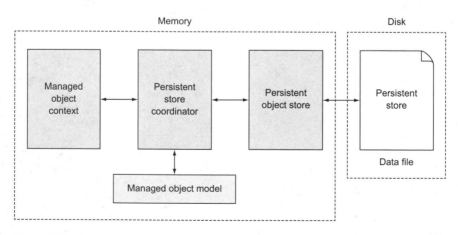

Figure 11.8   Core Data stack

Because the persistent container needs to be accessed globally, it's often added as a lazy computed property to the `AppDelegate` class.

1 Add a *persistent container* to your `AppDelegate` class now. Instantiate it with the name of your data model, and then load up any persistent stores.

Basic error handling has been included for now, but you should include more-relevant error handling when shipping your app.

```
// MARK: - Core Data stack                                          Lazy computed
lazy var persistentContainer: NSPersistentContainer = {            property
    let container = NSPersistentContainer(name: "Model")
    container.loadPersistentStores(
            completionHandler: { (storeDescription, error) in
        if let error = error as NSError? {
            fatalError("Unresolved error")                          Completion
        }                                                          handler
    })
    return container
}()
```

Instantiates with data model

Improve error handling here

Changes to data are performed in memory (via the managed object context) and aren't automatically saved to disk. To persist changes, you need to ask the managed object context to save the changes to the persistent store.

2 Add a method to the `AppDelegate` for committing unsaved changes.

```
// MARK: - Core Data Saving support
func saveContext () {                                               Gets managed
    let context = persistentContainer.viewContext                  object context
    if context.hasChanges {
        do {                                                       do-catch
            try context.save()                                     statement
        } catch {
            fatalError("Unresolved error")E                        Improve error
        }                                                          handling here
    }
}
```

Only saves if necessary

Saves changes to store

This method will come in handy every time you save data in the app. You can also ensure that unsaved data is saved to disk before the app terminates.

3 Add a call to the `saveContext` method in the `AppDelegate`'s `application-WillTerminate` method.

```
self.saveContext()
```

4 Add a reference to the application delegate in the `BooksTableView-Controller`, so that it can easily access the `saveContext` method you created. The `UIApplication` class has a singleton, `shared`, that refers to the application instance. Use the `delegate` property to access the app's `AppDelegate`.

```
let appDelegate = (UIApplication.shared.delegate as! AppDelegate)
```

The table view controller will also need a reference to the managed object context to perform updates and fetches on the database.

5 Use the reference to the `AppDelegate` to keep a reference to the *managed object context* via the *persistent container*.

```
lazy var context:NSManagedObjectContext = {
    return self.appDelegate.persistentContainer.viewContext
}()
```

That's all for the boilerplate setup; now, let's do a little cleanup on your Bookcase app.

CLEANUP

Core Data manages many operations on the data for you, making part of your existing code redundant. For those following along in Xcode, before we get into the details of using Core Data in your app's code, you'll need to perform a little cleanup of code that won't be required.

It may surprise you that you won't need the `BooksManager` class. Core Data will be handling the management of your books data!

1 Delete the `BooksManager` class, leaving the BooksManager.swift file with just the `SortOrder` enum. This will generate several errors elsewhere—not to worry, we'll attend to these in time. Rename the file SortOrder.swift.

2 Because you no longer have a `BooksManager` class, you won't need to inject it into the table view controller. Because injecting the `BooksManager` class was the whole point of the `TabBarController`, you can remove this file.

3 In the storyboard, remove the `TabBarController` from the custom class for the tab bar controller in the Identity Inspector.

4 Remove the `inject` method from the `BooksTableViewController`.

5 Comment out the whole `BooksCollectionViewController` class for now, so you can focus on the `BooksTableViewController` class without being concerned about errors elsewhere. Temporarily remove this class from the identification of this view controller in the storyboard.

6 Because you removed the original `Book` structure, you also removed a reference to the `defaultCover`. For simplicity, let's add this back in the `Books-TableViewController` class.

```
static let defaultCover = UIImage(named: "book.jpg")!
```

Great! Tidy-up complete, you're finally ready to start adding managed objects to Core Data for your app.

ADDING MANAGED OBJECTS

Now that you've set up the data model and the Core Data stack, how can you add an object to the persistent store for your app on a device?

Since iOS 10, it's too easy! All you need to do is instantiate a new model object, passing in the managed object context, set its properties like you would any Swift object, and then call the `AppDelegate`'s `saveContext` method. Believe it or not, that's it!

The following listing, for example, would create a new book with a title of *Great Expectations*.

Listing 11.2   Create managed object

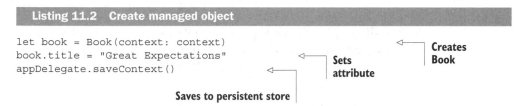

```
let book = Book(context: context)
book.title = "Great Expectations"
appDelegate.saveContext()
```

If you need to consider users with earlier versions of iOS, the first line blows out to the following:

```
let book = NSEntityDescription.insertNewObject(
    forEntityName: "Book", into: context) as! Book
```

As you can see, the syntax prior to iOS 10 was unwieldy. For brevity and clarity, I'll assume at least iOS 10 for the rest of this section. If you need to update the deployment target of your app to iOS 10, you can find this in the General properties for your app's main target.

If the user is creating a new book object, the `BookViewController` class will need a reference to the managed object context.

1   Add an implicitly unwrapped optional for the managed object context in the `BookViewController` class.

```
var context:NSManagedObjectContext!
```

2   Pass this context into the `BookViewController` in the `prepareForSegue` method in the `BooksTableViewController` class:

```
viewController.context = context
```

3   Now you can update the `touchSave` method in `BookViewController` to save a book. Each `Book` object is uniquely identifiable internally for Core Data.

When the user taps the Save button in the detail view controller, you want to first check if the book already exists. If it doesn't, you want to create a new `Book` managed object. If it does, you want to *update* the existing `Book` object.

```
@IBAction func touchSave(_ sender: AnyObject) {
    let bookToSave: Book
    if let book = book {                          Gets book
        bookToSave = book                         to update
    } else {
        bookToSave = Book(context: context)       Creates
    }                                             book
```

```
bookToSave.title = titleTextField.text!
bookToSave.author = authorTextField.text!
bookToSave.rating = 3
bookToSave.isbn = isbnTextField.text!
bookToSave.notes = notesTextView.text!
delegate?.saveBook(book: bookToSave)
dismissMe()
}
```

Updates book attributes

4   Back in the `saveBook` method in the table view controller class extension, you can now call the `saveContext` method on the `AppDelegate`, to commit unsaved changes to the persistent store.

```
func saveBook(book: Book) {
    appDelegate.saveContext()
}
```

You no longer want to update the table view in this method. Instead, you'll soon be setting up the `BookTableViewController` class to receive notifications of updates to the data and update the interface.

FETCHING MANAGED OBJECTS

Now that you know how to store managed objects in the persistent object store, you need to retrieve these objects to display to the user. Use a *fetch request* to define how to fetch these managed objects. You can request an `NSFetchRequest` object directly from your managed object with the `fetchRequest` method. Using generics, you can specify that your `NSFetchRequest` contains a fetch request of your `Book` managed object.

The `NSFetchRequest` can specify

- *Batch size*—The number of managed objects to return.
- *Search criteria*—Use the `NSPredicate` class to define search criteria.
- *Sort order*—Use an array of instances of the `NSSortDescriptor` class to define the sort order.

For example, a basic `NSFetchRequest` with a batch size of 20 items that searches for *all* books and sorts by title would look like the following listing.

Listing 11.3   Simple fetch request

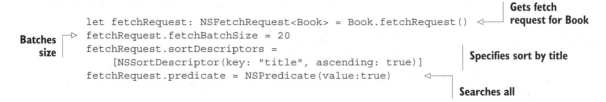

```
let fetchRequest: NSFetchRequest<Book> = Book.fetchRequest()        Gets fetch
fetchRequest.fetchBatchSize = 20                                    request for Book
fetchRequest.sortDescriptors =
    [NSSortDescriptor(key: "title", ascending: true)]
fetchRequest.predicate = NSPredicate(value:true)                    Specifies sort by title

                                                                    Searches all
```

Batches size

We'll look at sorting with `NSSortDescriptor` and searching with `NSPredicate` in more detail shortly.

Now that you have a fetch request, you can pass it and the managed object context into a *fetched results controller*. A fetched results controller can perform the fetch and manage the results of the fetch request.

You're going to use the delegate of the fetched results controller to respond to changes in the data and update your table view. You also have the option to request the fetched results controller to *cache* the results of the query to avoid recalculating the same fetch request.

1 Store a fetched results controller of your fetch request in a lazy computed property in your `BooksTableViewController`. Set `self` as the delegate and perform the fetch.

```
// MARK: FetchedResultsController
lazy var fetchedResultsController: NSFetchedResultsController<Book> =
        self.getFetch()

func getFetch() -> NSFetchedResultsController<Book> {
    let fetchRequest: NSFetchRequest<Book> = Book.fetchRequest()
    fetchRequest.fetchBatchSize = 20
    fetchRequest.sortDescriptors =
        [NSSortDescriptor(key: "title", ascending: true)]
    fetchRequest.predicate = NSPredicate(value: true)
    fetchedResultsController = NSFetchedResultsController(
        fetchRequest: fetchRequest,
        managedObjectContext: self.context,
        sectionNameKeyPath: nil,
        cacheName: nil
    )
    fetchedResultsController.delegate = self
    do {
        try fetchedResultsController.performFetch()
        return fetchedResultsController
    } catch {
        fatalError("Error \(error)")
    }
}
```

Creates lazy var — lazy var fetchedResultsController

Returns fetched results controller — func getFetch()

Creates fetched results controller — fetchedResultsController = NSFetchedResultsController(

Specifies cache name — cacheName: nil

Specifies delegate — fetchedResultsController.delegate = self

do-catch statement — do {

Performs fetch — try fetchedResultsController.performFetch()

The table view controller now needs to adopt the protocol associated with the fetched view controller's delegate. Methods in this delegate will be triggered when changes occur in the data. You could use the data returned in these protocol methods to perform specific operations in the table, such as *insert, delete,* and *update*. For this example, you'll keep it simple, however, and reload the table when content changes.

2 Add an extension to the `BooksTableViewController` that adopts the `NSFetchedResultsControllerDelegate` protocol and implement the `controllerDidChangeContent` method, reloading the table.

```
extension BooksTableViewController: NSFetchedResultsControllerDelegate {
    func controllerDidChangeContent(_ controller:
            NSFetchedResultsController<NSFetchRequestResult>) {
```

```
        self.tableView.reloadData()
    }
}
```

You can use your fetched results controller to display the data to the user in the table by responding to the `UITableViewDelegate` methods.

Let's start by defining the number of items in each section. The `NSFetched-ResultsController` class contains a sections property with information about each section. As you know, your results will have one section; you can get information about the first section and extract the number of objects.

3 Return the number of objects from the fetched results controller in the `numberOfRowsInSection` table view delegate method.

```
override func tableView(_ tableView: UITableView,
        numberOfRowsInSection section: Int) -> Int {
    let sectionInfo = self.fetchedResultsController.sections![section]
    return sectionInfo.numberOfObjects
}
```

Now, you need to extract actual book data from the fetched results controller to display in the table. It's straightforward to get a `Book` managed object from the fetched results controller by calling the `object` method and passing in an `indexPath`.

4 Update the `cellForRowAt` method of the table view delegate protocol. Don't forget to update the location of the image because you're no longer storing this constant in the `Book` structure.

```
override func tableView(_ tableView: UITableView,
        cellForRowAt indexPath: IndexPath) -> UITableViewCell {
    let cell = tableView.dequeueReusableCell(
        withIdentifier: "bookCell", for: indexPath)
    let book = self.fetchedResultsController.object(at: indexPath)
    cell.textLabel?.text = book.title
    cell.detailTextLabel?.text = book.author
    cell.imageView?.image = BooksTableViewController.defaultCover
    return cell
}
```

UPDATING AND DELETING MANAGED OBJECTS

Now that you can extract a managed object at an index of the table, you can use the same method to pass this object to the detail view controller in the `prepareForSegue` method, when the user selects a book in the table to update.

1 Pass in the book to update to the `BookTableViewController`, in the `prepareForSegue` method of `BooksTableViewController`.

```
viewController.book = self.fetchedResultsController.object(
    at: selectedIndexPath)
```

Implementing deletion of a managed object is equally straightforward. Call the managed object context's `delete` method, passing in the `Book` object to delete from the fetched results controller. To persist the changes to the store, finish by calling the `saveContext` method. It's not necessary to request the table view to update because this update will be triggered in the fetched results controller delegate.

2   Update the delete portion of code in your `BooksTableViewController` class to delete a `Book` managed object:

```
override func tableView(_ tableView: UITableView,
    commit editingStyle: UITableViewCellEditingStyle,
    forRowAt indexPath: IndexPath) {
  if editingStyle == .delete {
    context.delete(fetchedResultsController.object(at: indexPath))
    appDelegate.saveContext()
  }
}
```

SORTING FETCH REQUESTS

Rather than the `BooksManager` sorting the data in memory, you'll use the `sortDescriptors` attribute of the `NSFetchRequest`.

Sort descriptors describe how you'd like a sort operation of your data to be performed. A sort descriptor specifies a field to sort and the direction of the sort. The `sortOrder` property of `NSFetchRequest` is an array so that your fetch request can have multiple sort operations for multiple fields.

The sort descriptor can also specify an optional method to customize the comparison. The `NSString` method has a convenient method called `localizedCaseInsensitiveCompare` for comparisons that ignore case and localization differences.

Here's an example sort descriptor that will sort the `title` field in an ascending order, ignoring case and localization:

```
NSSortDescriptor(key: "title",
    ascending: true,
    selector: #selector(NSString.localizedCaseInsensitiveCompare(_:)))
```

You need two sort descriptors in the Bookcase app—one that sorts by title and another that sorts by author.

If the user selects to sort by title, the fetch request should prioritize the title sort descriptor. Conversely, if the user wants to sort by author, the author sort descriptor should take priority.

You'll need to get the user's currently selected segment in the sort order segmented control. If you haven't yet created one (you may have for the user defaults challenge at the end of section 11.1.2), connect an outlet for it in the `BooksTableViewController`.

```
@IBOutlet weak var sortSegmentedControl: UISegmentedControl!
```

1 Replace the simple sort descriptor in the creation of the fetch request with one
that takes the user's preferred sort order into consideration.

Gets segmented control index →
Gets preferred Sort Order →
Title sort descriptor →
Author sort descriptor →
User wants sort by title →
Prioritizes title
Prioritizes author

```
let segmentIndex = sortSegmentedControl.selectedSegmentIndex
guard let sortOrder = SortOrder(rawValue: segmentIndex)
    else {fatalError("Segment error")}
let titleDescriptor = NSSortDescriptor(key: "title",
    ascending: true,
    selector: #selector(NSString.localizedCaseInsensitiveCompare(_:)))
let authorDescriptor = NSSortDescriptor(key: "author",
    ascending: true,
    selector: #selector(NSString.localizedCaseInsensitiveCompare(_:)))
if self.sortOrder == .title {
    fetchRequest.sortDescriptors =
        [titleDescriptor,authorDescriptor]
} else {
    fetchRequest.sortDescriptors =
        [authorDescriptor,titleDescriptor]
}
```

Now, when the user selects a new segment of the segmented control, you should
regenerate the fetch results controller before updating the table.

2 Update the `changedSegment` method.

```
@IBAction func changedSegment(_ sender: UISegmentedControl) {
    fetchedResultsController = getFetch()
    self.tableView.reloadData()
}
```

SEARCHING FETCH REQUESTS

Rather than the `BooksManager` searching through your data in memory, you're
going to take advantage of searching via *predicates* as a built-in feature of `NSFetch-`
`Request`.

Predicates allow you to define the criteria for filtering your data using a natural
language interface. You can use all the basic operators, such as = or <, and similar to
SQLite queries, you have English comparisons such as `LIKE`, `CONTAINS`, or
`BEGINSWITH`, and logical operations such as `AND` or `OR`.

All you need to do is instantiate the `NSPredicate` class, passing in the filtering criteria via the `format` property. For example, here's a predicate that returns books with
a rating of 4:

```
NSPredicate(format: "rating = 4")
```

A predicate that returns books that contain "the" in the title looks like this:

```
NSPredicate(format: "title CONTAINS 'the'")
```

Notice that strings need to be contained in quotes.

NOTE If you want your search to ignore differences such as letter case
(upper- or lowercase) or letter *accents* (called *diacritics*), you can use the `CON-`
`TAINS[CD]` comparison (*CD* stands for *case diacritics*).

The predicate you added to the `fetchRequest` earlier returned *all* books, but if text is in the search bar, you only want books that match this text.

1 Replace the fetch request predicate with a predicate that fetches books whose `title` or `author` fields contain the text in the search bar.

```
guard let searchText = searchController.searchBar.text
    else { fatalError("No search bar") }
if searchText != "" {
    fetchRequest.predicate =
        NSPredicate(format: "(title CONTAINS[CD] '\(searchText)')
        ➡ OR (author CONTAINS[CD] '\(searchText)')")
}
```

When a change is made to the text in the search bar, the fetched results controller should be regenerated before reloading the table view.

2 Update the `updateSearchResults` method in the extension.

```
func updateSearchResults(for searchController: UISearchController) {
    fetchedResultsController = getFetch()
    tableView.reloadData()
}
```

Well, it's been a journey, but you're there! Core Data should now be set up and ready to use in your table view controller. You can view, add, delete, and update managed objects, and search and sort the data.

CHALLENGE   Add a fetched results controller to the collection view controller. Make the necessary changes to display, add, edit, search, and sort book managed objects from this tab. You will find interesting challenges when setting up the collection view controller, because you'll be displaying items in section 2, but requesting them in section 1 of the fetched results controller.

✓ **CHECKPOINT**   If you'd like to compare your project with mine at this point, you can check it out at https://github.com/iOSAppDevelopmentwithSwiftinAction/Bookcase.git (Chapter11.7.StoreDataCoreData).

In the next chapter, we'll take data persistence to the next level—in iCloud!

11.3   Summary

In this chapter, you learned the following:

- Preserve app state to restore the app the way the user left it.
- User defaults can be used to store small, discrete pieces of information, such as username, high score, or user preferences such as sound on or off.
- Respond to app-level events in the app delegate.

- To include Objective-C classes in a Swift project, add a bridging header and import their Objective-C header files.
- Store smaller amounts of data in their entirety locally (also known as an *atomic store*) using technologies such as XML, property lists, or archiving objects.
- For apps with greater data requirements, such as creating relationships between objects and sophisticated queries, consider storing data using a *transactional store* such as SQLite.
- If your app has large data requirements with relationships and sophisticated queries, you might also want to consider Core Data. Core Data also provides additional features such as creating relationships between objects, tracking changes, caching, and validation.

Data persistence
in iCloud

This chapter covers

- Storing user preferences in iCloud
- Storing data in iCloud using CloudKit

In this chapter, you'll take storing data to the next level—iCloud.

Until now, you've only stored user defaults locally on the device. What happens if the user opens your app on another device they own?

In this chapter, you'll explore iCloud, a convenient cloud data storage service provided by Apple, which can be used by developers to automatically share data and give your user the same experience between multiple devices. You'll look at storing discrete values such as user preferences in iCloud using the *ubiquitous key-value store*. You'll also explore *CloudKit*, an essential framework for storing structured data in iCloud.

Along the way, you'll encounter additional concepts:

- Concurrent programming in iOS
- Indicating background tasks
- Displaying alerts

- Refreshing a table view
- Receiving remote notifications

NOTE   If you haven't enrolled in the Apple Developer Program yet, be aware that membership is necessary to use iCloud. If you need to enroll, you'll want to click here and follow Apple's instructions: https://developer.apple.com/programs/enroll/. We'll go into this process in more detail in chapter 16. If you're not ready to enroll, you might want to skip this chapter for now.

12.1   *Setting up your app for iCloud*

In this chapter, you'll store book data and user preference data for the Bookcase app in iCloud.

✔ **CHECKPOINT**   Open the app after adding user preferences in the last chapter, or check it out at https://github.com/iOSAppDevelopment-withSwiftinAction/Bookcase.git (Chapter11.1.UserPreferences).

Setting up your app to use iCloud is straightforward.

1 First, you need to ensure your team is specified in your target's General preferences. (Even if you're a solo developer, you're defined as a development *team* by Apple.)
2 While you're in the General preferences, you'll want to also change the bundle identifier for your app. iCloud uses this bundle ID to uniquely identify your app.
3 Open the Capabilities tab to turn on iCloud (see figure 12.1). You have three services to choose from:

- *Key-value Storage*—Store small, discrete values such as user preferences.
- *iCloud Documents*—Store complete documents.
- *CloudKit*—Store structured data. In this chapter, we'll look at key-value storage and CloudKit.

4 For now, just keep *Key-value Storage* selected.

You'll find that when you activate iCloud, Xcode creates an entitlements file— a property list file representing the new capability that you introduced for your app—in your Project Navigator.

Now that you have iCloud set up for your application, you can use iCloud's key-value storage to store user defaults.

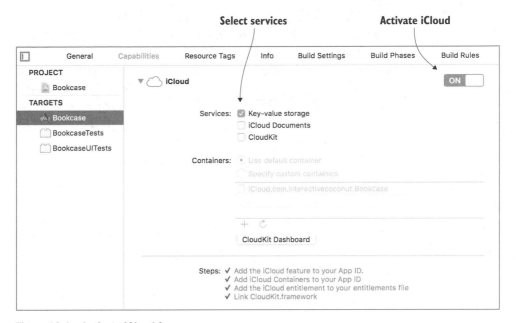

Figure 12.1   Activate iCloud for your app

12.2   *Persisting data with ubiquitous key-value store*

To persist user preferences data in iCloud, you'll want to use the ubiquitous key-value store. The ubiquitous key-value store stores data locally on the device and then requests this data to be synced with iCloud. Unlike user defaults, the ubiquitous key-value store doesn't immediately store data to iCloud from memory. Rather, it waits a few seconds, or until the app moves to the background. If you want the local storage and memory to sync immediately after setting a value, you can call the synchronize method.

Let's use the ubiquitous key-value store to sync the Bookcase app across a user's devices, tracking the user's preference for the ISBN field in the book detail view.

Implementing the ubiquitous key-value store rather than user defaults is surprisingly simple—you can replace any reference to UserDefaults.standard with NSUbiquitousKeyValueStore.default.

1 Replace references to setting and getting user defaults in your earlier BookViewController code with the ubiquitous key-value store. You'll find these in the toggleISBN and viewDidLoad methods.

```
NSUbiquitousKeyValueStore.default.set(                        Sets value (toggleISBN)
    isbnStackView.isHidden, forKey: isbnKey)
isbnStackView.isHidden =
    NSUbiquitousKeyValueStore.default.bool(forKey: isbnKey)
```

Gets value (viewDidLoad) labels the second statement.

2 Run the app to test this.

3 In the running app, hide the ISBN field, tap the Home button to send the app to the background, and then run the app again. You should find that the app has preserved your preference, the way it did with user defaults.

Preferences will be stored locally regardless of whether the user has iCloud set up on their device! If the user has registered their device to use iCloud, the app will let iCloud know that it has new values waiting to be uploaded, and they'll be uploaded at the next convenient moment. See figure 12.2 for a diagram showing how this change finds its way to the ubiquitous key-value store and is propagated to other devices.

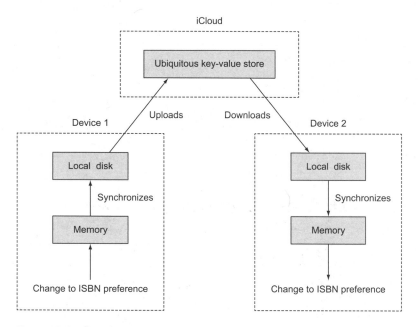

Figure 12.2 Ubiquitous key-value store

NOTE Don't depend on values being immediately updated. It can take several seconds to upload data to iCloud! Don't worry if your app loses connection to the internet or iCloud temporarily—the update will automatically upload when your device reconnects.

To fully appreciate the ubiquitous key-value store, you'll ideally test on two devices. If you only have one device, you can use the simulator for one device, but be sure to log in to iCloud on the simulator.

4 If you're using the simulator, log in now. With the simulator open, tap the Home button to return to the home screen. Find the Settings app, select "Sign in to your iPhone," and follow the prompts. It's not necessary to merge your contacts.

NOTE Because each device has a different simulator, if you want to run your app on a simulator for a different device, you'll need to log in again to iCloud.

5 Run the app on one device, make a change to the ISBN field, and send the app to the background. Now run the app on the second device.

You should notice that the change persists on both devices. But what if both apps are running simultaneously? An app can be notified that the app running on another device has updated the ubiquitous key-value store via a notification from the notification center.

6 In the `viewDidAppear` method of the `BookViewController` class, add an observer that will respond to changes in the ubiquitous key-value store.

```
NotificationCenter.default.addObserver(self,
    selector: #selector(uKVSChanged),
    name: NSUbiquitousKeyValueStore.didChangeExternallyNotification,
    object: nil)
```

When this notification is triggered, the data in memory will automatically be synchronized with the data that has recently been downloaded from iCloud. In case of conflict, the value that was set most recently is given priority, and the older value is discarded.

7 Create a method that will be triggered by this notification. Once you know that the data is up to date, you can update the ISBN field with the updated value.

Observer method

Shows/Hides ISBN field

```
@objc func uKVSChanged(notification: Notification) {
    isbnStackView.isHidden =
        NSUbiquitousKeyValueStore.default.bool(forKey: isbnKey)
}
```

Run the app on two devices with iCloud installed. Navigate to the book view controller on both apps. Hide or show the ISBN field on one device. (If one of your devices is a simulator, do this step on the simulator, because the simulator doesn't reliably receive key-value store change notifications.) Be patient, it can take time—eventually you should notice that the change synchronizes on the other device. Magic!

CHALLENGE Using the ubiquitous key-value store, record the user's choice of sort order in the segmented controls in the books table and books collection scenes.

✓ **CHECKPOINT** If you'd like to compare your project with mine at this point, you can check mine out at https://github.com/iOSApp-DevelopmentwithSwiftinAction/Bookcase.git (Chapter12.1.UbiquitousKey-ValueStore).

12.3 *Storing data using CloudKit*

CloudKit is a service provided by Apple for storing data as records in a database in iCloud, ready to be accessed by your app from different devices.

Unlike the ubiquitous key-value store, CloudKit doesn't perform any local storage. It's up to you to determine whether your app requires an internet connection to access CloudKit data, or whether you want to maintain local storage in addition to CloudKit, and manage synchronization of the two. To keep things as simple as possible, in this section we'll explore storage of data in iCloud using CloudKit without any local storage.

The same way the file system for your app on the device is sandboxed, your app has a sandboxed area in iCloud, called a *container*. When you activate iCloud for your app, Apple automatically creates a container for it, ready to store data using CloudKit.

Inside your app's container, you have access to a *public* database that all users of your app can access. Your app's users can write to the public database if they're logged in to iCloud. A public database could be useful for an app that allows users to post restaurant reviews, for example, where reviews would be useful to other users. Logged-in users will also have access to a *private database*, relevant only to a single user. A private database will be perfect for the Bookcase app, where a user's data should be private and only relevant to them.

Database tables in CloudKit are called *record types*. Each *record type* contains *records* that are key-value dictionaries storing the *fields* of the record, and identified by a *record ID*. In your Bookcase app, a *books record type* would be perfect for storing book records. The book record fields would represent book properties (see figure 12.3).

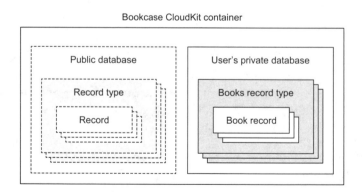

Figure 12.3   CloudKit container

NOTE   Within a private database, record types can also be grouped into *zones*.

As you've probably guessed, you're going to explore using a private database in Cloud-Kit to store your app's books data in iCloud.

1. Return to the iCloud capabilities for your app, and turn on CloudKit services (see figure 12.4). Use the CloudKit dashboard to manage your app's container or its contents.

Select services

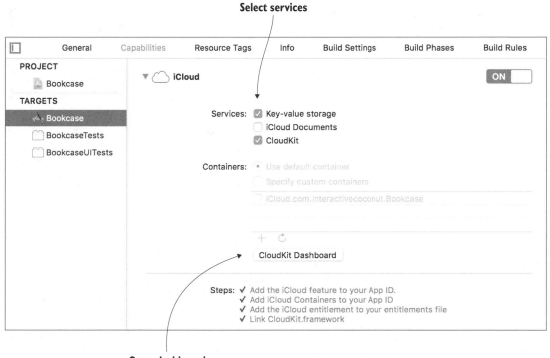

Open dashboard

Figure 12.4   Activate CloudKit, and open dashboard

2. Select the CloudKit dashboard.
3. Select your app, select Development Data, and explore the dashboard for your app.

You won't see any records in your app's container yet, but by the end of this section, you'll have a Books record type in your private database containing book data (see figure 12.5).

Great, let's get started by updating your model!

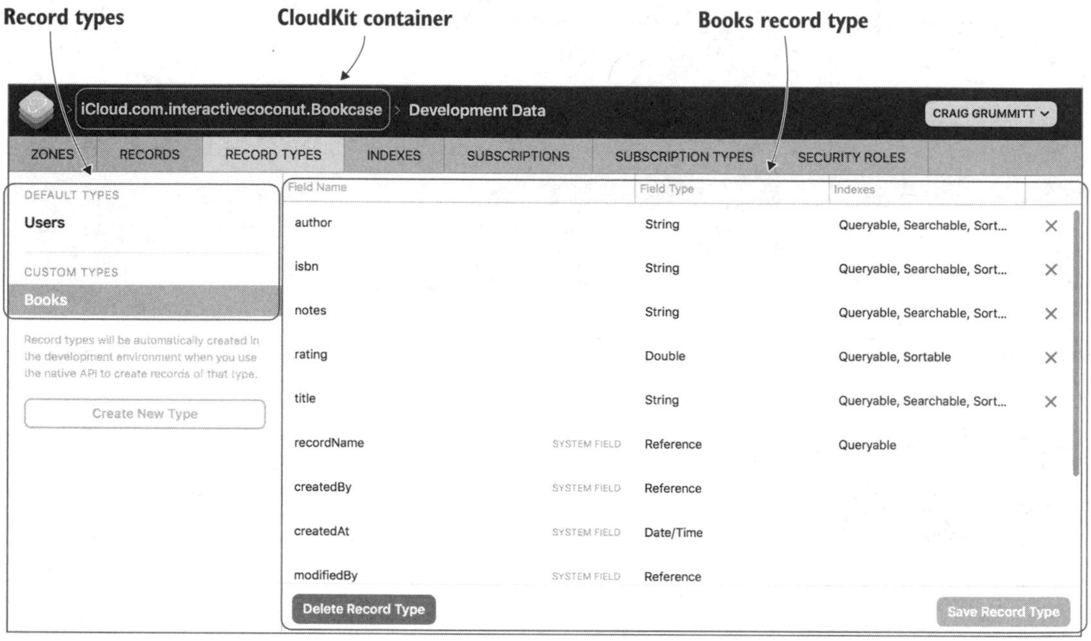

Record types   **CloudKit container**   **Books record type**

Figure 12.5   CloudKit dashboard

12.3.1 *Updating the model for CloudKit*

Records are represented in your code by the CKRecord class. Like a dictionary, the CKRecord class can store values with keys. There are, however, only certain Objective-C data types that can be stored: NSString, NSNumber, NSData, NSDate, and NSArray. To store Swift data types, you need to cast them first to their Objective-C equivalent. Easy enough—you need to cast String to NSString, Int or Double to NSNumber, Data to NSData, Date to NSDate, and Swift arrays as NSArray.

CloudKit records can also store three special data types:

- CLLocation—Geographical locations.
- CKAsset—Large files, such as images, sounds, or video.
- CKReference—A reference to another record. Using a CKReference, you can build relationships between record types.

When you create a new record, CloudKit automatically assigns it a record ID. To update a record, you need a reference to the CKRecord object you need to change. One way to do this is to fetch the record using its record ID, but for simplicity, you'll store CKRecord objects for each book in memory.

1 Add a record optional property to the Book structure to store the record for each book:

```
var record: CKRecord
```

2 You'll need to import CloudKit, because `CKRecord` comes from the CloudKit framework.

```
import CloudKit
```

To identify a record type, it needs a name.

3 Add a constant to specify the record type's name:

```
static let recordType = "Books"
```

Now, you can include a reference to a record when instantiating a Book structure. When you're first creating a `Book` object, you won't yet have a reference to a `CKRecord`, so this should be an optional, and the `Book` initializer can handle instantiating a `CKRecord` with the record type you set up.

4 Add the code in bold in the following listing to the `init` method of Book:

```
init(record: CKRecord? = nil, title: String, …) {
    if let record = record {
        self.record = record
    } else {
        self.record = CKRecord(recordType: Book.recordType)
    }
    // Continue setting properties
```

Now, you have a `CKRecord` object stored in the `Book` object that will be storing all of the `Book` properties. Because it would be redundant to store the same properties in the `Book` object *and* the `CKRecord` object, let's convert the `Book` properties to computed properties that set and get their values from `CKRecord`.

5 For example, change the title property to

```
var title: String {
    get { return record[Key.title] as! String }
    set { record[Key.title] = newValue as NSString }
}
```

CHALLENGE Convert the `Book` object's other properties—`author`, `rating`, `isbn`, and `notes`—to computed properties that derive their values from the `CKRecord`.

Shortly, you'll be querying CloudKit for all book records, which you'll want to convert to `Book` objects.

6 Add an initializer to the `Book` structure that instantiates a `Book` object from a `CKRecord`:

```
init(record: CKRecord) {
    self.record = record
}
```

12.3.2 *Adding a book record to CloudKit*

Now that the book objects you create have a `CKRecord` property, you can add this record to your app's private database.

1 Add a reference to your app container's private database in the `BooksManager` class.

```
let db = CKContainer.default.privateCloudDatabase
```

Use the `default` type method to return the container object for this app. Instances of `CKContainer` contain properties for both the private and public databases. Because you'll use the private database in Bookcase to store each user's private data, get a reference to it with the `privateCloudDatabase` method.

2 You'll need to import CloudKit here in `BooksManager` too, because `CKContainer` comes from the CloudKit framework.

```
import CloudKit
```

Adding a new record to iCloud is as simple as calling the database's `save` method, and passing in the new record. Because a call to iCloud occurs asynchronously, the response from iCloud is returned in a completion handler closure that receives the saved record, and an optional error object if something went wrong.

3 Set up an `addBookCloudKit` method in `BooksManager` that will add a new book:

```
func addBookCloudKit(book: Book) {
    db.save(book.record) { (record, error) in
        // Save complete or Error occurred
        // Do something here
    }
}
```

When you receive the response from iCloud, you want to either add the new book record to the table, or, if something went wrong, you probably want to notify the user. Both actions occur in the user interface, but there's a problem. Because the `save` method occurs asynchronously, its completion handler is performed on a background queue and therefore doesn't have access to the interface.

Using threads and queues in iOS

As you saw in chapter 4, the path of execution that code follows is called a *thread*. If all code were to execute in the same thread, as soon as a time-consuming operation were encountered, such as heavy-duty processing or a network operation, everything else including the user interface would freeze waiting for the operation to complete.

Multiple threads are the solution to this problem, where time-consuming operations can occur on *background threads* without holding up the *main thread*, where important work occurs, such as updating the user interface and responding to system events.

Apple provides developers with several alternatives for managing threads. One common solution is the concept of a *dispatch queue*. A dispatch queue is like a to-do list of tasks. Queues can dispatch their tasks in sequence (*serial* queues) or simultaneously (*concurrent* queues).

Serial and concurrent queues

The thread a queue performs its tasks on is managed by the system behind the scenes. One exception to this rule is a serial queue called the *main queue* that's intrinsically tied to the *main thread*, meaning that tasks you run on the main queue will be guaranteed access to the user interface.

You can create your own dispatch queue, but most commonly you'll use one of the system queues. In addition to the main queue, four global concurrent queues, with different *quality of service* (QOS), affect their priority and therefore the time the task takes to complete:

- *User-initiated* tasks are the highest priority, because the user is waiting on a response. Saving a file is an example of a task that should be given a QOS of user-initiated.
- *Utility* tasks are a medium priority, because they're time-consuming operations that aren't expected to return an immediate response. Downloading a file is an example of a utility task.
- *Background* tasks are a low priority, because they generally perform administrative tasks that aren't time critical, such as performing backups.

(continued)

Use the `DispatchQueue` syntax to pass in tasks to perform (as closures) to specific queues. Here's how you could request a background queue to perform a time-consuming operation on a global concurrent queue with a *utility* QOS and then request the main queue to display the result of the operation to the user:

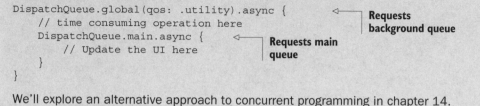

```
DispatchQueue.global(qos: .utility).async {          ◁──┐ Requests
    // time consuming operation here                      │ background queue
    DispatchQueue.main.async {        ◁──┐ Requests main
        // Update the UI here             │ queue
    }
}
```

We'll explore an alternative approach to concurrent programming in chapter 14.

4   Request the main queue before going any further to have access to the user interface. Once you're on the main thread, you can deal with errors, or (if the operation was successful) call the `addBook` method to add the book to the books array and sort.

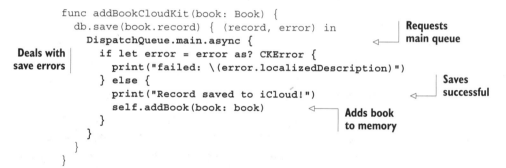

```
func addBookCloudKit(book: Book) {
    db.save(book.record) { (record, error) in         ◁──┐ Requests
        DispatchQueue.main.async {                          │ main queue
            if let error = error as? CKError {
                print("failed: \(error.localizedDescription)")
            } else {
                print("Record saved to iCloud!")       ◁── Saves
                self.addBook(book: book)   ◁──┐ Adds book    successful
            }                                   │ to memory
        }
    }
}
```

Deals with save errors

The `BooksManager` will now need to notify the view controller that the save operation has completed so that the view controller can update the view based on the result of updating the model. As you've seen, several options exist for achieving this. For instance, the `BooksManager` could use the delegation pattern, or it could dispatch a notification. This time, let's pass in a closure to the `BooksManager`, which it will call when the operation is complete.

5   Add in a completion handler parameter to the `addBookCloudKit` method that accepts an error variable. You can then call this closure to notify it that the save operation has either completed or failed.

```
func addBookCloudKit(book: Book,
    completion: @escaping (_ error: CKError?) -> Void) {   ◁── Passes in
    db.save(book.record) { (record, error) in                   closure
        DispatchQueue.main.async {
            if let error = error as? CKError {
                // Error occurred
```

```
        completion(error)
    } else {
        // Record saved to iCloud
        self.addBook(book: book)
        completion(nil)
    }
  }
 }
}
```

◁ ── Notifies failure with error

◁ ── Notifies success with nil

Because the completion handler closure is called within a dispatch queue, it needs to *escape* its function.

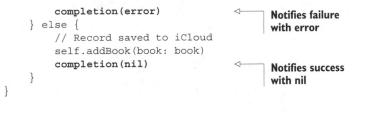
Escaping closures
By default, a closure passed in to a function can't *escape* that method: it can't be stored in a property outside the function, used as an argument when calling another function, or added to a dispatch queue. Think of the function as a walled area—once a closure is passed in, it can't get out, with one exception: you can specify that you're okay with a closure escaping its function by marking it `@escaping`.

6 Back in the `saveBook` method in the `BooksTableViewController` extension, you can now call the new `BooksManager` method you set up, and pass in a completion closure:

```
booksManager.addBookCloudKit(book: book,
    completion: { (error) in
        // Add book operation is complete
    }
)
```

While the save operation is being performed, you'll prevent the user from performing additional operations by displaying an indicator to signal to the user that something is happening.

Indicating background tasks
UIKit provides you with two alternatives for indicating to the user that a background task is in progress:

- The *Activity Indicator* is a view containing infinitely animating spinning spokes that indicate a task is in progress. Use an activity indicator when a task has an indeterminate finish time.
- The *Progress View* is a view containing a progress bar, illustrating the progress of a background task. Use a progress view when it's possible to estimate the progress of a task.

Because you can't accurately estimate when a save operation will complete, let's use an activity indicator.

7 Create an activity indicator in a lazy stored property. When it's first referenced, you can also add it to the root view's subviews and center it.

```
lazy var activityIndicator: UIActivityIndicatorView = {
    let indicator = UIActivityIndicatorView(activityIndicatorStyle: .gray)
        indicator.center = self.view.center
        self.view.addSubview(indicator)
    return indicator
}()
```

8 Now, when a cloud operation is in progress, you need a method to call that prevents the user from interacting with the interface and starts animating the activity indicator. By passing in a function parameter, the same method could be used to stop the activity indicator animating and reenable user interaction.

```
func cloudOperation(waiting: Bool) {
  if waiting {
    activityIndicator.startAnimating()
  } else {
    activityIndicator.stopAnimating()
  }
  tableView?.isUserInteractionEnabled = !waiting
  navigationController?.navigationBar.isUserInteractionEnabled =
  ➥ !waiting
  tabBarController?.tabBar.isUserInteractionEnabled = !waiting
}
```

NOTE The activity indicator will automatically hide itself when it isn't animating.

9 You can now call this method in the `saveBook` method both before requesting the CloudKit operation and in the completion handler:

```
cloudOperation(waiting: true)                          ◁────┐ Waits for response
booksManager.addBookCloudKit(book: book,                      from iCloud
    completion: { (error) in
        self.cloudOperation(waiting: false)            ◁────┐ Response received
        self.tableView.reloadData()                           from iCloud
    }
)
```
Reloads table ┌──▷

Your Bookcase app should now be ready to add a book record to iCloud.

10 Run your app, and from the table view controller, add a book and select Save. (Don't forget that if you're testing on the simulator, you need to log in to iCloud.) You should see an activity indicator appear for a second before the new book appears.

Let's see if your new book has been added in iCloud.

11 Open the CloudKit dashboard again, and select the Bookcase app and Development Data. Under Record Types, the Books record type should now appear, listing all the fields associated with this record type.

While you're in the record types section, take a look at the metadata that have been set up for this record. You should see metadata Created By, Date Created, Modified By, and Date Modified. Here, you can also find your record's automatically generated record name that the record ID is generated from.

While the fields in your record are automatically sortable, queryable, and searchable by default, the metadata by default is not. If you want to perform queries on specific metadata, you'll need to check that field here. In fact, to return all records in a query, you'll need to make the record name queryable.

12 Select the Indexes tab.

13 Select Add Field, recordName, Queryable, and Save Record Type (see figure 12.6).

Figure 12.6   Check CloudKit book record ID

14 Now, take a look at the book record data you added. Select Records, and with the Books record selected, select Query Records (see figure 12.7).

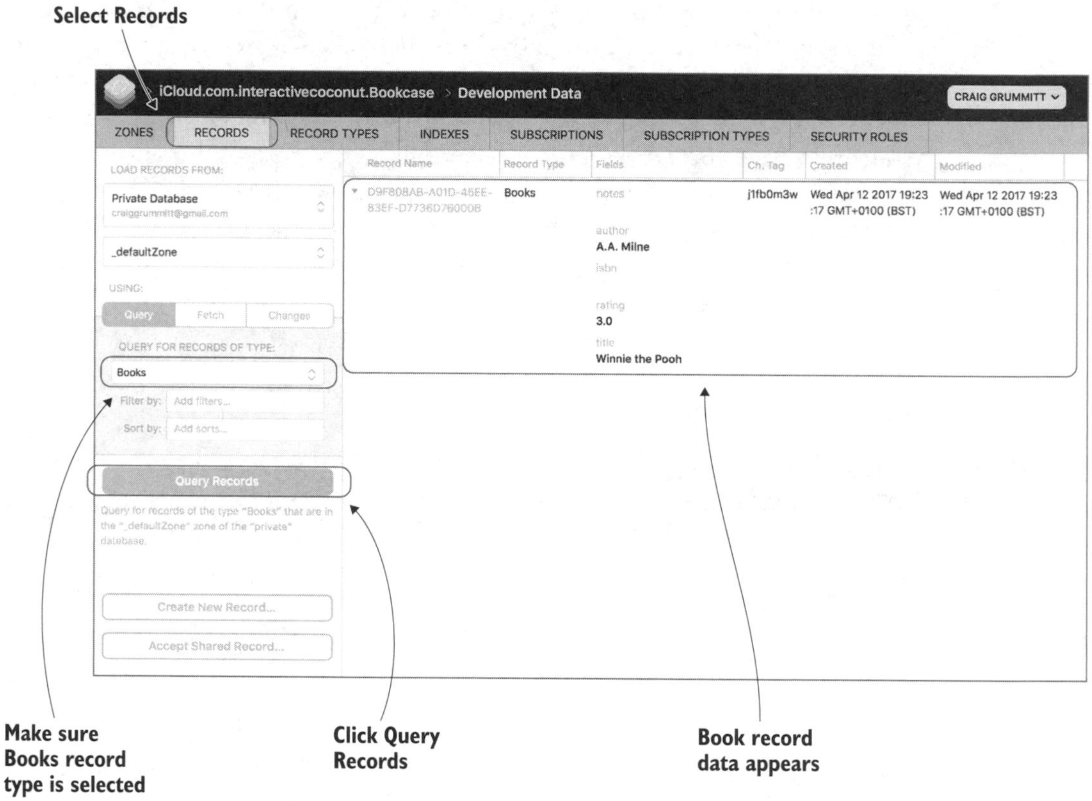

Figure 12.7 CloudKit book record data

12.3.3 *Updating a book record in CloudKit*

Updating a book is similar to adding one. If you fetch a record from CloudKit, update it, and then pass it in to the save method of CKDatabase, this record will be updated in iCloud.

When the user taps the Save button in the detail view controller, be sure that you're updating the CKRecord object if it exists, rather than generating a new one, by instantiating a Book object with the CKRecord object of the book the user is currently editing.

1 Include the current book's record when saving a book in the touchSave method of BookViewController.

```
let bookToSave = Book(record: book?.record,
    title: titleTextField.text!,
    ...
```

Now, the book object returned from the detail view controller contains a record to update rather than a newly generated record, and the call to save it in Cloud-Kit should perform an update rather than an add operation.

2   Add a method to update a book in `BooksManager` (which will look similar to adding a book).

```
func updateBookCloudKit(at index: Int, with book: Book,
    completion: @escaping (_ error: Error?) -> Void) {
    db.save(book.record) { (record, error) in
        DispatchQueue.main.async {
            if let error = error as? CKError {
                // Error occurred
                completion(error)
            } else {
                self.updateBook(at: index, with: book)
                completion(nil)
            }
        }
    }
}
```

3   Call the `updateBookCloudKit` method of `BooksManager` from the `saveBook` method of `BookTableViewController`. (This will look equally familiar.)

```
cloudOperation(waiting: true)
booksManager.updateBookCloudKit(at: selectedIndexPath.row, with: book,
    completion: { (error) in
        self.cloudOperation(waiting: false)
        self.tableView.reloadData()
})
```

Waits for response from iCloud

Response received from iCloud

Reloads table

12.3.4   Loading book records in CloudKit

Run the Bookcase app again, and you'll notice that the book you added earlier doesn't appear in the table. When the app first loads, you have to load all book records stored in CloudKit into memory.

1   Add a flag to the `BooksManager` to register whether the `books` array requires loading:

```
var booksRequireLoading = true
```

2   Change the initial state of `books` to an empty array and remove the `loadBooks` method:

```
var books:[Book] = []
```

To load all books, you need to perform a *query*. A query performs a search for records in a database via a `CKQuery` object. The search parameters in the

CKQuery object are configured via an NSPredicate object. CKQuery first specifies the record type you're interested in. If you're interested in *every* element in that record type, you'll specify an NSPredicate with a value of true, for example:

```
let query = CKQuery(recordType: Book.recordType,
    predicate: NSPredicate(value: true))
```

NOTE You might remember using the NSPredicate to filter your records using Core Data in the previous chapter. You should be aware that certain predicate operations aren't supported by CKQuery. Check the documentation for CKQuery for more details.

Once you have a CKQuery object, you can request your database to perform the query. Because you're not using zones, you can leave that parameter as nil. The response from CloudKit will be returned in a completion handler closure, containing an optional array of CKRecord objects that matched the query, and an optional error object if something went wrong.

```
db.perform(query, inZoneWith: nil) { (records, error) in
```

Because the response occurs on a background thread, you'll need to request the main thread before going any further. Unwrap the array of CKRecord objects, map them to Book objects, and set the loaded flag to true.

3 Wrap it all in a method in the BooksManager class that accepts a completion handler, loads books from CloudKit, and then calls the closure to notify it of the success of the load operation.

```
func loadBooksCloudKit(
        completion: @escaping (_ error: Error?) -> Void) {        Requests
    let query = CKQuery(recordType: Book.recordType,             database
        predicate: NSPredicate(value: true))                     perform
    db.perform(query, inZoneWith: nil) { (records, error) in  ◄— query
        DispatchQueue.main.async {                        ◄——┐ Requests
            if let error = error as? CKError {                 │ main thread
                // Error occurred
                completion(error)
            } else if let records = records {
                self.books = records.map { Book(record: $0) }  ◄—┐
                self.booksRequireLoading = false  ◄——┐
                completion(error)                     │      Maps records
            }                              Sets books  │    to Book objects
        }                                  to loaded  │
    }
}
```

Creates query of Book — let query = CKQuery...

Error handling goes here — if let error = error as? CKError {

Unwraps records in the query response — } else if let records = records {

4 Set up a method in the BooksTableViewController class that will request the books to be loaded if they haven't yet been loaded. Be sure to disable the

user interface and display an activity indicator while the data loads. After loading the data, ensure the data is sorted correctly and reload the table.

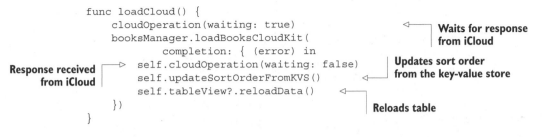

```
func loadCloud() {
    cloudOperation(waiting: true)                       ◁─┐  Waits for response
    booksManager.loadBooksCloudKit(                       │  from iCloud
            completion: { (error) in
        self.cloudOperation(waiting: false)             ◁─┐  Updates sort order
        self.updateSortOrderFromKVS()                     │  from the key-value store
        self.tableView?.reloadData()                    ◁─┐
    })                                                    │  Reloads table
}
```

Response received from iCloud ──▷ `self.updateSortOrderFromKVS()`

5 Call the `loadCloud` method in the `viewDidAppear` method, if the books haven't been loaded yet.

```
if booksManager.booksRequireLoading {
    loadCloud()
}
```

6 Run the app, and the book you added earlier should appear in the table!

7 Edit the book and save; back in the table, the book should update.

8 Double-check in the dashboard that everything updated correctly in CloudKit.

12.3.5 Deleting a book record in CloudKit

It won't surprise you that deleting a book in CloudKit follows a similar pattern to adding and updating.

Use the `delete` method of `CKDatabase`, passing in the record ID of the record you wish to delete. The response will be returned in a completion handler closure, where you can delete the book from the `books` array in memory.

1 Wrap all of this in a method in the `BooksManager` class with a completion handler to notify that the delete operation is complete.

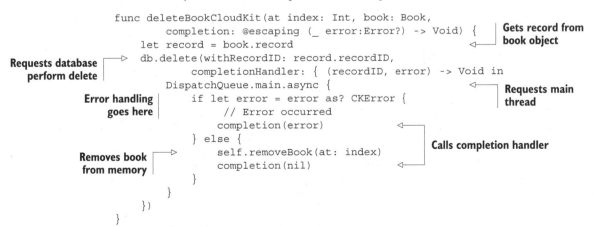

```
func deleteBookCloudKit(at index: Int, book: Book,
        completion: @escaping (_ error:Error?) -> Void) {   │  Gets record from
    let record = book.record                              ◁─┘  book object
    db.delete(withRecordID: record.recordID,
            completionHandler: { (recordID, error) -> Void in
        DispatchQueue.main.async {                        ◁─┐  Requests main
            if let error = error as? CKError {              │  thread
                // Error occurred
                completion(error)                         ◁─┐
            } else {                                        │  Calls completion handler
                self.removeBook(at: index)
                completion(nil)                           ◁─┘
            }
        }
    })
}
```

Requests database perform delete ──▷ `db.delete(withRecordID: record.recordID,`

Error handling goes here

Removes book from memory ──▷ `self.removeBook(at: index)`

2 You can now call this method from the table view controller in the table view `commitEditingStyle` method.

```
let book = booksManager.getBook(at: indexPath.row)
cloudOperation(waiting: true)
booksManager.deleteBookCloudKit(at: indexPath.row, book: book,
➥ completion: { (error) in
    self.cloudOperation(waiting: false)
    tableView.deleteRows(at: [indexPath], with: .fade)
})
```

12.3.6 Managing CloudKit errors

To keep things simple, I've basically ignored errors returned from CloudKit, but for a functional app, it's vital to manage these responsibly. I can't go into all the possible CloudKit errors here (28 possible CloudKit errors to be exact, at the time of writing!) but let's look at several example CloudKit errors, as shown in table 12.1, and how to deal with them.

Table 12.1 Example CloudKit errors

Error	Description
notAuthenticated	User isn't authenticated to perform the operation. Could indicate that the user isn't logged in to iCloud.
networkUnavailable, networkFailure	Problems with user's network.
serviceUnavailable, zoneBusy, requestRateLimited	Problems with the CloudKit service.
serverRecordChanged	A conflict encountered between the server and the request, for example, when two devices try to update the same record.
unknownItem	Record doesn't exist.

Now that you know what sort of errors to expect, how can you deal with them?

RESOLVING CONFLICTS

If you receive a serverRecordChanged error, indicating a conflict between the local updates to a record and the server version of the same record, your app will need to decide how to deal with the conflict.

For convenience, the `userInfo` property for the error will return three versions of the same record:

- The original record your user made changes to
- The record after your user made changes
- The record stored on the server

With this information, your app is in the best position to decide how to resolve the conflict between the three record objects.

For example, if you decide that the server's version of the record should win the conflict, you could reset the book record to the record stored on the server.

1 Add the following to the error-handling code of the `updateBookCloudKit` method in the `BooksManager` class:

```
if error.code == .serverRecordChanged {
  if let serverRecord =
          error.userInfo[CKRecordChangedErrorServerRecordKey] as?
      ⮡ CKRecord {
    book.record = serverRecord
    self.updateBook(at: index, with: book)
  }
}
```

2 To test this, run the app.
3 While the app is running, make a change to a record in the dashboard.
4 Back in the app, try to make a change to the same record.
5 Select the Save button.

Your change will be rejected and the record will revert to the version of the record on the server.

This may or may not be the best approach for conflict resolution for your app, but this gives you an idea of how you can handle resolving such conflicts.

RETRYING OPERATIONS

Sometimes an operation fails, but this doesn't mean you should give up trying! Certain types of operations, such as problems with the CloudKit service, are worth retrying. The question is, how long should you wait before trying again? Apple has a suggestion for you, and they include the suggestion in the CKErrorRetryAfterKey property in the userInfo property for the error object.

You should check if this `CKErrorRetryAfterKey` interval exists in the `userInfo` property, as shown in the following listing. You can wait a specified suggested time with the `DispatchQueue`'s asyncAfter method.

Listing 12.1 Retry operation

```
if let retryInterval = error.userInfo[CKErrorRetryAfterKey]
    as? TimeInterval {
  DispatchQueue.main.asyncAfter(deadline: .now() + retryInterval) {
    self.updateBookCloudKit(at: index, with: book, completion: completion)
  }
  return
}
```

CHALLENGE Add a retry operation to error-handling sections of the addBook-CloudKit, updateBookCloudKit, and deleteBookCloudKit methods.

NOTIFYING THE USER OF THE ERROR

For certain errors, you probably want to provide the user with error information. A useful technique for providing information to the user is via an alert controller.

Displaying alert controllers

An alert controller is a modal popup window that contains a title, message, and buttons. Two styles of alert controller exist:

- *Alerts* display in the center of the screen.
- *Action sheets* display at the bottom of the screen.

To display an alert controller, you need to

- Instantiate a `UIAlertController` with the required title, message, and style.
- Add any buttons required with `UIAlertAction` objects that can optionally define a handler closure that will execute when the user selects the button.
- Present the alert controller.

In code, this looks like the following:

```
let alertController = UIAlertController(
        title: "CloudKit error",                          Creates alert controller
        message: "The request timed out.",
        preferredStyle: .alert)
let tryAction = UIAlertAction(title: "Try again",        Creates action
        style: .default) { (action) in
    // User pressed button          ◄─── Action closure
                                                          Adds action to
}                                                         alert controller
alertController.addAction(tryAction)           ◄
self.present(alertController, animated: true)  ◄── Presents alert controller
```

The alert controller will need to be presented from a view controller.

1 Add a utility method to the `BooksTableViewController` that builds and presents a customized alert controller from an error object, which can also be passed an optional completion closure that will trigger when the user taps the alert's action.

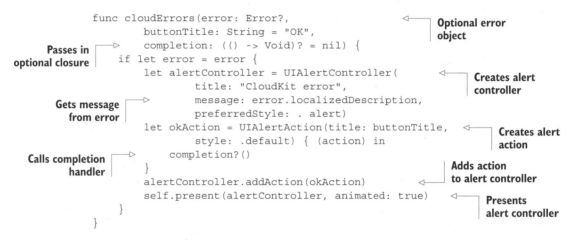

```
func cloudErrors(error: Error?,                           Optional error
        buttonTitle: String = "OK",                       object
        completion: (() -> Void)? = nil) {
    if let error = error {
        let alertController = UIAlertController(           Creates alert
            title: "CloudKit error",                      controller
            message: error.localizedDescription,
            preferredStyle: . alert)
        let okAction = UIAlertAction(title: buttonTitle,  Creates alert
            style: .default) { (action) in                action
            completion?()
        }                                                 Adds action
        alertController.addAction(okAction)               to alert controller
        self.present(alertController, animated: true)     Presents
    }                                                     alert controller
}
```

Passes in optional closure

Gets message from error

Calls completion handler

This method can now be called in the table view controller after responses have been received from CloudKit operations, to display an appropriate message to the user from the error object.

2 Add a call to `cloudErrors` in the completion handler of `addBookCloudKit`, `updateBookCloudKit`, and `deleteBookCloudKit` in `BooksTableView-Controller`.

```
self.cloudErrors(error: error)
```

3 Because the app has been built to require CloudKit access, if the `loadCloud` operation fails, give the user the option to try again, changing the button title to "Try again" and calling `loadCloud` again when the user taps the button:

```
self.cloudErrors(error: error, buttonTitle: "Try again") {
    self.loadCloud()
    return
}
```

RECORD DOESN'T EXIST

As you've seen, when you first store a book object, the books record type is added in iCloud for your app. If you ran your app for the first time and hadn't stored a book object yet, you'd find that your query to return books records would return an unknownItem error. The unknownItem error indicates that this record type doesn't yet exist.

Oh, but if any sort of error occurs when loading books data, you added a "Try again" alert. This creates an infinite loop; the app would never get past the query to return books records to the point where it can add a book and create a books record type.

If the books query in the `loadBooksCloudKit` method in `BooksManager` returns an `unknownItem` error, that's one error you can ignore.

Add this condition to the `if` statement in `loadBooksCloudKit` in `Books-Manager`:

```
if let error = error as? CKError,
   error.code != .unknownItem {
   //Error occurred
   completion(error)
...
```

12.3.7 *Refreshing CloudKit data*

As the app stands, the data is loaded from CloudKit only once—when the app is launched. If the app is running on two devices, a change on one device won't be represented on the other device and vice versa. Requiring the user to relaunch the app to refresh the data won't do! Let's look at two approaches for updating the data in the app:

- The user requests the data to refresh.
- The app subscribes to notifications of changes to the data.

The simplest mechanism for the user to request a refresh on the data in a table view controller is a built-in UIKit control called a refresh control. If you add a refresh control to a table view controller, the user can pull the table down to request a refresh, displaying an activity indicator. When the user releases the table by lifting their finger, a method in your code that can request new data for the table will be called. When the data has downloaded, you can reload the table and tell the refresh control to finish refreshing, and the table will automatically return to its place with data refreshed (see figure 12.8).

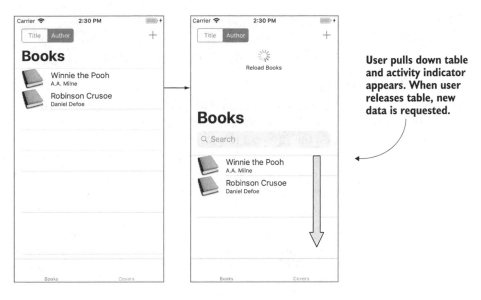

User pulls down table and activity indicator appears. When user releases table, new data is requested.

Figure 12.8   Refresh control

You'll add a refresh control to the table view controller in the Bookcase app to refresh the data when the user pulls down on the table.

1   Add the following to the `viewDidAppear` method of the table view controller:

```
refreshControl = UIRefreshControl()                    ⟵ Creates refresh control
refreshControl?.attributedTitle =
    NSAttributedString(string: "Reload Books")          Adds instruction to control
refreshControl?.addTarget(self,
    action: #selector(loadCloud), for: .valueChanged)
```

Specifies method to call

The `loadCloud` method will be called when the user pulls the table down.

2   Prefix `loadCloud` with the `@objc` attribute to make the method visible to the `#selector` keyword:

```
@objc func loadCloud() {
```

3   When data is returned from this method, hide the refresh control and stop it from animating by calling the `endRefreshing` method:

```
self.refreshControl?.endRefreshing()
```

4   Run the app.
5   Make a change to the data in the CloudKit dashboard.
6   Back in your app, pull the table down and release.

The data in the table should magically update to resemble your changes in the dashboard!

Let's look at the second approach for keeping the data in your app up to date.

12.3.8 Subscribing to changes

Giving the user the power to keep the table up to date is nice, but wouldn't it be great if the table would stay up to date without the user lifting a finger? (Hilarious pun intended!) This is achievable through database subscriptions.

A database subscription is how your app can be notified of any changes to the database. Your app is notified of these changes via remote notifications. To add subscriptions to your app, you need to follow three steps:

1 Add remote notifications to your app.
2 Save a database subscription to CloudKit to be notified of changes.
3 When you receive a subscription notification, update the data in memory and the user interface.

You'll add database subscriptions to the Bookcase app, to ensure that the data in the table is always as up to date as possible.

ADDING REMOTE NOTIFICATIONS TO YOUR APP

To receive remote (also called *push*) notifications, you need to turn on its capability.

1 Find the Capabilities tab in your project target's settings, and turn on Push Notifications (see figure 12.9).

Figure 12.9   Push notifications capability

> **NOTE**   If you're interested in running your app in the background to begin downloading any new content as soon as your app receives a notification, you should also turn on the Background Modes capability, and check Remote notifications.

2 Next, you need to register to receive remote notifications. Because your app only needs to do this once, this is commonly added to the `didFinishLaunching-WithOptions` method in the `AppDelegate`.

```
application.registerForRemoteNotifications()
```

This will request remote notifications to be sent to your app if it's running.

If you want alerts, sounds, or badges displayed on the app's icon when a remote notification arrives and your app is either in the background or not running, you need to register additional notification settings:

```
application.registerUserNotificationSettings(
    UIUserNotificationSettings(
        types: [.alert, .badge, .sound], categories: nil))
```

But be aware that requesting any of these additional notification types requires specific permission from the user that the user could decide to reject, crippling your app's ability to stay up to date (see figure 12.10).

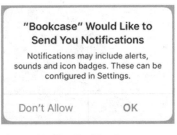

3 Your app will receive remote notifications in the AppDelegate's didReceiveRemote-Notification method. Implement that method now:

Figure 12.10   Notification permission

```
func application(_ application: UIApplication,
        didReceiveRemoteNotification userInfo: [AnyHashable: Any]) {
    print("Notification received")
}
```

We'll deal with any notifications this method receives in a moment, but first you need to set up the database subscription.

REQUEST A DATABASE SUBSCRIPTION

Now that your app is set up to receive notifications, it's ready to subscribe to notifications from CloudKit. Before you try this yourself, let's look at what's involved.

First, you create a CKQuerySubscription for a specific record type with search parameters configured with the NSPredicate. Use options to specify what types of operations you're interested in, and optionally identify the subscription with an ID.

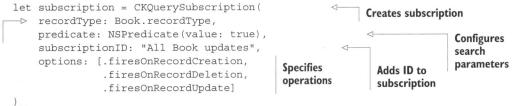

```
let subscription = CKQuerySubscription(
    recordType: Book.recordType,
    predicate: NSPredicate(value: true),
    subscriptionID: "All Book updates",
    options: [.firesOnRecordCreation,
              .firesOnRecordDeletion,
              .firesOnRecordUpdate]
)
```

Specifies record type — Specifies record type

Creates subscription

Configures search parameters

Specifies operations

Adds ID to subscription

Deprecated APIs

Prior to iOS 10, a CKSubscription object was used to subscribe to CloudKit notifications. CKQuerySubscription, a subclass of CKSubscription, was introduced in iOS 10, and CKSubscription initializers were deprecated, essentially converting CKSubscription into an abstract class.

(continued)

Deprecated APIs in iOS generally continue to work for a time, but there's no guarantee that they'll work indefinitely—at a point in the future, Apple might decide to make deprecated functions or classes obsolete.

Just as you did in chapter 10, you could choose to use the special keyword #available to check the user device's version of iOS. If the user has at least iOS 10, you'd instantiate a CKQuerySubscription object, using the newer API. If the user's still running a version of iOS lower than 10, you'd instead instantiate a CKSubscription object.

Because CKQuerySubscription is a subclass of CKSubscription, you can define the subscription value for either case as a CKSubscription.

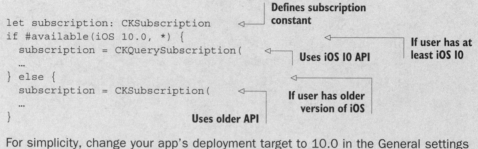

```
let subscription: CKSubscription          ← Defines subscription
if #available(iOS 10.0, *) {                 constant
  subscription = CKQuerySubscription(    ←                      If user has at
    ...                                      Uses iOS 10 API     least iOS 10
} else {                                  ←
  subscription = CKSubscription(        ←
    ...                                      If user has older
}                                            version of iOS
                          Uses older API
```

For simplicity, change your app's deployment target to 10.0 in the General settings to only support users with iOS 10 and to use the newer version of the CKQuerySubscription API without backward compatibility issues.

After defining a subscription object, you configure the data that the remote notification sends your app. If you want your notification to display a badge or alert, or play a sound, this is where you should specify the details. If you want a silent notification that doesn't require additional user permissions, you should include a shouldSendContentAvailable flag, as shown in the following listing.

Listing 12.2   Add notification info to subscription

```
                                              Creates
                                              notification info
let notificationInfo = CKNotificationInfo()  ←
notificationInfo.shouldSendContentAvailable = true      ←
notificationInfo.shouldBadge = true                  ←        Required for
notificationInfo.alertBody = "Your books have changed!"      silent notifications
notificationInfo.soundName = "default"
subscription.notificationInfo = notificationInfo    ←   Increments
                                                        badge
                                 Adds notification
                                 to subscription
```

Alert message (→ alertBody)
Default Sound (→ soundName)

Now, your subscription is ready to submit to the database, which you can do with a simple save operation. Your app only needs to subscribe once, so if your save operation is successful, you can store a UserDefaults preference to avoid unnecessarily requesting a subscription more than once.

Let's add a database subscription to the Bookcase app.

1 Add the complete `subscribe` method to the `BooksManager` class, and call it from its initializer.

```
init() {
    subscribe()
}
func subscribe() {
    let alreadySubscribed = "alreadySubscribed"
    if !UserDefaults.standard.bool(
        forKey: alreadySubscribed) {
        let subscription = CKQuerySubscription(
            recordType: Book.recordType,
            predicate: NSPredicate(value: true),
            subscriptionID: "All Book updates",
            options: [.firesOnRecordCreation,
                      .firesOnRecordDeletion,
                      .firesOnRecordUpdate]
        )
        let notificationInfo = CKNotificationInfo()
        notificationInfo.shouldSendContentAvailable = true
        subscription.notificationInfo = notificationInfo
        db.save(subscription) { (subscription, error) in
            if error == nil {
                UserDefaults.standard.set(
                    true, forKey: alreadySubscribed)
            }
        }
    }
}
```

Checks if already subscribed (annotation pointing to the `if !UserDefaults.standard.bool(forKey: alreadySubscribed)` line)

Requests subscription (annotation pointing to the `db.save(subscription)` line)

Set already subscribed (annotation pointing to the `UserDefaults.standard.set(true, forKey: alreadySubscribed)` lines)

Now that you've requested a subscription to your app's private database, the `didReceiveRemoteNotification` method in your app's `AppDelegate` will begin receiving notifications whenever a change occurs to the data.

2 Extract the CloudKit query notification from the `userInfo` argument that the `didReceiveRemoteNotification` method receives by instantiating a `CKQueryNotification` object.

```
guard let userInfo = userInfo as NSDictionary as? [String:NSObject]
    else {return}
let queryNotification = CKQueryNotification(
    fromRemoteNotificationDictionary: userInfo)
```

From the `CKQueryNotification` object, you can extract the affected `recordID` and the *reason* for the change (add, delete, or update), or verify that you're dealing with the correct subscription with the `subscriptionID` you set when you created the subscription.

```
let recordID = queryNotification.recordID
let reason = queryNotification.queryNotificationReason
let subscriptionID = queryNotification.subscriptionID
```

Now that you've received the remote notification from CloudKit, you need to update the data and user interface.

UPDATING THE DATA AND USER INTERFACE FOR THE CHANGE

The easiest way for the `AppDelegate` to inform all relevant classes that the data and user interface require an update is by requesting the Notification Center to broadcast a notification.

See figure 12.11 for a representation of the path a CloudKit subscription notification of a change to the books data in the database will take to eventually update the data and user interface in your app.

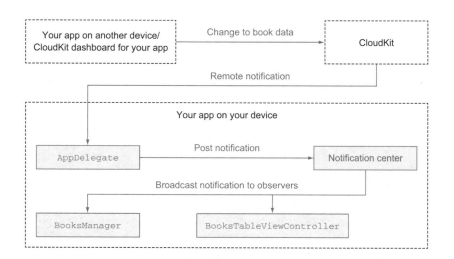

Figure 12.11   CloudKit subscription notification path

1. Set up a `struct` containing `Notifications` in the project, in the `Books-Manager` file (outside the `BooksManager` class).

```
struct Notifications {
    static let CloudKitReceived = Notification.Name("CloudKitReceived")
}
```

2. Back in the `didReceiveRemoteNotification` method in the `AppDelegate`, post this notification when the remote notification is received.

```
// Broadcast Notification
let notification = Notification(
    name: Notifications.CloudKitReceived,
    object: nil
)
NotificationCenter.default.post(notification)
```

Any interested classes can now observe this notification. The table view controller would be a great place to start. When the notification arrives from CloudKit, it could reload the books data and table.

3   Register the `BooksTableViewController` as an observer of the notification in its `viewDidAppear` method. When the notification is observed, it should reload the books data from CloudKit.

```
NotificationCenter.default.addObserver(self,
    selector: #selector(loadCloud),
    name: Notifications.CloudKitReceived,
    object: nil)
```

What happens if the notification arrives when the user is editing the book details in the book detail scene? It could be a dangerous moment to reload book data because you're currently editing a book. A better approach would be to flag that the books data is out of date and check this when you return to the table view controller. As it happens, the `BooksManager` already contains a flag, `booksRequireLoading`, that the table view controller checks in the `view-DidAppear` method to determine whether it should load the books data.

4   In the `init` method of `BooksManager`, add a closure as an observer of the CloudKit notification that flags that the books array needs reloading.

```
NotificationCenter.default.addObserver(
    forName: Notifications.CloudKitReceived,
    object: nil,
    queue: OperationQueue.main,
    using: { notification in
        self.booksRequireLoading = false
    }
)
```

NOTE   Notice that you used an alternative syntax—adding an observer that passes in a closure—rather than a selector method.

That's it! Run the app, and then make a change to the data in the CloudKit dashboard. After several moments, the app should receive the notification of a change, update the data, and reload the table. All automatic, and no table pulling necessary!

Why request data from CloudKit?

You may be wondering, why request the data from CloudKit if the query notification from CloudKit already contained information regarding the change?

While it's true that you could use the data from the `CKQueryNotification` object to derive details of the change, a problem exists: subscriptions aren't guaranteed to successfully notify your app of every change. If your device is disconnected from the internet at the moment several changes are made, the notifications may be consolidated into one notification. Though a subscription query notification describes one

(continued)

change, rather than accept this at face value, it's a good idea for your app to recognize that this notification indicates that one or more things may have changed and request the server for the exact details.

What data should you request from CloudKit? If you're implementing a local cache of the data being stored in CloudKit, it makes sense for you to request only the changes that have occurred since your last fetch. You can do this with `CKFetchRecord-ChangesOperation`, and then go through the local cache making the appropriate updates. This operation only works if your records are contained within a record zone.

For this example, we'll keep things simple, and reload all book records when the app receives a change notification.

NOTE   Before submitting your app to the App Store, you need to migrate the CloudKit environment for your app from development to production. You'll find this option in the lower-left corner of the CloudKit dashboard.

CHALLENGE   Up to now, you've added CloudKit to the table view controller. Make the necessary CloudKit changes to the collection view controller, too. It should load data from CloudKit, display an activity indicator and disable the user interface while loading, observe the CloudKit notification, and display information to the user about CloudKit errors. (Unfortunately, the refresh control only works in table view controllers, so leave that out.)

✓   **CHECKPOINT**   If you'd like to compare your project with mine at this point, you can check mine out at https://github.com/iOSApp-DevelopmentwithSwiftinAction/Bookcase.git   (Chapter12.2.StoreDataCloud-Kit).

CloudKit beyond iOS

Though the focus in this book is on iOS development, you may be curious to know what the prospects are of porting your CloudKit-connected iOS app to other environments. *CloudKit Web Services* and a JavaScript library called *CloudKit JS* make it possible to connect to your CloudKit data from anywhere—a web app, another server, or even an Android app.

One thing to consider is that your users will need to log in to (or register for) iCloud, a process with the potential to confuse or frustrate your Android users!

Perhaps you prefer to set up your own backend server to store data, or you have a preexisting service you want to connect to. Not to worry, in chapter 14 we'll look at connecting to your own or a third-party web service.

12.4 *Summary*

In this chapter, you learned the following:

- While the ubiquitous key-value store maintains sync with local data, CloudKit doesn't provide local syncing.
- When performing operations on a background thread, request the main queue to update the user interface.
- It's vital to respond appropriately to errors returned from CloudKit.
- Use alert controllers or action sheets to present the user with a message or present a choice of two or more options.
- When using remote notifications to update CloudKit data, avoid alerts, badges, or sounds, if possible, to avoid requesting user permissions.

Graphics and media

13

This chapter covers

- Adding images and app icons to your app bundle
- Drawing in your app and creating a reusable custom view
- Taking or selecting photos from the photo library
- Detecting barcodes
- Playing sounds

In this chapter, we'll look at making your apps more visual! Though you want your app to follow Apple standards for app consistency, you also want your app to stand out in the crowd. We'll explore changing the look of your app, from adding images and app icons to custom drawing. We'll also look at allowing the user to add their own images from the camera and photo library and even turn their device into a barcode scanner!

Along the way, you'll encounter additional concepts:

- Asset catalog and image sets
- Core graphics

- Core animation
- `UIImagePickerController`
- AVFoundation

13.1 *Adding images to your app with an asset catalog*

You've probably noticed the Assets.xcassets file in your Project Navigator. This is the default *asset catalog* for your app and a convenient place to store assets. Though it's possible to drag images directly to your Project Navigator to include them in your project bundle, an asset catalog is generally preferable. Why?

The asset catalog makes it easy for you to categorize your images into *image sets*, variations of the same image optimized for different environments. With different size classes, resolutions, and devices, you could potentially provide many variations of each image, but Apple makes it simpler for you with the distinction of *scale factor*. Variations of an image in an image set can be divided into three scale factor categories, as explained in table 13.1.

Table 13.1   Scale factor

Scale factor	Device types
1x	Non-Retina devices (for example: iPhone 3, iPad mini 1, iPad 2, and earlier)
2x	Retina devices (for example: iPhone 4–8, iPad mini, and iPad Pro)
3x	iPhone X, iPhone Plus range (for example: iPhone 8 Plus)

By providing variations for each scale factor, the appropriate variation for each image is automatically displayed for a device. iPhones in the *Plus* range, such as iPhone 7 Plus, automatically use 3x images, while most other iPhones and iPads on the market today use 2x images.

> **TIP** 1x scaled images for non-Retina devices apply to a small percentage of iOS devices in use today. (The last non-Retina device to be sold in stores, the 16GB iPad Mini 1, was discontinued in mid-2015.) In fact, if your deployment target is iOS 9 or later, your app won't even support non-Retina iPhones!

All that said, you don't even need to know which scale factor goes with each device type. You provide scale factor alternatives, and the correct image is used automatically—sorry for the cliché, but it just works!

> **NOTE** Asset catalogs are capable of holding other types of assets as well, such as textures or data. Similar to images, adding other types of assets to the asset catalog can prove useful in providing variations for different environments.

13.1.1 Adding image sets

Next, you'll add image sets to the asset catalog of the Bookcase app to display in the tab bar (see figure 13.1).

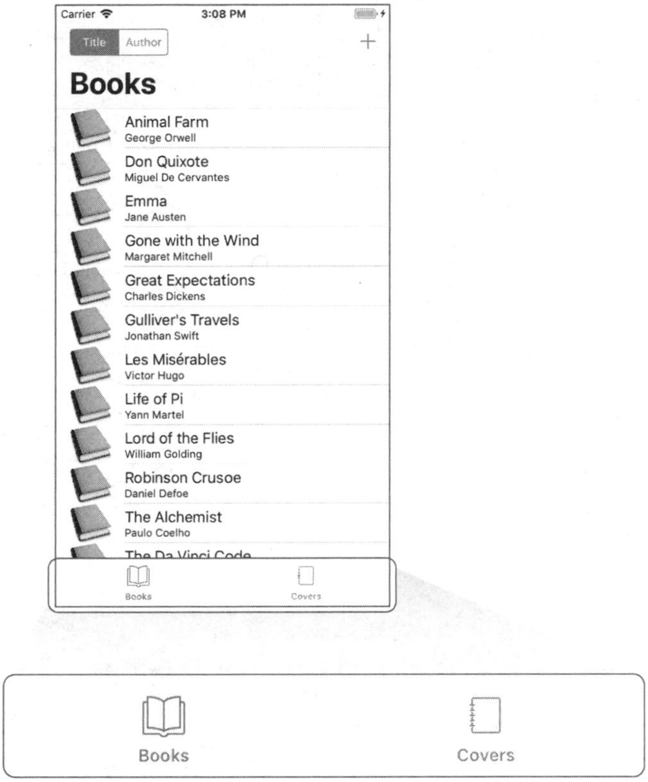

Figure 13.1   Tab bar icons

✅ **CHECKPOINT**   Open the Bookcase app where you left it after implementing the archiving data storage option, or check it out at https://github.com/iOSAppDevelopmentwithSwiftinAction/Bookcase.git (Chapter11.5.StoreDataArchiving).

---

1   Select Assets.xcassets in the Project Navigator. This opens the asset catalog editor. On the left, you'll find the asset *set list*, with the *set viewer* on its right. You'll find the project already has an asset set defined for the app icon. We'll look at this shortly.

2   Select the + button at the bottom of the set list to add a new image set, and select New Image Set (see figure 13.2).

Set list   **Set viewer**   **Attributes Inspector**

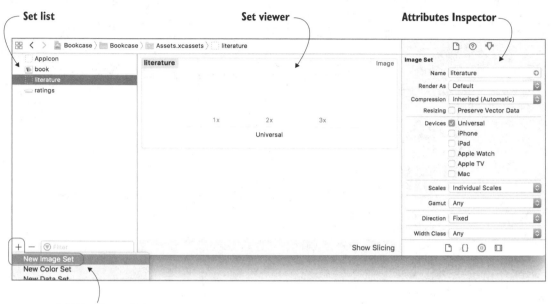

Add New Image Set

Figure 13.2   Asset catalog editor

3   Double-click on the name of the image set to rename it to "literature."

With the *literature* image set selected, you'll see the variations defined for the set in the set viewer. If you want additional variations (for device types, for example) you can add those in the Attributes Inspector for the image set. We'll stick with the three default scale factor variations.

Now, to add the actual images to the image set. Your designer has sent you a nice crisp design for both tabs, but the question is, what size should a tab bar image be? You'll find the answer in the *iOS Human Interface Guidelines*.

---

iOS Human Interface Guidelines

Apple provides a helpful site called the Human Interface Guidelines (https:// developer.apple.com/ios/human-interface-guidelines) that provides recommendations and advice direct from Apple to improve the interface of your apps, with an aim to make them more consistent and simple to use. I recommend you browse these guidelines (also known as the HIG), especially any areas with relevance to an app you hope to build.

According to the HIG (https://developer.apple.com/ios/human-interface-guidelines/icons-and-images/custom-icons/), tab bar icons should be 75 x 75 pixels for 3x images and 50 x 50 pixels for 2x images. The HIG doesn't mention the older 1x images, but through simple mathematics, 1x images should be 25 x 25 pixels.

4   Download the icons. You can find a package of media you'll use in this chapter at https://github.com/iOSAppDevelopmentwithSwiftinAction/Bookcase-Media.

5   In the *literature* and *cover* folders, you'll find the icons already exported into the three scale factor sizes. The 2x and 3x files have suffixes @2x and @3x to distinguish them from the 1x file.

NOTE   To avoid compression artifacts, PNG files are usually recommended in iOS development, especially for smaller images such as icons. In fact, app icons (which we'll explore shortly) accept *only* PNG files.

6   Drag the three literature icons from the Finder into their appropriate wells in the set viewer for the literature set list (see figure 13.3).

The suffixes of the image files can also help to automate this process.

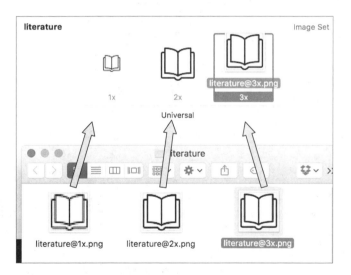

Figure 13.3   Add images to image set from Finder

7   Create the image set for the second icon by selecting all three files in the Finder and dragging them directly to the asset set list. A new image set will be created with the name *cover*, and, like magic, the files will automatically drop into the appropriate wells in the image set (see figure 13.4).

NOTE   It would probably be more consistent to give the cover 1x image the suffix @1x, but unfortunately Xcode doesn't work that way—leave the 1x file without a suffix if you want Xcode to automatically detect its scale factor.

Now that you've added both image sets, it's straightforward to add these images to the tab bar items of the tab bar.

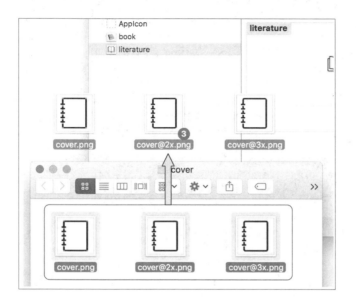

Figure 13.4   Add image set

8 Select the Books tab bar item.

TIP   There's a trick to selecting a tab bar item that can drive you *crazy* until you know what the problem is! Your instinct may be to select and configure tab bar items in the tab bar controller; but tab bar items can only be selected in the first view controller for each tab. In this example, because both tabs take you to navigation controllers, you'll need to select the tab bar items in each navigation controller.

9 In the Image item in the Attributes Inspector, select the literature image set (see figure 13.5).

10 Do the same for the Covers tab bar item, selecting the *cover* image set.

Optionally, you can include an image to display when the tab is selected, in the Selected Image item. If you don't include a separate image, the distinction is still clear, because selected tab bar items are automatically *tinted* blue. You can adjust the tint color in the attributes of the tab bar itself in the tab bar controller.

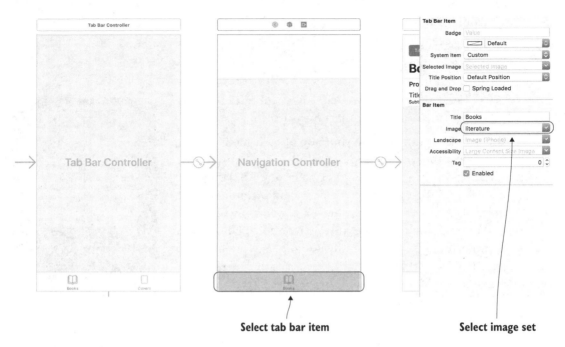

Figure 13.5   Add image to tab bar item

11   That's it! If you run your app now, you should find your tab bar has two icons representing each tab.

> **App slicing**
>
> Once you define variations for each asset, your app will automatically use this information to produce a variation of your app bundle appropriate for each device. This process is called *app slicing*. Only assets that are appropriate for a user's device will be included in the app's bundle when it's distributed to the user, reducing app size and download time.

13.1.2 Adding app icons

As you've seen, the asset catalog also contains an image set for the icon for your app. Unlike regular image sets, iOS app icons accept a range of sizes for different devices and purposes. In addition to the app icon displayed in the home screen, versions of the icon are needed for when your app turns up in a Spotlight search, when push notifications appear, or for adjusting settings for your app in the Settings app. You'll also need a large version of your app icon for the App Store (although this icon doesn't need to be included in your app bundle). Apple provides a template for app icons in the resources section of the HIG.

Apple also provides several guidelines in the HIG for app icons, such as these:

- Keep it simple.
- Avoid transparency.
- Don't include photos.
- Keep icon corners square. iOS will automatically provide rounded corners for your icon.

You may have noticed that your app already has a default icon consisting of grid lines and circles (see figure 13.6). This curious symbol is the grid system that Apple designers use to design icons for their apps and can be a great guide to consider in composing your own app icons.

You're going to update the app icon for the Bookcase app. Fortunately, your friendly designer has already prepared an icon and output it in a variety of image sizes. You can find a folder of app icon image files in the app icon folder of the same package you downloaded for image sets. All you need to do now is play "Match that file"!

Figure 13.6   Apple icon grid

1. As you did earlier, drag each file to the appropriate well. (Unfortunately, automating this process isn't as straightforward as simple image sets.) When you're finished, your app icon should look like figure 13.7 in the asset catalog.

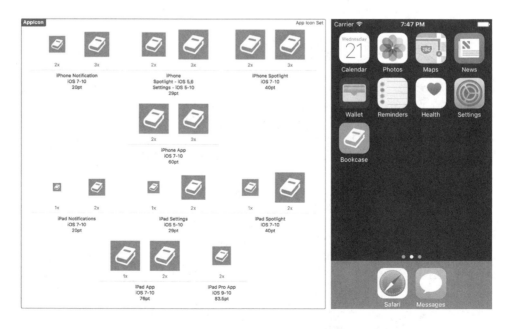

Figure 13.7   App icon in the asset catalog and device home screen

2 Run the app and close it again; you should now see your brand-new app icon in your device's home screen.

13.2 Displaying a launch screen

You may have noticed a moment of white screen after launching your app, before your app loads and the interface of your app appears. To indicate to the user that your app is loading, Apple recommends you prepare a *launch screen* to replace that moment of white screen that resembles the initial scene of your app. Let's look at how Apple has implemented the launch screen in two of their own apps to get a better idea of what they mean (see figure 13.8).

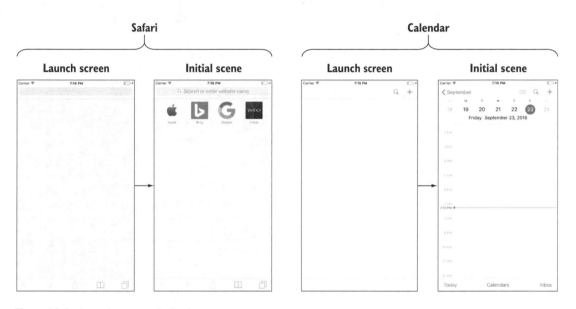

Figure 13.8 Launch screens in Apple apps

You can build your launch screen using the *LaunchScreen* storyboard that's generated automatically for you when you create your project. As with regular storyboards, you can add standard UIKit components from the Object Library to the launch screen storyboard and position views with auto layout and size classes.

As you'd expect, launch screen storyboards do have their limitations. To load up quickly, launch screens are static and noninteractive, don't animate, and are disconnected from the rest of your app. Launch screen storyboards don't permit you to subclass views or view controllers or perform segues or actions.

You can read more about Apple's recommendations for launch screens in the HIG at https://developer.apple.com/ios/human-interface-guidelines/icons-and-images/launch-screen/. For example, Apple suggests that text, in general, should be avoided, because launch screen text can't be localized.

TIP Though storyboards are the recommended approach for building up a launch screen, sometimes it can be difficult to build up an appropriate launch screen storyboard for your app using standard UIKit components, especially for games or other graphically intensive apps. If you prefer, you can create a launch screen with an image set of PNG files. Add a launch screen image set to the asset catalog, providing variations for all possible device types, orientations, and environments. To direct Xcode to the correct launch screen, you should then specify the image set you created in the launch screen file attribute in the General settings for your project target.

You'll modify the launch screen storyboard of the Bookcase app so that it resembles the app's initial screen. Following Apple's lead, let's implement a plain navigation bar, search bar, and tab bar, ready to create the illusion that these elements are completed when the first scene appears (see figure 13.9).

Figure 13.9 Bookcase launch screen

1 Select LaunchScreen.storyboard in the Project Navigator.
2 Drag a tab bar to the bottom of the launch screen. Remove any default tab bar items.
3 Drag a navigation bar to the top of the main scene of the launch screen. The navigation controller in the main storyboard increases the height of its navigation bar to 118 points.

4   Give your navigation bar a height constraint of 118 points to match, and while you're there, pin the navigation bar to the left, top, and right edges.

5   Drag a search bar below the navigation bar.

That's it! If you run your app now, you should catch a glimpse of your launch screen handiwork for a second before it's replaced by the real thing. Well done!

✅ **CHECKPOINT**   If you'd like to compare your project with mine at this point, you can check mine out at https://github.com/iOSApp-DevelopmentwithSwiftinAction/Bookcase.git   (Chapter13.1.AssetCatalog LaunchScreen).

13.3   *Drawing with Core Graphics*

Up to now, all the visuals you've used in apps have been standard UIKit components or PNG images from the asset catalog. What if you want to go a little further and *draw* your own 2D shapes in code? Perhaps you want to draw a simple shape such as a rectangle or circle or a more complicated path such as a star or even a custom button. One way to achieve drawing in Swift is with the Core Graphics framework.

You're going to explore Core Graphics by building a view in the Bookcase app that displays star-ratings for each book that the user can interact with to edit the rating (see figure 13.10).

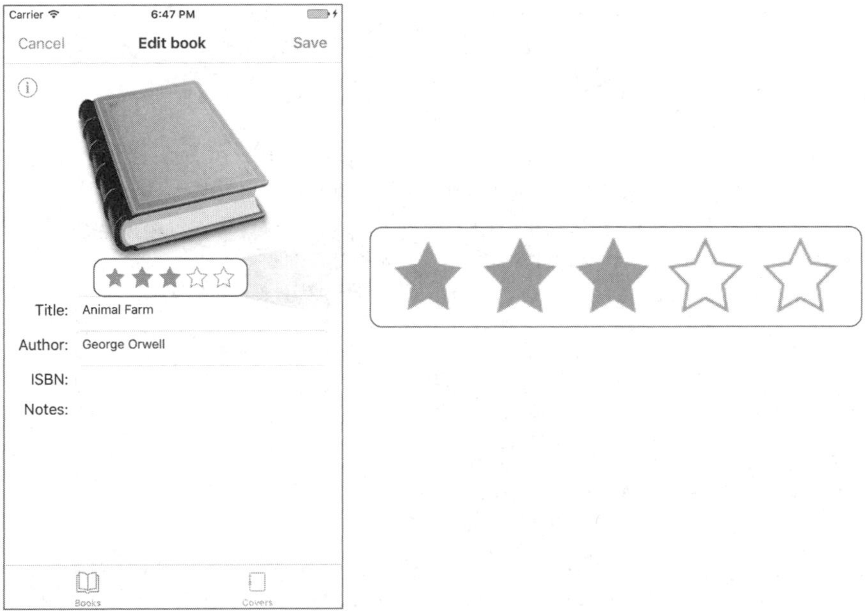

Figure 13.10   Star-ratings

First, let's build a view that will draw a yellow star.

13.3.1 *Overriding the draw method*

The most common place to draw using Core Graphics is in the `draw` method of `UIView`. This method is called when a view is first laid out and any time that the view needs to be redrawn.

1 Create a subclass of `UIView` called `Star`. The `draw` method shows up in the `UIView` template, but it's commented out.

2 Uncomment the `draw` method:

```
class Star: UIView {
    override func draw(_ rect: CGRect) {
        // Drawing code
    }
}
```

Note that the `draw` method is passed a `rect` parameter containing the dimensions available to you to draw in.

13.3.2 *Describing a path*

To draw both simple and complex shapes in Core Graphics, you first need to describe their paths. Paths are described with a `CGPath` object, but UIKit class `UIBezierPath` is often used, because it has additional functionality and can provide you with a `CGPath` object anyway, via its `cgPath` property.

Simple shapes are easy to define in `UIBezierPath`—it has initializers that define ovals, rectangles, rounded rectangles, and arcs. For example, the following will create a circle path that fits inside a rectangle:

```
UIBezierPath(rect: CGRect(x: 0, y: 0, width: 100, height: 100))
```

Complex shapes are easy, too. To create a complex path, after instantiating an empty `UIBezierPath` object, you'd move to the initial point of the path with the `move` method, draw lines to each point in the path with the `addLine` method, and finally close the path with the `close` method.

You'll use the `UIBezierPath` method to draw a star. Add the following method to your `Star` class that returns a `UIBezierPath` object that describes the path to draw a star:

```
func getStarPath() -> UIBezierPath {
    let path = UIBezierPath()
    path.move(to: CGPoint(x: 12, y: 1.2))
    path.addLine(to: CGPoint(x: 15.4, y: 8.4))
    path.addLine(to: CGPoint(x: 23, y: 9.6))
    path.addLine(to: CGPoint(x: 17.5, y: 15.2))
    path.addLine(to: CGPoint(x: 18.8, y: 23.2))
    path.addLine(to: CGPoint(x: 12, y: 19.4))
    path.addLine(to: CGPoint(x: 5.2, y: 23.2))
```

```
path.addLine(to: CGPoint(x: 6.5, y: 15.2))
path.addLine(to: CGPoint(x: 1, y: 9.6))
path.addLine(to: CGPoint(x: 8.6, y: 8.4))
path.close()
return path
}
```

How to get the path of a complex shape

Several paid programs out there, such as PaintCode, will automatically convert vector images to Swift code. Alternatively, if you already have a program that can export an XML-based vector format such as SVG, you can extract the points from the SVG file in a text editor and copy-paste away!

To draw the shape you defined with Core Graphics, you need a *graphics context*.

13.3.3 *Drawing into the graphics context*

The graphics context is where all your Core Graphics drawing is performed. You can get a reference to the current graphics context with the global `UIGraphicsGet-CurrentContext` method.

1 Add a reference to the current graphics context in the `draw` method:

```
let context = UIGraphicsGetCurrentContext()
```

Now that you have a graphics context, you can set the stroke or fill color, add the path you defined earlier, and then draw the path using either a fill, a stroke, or both.

2 Draw the star path into the current graphics context using an orange fill. Use the `cgColor` property of `UIColor` to pass in a `CGColor` object.

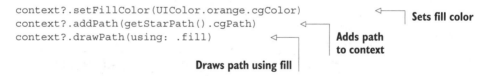

```
context?.setFillColor(UIColor.orange.cgColor)        ⟵⎤  Sets fill color
context?.addPath(getStarPath().cgPath)          ⟵    Adds path
context?.drawPath(using: .fill)           ⟵            to context
            Draws path using fill
```

Features of Core Graphics

Core Graphics isn't limited to drawing paths. It also offers additional features that we don't have time to delve into here, such as these:

- Drawing images
- Displaying text
- Adding shadows
- Transforms (We looked at view transforms in chapter 5.)
- Creating PDFs

13.3.4 *Saving and restoring graphics state*

Every time you make a change to an attribute in the graphics context (such as setting the fill color, font name, line width, anti-aliasing, or transforms—the list goes on) you're adjusting the *graphics state*, and any future graphics calls will be affected by these changes. If you only want to adjust the graphics state temporarily for the current operation you're performing, it's a good idea to *save* the graphics state to the stack first and then *restore* the graphics state from the stack when you're finished, to leave the graphics state as you found it.

Surround the drawing of the star path with saving and restoring the graphics state:

```
context?.saveGState()
//change graphics state
//draw operation (e.g. draw star)
context?.restoreGState()
```

13.3.5 *Drawing paths with UIBezierPath drawing methods*

An additional feature of the `UIBezierPath` wrapper for `CGPath` is the ability to stroke or fill a path into the current graphics context directly from the path object. Using the `UIBezierPath` drawing methods not only avoids the need for a reference to the graphics context, but will automatically perform the administrative detail of saving and restoring graphics state for you.

> **NOTE** Drawing paths with `UIBezierPath` methods will only work within the `draw` method of `UIView`, where drawing automatically updates the view's graphics context.

1   Replace the graphics context–focused code from earlier with the `UIBezierPath` drawing methods. You can set the fill on the `UIColor` class itself, and then fill the path by calling the `fill` method on the `UIBezierPath` object.

```
override func draw(_ rect: CGRect) {
    UIColor.orange.setFill()
    getStarPath().fill()
}
```

Notice the relative brevity of the `UIBezierPath` drawing methods. When you use these stars in the star-rating view, you need to display both filled and unfilled stars.

2   Add a `fill` property to the `Star` class, which determines whether the star should be filled or given a stroke.

```
var fill = false                          ⟵┐ Should star
override func draw(_ rect: CGRect) {        │ be filled?
    if fill {
        UIColor.orange.setFill()
        getStarPath().fill()
    } else {
        UIColor.orange.setStroke()
        getStarPath().stroke()
    }
}
```

When the `fill` property is set, the star should be redrawn. However, the star is being drawn in the `draw` method, and you should never call the `draw` method directly. Instead, you should notify the system that the view needs to be redrawn with the `setNeedsDisplay` method.

3 Add a `didSet` property observer to the `fill` property, which calls `setNeeds-Display`.

```
var fill: Bool = false {
    didSet {
        setNeedsDisplay()
    }
}
```

13.3.6 *Rendering views in Interface Builder*

It would be great to see the star you've drawn. Let's look at what you have so far in Interface Builder.

1 With the main storyboard open, drag in a temporary view controller and then drag a view into its root view.

2 In the Identity Inspector, give the view the custom class of `Star`, and you should see ... nothing change! Xcode needs to be notified that it should render your custom code for a view in Interface Builder. You can do this with the `@IBDesignable` attribute.

3 Add the `@IBDesignable` attribute before the class declaration for `Star`.

```
@IBDesignable class Star: UIView {
```

Return to the main storyboard, and the star view should now render nicely. But it's defaulting to not filled. It would be great if you could specify from the storyboard that you want to see the star filled (see figure 13.11).

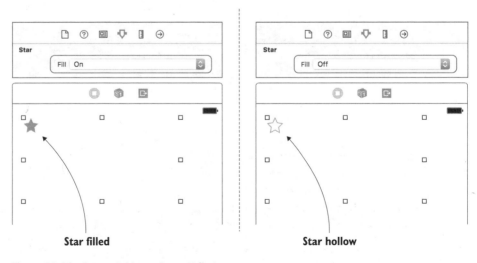

Star filled   **Star hollow**

Figure 13.11   Inspectable custom attribute

You can specify that a property be adjustable directly from Interface Builder by adding the `@IBInspectable` attribute before declaring the property.

4   Add the `@IBInspectable` attribute before the `fill` property in the `Star` class.

```
@IBInspectable var fill: Bool = false {
```

5   Return to the main storyboard and select the Attributes Inspector for the star view. You should find a new attribute, called "Fill."

6   Select On, and your star view should appear filled in the canvas!

CHALLENGE   Add inspectable properties for both the fill color and stroke color of the star view and check that they update in the storyboard.

13.3.7 *Creating a star-rating view*

Now that the star view is ready, you can set up your star-rating view. Similar to the star view, the star-rating view will render in Interface Builder, and will have inspectable properties to customize its appearance (see figure 13.12).

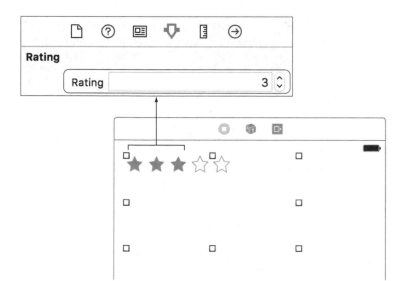

Figure 13.12   Star-rating view in Interface Builder

1   Create a `Rating` class that subclasses `UIView`, and make it render in the storyboard with the `@IBDesignable` attribute.

```
@IBDesignable class Rating: UIView {
```

2   Set up a property to define how many stars the rating view should fill. Make the property inspectable, and include a property observer that registers that the view requires layout when it is set.

```
@IBInspectable var rating: Double = 3 {
    didSet {setNeedsLayout()}
}
```

3   Add the star subviews in the `layoutSubviews` method of the star-rating view. Check that the `stars` array is empty. If it is, you need to create the star views, adding them to the view and the `stars` array. You need to clear the background color of each star view because it will default to black otherwise when generated from the `draw` method. Finally, use the `rating` property to determine how many stars should be filled.

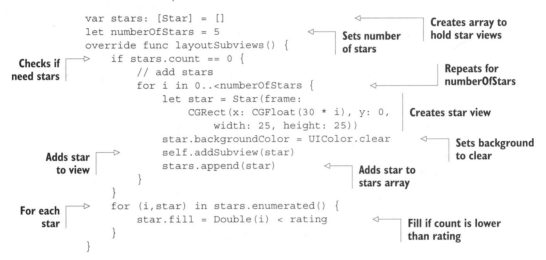

```
var stars: [Star] = []                          ←  Creates array to hold star views
let numberOfStars = 5                            ←  Sets number of stars
override func layoutSubviews() {
Checks if  →  if stars.count == 0 {
need stars        // add stars
              for i in 0..<numberOfStars {       ←  Repeats for numberOfStars
                  let star = Star(frame:
                      CGRect(x: CGFloat(30 * i), y: 0,    Creates star view
                          width: 25, height: 25))
                  star.backgroundColor = UIColor.clear    ←  Sets background to clear
Adds star  →      self.addSubview(star)
to view           stars.append(star)            ←  Adds star to stars array
              }
          }
For each  →   for (i,star) in stars.enumerated() {
star              star.fill = Double(i) < rating  ←  Fill if count is lower than rating
          }
}
```

4   Open the main storyboard, and in the Identity Inspector, change the subclass of your temporary view to your new `Rating` class. Your rating view should now render nicely in the storyboard.

5   Play with the number of stars and rating properties in the Attributes Inspector, and change the look of the rating view in the canvas.

    Now you want to make your ratings view interactive in your Bookcase app, so that the user can select ratings.

6   Override the `touchesBegan` method in the `Rating` class. Determine the index of the star view the user touched from the `stars` array, and use this index to set the rating property.

```
override func touchesBegan(_ touches: Set<UITouch>,
    with event: UIEvent?) {                              Gets touch object
Gets star        guard let touch = touches.first else {return}
view touched  →  guard let star = touch.view as? Star else {return}
```

Gets index of star →
```
guard let starIndex = stars.index(of: star) else {return}
rating = Double(starIndex) + 1          ←
}                                              **Sets rating**
```

Because the `rating` property calls `setNeedsDisplay` in its `didSet` property observer, setting the rating property is all that's needed for the star-rating view to update visually when the user selects a different rating.

For auto layout and scroll views to manage the size of the star-rating view correctly, you'll need to specify its intrinsic content size.

7 Override the `intrinsicContentSize` property in the `Rating` class.

```
override var intrinsicContentSize: CGSize {
    return CGSize(width: 30 * numberOfStars, height: 25)
}
```

Congratulations—you've completed a custom star-rating view, which you could reuse in other projects! Now that your star-rating view is interactive and operational, you can move it to the book edit form.

8 Delete the temporary view controller where you've been experimenting, and replace the placeholder ratings image in the book edit form with the star-rating view.

9 Connect the star-rating view up to an outlet in the `BookViewController` class. Give it the name `starRatings`.

10 After unwrapping the `book` object in the `viewDidLoad` method, set the rating in the star-rating view in `viewDidLoad` to the current book rating.

```
starRatings.rating = book.rating
```

11 When saving a new book in the `touchSave` method, instead of hardcoding the rating to 3, use the current rating in the star-rating view.

```
let bookToSave = Book(title: titleTextField.text!, …
    rating: starRatings.rating, …)
```

12 Run the app, select a book, and you should find your new star-rating view appear below the book cover.

13 Select a different rating, select Save, and then return to the book. You should see the rating appear as you left it.

✓ **CHECKPOINT** If you'd like to compare your project with mine at this point, you can check mine out at https://github.com/iOSApp-DevelopmentwithSwiftinAction/Bookcase.git (Chapter13.2.StarRatings-View).

13.4 *Drawing with Core Animation*

It's also possible to draw in a view in iOS using the Core Animation framework. All UIKit views and subclasses are backed by a Core Animation layer, represented by the CALayer class from the Core Animation framework. The CALayer describes everything visual about a view that needs rendering and can be used to animate these visuals.

You can access a view's layer with its layer property. With the reference to the layer, you can then modify its appearance. For instance, properties are available to adjust background color, border, corner radius, shadow, mask, transform, and anti-aliasing.

Certain CALayer properties are available in UIView already, while others aren't. If you want to give a UIView a background color of yellow, you could set this directly on the view in Interface Builder without needing to reference its layer. But if you want to give your UIView a black border of 1 pixel and a gray shadow (see figure 13.13), you need to manipulate its layer properties, as shown in the following listing.

Figure 13.13 View layer with border and shadow

Listing 13.1 Add border and shadow to view layer

```
layer.borderColor = UIColor.black.cgColor
layer.borderWidth = 1
layer.shadowColor = UIColor.gray.cgColor
layer.shadowOffset = CGSize(width: 2, height: 2)
layer.shadowOpacity = 1
layer.shadowRadius = 2.0
```

If you find that you need to adjust a layer property frequently, you could add it to the inspectable attributes for all views by creating an extension for UIView and adding it as an inspectable computed property. The following extension for UIView adds a corner radius inspectable property (see figure 13.14).

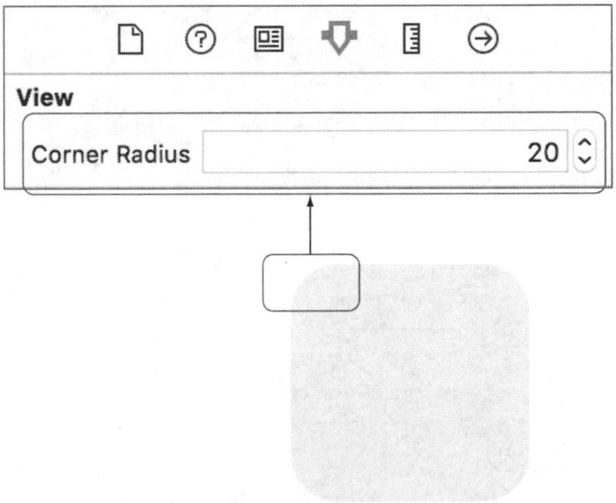

View

Corner Radius   20

Figure 13.14 Corner radius

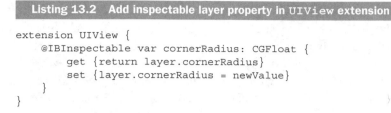

Listing 13.2 Add inspectable layer property in `UIView` extension

```swift
extension UIView {
    @IBInspectable var cornerRadius: CGFloat {
        get {return layer.cornerRadius}
        set {layer.cornerRadius = newValue}
    }
}
```

NOTE If you want your Attributes Inspector adjustments to show up in Interface Builder, views still need to be attached to a subclass of `UIView` that contains the `@IBDesignable` attribute.

Core Animation layers not only provide customizable properties, they're ready and primed for animation; and though it's true you can customize animations explicitly using `CATransaction` objects, the exciting thing about Core Animation layers is that adjusting layer properties will *implicitly* trigger an animation of the transition between the properties, and you don't have to do a thing!

You'll update the star object in your star-rating view to use the `CALayer` and take advantage of this fancy built-in animation. Rather than an immediate change when the star's `fillColor` is set, there will be a smooth transition from white to orange.

Layer hierarchy

Similar to the way you can add subviews to views to create a hierarchy of views, you can also add sublayers to layers. Every view and subview of a view has its own layer property that, in turn, can contain a hierarchy of layers.

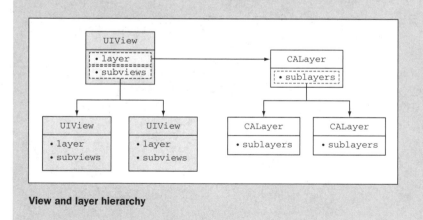

View and layer hierarchy

The Core Animation framework contains many `CALayer` subclasses that offer additional functionality beyond the basic `CALayer`. You'll find layer subclasses that help you to display gradients, text, tiles, video; you'll even find an emitter layer that displays particle systems, which you could use to simulate fire or smoke.

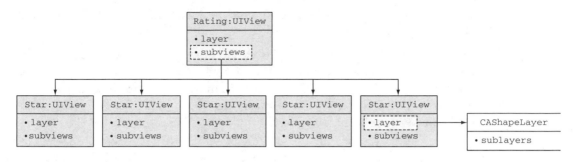

Figure 13.15   View and layer hierarchy of rating view

A subclass of `CALayer` specializes in drawing paths; it's called `CAShapeLayer`. You'll use shape layers to draw star shapes, and then add them to each star view's layer (see figure 13.15).

1 Refactor the `draw` method of the `Star` class in the Bookcase app to create a `CAShapeLayer` object and build up the star shape. Then add the shape layer as a sublayer to the main layer for the view.

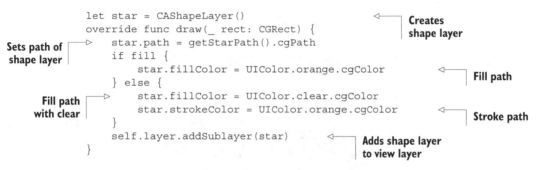

2 Run the app again, select a book, and change the rating. You should find, this time, that the change causes an animation between the filled and unfilled states of the star. Fancy!

✅ **CHECKPOINT**   If you'd like to compare your project with mine at this point, you can check mine out at https://github.com/iOSApp-DevelopmentwithSwiftinAction/Bookcase.git (Chapter13.3.StarRatingsView-CoreAnimation).

13.5 *Using the camera*

In addition to including images in your app catalog or drawing them with Core Graphics or Core Animation, an app can also use images from external sources, such as the device's camera or the user's photo library.

Here are two main ways of allowing the user to access the device's camera from your app:

- The `UIImagePickerController` from the Cocoa Touch Layer is the simplest approach. It provides a default interface for taking photos and videos, or selecting photos from the photo library that you can "drop in" to your app. You don't need to concern yourself with too many details, though customization of the image picker interface is possible.
- If you need to go beyond the default possibilities of `UIImagePickerController`, use the AVFoundation framework from the iOS SDK's Media layer.

13.5.1 *Taking photos with the image picker controller*

We'll come back to the AVFoundation framework shortly, but for now you'll use the simpler `UIImagePickerController` in the Bookcase app to allow users to add cover images to their books.

The user will select a camera button in the book edit scene, which will open the default image picker controller. After taking and accepting the photo, the image will appear instead of the default cover image (see figure 13.16).

Figure 13.16   Using `UIImagePickerController` to photograph a book cover

REQUESTING PERMISSION TO USE THE CAMERA

Before you can use the camera, you need user permission, and to get permission you must explain why you need it! This explanation will be included in a dialog that requests authorization from the user when you first access the camera (see figure 13.17).

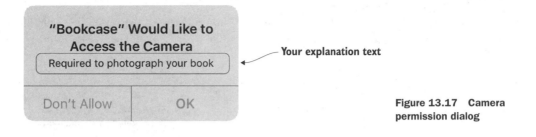

Figure 13.17 Camera permission dialog

You can provide the explanation text by adding a value to the Info.plist file:

1 Select the Info.plist file in the Project Navigator.
2 Right-click anywhere on the Property List Editor, and select Add Row.
3 Select Privacy - Camera Usage Description from the key drop-down.
4 Add a value describing why you need access. I went with Required to Photograph Your Book (see figure 13.18).

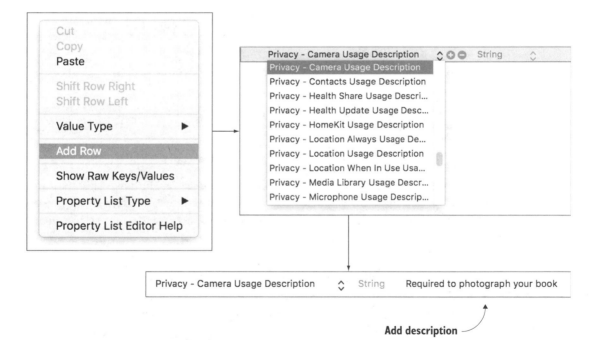

Figure 13.18   Add row to property list

NOTE   Be careful not to forget to add this value to the Info.plist file—without it, your app will crash in iOS 10 when it attempts to access the camera!

ADDING A CAMERA BUTTON

For the user to take a photo, you need to add a camera button to the interface. Let's add a bar button item to the navigation bar of the book edit scene (see figure 13.19).

Figure 13.19   Camera button item added to the navigation bar

1   Find the book edit view controller in the main storyboard.
2   Drag a bar button item from the Object Library to the left of the Save button.
3   Conveniently, bar button items already have a camera symbol available. In the System Item attribute for the bar button item, select Camera.

ENSURING THE CAMERA IS AVAILABLE

It's good practice to make sure the camera is available before using it.

You'll disable the camera button when the device doesn't have access to a camera.

1   Open the main storyboard in the Assistant Editor, and create an `IBOutlet` for the camera button and call it `cameraButton`. You can use the `isSource-TypeAvailable` method of the `UIImagePickerController` class to check a source type's availability.
2   Add the following to the `viewDidLoad` method of the `BookViewController` class:

```
if !UIImagePickerController.isSourceTypeAvailable(.camera) ⟵   Checks
    cameraButton.isEnabled = false                            camera is
}                                                             unavailable
```
Disables camera button

TAKING A PHOTO

Finally, you're set to take a photo! The `UIImagePickerController` class handles the interface for taking pictures, but you need to instantiate it and present it. Because the `UIImagePickerController` can also be used to record video or choose from images already saved on the device, you'll need to specify that you want the camera to be the source.

1   With the storyboard open in the Assistant Editor, create an `IBAction` for the camera button in the `BookViewController` class, and call it `takePhoto`.
2   Inside the `takePhoto` method, instantiate a `UIImagePickerController` with a camera source and present it.

```
let imagePicker = UIImagePickerController()                    ⟵  Creates image
imagePicker.sourceType = .camera                                  picker controller
present(imagePicker, animated: true, completion: nil)  ⟵
```
Sets source to camera

Presents full screen

You can get notification that the user has taken a photo through the image picker controller's delegate.

3 Set the BookViewController as the delegate of the imagePicker.

```
imagePicker.delegate = self
```

The delegate of UIImagePickerController must adopt two protocols, UIImagePickerControllerDelegate and UINavigationController-Delegate.

4 Adopt these protocols in an extension of BookViewController.

```
extension BookViewController: UIImagePickerControllerDelegate,
        UINavigationControllerDelegate {
    // Implement protocol methods here
}
```

When the user has taken a picture, the delegate's didFinishPickingMedi-aWithInfo method is called and passed a reference to the image. Be sure to dismiss the image picker controller from this method.

5 Implement the didFinishPickingMediaWithInfo delegate method:

```
func imagePickerController(                              Delegate
    _ picker: UIImagePickerController,                   method
        didFinishPickingMediaWithInfo info: [String: Any]) {
    dismiss(animated: true, completion: nil)    ◁─── Dismisses image
    // Store image                                      picker controller
}
```

The image picker controller should be working now, but your app isn't doing anything with the photo the user takes! First, you need a property to store the image.

6 Define an optional property to store the image in the BookViewController class.

```
var coverToSave: UIImage?
```

The image the user takes is passed into the delegate method as an element in the info dictionary and stored against the UIImagePickerController-OriginalImage key.

7 In the didFinishPickingMediaWithInfo method, extract the image from the info dictionary, store it in the coverToSave property, and use it to replace the default image in the book edit form.

```
if let image = info[UIImagePickerControllerOriginalImage]    Unwraps picked image
        as? UIImage {                                        from the dictionary
    coverToSave = image
    bookCover.image = image              ◁─── Displays image
}                                             in form
```

Stores image in
the book object

Now, when the user selects to save the book they've edited, you can also use the coverToSave property to generate the Book object to save.

8 Add in the cover property when saving a book.

```
let bookToSave = Book(title: titleTextField.text!,
    author: authorTextField.text!,
    rating: starRatings.rating,
    isbn: isbnTextField.text!,
    notes: notesTextView.text!,
    cover: coverToSave
)
```

Next, you'll set up the Book structure to store cover images to disk.

Unfortunately, the UIImage class does not adopt the Codable protocol. Fortunately, the Data structure does adopt the Codable protocol, and it's fairly straightforward to convert a UIImage to the Data format and vice versa.

Instead of using the init and encode methods that the Codable protocol automatically generates, you're going to implement your own version. It will be mostly identical to the synthesized version, but yours will also manage converting your image to image data and back. (If you need reminding about the Codable protocol, revisit section 11.2.3, "Archiving objects.")

9 Implement your own init method in the Book struct that works with the decoder to generate a Book object. Use the NSKeyedUnarchiver class to unarchive image data to a UIImage object.

```
init(from decoder: Decoder) throws {
  let container = try decoder.container(keyedBy: CodingKeys.self)
  title = try container.decode(String.self, forKey: .title)
  author = try container.decode(String.self, forKey: .author)
  rating = try container.decode(Double.self, forKey: .rating)
  isbn = try container.decode(String.self, forKey: .isbn)
  notes = try container.decode(String.self, forKey: .notes)

  if let imageData =
    try container.decodeIfPresent(Data.self, forKey: .imageData) {
      image = NSKeyedUnarchiver.unarchiveObject(with: imageData)
        as? UIImage
  } else {
    image = nil
  }
}
```

Identical to synthesized init — (annotation for the title through notes decode block)

Decodes image data — (annotation for the `if let imageData` line)

Unarchives to UIImage — (annotation for the NSKeyedUnarchiver line)

Sets to nil if no image data — (annotation for the `image = nil` line)

10 Implement your own encode method in the Book structure that works with the encoder to encode Book data. Use the NSKeyedArchiver class to archive the image to the Data format.

```
func encode(to encoder: Encoder) throws {
  var container = encoder.container(keyedBy: CodingKeys.self)
  try container.encode(title, forKey: .title)
  try container.encode(author, forKey: .author)
```

Identical to synthesized encode — (annotation for the encode block)

Identical to synthesized encode →

```
        try container.encode(rating, forKey: .rating)
        try container.encode(isbn, forKey: .isbn)
        try container.encode(notes, forKey: .notes)
```

Unwraps image ←

```
        if let image = image {
            let imageData = NSKeyedArchiver.archivedData(withRootObject: image)
            try container.encode(imageData, forKey: .imageData)
        }
    }
```

Archives image to Data →

Encodes image data ←

11 Add an `imageData` constant to the `CodingKeys` structure in Book.swift to use as a key when encoding your data for archiving.

```
enum CodingKeys: String, CodingKey {
    case title
    case author
    …
    case imageData
}
```

That's it! Now, if you run your app on a device, select the camera button, select the camera shutter button, and select Use Photo, you should see the photo appear as a cover for the book. If you select Save, the book cover should appear in the table or collection views and persist for the next launch of your app.

NOTE The simulator doesn't have access to your Mac's camera, so you need to test taking photos with an actual device. The simulator will come in handy, however, for testing that your camera button is disabled if the camera is unavailable!

13.5.2 *Selecting photos from photo library with the image picker controller*

The `UIImagePickerController` can handle selecting images from a user's photo library too! Although the interface is vastly different from the interface for taking photos, the code you need to implement is quite similar, with three main differences:

- Access to the photo library requires a different permission, and so a different explanation. You need to set the explanation in your app's Info.plist file under Privacy - Photo Library Usage Description.
- You need to adjust the `sourceType` of the image picker controller to `photo-Library`.

```
imagePicker.sourceType = .photoLibrary
```

Alternatively, you can use `savedPhotosAlbum`, which only shows the device's camera roll.

- Apple recommends in the documentation for `UIImagePickerController` that you present your image picker as a *popover* when picking from a photo library or saved photos album. As you saw in chapter 9, popovers appear as a bubble with an arrow pointing to an anchor point.

You need to present your image picker as a popover simply by updating its *modal presentation style*, and specifying the popover's *anchor point*:

```
imagePicker.modalPresentationStyle = .popover
imagePicker.popoverPresentationController?.barButtonItem
    = galleryButton
```

CHALLENGE   Add a custom bar button item to the navigation bar next to the camera button, using the *gallery* image from the media package. If the user selects the Gallery button, the device's photo library should open. The selected photo should replace the current book's cover image (see figure 13.20).

UIImagePickerController

Figure 13.20   Using `UIImagePickerController` to select a photo from the photo library

✓ **CHECKPOINT**   If you'd like to compare your project with mine at this point, you can check mine out at https://github.com/iOSApp-DevelopmentwithSwiftinAction/Bookcase.git (Chapter13.4.UIImagePicker-Controller).

13.5.3 *Taking photos with AVFoundation*

The `UIImagePickerController` is the simplest approach for taking photos and videos, and selecting photos from the device, and is appropriate for many circumstances, but sometimes you might need to dig a little deeper with the AVFoundation framework.

The AVFoundation framework is useful for recording, editing, and playing back audio and video. With AVFoundation, you can get lower-level access to the device's camera to do things such as adjust white balance, focus, and exposure; add effects; access raw picture data; or detect patterns such as faces, barcodes, or QR codes.

You'll use the AVFoundation framework in your Bookcase app to use the camera to automatically detect barcodes for the book and fill in the ISBN field. (Book barcodes are derived from their ISBN.) Your users will thank you for not making them laboriously type in the ISBN for each book! See figure 13.21.

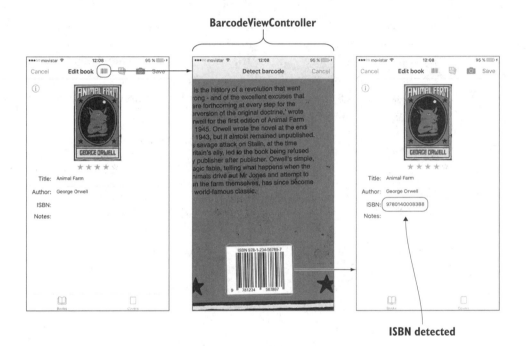

Figure 13.21   Using AVFoundation to detect barcodes

SETTING UP THE BARCODE DETECTION VIEW CONTROLLER

Because you'll use AVFoundation to access the camera, you need to build your own interface. None of this will be too new to you, so if you prefer, you can skip to the next checkpoint where you'll begin using AVFoundation. Alternatively, following the steps to set up the barcode detection view controller could be an interesting revision.

First, you'll need a scene to display the video preview for barcode detection.

1   In the main storyboard, drag another view controller into the right of the book edit form. Next, you need a button in the book edit form that opens the barcode detection scene.

2   Add the barcode icon from the media package to the asset catalog.

3 Drag in another bar button item to the top right of the book edit form's navigation bar. Give it the barcode image.

4 Add a popover segue from the barcode button to the barcode detection scene. To implement the barcode detector scene, you'll need to create a view controller subclass.

5 Create a new Cocoa Touch class called `BarcodeViewController` that subclasses UIViewController. The `BarcodeViewController` will display the preview of the camera and handle detection of barcodes. We'll look at how to do this shortly, but first, the `BarcodeViewController` will also need a way for the user to cancel this operation.

6 In the main storyboard, embed the barcode detection scene in a navigation controller. Give the barcode scene the title "Detect barcode" and add a Cancel bar button item to the right of the navigation bar. The Cancel button should dismiss the barcode view controller.

7 Link the Cancel button to an `@IBAction` in the `BarcodeViewController` class.

```
@IBAction func touchCancel(_ sender: AnyObject) {
    dismiss(animated: true, completion: nil)
}
```

If the barcode detection scene detects a barcode, it will need to communicate the ISBN back to the book edit form. You'll implement a delegation pattern to handle this communication.

8 Add a delegation protocol to the BarcodeViewController.swift file that contains a foundBarcode method. The BarcodeViewController class can use this method to notify its delegate that it has found a barcode.

```
protocol BarcodeViewControllerDelegate {
    func foundBarcode(barcode: String)
}
class BarcodeViewController
    var delegate: BarcodeViewControllerDelegate?
...
```

9 The BookViewController can set itself as the delegate of the `BarcodeView-Controller`, to be notified when a barcode is detected and then update the ISBN field in the book edit form.

```
extension BookViewController: BarcodeViewControllerDelegate {
    func foundBarcode(barcode: String) {
        isbnTextField.text = barcode
    }
}
```

10 In the `BookViewController` class, set up a `prepareForSegue` method, dig down through the barcode detection scene's navigation controller to get a reference to the `barcodeViewController`, and set the `BookView-Controller` as the delegate of the `barcodeViewController`.

```
override func prepare(for segue: UIStoryboardSegue, sender: Any?) {
    if let navController = segue.destination as?
            UINavigationController,
        let barcodeViewController = navController.topViewController
            as? BarcodeViewController {
        barcodeViewController.delegate = self
    }
}
```

11 If you run your app now, you can open the barcode detection scene and cancel it, but you haven't implemented any barcode detection yet! Let's do that now.

✓ **CHECKPOINT** If you'd like to compare your project with mine at this point, you can check mine out at https://github.com/iOSApp-DevelopmentwithSwiftinAction/Bookcase.git (Chapter13.5.PreAVFoundation)

DETECTING A BARCODE

As is often the case in iOS, there isn't just one way to solve a problem. To detect barcodes you could use

- The Vision framework, a powerful new framework introduced in iOS 11 that performs object detection, taking advantage of the new machine learning framework, CoreML.
- The AVFoundation framework itself provides object detection. Some object detection such as faces can be more accurate with the Vision framework and machine learning, but on the other hand, AVFoundation has a faster processing time.

We'll explore barcode detection using the AVFoundation framework.

The AVFoundation framework contains several classes that work together to capture, play, edit, and write video and audio. To detect book barcodes, we'll look specifically at using AVFoundation to capture metadata from the device's camera.

At the center of capturing media with AVFoundation is an instance of an `AVCaptureSession`. You can imagine your `AVCaptureSession` as a sort of black box where you can make connections between inputs and outputs. First, you hook up a device (such as a camera or microphone) to its own *input* that captures data from the device. You then connect this input to the *capture session*, which then directs this

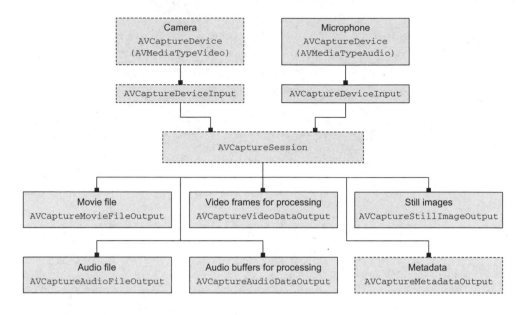

Figure 13.22   `AVCaptureSession` **with inputs and outputs**

data to appropriate *outputs* (such as writing to file, still images, or metadata). See figure 13.22 for more detail on this process and the classes involved.

Notice the boxes with broken lines—these are the objects you're going to need to use to capture input data from the camera, output it to metadata, and detect barcodes.

1   In the `BarcodeViewController` class, define a capture session instance property ready to accept inputs and dispatch appropriate data to outputs.

```
var captureSession: AVCaptureSession = AVCaptureSession()
```

2   In `viewDidLoad`, get a reference to the default capture device for the camera.

```
let cameraDevice = AVCaptureDevice.default(for: AVMediaType.video)
```

NOTE   The default device for video happens to be on the back camera, which is perfect for barcode detection. If you wanted the front camera (aka selfie camera) instead—perhaps for face detection—you'd use the `devices` method, which you could use to return an array of *all* available cameras. You could then use the `position` property on the `AVCaptureDevice` objects to find the front camera.

3   Instantiate an input object, passing it the camera. This operation can throw an error, so you'll need to implement error handling. Use an *optional try* to trap

any errors, call a `failed` method if you need to notify the user of the error with an alert (see chapter 11 if you need a reminder on alerts), and exit the method.

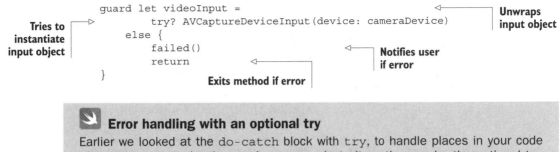

Tries to instantiate input object

```
guard let videoInput =
        try? AVCaptureDeviceInput(device: cameraDevice)
    else {
        failed()
        return
}
```

Unwraps input object

Notifies user if error

Exits method if error

> **Error handling with an optional try**
>
> Earlier we looked at the `do-catch` block with `try`, to handle places in your code where an error can be thrown. A more succinct alternative can be the optional try, represented by `try?`. An optional try will return an optional for the value that a throwable operation returns. It's then up to you to unwrap the optional. If you're confident that an error will never be thrown, you also have the option to use an *implicitly unwrapped optional try*, represented by `try!`.

4   Now, you can plug the camera's video input into the capture session black box, but first, you need to check that the capture session can accept this type of input. Again, if there's a problem, you should notify the user and exit the method.

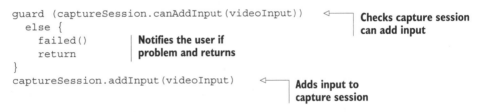

```
guard (captureSession.canAddInput(videoInput))
    else {
        failed()
        return
}
captureSession.addInput(videoInput)
```

Checks capture session can add input

Notifies the user if problem and returns

Adds input to capture session

Now that you've plugged your input into your capture session, it's time to plug in the output to extract barcode metadata. Similar to adding inputs, you need to check if the capture session is capable of adding this type of output, and if not, notify the user.

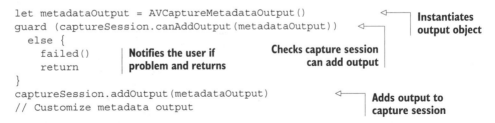

```
let metadataOutput = AVCaptureMetadataOutput()
guard (captureSession.canAddOutput(metadataOutput))
    else {
        failed()
        return
}
captureSession.addOutput(metadataOutput)
// Customize metadata output
```

Instantiates output object

Checks capture session can add output

Notifies the user if problem and returns

Adds output to capture session

Not only are there several types of metadata, there are several barcode formats. Fortunately, a standard 13-character barcode format exists that books implement these days.

5 Let the output object know what sort of metadata to look for.

```
metadataOutput.metadataObjectTypes = [AVMetadataObject.ObjectType.ean13]
```

When the output object discovers a barcode, it will notify its delegate. To receive callbacks from the metadata output, your `BarcodeViewController` class will need to specify itself as the delegate. You also need to specify which *queue* to receive callbacks on. Because you'll be updating the user interface, it makes sense to receive callbacks on the main queue.

6 Specify the delegate and the queue with the `setMetadataObjectsDelegate` method.

```
metadataOutput.setMetadataObjectsDelegate(self,
  queue: DispatchQueue.main)
```

Great—your black box is all set up with inputs and outputs, ready to start detecting barcodes, but there's one thing left to do—you need to turn it on!

7 Turn on the capture session:

```
captureSession.startRunning()
```

Because the `BarcodeViewController` is the delegate of the metadata output object, it will need to adopt the delegation protocol. The `captureOutput` delegate method will be notified whenever the metadata output object finds a barcode, and any information on barcodes found will be passed into the `metadataObjects` array. For simplicity, you'll use the first object in the array, and cast it as a special class for barcodes called `AVMetadataMachineReadable-CodeObject`, which stores the barcode value in its `stringValue` property.

Now that you've detected a barcode, you can stop the capture session, report the barcode back to the `BookViewController` using the delegate you created earlier, and dismiss the `BarcodeViewController`.

8 Create an extension of `BarcodeViewController` that adopts the output object's delegate, implements the `captureOutput` method, and deals with barcodes detected.

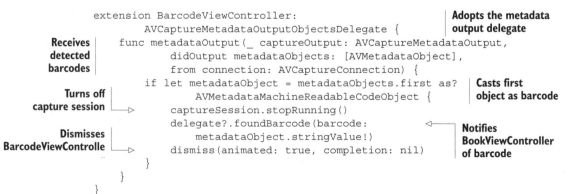

If you ran your app now, you'd find that barcodes are being detected correctly, but you won't yet see a preview of the camera—not exactly user friendly! To preview the camera, you need to generate a special type of `CALayer` that will preview the video from the `AVCaptureSession`.

9 Add a preview layer instance property to the `BarcodeViewController`.

```
var previewLayer: AVCaptureVideoPreviewLayer!
```

10 Back in the `viewDidLoad` method, instantiate the preview layer, passing in the capture session.

```
previewLayer = AVCaptureVideoPreviewLayer(session: captureSession)
```

11 Set the frame of the preview layer to the frame of the root view's layer. Then, set the preview layer's scaling to maintain its aspect ratio but fill the frame, with the strangely named `videoGravity` property.

```
previewLayer.frame = view.layer.frame
previewLayer.videoGravity = AVLayerVideoGravity.resizeAspectFill
```

12 Finally, add the preview layer to the layer of the `BarcodeViewController`'s root view.

```
view.layer.addSublayer(previewLayer)
```

13 That's it! Run your app, open a book, and select the Barcode button. The barcode detector scene should appear, previewing the camera.

14 Point the camera at a book barcode; the barcode scene should disappear, and the ISBN field should fill with the book's ISBN, like magic!

✓ **CHECKPOINT** If you'd like to compare your project with mine at this point, you can check mine out at https://github.com/iOSAppDevelopmentwithSwiftinAction/Bookcase.git (Chapter13.6.AVFoundation).

13.6 *Playing sounds*

The AVFoundation framework contains an area dedicated to audio. If you're interested in audio features, such as managing audio interruptions or playing audio in the background, look into the `AVAudioSession`. If you're interested in mixing audio and applying different audio effects, you should check out the `AVAudioEngine`. If, on the other hand, you only need the basic features of recording and playing audio, you can use the `AVAudioRecorder` and `AVAudioPlayer` classes.

We'll keep it simple here and play a sound in the Bookcase app, using an `AVAudioPlayer` instance.

You may have noticed that a default camera shutter sound already plays when you take a photo, as part of the image picker controller. Let's play a short sound as well to indicate that a barcode has been detected.

1   Grab the barcode scanning sound (scanner.aiff) out of the media package, and drag it into your Project Navigator.

2   To keep your project organized, you might want to create a group in the Project Navigator called "Media" and move in the sound file and asset catalog.

You'll play the barcode sound when the book edit form scene is notified by the barcode detection scene that it has found a barcode.

3   In the `foundBarcode` method for the `BookViewController` class, call the `playBarcodeSound` method.

4   Create the `playBarcodeSound` method. Get a URL reference to the sound file via the main bundle.

```
func playBarcodeSound() {
    guard let url = Bundle.main.url(
    forResource: "scanner",
    withExtension: "aiff") else {return}
    // Play sound
}
```

5   Add an `AVAudioPlayer` instance property to the `BookViewController` class to play the sound. This property mustn't only be defined locally within the method, or the property could be released while the sound is playing.

```
var barcodeAudio: AVAudioPlayer!
```

6   Back in the `playBarcodeSound` method, instantiate the `barcodeAudio` property with the URL you generated. Trap any errors with an optional `try`.

```
barcodeAudio = try? AVAudioPlayer(contentsOf: url)
```

7   Now that you have a sound file generated, you can go ahead and play it.

```
barcodeAudio?.play()
```

8   Run the app again, and this time the app should indicate when it detects a barcode with a simple barcode sound.

✓   **CHECKPOINT**   If you'd like to compare your project with mine at this point, you can check mine out at https://github.com/iOSApp-DevelopmentwithSwiftinAction/Bookcase.git (Chapter13.7.AVAudioPlayer).

13.7 *Summary*

In this chapter, you learned the following:

- Including variations for your assets in the asset catalog helps streamline your app bundle through app slicing.
- App icons you add to your asset catalog should be square—Apple will round the corners for you.
- Include a launch screen that resembles the first screen of your app to give the illusion that your app's interface is loading.
- When subclassing `UIView`, perform your drawing in the `draw` method.
- Consider Core Animation layers for drawing if a hierarchy of layers makes sense for your drawing or if you want to use animation features.
- `UIImagePickerController` is the simplest approach to giving the user access to the camera in your app. For a more advanced feature set, use `AVFoundation`.

Networking

14

This chapter covers

- Connecting to web services
- Requesting data from a web service
- Downloading from a web service
- Parsing JSON data
- Using dependency managers

Without a doubt, web services can transform an everyday app into an extraordinary experience. By hooking into the vast and diverse number of services and information online, or using the processing power of virtual servers, connecting to third-party web services can turn your humble app into an app that astounds!

You may be interested in connecting to your own web service, too. Perhaps Apple's iCloud and CloudKit services don't meet your needs precisely; maybe you need a more sophisticated back-end solution; or perhaps you already have a web service built that you hope to use.

In this chapter, we'll focus on using iOS networking capabilities to connect your app with online web services. Along the way, you'll encounter additional concepts:

- URL sessions and URL session tasks
- JSON serialization and SwiftyJSON
- CocoaPods and Carthage
- Operation queues
- App Transport Security

14.1   *Using a web service*

Most of the big players such as Google, Amazon, Twitter, and Facebook offer a range of web services such as mapping, cloud computing, login, analytics, or mobile advertising. Many of these services also provide their own SDK for iOS to simplify the process of using their service. In fact, basic social interactions such as posting to Facebook or Twitter are built right into the iOS SDK via the Social framework. Plenty of small players are out there though, and directories such as http://programmableweb.com can help you discover that potential.

In the previous chapter, you implemented bar code detection in your Bookcase app, which automatically filled in the ISBN field. How cool would it be if, by scanning a book's bar code, the book's details were automatically filled in as well! See figure 14.1.

In this chapter, you'll improve your Bookcase app by integrating it with the Google Books web service (https://developers.google.com/books/). You'll download

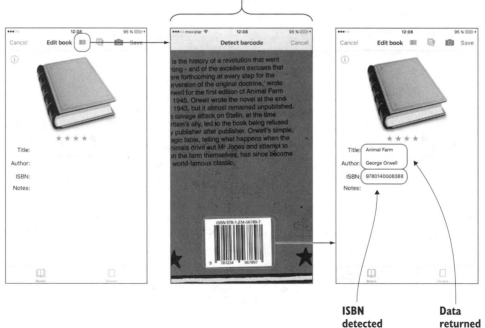

Figure 14.1   Request book data from a web service.

JSON data for scanned books, parse the data, and download cover images for scanned books.

✔ **CHECKPOINT** Open the Bookcase app where you left it at the end of the last chapter, or you can check it out at https://github.com/ iOSAppDevelopmentwithSwiftinAction/Bookcase.git (Chapter13.7.AVAudio-Player).

14.2 Setting up a books service

When the `BookViewController` receives the bar code, it will send this code to the books web service to request data on the book.

The temptation might be to add networking code directly to the `BookViewController`, but to keep code nicely organized, testable and reusable, you're going to set up a model class to connect with the books web service, and return the book data to the `BookViewController`, which will then update the views (see figure 14.2).

Figure 14.2 Model view controller getting book data

1 Right-click on the Model group in the Project Navigator, select New File > Swift File, and name the new file "GoogleBooksService."

2 Set up a class to connect with the Google Books web service:

```
class GoogleBooksService {
}
```

The `BookViewController` class needs to call a method on this class to get the data on a book. Because the networking code will be performed on a background thread, this method needs to be passed a closure that will receive the response from the server.

3 Add to the `GoogleBooksService` a `getBook` method that receives the bar code and a completion handler to notify the `BookViewController` when it has finished. We'll fill the details of this method later.

```
func getBook(with barcode: String,
    completionHandler: @escaping (Book?, Error?) -> Void) {
```

```
        // Get book from web service
}
```

Because the completion handler will be called from an asynchronous operation, it needs to be defined as @escaping.

4 Add a cancel method, if you need to cancel an operation. You'll fill in the details of this method later, too.

```
func cancel() {
    // Cancel any web service operations
}
```

One day, who knows—Google might close their web service to developers or you might decide an alternative web service does a better job. Let's ensure with a protocol that, from the perspective of your view controllers, the internal details of the web service are irrelevant.

5 Before the GoogleBooksService class definition, set up a protocol that defines the two main public methods of this class.

```
protocol BooksService {
    func getBook(with barcode: String,
        completionHandler: @escaping (Book?, Error?) -> Void)
    func cancel()
}
```

6 Now, set the GoogleBooksService to adopt the BooksService protocol.

```
class GoogleBooksService: BooksService {}
```

The BookViewController will request data from the BooksService when the user scans a barcode.

7 Instantiate a GoogleBooksService object instance property in the BookViewController. Define the variable with the BooksService protocol, so it can be easily swapped out if you go with a different service in the future.

```
var booksService: BooksService = GoogleBooksService()
```

Now, when a barcode is detected, the BookViewController can request the booksService to get the details of the book, and use these details to fill in the details of the book in the form, ready for the user to either save this information or cancel.

8 Add the request to get the book details to the end of the foundBarcode method in the BookViewController extension.

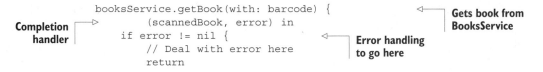

```
booksService.getBook(with: barcode) {                    ◁─── Gets book from
    (scannedBook, error) in                                      BooksService
    if error != nil {                            ◁─── Error handling
        // Deal with error here                        to go here
        return
```

Completion
handler

```
        } else if let scannedBook = scannedBook {
            self.titleTextField.text = scannedBook.title
            self.authorTextField.text = scannedBook.author
            self.bookCover.image = scannedBook.cover
            self.coverToSave = scannedBook.cover
            self.saveButton.isEnabled = true
        }
    } else {
        // Deal with no error, no book!
    }
```

Moves book information into form fields

Ensures Save button enabled

Now that the skeleton of the `GoogleBooksService` is ready, and it's communicating with the `BookViewController`, you can focus on setting up communication with the web service itself.

14.3 Communicating with the web service

We'll look in detail shortly about how to communicate with the web service using the `URLSession` API. As an overview, you'll want to follow these steps:

1 Create or access a `URLSession` object (optionally configured with a `URL-SessionConfiguration` object).

2 Create a `URL` object (optionally using a `URLComponents` object to customize the URL).

3 Optionally create a `URLRequest` object to further customize the URL request.

4 Use the `URLSession` object and the `URL` (or `URLRequest`) object to create a *task*.

5 Resume (begin) the task.

6 Receive responses from the web service either in a completion callback or with delegate methods.

See figure 14.3 for a broad overview of the path for creating and configuring all objects that are involved in communicating with a web service.

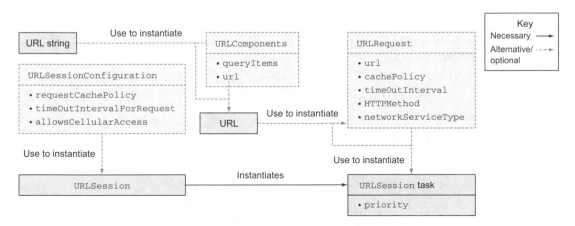

Figure 14.3   Create and configure objects for communicating with the web service.

14.4   *Creating a URL Session*

First, you'll need a URLSession object to coordinate communication with the web service.

Most of the configuration of your URLSession object is performed with a URL-SessionConfiguration object.

14.4.1 *URLSessionConfiguration*

URLSessionConfiguration objects come in three flavors:

- *Default*—Caches responses to requests to disk
- *Ephemeral*—Performs no caching
- *Background*—Permits tasks to be performed when the app is in the background

The following sets up a default session configuration object:

```
let configuration = URLSessionConfiguration.default
```

Once you have a standard URLSessionConfiguration object, you can configure it further by modifying properties such as

- requestCachePolicy—Determines when requests in this session check for cached data. The following, for example, requests that local caches are ignored:

  ```
  configuration.requestCachePolicy = .reloadIgnoringLocalCacheData
  ```

- timeoutIntervalForRequest—The acceptable waiting time before a request times out. The following, for example, changes the timeout interval from 60 (the default) to 30:

  ```
  configuration.timeoutIntervalForRequest = 30
  ```

- allowsCellularAccess—Specifies whether this session should connect via cellular networks. The following, for example, prevents your session from connecting via cellular networks:

  ```
  configuration.allowsCellularAccess = false
  ```

14.4.2 *URLSession*

There are three ways to access a URLSession, which range from basic access to the session to broader access to configure the session and receive session events.

- Shared session. URLSession contains a type property called shared which contains a reference to a URLSession singleton.

  ```
  let session = URLSession.shared
  ```

  This shared session is appropriate for basic network tasks because it can't be customized beyond the default configuration, and doesn't have access to more-advanced session events. As the shared session is a singleton, multiple sessions aren't available via this property.

- Instantiated with a session configuration object.

```
let session = URLSession(configuration: configuration)
```

- Instantiated with a session configuration object, delegate, and queue.

```
let session = URLSession(configuration: configuration, delegate: self,
    delegateQueue: OperationQueue.main)
```

In addition to a configuration object, you can specify a *delegate* to receive additional session notifications and permit additional configuration. Because network operations are performed on a background thread, when you receive notifications from the server, you can't be sure to be on the main thread. Specifying a queue when instantiating the session configuration object can request that responses from the server be served on a specific queue (often, this would be the *main* queue to be able to update the user interface).

1   Add a URLSession as a lazy property to the GoogleBooksService class that is instantiated with a default URLSessionConfiguration object, sets the GoogleBooksService class as the session's delegate, and specifies that session responses are sent to the main queue.

```
lazy var session: URLSession = {
    let configuration = URLSessionConfiguration.default
    return URLSession(configuration: configuration,
        delegate: self, delegateQueue: OperationQueue.main)
}()
```

Because you've made GoogleBooksService the delegate of the URLSession, it needs to adopt the URLSessionDelegate. Because the URLSession-Delegate inherits from NSObjectProtocol, your class also needs to adopt this protocol. The easiest way to inherit NSObjectProtocol is to subclass NSObject.

2   Update the GoogleBooksService class definition.

```
class GoogleBooksService: NSObject, BooksService, URLSessionDelegate {
```

TIP   When defining a subclass, the class it subclasses always precedes protocols in its definition.

Operation queue

In chapter 12, we looked at one approach for managing threads, called the *dispatch queue*. The API for using dispatch queues is known as Grand Central Dispatch, or GCD. An alternative approach to GCD is what's known as the *operation* queue. Built on top of the GCD API, the operation queue provides additional features and control.

Similar to dispatch queues, you either create a background operation queue with a certain quality of service or request access to the main queue, which has access to

(continued)

the main thread. You then add operations (known in GCD as *tasks*) to the operation queue. You can build up an operation either by subclassing `Operation` or by using one of Apple's subclasses such as the `BlockOperation` class, which creates an operation from one or more closures. You can also add an operation directly to the `OperationQueue` via a closure.

Here's one way you could request a background operation queue to perform a time-consuming operation and then request the main queue to display the result of the operation to the user:

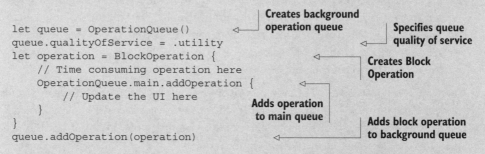

```
let queue = OperationQueue()
queue.qualityOfService = .utility
let operation = BlockOperation {
    // Time consuming operation here
    OperationQueue.main.addOperation {
        // Update the UI here
    }
}
queue.addOperation(operation)
```

Creates background operation queue

Specifies queue quality of service

Creates Block Operation

Adds operation to main queue

Adds block operation to background queue

Here are several advantages to operation queues over dispatch queues:

- Unlike GCD tasks, the state of operations can be monitored, and operations can be cancelled.
- The quality of service of specific operations can be changed independently of the operation queue they're in.
- An operation's readiness to execute can also be dependent on the completion of other operations.

These additional features also add overhead, so in situations where only the more basic features of GCD are required, an argument could be made for using GCD.

Because the `URLSession` class makes use of the `OperationQueue` API under the hood, it expects a reference to an *operation* queue in the `delegateQueue` parameter.

14.5   *Setting up the URL request*

To connect to the books web service, you need to pass a URL to the `URLSession`. According to the API documentation at the Google Books web service page (https://developers.google.com/books/docs/v1/using#WorkingVolumes), you can get information on a book by passing its ISBN in a URL that looks something like this: https://www.googleapis.com/books/v1/volumes?q=9780767926034

NOTE   You can check this URL in the browser to see what sort of data you should expect to see returned. You should see a JSON structure with information about the book requested.

1 Create a constant in the `GoogleBooksService` class containing the URL of the Google Books web service as a String, minus the query string.

```
let googleUrl = "https://www.googleapis.com/books/v1/volumes"
```

To get data on a specific book, you will need to pass in the ISBN in a parameter named q. One way to do this is to build this parameter directly into the URL itself with a query string, when instantiating the URL object. You can then see the query string in the `query` property.

```
let url = URL(string: "\(googleUrl)?q=9781617294075")!
print(url.query!) //q=9781617294075
```

The `query` property of URL is read only. If you prefer to construct the components of your URL object (such as the query string), you can instead build your URL object with a `URLComponents` object.

To define each parameter of the query, for example, you could pass in an array of `URLQueryItem` to the `queryItems` property. You'll use a `URLComponents` object to build up your URL.

2 Create a URL object from a `URLComponents` object, in the `getBook` method of the `GoogleBooksService` class:

Gets URL string →

Creates URL components from URL string

Sets URL components query items

```
var components = URLComponents(string: googleUrl)!   ◄
components.queryItems = [
    URLQueryItem(name: "q", value: barcode)]
guard let url = components.url else {return}
print(url.query!) // q=9781617294075 for example
```

The `URLComponents` object has a `url` property that, in this case, would be identical to the URL created in the previous code listing. You can pass this URL object directly to the `URLSession`, or you can customize the request with a `URLRequest` object (see figure 14.3).

3 Create a `URLRequest` object from the URL object.

```
let request = URLRequest(url: url)
```

A `URLRequest` object can customize features of the request such as

- `cachePolicy`—Determines whether the request checks for cached data.
- `timeOutInterval`—The acceptable waiting time before a request times out.
- `HTTPMethod`—The request method. GET is the default; then, there's POST.

4 `networkServiceType`—Specifies the type of data, to help iOS to prioritize network requests. Options are `default`, `voip`, `video`, `background`, and `voice`.

NOTE These customizations only override the configuration of URL-Session if they're stricter than the configurations set in the `URLSession-Configuration` object.

Now that you have either a `URL` or a `URLRequest`, you can use this to create a *task*. A *URL session task* is the object that performs a request from the web service.

14.6   *Requesting data from a web service*

With the `URL` or `URLRequest` you just created, the `URLSession` object will create and coordinate one or more *tasks* for you. You have three types of tasks available:

- *Data tasks* are used for requesting small amounts of data, such as text-based data. The data will be delivered to you as a `Data` object, either in small chunks via a delegate method or all at once via a completion closure.
- *Download tasks* download larger amounts of data and will be delivered to you via a file.
- *Upload tasks* are used to upload data as a file.

We'll look at download tasks shortly, but for now, let's use a data task to get data about a book from the Google Books web service.

1 Create a `URLSessionDataTask` by passing in the `URLRequest` object to the `URLSession`. A completion handler will receive the response from the server, which contains data, response, and error optional objects. Because all tasks begin life by default in a suspended state, you must trigger them to start by calling the `resume` method to activate them.

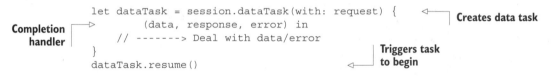

```
                                                                        Creates data task
let dataTask = session.dataTask(with: request) {
Completion        (data, response, error) in
handler      // -------> Deal with data/error
             }                                               Triggers task
             dataTask.resume()                               to begin
```

TIP Tasks have an additional property called `priority` that allows you to adjust the priority of certain tasks relative to others.

2 If there's an error, call the `getBook` method's completion handler, passing the `error` object. Otherwise, unwrap the data object, ready to extract book information.

```
                    if let error = error {                   Unwraps
Calls getBook           completionHandler(nil, error)        error object
completion handler  }
                    guard let data = data else { return }    Unwraps
                    // Get book information                   data object
```

14.7   *Examining the data*

You now have a `Data` object returned from the web service in the `dataTask` completion handler. Because `Data` objects are binary, conversion will be necessary.

To convert the `data` object to text, you could instantiate a String, pass in the data object, and specify the most frequently used character encoding, UTF-8.

```
let dataAsString = String(data: data, encoding: String.Encoding.utf8)
```

Open an example book in the browser to see what results you expect the Google Books service to return. (Here's the link again: https://www.googleapis.com/books/v1/volumes?q=9780767926034.) Notice that the data you get back is in JSON format.

To better analyze the structure of the data returned, it can be useful to view it in an online JSON viewer. See figure 14.4 for the raw JSON returned and how it looks in the JSON viewer at http://jsonviewer.stack.hu/.

Raw JSON

```json
{
 "kind": "books#volumes",
 "totalItems": 6,
 "items": [
  {
   "kind": "books#volume",
   "id": "dUaUAAAACAAJ",
   "etag": "N//rvwa2+Oo",
   "selfLink": "https://www.googleapis.com/books/v1/volumes/dUaUAAAACAAJ",
   "volumeInfo": {
    "title": "The Da Vinci Code",
    "authors": [
     "Dan Brown"
    ],
```

JSON formatter

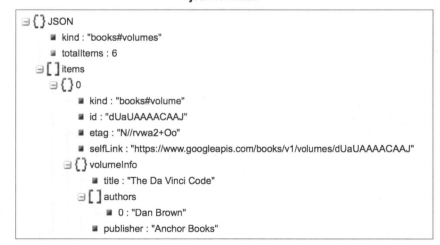

Figure 14.4 JSON data returned

We'll look at three different approaches for parsing this JSON data to a `Book` object. The API returns multiple books that contain the requested barcode. For simplicity for now, we'll assume the first book returned is correct.

14.8   *Parsing JSON data with JSONSerialization*

First, let's see what parsing the data object as JSON using the `jsonObject` method of the `JSONSerialization` class looks like:

```
let dataAsJSON = JSONSerialization.jsonObject(with: data, options: [])
```

This method serializes the JSON object into Foundation data types. Because this method by default returns an `Any` type, and we know to expect a dictionary at the top level of the JSON data, you can downcast this result to `[String: Any]`. Because this method can throw an error, surround it with a `do-catch` method and unwrap the result.

1   Parse the JSON data in a `parseJSON` method in the `GoogleBooksService` class, that receives a completion handler for returning the result.

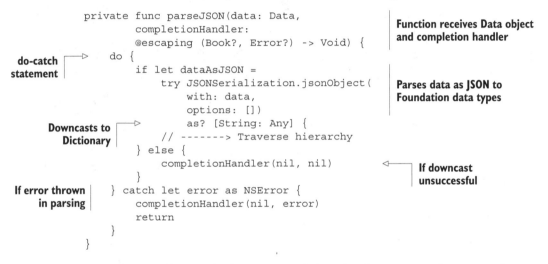

Now that you have a dictionary containing the data returned, you need to traverse the hierarchy down to the data you're after.

To extract the title and author from the first book in the JSON structure returned, you can follow this path:

```
dataAsJSON["items"][0]["volumeInfo"]["title"]
dataAsJSON["items"][0]["volumeInfo"]["authors"]
```

Because Swift is a strictly typed language, you need to *downcast* each value to the type of data you expect.

2   Continue to traverse the hierarchy in the `do` clause, using optional binding and downcasting to Foundation data types:

```
if let dataAsJSON =
    try JSONSerialization.jsonObject(
        with: data,
```

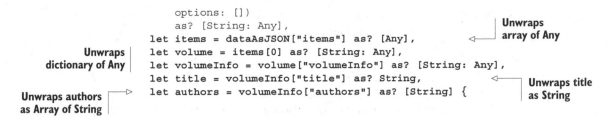

```
        options: [])
        as? [String: Any],
    let items = dataAsJSON["items"] as? [Any],
    let volume = items[0] as? [String: Any],
    let volumeInfo = volume["volumeInfo"] as? [String: Any],
    let title = volumeInfo["title"] as? String,
    let authors = volumeInfo["authors"] as? [String] {
```

Unwraps array of Any

Unwraps dictionary of Any

Unwraps title as String

Unwraps authors as Array of String

Finally, you've dug down into the hierarchy of the data to the book's title and authors and can use this information to generate a Book object.

3 Instantiate a Book object from the JSON data and call the completion handler.

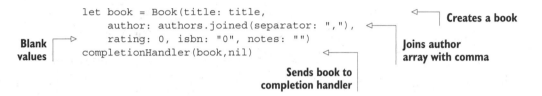

```
let book = Book(title: title,
    author: authors.joined(separator: ","),
    rating: 0, isbn: "0", notes: "")
completionHandler(book,nil)
```

Creates a book

Joins author array with comma

Blank values

Sends book to completion handler

4 The getBook method can now call the parseJSON method, passing it the completion handler to call when it's done.

```
self.parseJSON(data: data, completionHandler: completionHandler)
```

Now, if you run the app, create a new book, and scan a book barcode, the form fields should automatically fill with the data returned from the Google Books web service. Hooray!

14.9 *Parsing JSON data with JSONDecoder*

Let's look at parsing the JSON data using the JSONDecoder. The JSONDecoder can automatically decode data to native Swift types that are set up using the Decodable (or Codable) protocol.

You may remember you encountered encoding and decoding data to JSON using the Codable protocol back in chapter 11, but the data you used was fairly straightforward. How can data that has a complex structure be decoded, such as the data being returned from the Google Books service?

First, you need to set up a ServerResponse type that manages the data that's returned from the server.

1 Create a ServerResponse.swift file. Because you're only going to decode this server response, adopt the Decodable protocol. The ultimate aim of this ServerResponse is to retrieve a Book object, so set up a book property.

```
struct ServerResponse: Decodable {
  var book:Book
}
```

2 Because you're only interested in the array of items returned in the JSON data, set up a CodingKeys enum.

```
enum CodingKeys: String, CodingKey {
  case items
}
```

3 Next, you need to set up custom implementation of the Decodable protocol's init method that works with the Decoder to decode the data. Get a reference to the items array with the nestedUnkeyedContainer method and loop through the array, digging out Book objects. As mentioned earlier, you'll use the first book in the array for simplicity.

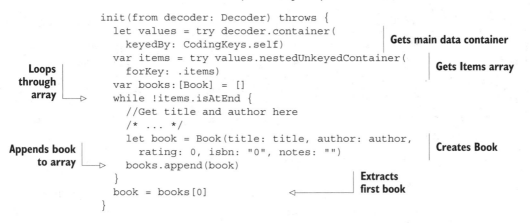

```
init(from decoder: Decoder) throws {
  let values = try decoder.container(
    keyedBy: CodingKeys.self)          Gets main data container
  var items = try values.nestedUnkeyedContainer(
    forKey: .items)                    Gets Items array
  var books:[Book] = []
  while !items.isAtEnd {
    //Get title and author here
    /* ... */
    let book = Book(title: title, author: author,
      rating: 0, isbn: "0", notes: "")   Creates Book
    books.append(book)
  }
  book = books[0]                      Extracts first book
}
```

Loops through array

Appends book to array

4 In the raw JSON data, each item contains a volumeInfo property. Set up another keys enum called ItemKeys.

```
enum ItemKeys: String, CodingKey {
  case volumeInfo
}
```

5 Use the ItemKeys enum in the init method to define the data you expect.

```
let item = try items.nestedContainer(keyedBy: ItemKeys.self)
```

6 The volumeInfo data in the raw JSON contains the title and author properties. Set up another keys enum to describe this.

```
enum VolumeKeys: String, CodingKey {
  case title
  case authors
}
```

7 Back in the init method, use this VolumeKeys enum to define the structure that you expect in the volumeInfo property.

```
let volumeInfo = try item.nestedContainer(keyedBy: VolumeKeys.self,
  forKey: .volumeInfo)
```

8 You can now extract the `title` and `author` from this `volumeInfo` container. Because `author` is an array of `String` for cases of multiple authors, merge these to make one `String`, separated by a comma.

```
let title = try volumeInfo.decode(String.self, forKey:.title)
let authors:[String] = try volumeInfo.decode([String].self,
➥ forKey:.authors)
let author = authors.joined(separator: ",")
```

9 Let's look at the completed `ServerResponse` structure, ready to decode data returned from the Google Books service:

```
import Foundation
struct ServerResponse:Decodable {          ◁──── Adopts
  var book:Book                                     Decodable

  enum CodingKeys: String, CodingKey {
    case items
  }
  enum ItemKeys: String, CodingKey {
    case volumeInfo
  }                                        Sets up Coding Keys
  enum VolumeKeys: String, CodingKey {
    case title
    case authors
  }

  init(from decoder: Decoder) throws {
    let values = try decoder.container(
      keyedBy: CodingKeys.self)             Gets main data container
    var items = try values.nestedUnkeyedContainer(
      forKey: .items)
    var books:[Book] = []                   Loops through
    while !items.isAtEnd {             ◁──── array
      let item = try items.nestedContainer(
        keyedBy: ItemKeys.self)
      let volumeInfo = try item.nestedContainer(     Gets volumeInfo
        keyedBy: VolumeKeys.self, forKey: .volumeInfo)  container
      let title = try volumeInfo.decode(
        String.self, forKey:.title)
      let authors:[String] = try volumeInfo.decode(   Gets authors
        [String].self, forKey:.authors)               String array
      let author = authors.joined(separator: ",")
      let book = Book(title: title, author: author,
        rating: 0, isbn: "0", notes: "")    Creates Book
      books.append(book)
    }                                   ◁──── Appends book
    book = books[0]                            to array
  }                          ◁──── Extracts
}                                  first book
```

Gets items array — `var items = try values.nestedUnkeyedContainer(forKey: .items)`

Gets item container — `let item = try items.nestedContainer(keyedBy: ItemKeys.self)`

Gets title string — `let title = try volumeInfo.decode(String.self, forKey:.title)`

Joins authors — `let author = authors.joined(separator: ",")`

Now that you have the `ServerResponse Decodable` structure set up, you can use it to parse data returning from the Google Books service.

10 Create a method in the `GoogleBooksService` class that parses the JSON using a combination of the `JSONDecoder` and your `ServerResponse` struct.

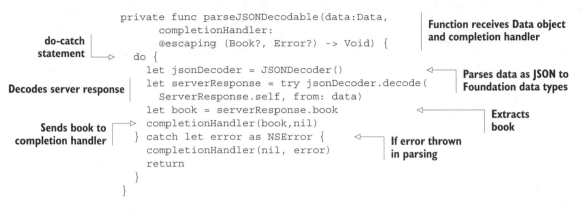

```
private func parseJSONDecodable(data:Data,
    completionHandler:
    @escaping (Book?, Error?) -> Void) {
  do {
    let jsonDecoder = JSONDecoder()
    let serverResponse = try jsonDecoder.decode(
      ServerResponse.self, from: data)
    let book = serverResponse.book
    completionHandler(book,nil)
  } catch let error as NSError {
    completionHandler(nil, error)
    return
  }
}
```

do-catch statement →

Decodes server response

Sends book to completion handler →

Function receives Data object and completion handler

Parses data as JSON to Foundation data types

Extracts book

If error thrown in parsing

11 Last, the `getBook` method can now call the `parseJSONDecodable` method.

```
self.parseJSONDecodable(data: data, completionHandler:
➥ completionHandler)
```

14.10 *Parsing JSON data with SwiftyJSON*

You may have noticed that both techniques we've looked at for parsing JSON have required a number of lines of code:

- With `JSONDecoder`, because the structure of the raw JSON data differs significantly from the model's structure in code, you had to define your own decoding logic in your custom implementation of `Decodable`, missing out on the convenience of automatically generated decoding.
- With `JSONSerialization`, due to Swift's type safety, the code involved in extracting information from JSON data can also be verbose. With the data returned from the `JSONSerialization` class, it's then necessary to unwrap and downcast every object as you traverse the data hierarchy.

Several third-party solutions out there address this problem and try to reduce the number of lines required to extract data from JSON. Probably the most popular at present is SwiftyJSON (https://github.com/SwiftyJSON/SwiftyJSON).

Let's explore using SwiftyJSON to parse the same JSON data. To use SwiftyJSON, you need to integrate it with your project.

In previous chapters, when you integrated third-party code into your projects, you downloaded the relevant files and dragged them into the Project Navigator. But what happens when you come back to tweak your code in six months and find that all your third-party frameworks are out of date? You'd need to manually step through each of your dependencies, repeating the process. This time, you're going to integrate third-party code into your project using a *dependency manager* to help automate this process.

Dependency managers

Dependency managers specify a list of third-party code, called *dependencies*, that your app requires. They then provide a mechanism for you to automatically load and update this third-party code. They may also integrate this code into your Xcode project for you.

At the time of writing, three main dependency managers are available for your Xcode projects.

Swift Package Manager

Because the Swift Package Manager is being developed by Apple, you'd think that it would be the safest option, but (at the time of writing) it's still a work in progress, and doesn't yet support iOS.

CocoaPods

CocoaPods, with a long history since its release in 2011, is probably the most popular dependency manager. CocoaPods isn't only a dependency manager, but it maintains a central database of third-party libraries at http://cocoapods.org that you can browse to find what you're looking for. It's compatible with Swift and Objective-C and automatically integrates dependencies (called *pods*) into your project.

As pods are managed by a CocoaPods project, something called a *workspace* is created to contain both your project and the CocoaPods project.

All that sounds great, but CocoaPods does have several cons:

- The CocoaPods software can be a pain to set up, requiring you to install the correct version of several command-line tools such as Gem and Ruby.
- Complete automation to integrate dependencies in a workspace can feel inflexible, and, ironically, add complexity, especially when something goes wrong.
- Removing CocoaPods from a project can be laborious.

Carthage

Carthage, released in 2014, is a little newer than CocoaPods, but has been steadily gaining in popularity. Carthage is less feature-heavy than CocoaPods; Carthage merely manages your dependencies and leaves it up to you to integrate them into your Xcode project. This lack of automation could be seen as a negative, but supporters of Carthage would say it reduces complexity and increases flexibility. A couple more points in favor of Carthage:

- Carthage is easier to install than CocoaPods, only requiring the running of an installer package.
- Carthage is *decentralized*, and unlike CocoaPods, it doesn't have a central database of frameworks.

In the end, which dependency manager you use (if any) can come down to personal preference, but it's definitely worth exploring the options. We're going to explore using dependency managers with the simplest of the three main options, Carthage.

14.10.1 Integrating SwiftyJSON with Carthage

You're going to integrate SwiftyJSON with your project, using the Carthage dependency manager.

1   First, you need to install the software for Carthage via an installer package or Homebrew. You can find instructions for installing Carthage at https://github.com/Carthage/Carthage#installing-carthage.

   To add dependencies to your project, you need what Carthage calls a *Cartfile*. A Cartfile is basically a list of your project's dependencies that you want Carthage to manage.

2   With your favorite text editor, create a file called Cartfile and save it your project folder. The basic syntax for adding a dependency to your Cartfile is straightforward:

```
github "profile name/repository name"
```

3   Add SwiftyJSON as a dependency in your Cartfile.

```
github "SwiftyJSON/SwiftyJSON"
```

Now, it's time to request that Carthage automatically download your requested dependencies. You'll do this from the Terminal.

4   Find the Terminal application in the Application/Utilities folder—or, even better, keep it conveniently in the dock. Drag your project folder from the Finder to the Terminal icon, and the Terminal should open, ready to go at the right path (see figure 14.5).

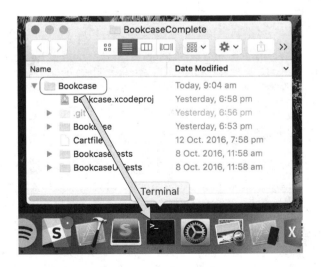

Figure 14.5   Drag folder to the Terminal

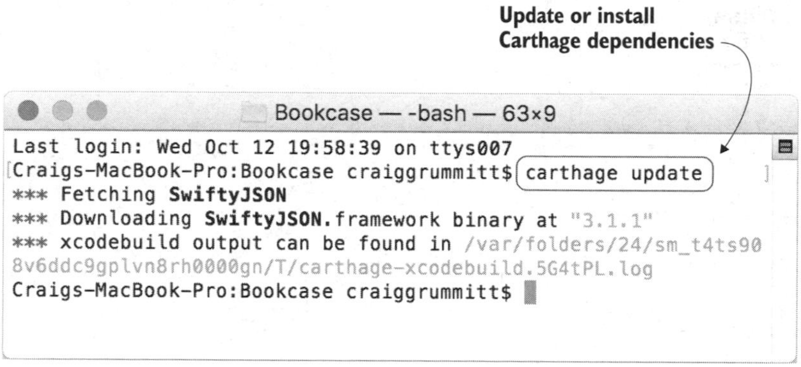

**Update or install
Carthage dependencies**

```
●  ●  ●       Bookcase — -bash — 63×9
Last login: Wed Oct 12 19:58:39 on ttys007
[Craigs-MacBook-Pro:Bookcase craiggrummitt$ carthage update ]
*** Fetching SwiftyJSON
*** Downloading SwiftyJSON.framework binary at "3.1.1"
*** xcodebuild output can be found in /var/folders/24/sm_t4ts90
8v6ddc9gplvn8rh0000gn/T/carthage-xcodebuild.5G4tPL.log
Craigs-MacBook-Pro:Bookcase craiggrummitt$ ▌
```

Figure 14.6   Fetch Carthage dependencies.

5 Run the command `carthage update` in the Terminal (see figure 14.6).

NOTE   If you're building only for iOS, you can specify that you want only iOS frameworks to download by adding the flag `--platform iOS` to the Terminal command.

Like magic, all your project's dependencies (that is, the SwiftyJSON framework!) should appear in the Carthage/Build folder in your project. Later, when you want to update your dependencies, you should run this command again.

Unlike CocoaPods, Carthage doesn't integrate your dependencies into your Xcode project for you. Not to worry, doing so is straightforward; you have a few simple steps left to complete this process.

6 First, you need to add the SwiftyJSON framework to your project. Open the project in the Finder. In the Carthage/Build folder, you should find an iOS folder, which contains the SwiftyJSON framework relevant to the iOS platform.

7 Back in Xcode, open the General settings for the main project target. At the bottom, you should find Linked Frameworks and Libraries. Drag the Swifty-JSON.framework file from the Carthage/Build/iOS folder in the Finder to the Linked Frameworks and Libraries section in the General settings (see figure 14.7).

Next, you need to add a special script that will run when your project builds and copy debug information from the SwiftyJSON framework to your project.

Open General settings in Xcode for main project target

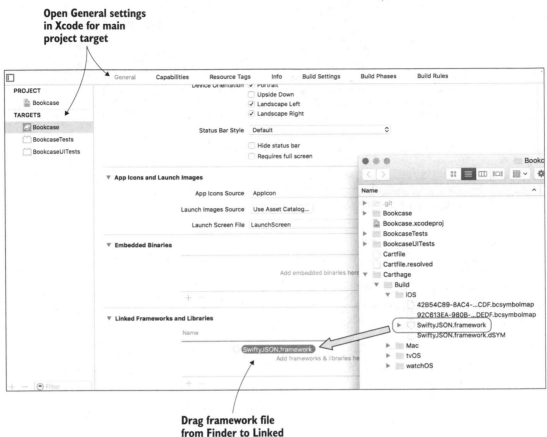

Drag framework file from Finder to Linked Frameworks and Libraries

Figure 14.7 Add linked framework

8 Open the Build Phases tab of the settings for the main project target. Select the plus (+) symbol at the top left of the window, and select New Run Script phase (see figure 14.8).

9 Add the following text to the script area (figure 14.8):

```
/usr/local/bin/carthage copy-frameworks
```

10 Now, in the same area, add the SwiftyJSON framework to be copied, by selecting the plus (+) symbol beneath the Input Files title and pasting in the location of the framework, using a shortcut variable to the root path of the project (figure 14.8).

```
$(SRCROOT)/Carthage/Build/iOS/SwiftyJSON.framework
```

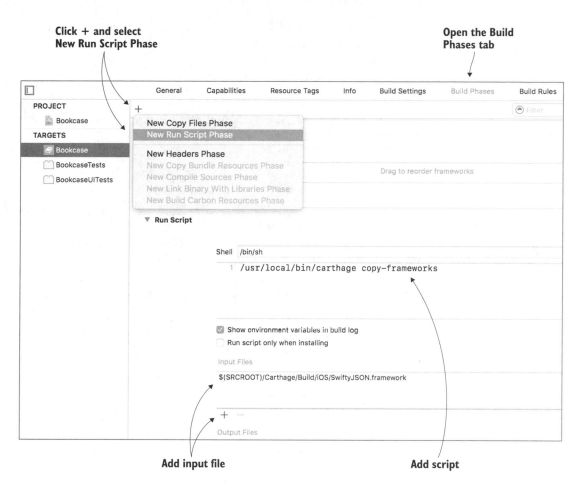

Figure 14.8   Add run script to build phases

NOTE   If you want to know more about project settings, check appendix A.

14.10.2 Using SwiftyJSON

Now that you have SwiftyJSON integrated into your Xcode project, parsing your JSON and digging down to the data you need is a piece of cake!

First, any Swift file that uses the SwiftyJSON framework will need to import it.

1 Add a line to import the SwiftyJSON framework at the top of the `Google-BooksService`.

```
import SwiftyJSON
```

Now, create a new method to parse the JSON with SwiftyJSON, so that you can compare it with the other JSON parsing methods we've looked at.

2 Add a new method called `parseSwiftyJSON`, with the same definition as the other JSON parsing methods you've created.

```
private func parseSwiftyJSON(data:Data,
    completionHandler: @escaping (Book?, Error?) -> Void) {
}
```

3 Parse the JSON in the `parseSwiftyJSON` method by instantiating SwiftyJSON's JSON class, passing in the data object.

```
let dataAsJSON = JSON(data: data)
```

Using SwiftyJSON, you can now drill down to the data you're after using familiar dictionary and array syntax. To finally extract a foundation type, use the property relevant to the type. For example, to extract a `String`, `Double`, `Int`, or `Array` you would use the properties `string`, `double`, `int`, or `arrayObject`. (If you prefer a default value to an optional, add the suffix `Value` to the property, that is, `stringValue`, `doubleValue`, `intValue`, or `arrayValue`.)

4 Extract and unwrap the `title` and `authors` properties from the parsed JSON. Like before, if this is successful, create a `book` object and pass it in a call to the completion handler; otherwise, call the completion handler, passing `nil` to indicate the method was unsuccessful in extracting a book from the JSON data.

```
if let title = dataAsJSON["items"][0]["volumeInfo"]         ── Extracts title
              ➥ "title"].string,
   let authors = dataAsJSON["items"][0]["volumeInfo"]        ── Extracts authors
              ➥ "authors"].arrayObject as? [String] {
       let book = Book(title: title,
           author: authors.joined(separator: ","),
           rating: 0, isbn: "0", notes: "")                  ── Creates book
       completionHandler(book,nil)                           ◄── Sends book to
} else {                                                         completion handler
       completionHandler(nil, nil)                           ── If parsing unsuccessful
}
```

Notice the difference in the amount of code required with SwiftyJSON. You'll most likely find that because the SwiftyJSON method is much more succinct, it's clearer at a glance.

5 Finally, you need to call your new `parseSwiftyJSON` method from the `get-Book` method:

```
self.parseSwiftyJSON(data: data, completionHandler: completionHandler)
```

6 Run the app, and test your barcode detection. You should find the app fills the `title` and `authors` fields the way it did before, but this time using the Swifty-JSON framework to parse the JSON returned from the Google Books web service. You'll still need to give your book a title to save it.

CHALLENGE Because the Google Books web service searches for any incidence of the ISBN number in the book data, it can sometimes return multiple books for a search query if the same number coincidentally occurs in a different field. Your challenge (if you choose to accept it!) is to ensure that the book data you use has the correct ISBN. You need to analyze the structure of the data being returned from Google Books web service to find the ISBN for each book. Remember, you're detecting barcodes with standard 13-character ISBNs.

CHECKPOINT If you'd like to compare your project with mine at this point, you can check mine out at https://github.com/iOSApp-DevelopmentwithSwiftinAction/Bookcase.git (Chapter14.1.WebServiceData).

14.11 Downloading data from a web service

How cool would it be if you could automatically load the cover art for a book when the user scans the book's ISBN? In this section, you're going to explore using a *download task* to download a book cover image (see figure 14.9).

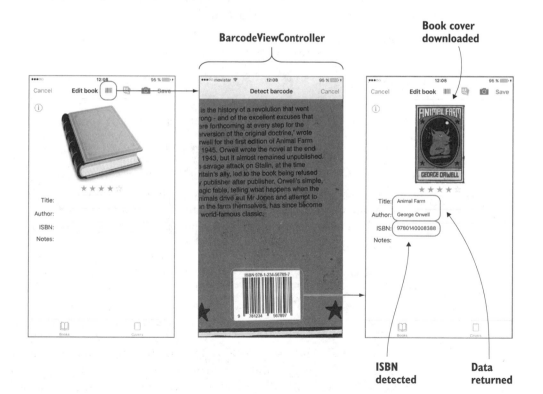

Figure 14.9 Download book cover

Looking at the data being returned from the Google Books web service, you'll see you're already receiving a URL with a thumbnail for the book at the following path:

```
dataAsJSON["items"][0]["volumeInfo"]["imageLinks"]["thumbnail"]
```

1 Extract the URL for the book cover thumbnail in the `parseSwiftyJSON` method after extracting the title and author.

```
let thumbnailURL = volumeInfo["imageLinks"]?["thumbnail"].string {
```

Now, instead of calling the completion handler, you have more work to do!

2 Call a `loadCover` method that you'll define next. Pass in the `book` object that you generated, the `thumbnailURL` that you extracted from the JSON, and the completion handler.

```
loadCover(book: book,
    thumbnailURL: thumbnailURL,
    completionHandler: completionHandler)
```

3 Create the stub of the method to load the cover art in the `GoogleBooksSer-vice` class. Because you eventually want to modify the `book` parameter by passing it the image, you'll need to reassign it as a variable.

```
func loadCover(book: Book,
    thumbnailURL: String,
    completionHandler: @escaping (Book?, Error?) -> Void) {
  var book = book
}
```

4 Set up a `URL` object using the `thumbnailURL` string.

```
guard let url = URL(string: thumbnailURL) else {return}
```

Because an image is a larger chunk of data that makes sense to receive as a file, you're going to get the book cover using a *download task* from the `URLSession`. Because you'll use the default configuration, this time let's not instantiate a `URLRequest`, and instead instantiate the task passing the `URL` object directly.

5 Create a download task, and activate it by calling the `resume` method.

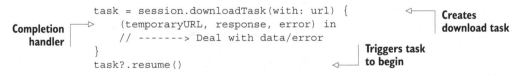

```
                 task = session.downloadTask(with: url) {              Creates
Completion          (temporaryURL, response, error) in               download task
 handler            // -------> Deal with data/error
                 }                                            Triggers task
                 task?.resume()                               to begin
```

The download task works somewhat differently from the data task. Instead of the completion handler providing you with a data object that was returned from the web service, the download task provides a URL that links to a file stored in the local temporary directory.

6 Unwrap the optional URL and use it to create a `Data` object. (Creating a data object can throw an error, so prefix this with an optional `try`.) Use the data object to generate a `UIImage` object, which you can use to set the `cover` property on the `book` object. Finally, regardless of the success of the task, you should call the completion handler, passing it the `book` object.

```
                                                                    Unwraps URL
                  if let imageURL = temporaryURL,
Extracts UIImage       let data = try? Data(contentsOf: imageURL),       Extracts Data
from data              let image = UIImage(data: data) {                 from local URL
                           book.cover = image                      Sets book cover
                  }                                                to image
                  completionHandler(book, error)
```

NOTE Because you're using `UIImage`, ensure that the `GoogleBooks-Service` class imports UIKit.

7 Run the app, add a book, and scan a book barcode. The details of the book should appear—but the cover? Nothing changes. What's going on?

Check the console and you'll find the error:

```
App Transport Security has blocked a cleartext HTTP (http://) resource load
    since it is insecure. Temporary exceptions can be configured via your
    app's Info.plist file.
```

14.11.1 Accessing insecure domains

By default, apps aren't permitted to connect to insecure domains. *Secure* domains are defined as those using HTTPS that use a Transport Layer Security of at least 1.2. If you look at the URLs for the book cover art, you'll notice that they're only HTTP and so are blocked from loading.

As the error indicates, you can specify that you want to make an exception for specific (or all) insecure domains by editing the Info.plist file.

As you saw in chapter 11, the XML representing the attributes in the Info.plist file consists of key tags followed by data type tags. To add exceptions, you'll add an `NSAppTransportSecurity` key that contains a dictionary describing the security level you want in your app. This dictionary accepts the keys shown in table 14.1.

Table 14.1 App Transport Security keys

Key	Type	Default	Description
NSAllowsArbitraryLoads	Boolean	false	Disables security on all domains. This option requires justification when you publish your app to the App Store.
NSAllowsArbitraryLoadsInMedia	Boolean	false	Disables security on media loaded with `AVFoundation`.

Table 14.1   App Transport Security keys *(continued)*

Key	Type	Default	Description
NSAllowsArbitraryLoadsInWebContent	Boolean	false	Disables security on content loaded into web views.
NSAllowsLocalNetworking	Boolean	false	Disables security on loading local resources.
NSExceptionDomains	Dictionary	None	Disables security for specific domains.

Make domain exceptions by adding them as keys to the NSExceptionDomain dictionary. You then add a dictionary describing how this domain should be treated, using the keys shown in table 14.2.

Table 14.2   Exception domain keys

Key	Type	Default	Description
NSIncludesSubdomains	Boolean	false	Exception applies to subdomains
NSRequiresCertificateTransparency	Boolean	false	Requires valid certificate transparency timestamps
NSExceptionAllowsInsecureHTTPLoads	Boolean	false	Allows insecure HTTP loads*
NSExceptionRequiresForwardSecrecy	Boolean	true	Requires cyphers that support forward secrecy
NSExceptionMinimumTLSVersion	String	TLS v1.2	Specifies the minimum Transport Layer Security version*

* These options require justification when you publish your app to the App Store.

All the book cover art seems to be derived from the same insecure HTTP domain at http://books.google.com, so you'll make this domain an exception.

1   Open the Info.plist file, this time as raw XML. Right-click on the Info.plist file in the Project Navigator, and select Open As > Source Code. Add books.google .com to the NSAppTransportSecurity dictionary in the NSAppTransport- Security dictionary, and request that insecure HTTP loads for this domain be permitted.

```
<dict>
    …
    <key>NSAppTransportSecurity</key>
    <dict>
        <key>NSExceptionDomains</key>
        <dict>
            <key>books.google.com</key>
            <dict>
```

```
            <key>NSExceptionAllowsInsecureHTTPLoads</key>
                <true/>
            </dict>
        </dict>
    </dict>
</dict>
```

NOTE If you view the Info.plist file in the property list editor, you'll see more human-readable names for these keys by default. `NSAppTransportSecurity`, for example, is called "App Transport Security Settings."

2 Run the app, add a book, and scan a book barcode. This time, because you've added the `books.google.com` domain to the list of exception domains, the cover art should appear.

3 Select Save, and you've added a book's details and cover art by scanning a barcode—too easy!

Session task delegate

Managing session tasks by implementing a custom delegate has an alternate approach. This approach provides greater configuration and control over the session task.

To use this approach, you'll want to instantiate the task without a callback and implement the delegate for the specific task type.

For example, to use the custom delegate approach to download the book cover, you'd take these steps:

1 Instantiate the task without a completion handler.

```
task = session.downloadTask(with: url)
```

2 `GoogleBooksService` would adopt the `URLSessionDownloadDelegate`. (This protocol subclasses `URLSessionDelegate`, so you don't have to specify that delegate.)

```
class GoogleBooksService: NSObject, BooksService,
    URLSessionDownloadDelegate
```

3 `GoogleBooksService` then implements required protocol methods. The `URLSessionDownloadDelegate` requires you to respond to when the data has finished downloading. This is where you would generate an image from the data downloaded to the temporary URL at `location` and update the book object.

```
public func urlSession(_ session: URLSession,
        downloadTask: URLSessionDownloadTask,
        didFinishDownloadingTo location: URL) {
    //Set book cover from image downloaded
}
```

(continued)

4   `GoogleBooksService` could then implement any optional protocol methods. For example, the `URLSessionDownloadDelegate` and its subclasses permit additional customization of the task, such as providing authentication details to the server and managing HTTP redirects. The delegate can also be used to provide notifications, such as if a session becomes invalidated or of a download's progress (this is useful for showing percentage downloaded in a progress bar for downloads of larger file sizes).

14.12 Displaying the network activity indicator

If a networking task can take more than a couple of seconds, it's a good idea to indicate this to the user with a network activity indicator in the status bar (see figure 14.10).

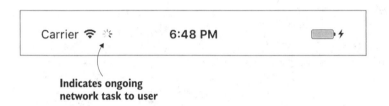

Figure 14.10   Network activity indicator

Displaying the network activity indicator is straightforward—all that's needed is to set the `isNetworkActivityIndicatorVisible` property of the `UIApplication` to `true`.

1   In the `foundBarcode` method in `BookViewController`, get a reference to the `UIApplication` with its singleton type property `shared` and turn on the activity indicator.

```
UIApplication.shared.isNetworkActivityIndicatorVisible = true
```

2   In the completion handler of `getBook`, when network activity is complete, hide the indicator by setting the same property to `false`:

```
UIApplication.shared.isNetworkActivityIndicatorVisible = false
```

14.13 Cancelling a task

It may have occurred to you that the user is currently able to exit the book edit form while a data or download task is in progress.

If the user exits the book view controller by saving or cancelling while the `BooksService` is still waiting for a response from the web service, you should cancel any ongoing operations.

1 Add a request to cancel web operations in the `viewDidDisappear` method of `BookViewController`.

```
booksService.cancel()
```

2 In the `GoogleBooksService` class, fill out the `cancel` method by cancelling the current task.

```
func cancel() {
    task?.cancel()
}
```

✓ **CHECKPOINT** If you'd like to compare your project with mine at this point, you can check mine out at https://github.com/iOSApp-DevelopmentwithSwiftinAction/Bookcase.git (Chapter14.2.WebService-Download). You may need to call `carthage update` in the Terminal to update SwiftyJSON to the latest version.

14.14 Summary

In this chapter, you learned the following:

- You can optionally use `URLRequest` to configure your URL request beyond the defaults and `URLSessionConfiguration` to configure your `URLSession` beyond the defaults.
- Use the URL session task delegate for fine-grained control over a task. Alternatively, for basic requirements, use the completion handler when instantiating the URL session task.
- Use a third-party JSON parser such as SwiftyJSON to access more-complex JSON data with a more readable syntax.
- You can use operation queues instead of dispatch queues to manage threads for additional control, such as dependencies between operations.
- You can use dependency managers such as Carthage and CocoaPods to maintain third-party code and keep it conveniently updated.
- Configure your app's App Transport Security to be able to connect to insecure domains.

Debugging and testing

This chapter covers

- Debugging using different techniques, tools, gauges, and instruments in Xcode
- Testing your app
- Testing your app interface

All's well and good reading a book or following a tutorial, but in the real world things go wrong. And often! This is your chance to put your detective hat on and investigate.

In this chapter, we'll look at what to do when things go wrong by using debugging. We'll also look at how to prevent things from going wrong with testing.

Along the way, we'll explore additional concepts:

- The console
- Variables view
- Breakpoints and the breakpoint navigator
- The debug navigator and gauges
- Instruments
- Unit tests and UI tests

439

15.1   *The setup*

A friend has kindly offered to look at your app and see if they can find any bugs. You sent them a link to the GitHub repo for your Xcode project, and a few days later you got this email in return:

Hey—I've had a look at the app for you. It's looking good, but I also found a few odd problems:

- *The book edit form was working well to begin with, but then it started crashing. Don't know what that's about.*
- *The Cancel button in the book edit form crashes the app.*
- *After you add an image and save it, the next time you edit the book and save it, the book cover seems to disappear … strange?*

Oh, I also made a couple of little improvements here and there. Hope that's okay!

- *I used a cool third-party framework to detect a nice color palette in the cover art of each book, to use in styling the table view cells and the book edit form. I've also added properties for these colors in the* Book *class. The app seems to freeze, though, for a couple of seconds when you add an image. Is there something you can do about that?*
- *I added a nice little three-page help section to onboard the app, using a page view controller. It automatically triggers when you first open the app, and you can reopen it with a Help button. There should be a title, blurb, and image, but for some weird reason, only the images are displaying.*

Oh, and you should probably add some tests.

Sorry I ran out of time to fix everything up. All the best with it, I look forward to downloading it from the App Store!

Oh, here's the repo with my updates: https://github.com/iOSAppDevelopmentwithSwift-inAction/Bookcase.git (Chapter15.1.UpdatesNeedFixing).

Well, that was a nice surprise. Your friend made a couple of nice additions to the app. Great! But it seems the app has been left in a buggy state. That email contains a lot of information; let's go through it step by step, check out what they've done, and explore what needs fixing.

15.2   *Debugging mode*

The book edit form was working well to begin with, but then it started crashing. Don't know what that's about.

Let's confirm what your friend is saying about the app crashing.

1. Download your friend's repo update.
2. As usual, run `carthage update` in the Terminal to update third-party code in the project.
3. Run the app. Your friend's onboarding section should appear.
4. Select the Skip button.
5. Select the + button to add a book.

Bam! Your friend was right—the app crashes!

When Xcode crashes, it automatically enters debugging mode (see figure 15.1). Debugging mode can be intimidating, especially at first. Let's break it down.

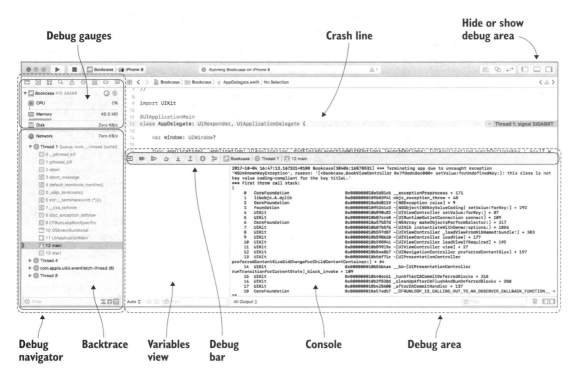

Figure 15.1 Xcode debugger in a crash

Debugging mode consists of

- A red line that appears in the source editor indicating the most recent line of your code that ran before the crash occurred.
- The *debug navigator* appears in the navigator panel, consisting of
  - Gauges for measuring the current state of your device or simulator's CPU, memory, disk, and network activity.
  - A path of how you arrived at the current line of code in each active thread. This is called the *backtrace* (people also call this the *call stack* or *stack trace*).
- The *debug area* appears below the source editor, consisting of
  - The *debug bar* with several debug controls including stepping through your app.
  - The *variables view* showing the current state of variables from the scope of the line in the source editor.
  - The *console*, which outputs the reason for the crash and a printed call stack.

Don't worry, this has only been a short summary of these tools. In a moment, we'll look at each in turn.

Xcode behaviors

How does Xcode know to automatically show you the debug navigator and the debug area when the app crashes? Well, it's all defined in special Xcode preferences called *behaviors*. Use behaviors to request that Xcode performs specific actions when specific events occur. Xcode comes with certain behaviors already set up for you by default.

Let's look at the default behavior that opens the debug navigator and debug area. Select Xcode > Behaviors > Edit Behaviors. In the events menu on the left, select Running > Pauses. This behavior is triggered when a running app is paused, such as when the app crashes! In the actions menu on the right, you can specify actions to perform when this event occurs. In addition to showing the debug navigator and debug area, you could, for example, play a sound, display a system notification, or even have an announcement spoken to you.

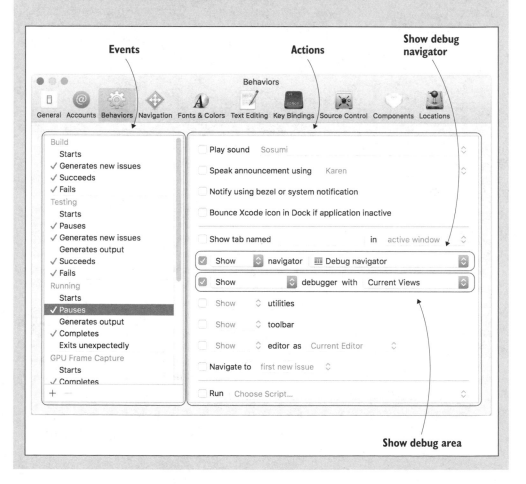

Sometimes, such as in this case, the red line freezes on your `AppDelegate` class, indicating that the problem probably occurred in initial setup. One common reason for this is a problem with the storyboard. Let's look at the console for clues.

15.3 Debugging crash logs in the console

At first glance, the output in the console after a crash looks crazy complicated. To give yourself a shock, take a glance at figure 15.2. But don't panic! You'll see a number of strange symbols, numbers, and unfamiliar syntax. Where to start?

```
2017-10-04 16:54:52.138072+0100 Bookcase[38828:16887511] *** Terminating app due to uncaught exception 'NSUnknownKeyException', reason:
'[<Bookcase.BookViewController 0x7fd4a307e200> setValue:forUndefinedKey:]: this class is not key value coding-compliant for the key titleL.'
*** First throw call stack:
(
    0   CoreFoundation                      0x000000010d7ab1cb __exceptionPreprocess + 171
    1   libobjc.A.dylib                     0x000000010ccd6f41 objc_exception_throw + 48
    2   CoreFoundation                      0x000000010d7ab119 -[NSException raise] + 9
    3   Foundation                          0x000000010c6f91e3 -[NSObject(NSKeyValueCoding) setValue:forKey:] + 292
    4   UIKit                               0x000000011054fc82 -[UIViewController setValue:forKey:] + 87
    5   UIKit                               0x0000000011083bc40 -[UIRuntimeOutletConnection connect] + 109
    6   CoreFoundation                      0x000000010d74e57d -[NSArray makeObjectsPerformSelector:] + 317
    7   UIKit                               0x0000000011083a5f6 -[UINib instantiateWithOwner:options:] + 1856
    8   UIKit                               0x0000000110556d07 -[UIViewController _loadViewFromNibNamed:bundle:] + 383
    9   UIKit                               0x0000000110557610 -[UIViewController loadView] + 177
    10  UIKit                               0x0000000110557941 -[UIViewController loadViewIfRequired] + 195
    11  UIKit                               0x000000011055819e -[UIViewController view] + 27
    12  UIKit                               0x00000001105ad8b7 -[UINavigationController preferredContentSize] + 197
    13  UIKit                               0x000000011052e71c -[UIPresentationController preferredContentSizeDidChangeForChildContentContai
    14  UIKit                               0x000000011052a4ae __56-[UIPresentationController runTransitionForCurrentState]_block_invoke + 1
    15  UIKit                               0x00000001103c5c61 _runAfterCACommitDeferredBlocks + 318
    16  UIKit                               0x00000001103b430d _cleanUpAfterCAFlushAndRunDeferredBlocks + 280
    17  UIKit                               0x00000001103e4600 _afterCACommitHandler + 137
    18  CoreFoundation                      0x000000010d74ddb7 __CFRUNLOOP_IS_CALLING_OUT_TO_AN_OBSERVER_CALLBACK_FUNCTION__ + 23
    19  CoreFoundation                      0x000000010d74dd0e __CFRunLoopDoObservers + 430
    20  CoreFoundation                      0x000000010d732324 __CFRunLoopRun + 1572
    21  CoreFoundation                      0x000000010d731a89 CFRunLoopRunSpecific + 409
    22  GraphicsServices                    0x000000114e029c6 GSEventRunModal + 62
    23  UIKit                               0x0000000113b9d30 UIApplicationMain + 159
    24  Bookcase                            0x000000010c2d1557 main + 55
    25  libdyld.dylib                       0x00000001102b8d81 start + 1
    26  ???                                 0x0000000000000001 0x0 + 1
)
libc++abi.dylib: terminating with uncaught exception of type NSException
(lldb)
```

Figure 15.2   Crash log in console

The trick in interpreting this output is learning what you can ignore 90% of the time and where to find the most relevant information.

The text that automatically outputs to the console when your app crashes is made of two main parts that answer two important questions:

- *Exception information*—What caused the problem?
- *Call stack*—What was happening at the time?

I've organized the console output in figure 15.3. I separated the two main parts and emphasized part of the output to help you focus on what's most important.

First, what caused the problem? The *exception information* should answer this important question, and ironically, it's often scrolled offscreen by the call stack! Ignore the time codes and memory addresses and look for the description of the exception in English. According to the exception information in this case, there was an `NSUnknownKeyException` for the key `titleL` in the `BookViewController`.

Exception
information

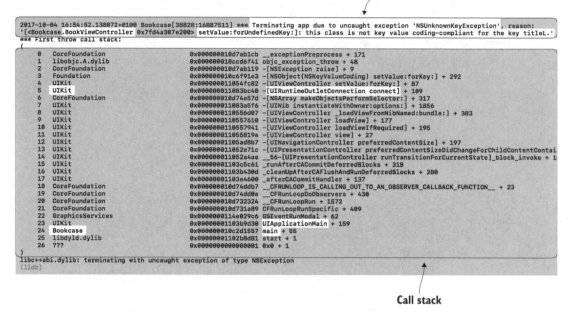

Figure 15.3   Crash log in console

Great—the English description of the exception information is often all you'll need to look at after a crash, but sometimes it helps to also look at what was happening at the time of the crash. The call stack is a path of method calls called *frames* that lead to a certain location in the code. You can use the call stack to trace the path backward from the most recent frame marked with a 0 at the top, down to the least recent frame at the bottom.

To identify each frame in the call stack, each line gives you the framework, origin (usually object and method), line number, and even the memory address of each call. See figure 15.4 for a close-up of frame 5.

Figure 15.4   Frame in call stack

Calls originating from your own code will have your project name at the left. Note in the call stack that only one call originates from your project, indicated by the project name Bookcase. Look for *main* at line 29 of figure 15.3.

> **NOTE** The *main* call is a special one—*main* represents the main entry point for your app, which in your project (and most others as well) is the App-Delegate class. If you take a close look at the AppDelegate class in your project, you'll notice that it's preceded by the keyword @UIApplication-Main. This keyword defines the AppDelegate as your app's entry point. You'll find this in the call stack too, at line 28.

Sometimes the call stack can give you a peek behind the curtain of certain classes in the iOS SDK that aren't available to developers. If you look through the objects and method calls in the call stack, you might get an idea as to what was happening when the unknown key exception occurred. Perhaps the connect call to the UIRuntime-OutletConnection object at line 5 could be a clue. Although you don't have documentation for this object, you could make a reasonable guess by its name that this object is involved in connecting outlets, and perhaps this has something to do with your crash. The plot thickens!

15.3.1 Solving a crash caused by an outlet

Let's revise your clues. You know that an outlet problem likely exists in BookView-Controller related to the key titleL. Let's look at the storyboard and try to dig deeper.

1   Open the storyboard, and select the book edit form scene.
2   Open the Connections Inspector to explore problems with outlets. As expected, it appears there's a problem with the titleL property—the Connections Inspector shows it with an exclamation mark within a yellow triangle, indicating a broken connection (see figure 15.5).

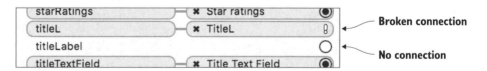

Figure 15.5 IBOutlet **issues**

Below the broken outlet connection is another outlet called titleLabel with a hollow circle, indicating that a property in the BookViewController class called titleLabel has been defined with the @IBOutlet keyword, but hasn't been connected to a view in the storyboard.

It appears that your friend set up an outlet called `titleL` and then decided to give it the name `titleLabel`, probably to ensure good naming practices. They renamed it in the code, but didn't update the connections! Let's fix it and see if that resolves the crash.

3   Remove the old connection by selecting the X next to `TitleL`.

4   Now, set up a new connection to `titleLabel` in the Connections Inspector. You could do this in the Assistant Editor as you've done previously, but since you're already in the Connections Inspector, drag from the circle beside `titleLabel` to the title label in the storyboard (see figure 15.6).

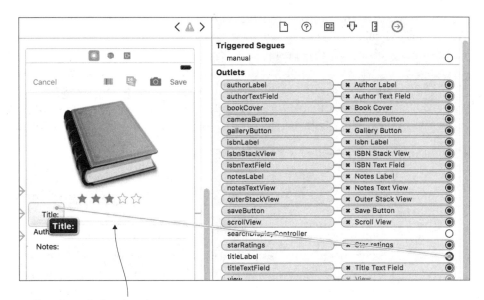

Drag from Connections Inspector to appropriate element in storyboard

Figure 15.6   Connect `IBOutlet` into the Connections Inspector.

You should see the title label with a filled circle in the Connections Inspector, indicating that it's now connected to a view in the storyboard. If you open the `BookViewController` class, you'll see the same filled circle indicator there as well (see figure 15.7).

Connected ────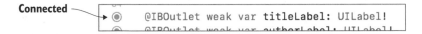

```
@IBOutlet weak var titleLabel: UILabel!
@IBOutlet weak var authorLabel: UILabel!
```

Figure 15.7   `IBOutlet` connected in the source editor

Now, all that's left is to run the app and see if you've solved the problem!

5 Run the app, select or add a book, and ... no crash!

First problem solved, what's next?

15.3.2 Solving a crash caused by an action

The Cancel button in the book edit form crashes the app.

With the app running and the book form open, select the Cancel button. Your friend was right!

Another long crash log fills the console, but this time you have a better idea of what to look for. Let's start with what caused the problem. With memory addresses removed, the exception information reads thus:

```
-[Bookcase.BookViewController touchCancel:]: unrecognized selector sent to
    instance
```

It appears that in the BookViewController class, a selector (that is, a method) called touchCancel is being called but not recognized. Why would that be, and what was happening at the time? You probably have enough information to take a good, educated guess, but let's look at a portion of the call stack for more clues. See figure 15.8—again, I've emphasized part of the output to help you focus on more-interesting details.

```
 4   CoreFoundation        0x0000000108713798 _CF_forwarding_prep_0 + 120
 5   UIKit                 0x00000001076035b8 -[UIApplication sendAction:to:from:forEvent:] + 83
 6   UIKit                 0x0000000107a44405 -[UIBarButtonItem(UIInternal) _sendAction:withEvent:] + 149
 7   UIKit                 0x00000001076035b8 -[UIApplication sendAction:to:from:forEvent:] + 83
 8   UIKit                 0x0000000107788edd -[UIControl sendAction:to:forEvent:] + 67
 9   UIKit                 0x0000000107891f6 -[UIControl _sendActionsForEvents:withEvent:] + 444
10   UIKit                 0x0000000107789380 -[UIControl _sendActionsForEvents:withEvent:] + 838
11   UIKit                 0x0000000107788f2 -[UIControl touchesEnded:withEvent:] + 668
12   UIKit                 0x0000000107670ce1 -[UIWindow _sendTouchesForEvent:] + 2747
13   UIKit                 0x00000001076723cf -[UIWindow sendEvent:] + 4011
14   UIKit                 0x0000000107611f63f -[UIApplication sendEvent:] + 371
15   UIKit                 0x0000000107c1171d _dispatchPreprocessedEventFromEventQueue + 3248
```

Figure 15.8 Crash log in the console

Note that sending an action for an event triggered by a UIControl seems to be a theme. The event itself seems to be a touch, according to frame 11, and the control seems to be a UIBarButtonItem.

Let's revise all of our clues again. When a bar button item in the scene connected to the BookViewController class (assumedly the Cancel button) tries to call the touchCancel method, it's not recognized. Let's look at the storyboard to get a clearer idea of the problem.

1 Open the storyboard, select the book edit form scene, and open the Connections Inspector to explore problems with actions. Similar to earlier, there seems to be a problem with the touchCancel method (see figure 15.9).

Figure 15.9 `IBAction` **issues**

There seems to be a broken connection between the Cancel button and the `touchCancel` action method. Curiously, there seems to be an unconnected action method called `touchCancelzzzz`!

2 Open the `BookViewController` class and see what's going on in the code (see figure 15.10).

Figure 15.10 `IBActions` **in the source editor**

It's true! There's a `touchCancelzzzz` method in the `BookViewController`, and there isn't a `touchCancel` method to be seen. Your "helpful" friend must have leaned on the keyboard and inadvertently renamed the method. As the hollow circle indicates, this caused the `touchCancelzzzz` method to disconnect from the storyboard.

3 Remove the extra z's from the method name and rebuild the project. The circle should fill in, indicating that all is well in the world again, and the Cancel button in the storyboard is reconnected with the `touchCancel` action in your `BookViewController` class.

4 To be sure, rerun the app, open a book, and select Cancel.

This time, the app should act as expected, closing the book edit form scene.
    What's next, detective?

15.4 *Examining variables and breakpoints*

After you add an image and save it, the next time you edit the book and save it, the book cover seems to disappear … strange?

First, check that you can replicate the problem.

    Run the app, open a book with a cover image (you'll have to add a cover image for a book first if none of your sample books have cover art), and select Save. The book image returns to the default cover image. "Strange" is right! What could be happening?

Your immediate suspicion is that for some reason, an existing book cover isn't being used when the `BookViewController` generates a book to save. Let's confirm that by examining the `bookToSave` variable in the `BookViewController` class in the `touchSave` method.

As is so often the case in Xcode, there are many different ways to examine the contents of a variable. Let's look at a few now, beginning with a method that you've seen before, the `print` method.

15.4.1 *Examining a variable with print*

To examine the `bookToSave` variable, let's print its contents to the console with the `print` method.

1 Before the `touchSave` method calls `dismissMe`, print the `bookToSave` variable.

```
print("Saving book: \(bookToSave)")
```

2 Run the app again, once again open a book with a cover image, and select Save. This time, the book object should print to the console, looking something like this:

```
Saving book: Book(title: "Five on Brexit Island", author: "Enid
  Blyton", rating: 3.0, isbn: " 9781786488077", notes: "", image:
  Optional(<UIImage: 0x1c02aeb20>, {128, 202}), backgroundColor:
  UIExtendedGrayColorSpace 1 1, primaryColor: UIExtendedGrayColorSpace 0
  1, detailColor: UIExtendedGrayColorSpace 0 1)
```

Well, that's great. By default you're seeing the value of every property of the object, down to its background color. Sometimes, however, when you print an object, you might not need to see its every last detail. You might prefer to see just the important stuff. It would probably be sufficient detail to identify a book, for example, by the title and author. To resolve this bug, you might also want to see whether or not this book has a cover image.

There's a neat little trick for adjusting the string that's output when you print an object. If your custom type adopts the `CustomStringConvertible` protocol, you can provide a description property that describes your object as a String, and it will automatically be used by `print`.

3 Add a description property to the `Book` class that returns the `title`, `author`, and a message about whether the book has a cover image.

```
override var description: String {
    return "\(title) by \(author) :
        ➥ \(hasCoverImage ? "Has" : "No") cover image"
}
```

4 Run the app again, and save a book with a cover image. This time, you should see more meaningful information about the book being saved in the console:

```
Saving book: Five on Brexit Island by Enid Blyton : No cover image
```

It appears that your suspicion was correct. For some unknown reason, the book object to be saved isn't being generated with its cover image.

> **TIP**   Classes that subclass NSObject, such as UIView, automatically adopt the CustomStringConvertible protocol and contain a description property. To provide your own description, you'll have to override the default description property.

Sometimes, adding print statements everywhere in your code to help diagnose a problem can get out of hand, and more-sophisticated debugging techniques would be more appropriate.

> **TIP**   An alternative approach to print that certain developers prefer is the NSLog statement. While NSLog is a little slower, it does add a timestamp to the log and stores logging data to disk. Having a log history can be useful, but makes it even more important to ensure you remove all NSLog calls from your code before publishing your app to the App Store.

Remove the print statement now. We're going to explore other debugging techniques to diagnose the source of this problem further.

15.4.2   *Pausing your app with a breakpoint*

To diagnose problems in your app, sometimes it can help to use a file and line breakpoint to pause execution at a line in your code. File and line breakpoints are ultra-useful for

- *Checking the current state of the app.* This is useful for taking a closer look at variables, the call stack, threads, the user interface (UI), or the app's use of system resources at a specific point in time.
- *Stepping through your app.* You can use the step controls to run your app step by step and diagnose any problems with the flow of your app.

You'll use file and line breakpoints to analyze why books aren't being saved with their images. Let's start by looking at right after a book object is generated for saving data from the book edit form.

1   Add a breakpoint to your code after setting the bookToSave variable in the touchSave method in BookViewController. Adding a breakpoint is simple; click to the left of the line where you want execution to be paused. A dark blue pointed rectangle should appear where you clicked, indicating an active breakpoint (see figure 15.11).

Breakpoint indicator →

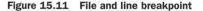
Figure 15.11   File and line breakpoint

NOTE   Be careful not to click on the breakpoint again; this will cause the indicator to turn light blue and the breakpoint will toggle to a disabled state.

Another place that could be interesting to analyze is when a view is loaded and the `BookViewController` class receives a `Book` object to edit.

2 Using the same technique, add a second breakpoint to the `viewDidLoad` method of `BookViewController` after unwrapping the book object.

3 Run your app again, and this time tap on a book that does *not* have a cover image. The app should pause immediately at the breakpoint you specified in the `viewDidLoad` method.

The same way it did earlier when the app crashed, the Running > Pauses behavior launches into action, automatically opening the debug navigator and debug area for you. One difference you may notice is that the paused line of execution is green this time (see figure 15.12).

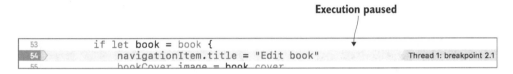

Figure 15.12   Breakpoint pausing execution

Advanced breakpoints

Most commonly, you'll use breakpoints to pause execution at a specific line of code, but they're capable of doing so much more.

For example, *exception breakpoints* break execution whenever specific types of exceptions occur, and *symbolic breakpoints* break execution whenever a specific *method* is called on all subclasses of a certain type of class. You have to add these types of breakpoints in the *breakpoint navigator*.

Your breakpoint could be set up to trigger only if a certain condition is true or after a certain number of times. Breakpoints can also be set up to perform one or more *actions*, such as output to the console or play a sound. Ironically, breakpoints don't necessarily *break* execution. If you like, after performing an action, a breakpoint can automatically continue.

Edit your breakpoints by double-clicking on the breakpoint indicator in the source editor or the breakpoint navigator.

Now that your app has paused execution, you can examine the state of the app's variables. Checking the book object at this point may help diagnose the problem with saving a book cover.

You can use several approaches for examining the state of variables while the app is paused:

- The variables view
- Quick Look
- Print description
- Command line in the lower-level debugger
- Datatips

We'll look at each of these in turn. Let's look first at the variables view.

15.4.3 *Examining a variable with the variables view*

The *variables view* contains variables in the context of where the app is currently paused. Instance variables of `BookViewController` will be contained within the `self` property, while local variables are shown at the top level. As the book object is unwrapped with optional binding, it's considered a local variable.

At the left of several variables, you'll see a *disclosure triangle*, indicating that you can "open up" the variable to have a closer look at its contents.

1 Click on the disclosure triangle for the book object to inspect the value of its properties (see figure 15.13).

Disclosure triangle

Book image

Figure 15.13   Variables view

2 Note that the book image is nil.

This makes sense, as you selected a book with no cover.

Now, let's resume execution so that you can add an image to this book.

15.4.4 *Controlling the app's execution using the debug bar*

Above the variables view, you'll find the debug bar, which contains several controls useful for controlling the execution of your app (see figure 15.14).

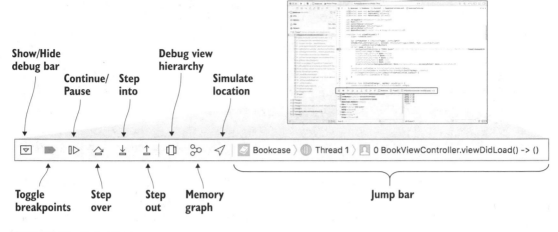

Figure 15.14   Debug bar

Table 15.1 lists several elements that could use extra explanation.

Table 15.1   Debug bar elements

Element	Description
Toggle breakpoints	For convenience, toggle all breakpoints on or off.
Continue/Pause	Continue execution of the app.
Step buttons	Three skip buttons allow you to execute your code step by step. *Step over* and *step into* differ as to how they act when there's a method call in the current line. *Step into* will step through every line of the method, whereas *step over* will interpret the entire method as one step. *Step out*, on the other hand, executes the rest of the current function as one step and pauses execution again when it exits the function.
Debug view hierarchy	View the hierarchy of views in the app. We'll come back to this soon.
Memory graph	Visualize the memory allocations in the app.
Simulate location	Simulate that your app is running from an alternative location.
Jump bar	Use the jump bar to examine your app state from the context of different threads and stack frames.

Let's use the controls in the debug bar to resume execution of the app.

1 Tap the Continue button.
2 Add a cover image to the app.
3 Save the book with the new image by tapping the Save button.

The app should pause execution again after generating a new book to save in the local `bookToSave` variable. Let's examine this variable for more clues.

15.4.5 *Examining a variable with Quick Look*

Let's explore examining variables using another technique, called *Quick Look*.

1 First, focus once again on the variables view, and select the disclosure triangle beside the `bookToSave` variable to open it up.

2 Note that this time, the book image shows a memory address. You can reasonably assume that this means that your book contains an image, but how can you know which?

Certain variables are visual in nature, and the variables view may not be sufficient to describe a variable. *Quick Look* provides you with a *visualization* of the contents of a variable. (You may remember Quick Look from playgrounds, way back in chapter 2.)

3 Select the `image` property of `bookToSave`.

4 To open a visualization of the image property and select the button that looks like an eye, located below the variables view (see figure 15.15).

Figure 15.15
Quick Look

Well, that seems to have worked correctly. The image you added to the book edit form is stored in the image you're saving. But the problem was presenting itself in books that already have an image. You'll need to go through this process again, with the same book now that you know it contains an image, and find the source of this problem.

5 Tap the Continue button, which should return you to the main screen.

6 Choose the same book you added a cover image to.

The app should pause once again at the breakpoint in the `viewDidLoad` method after unwrapping the book object to edit.

Let's use yet another technique for examining the contents of the book object.

15.4.6 Examining a variable with print description

Next to the *Show Quick Look* button, is another useful button that appears as an "i" in a circle. This is called the *Print Description* button. If you select a variable in the variables view, and select the Print Description button, you get exactly the same output in the console as you did earlier when you printed a variable in code.

This time, you'll examine the contents of the book object with the Print Description button.

1 Select the book object in the variables view.

2 Select the Print Description button.

The description property of the `Book` object that you set up earlier will output to the console (see figure 15.16). Covering all bases, the properties of the `Book` object also output to the console.

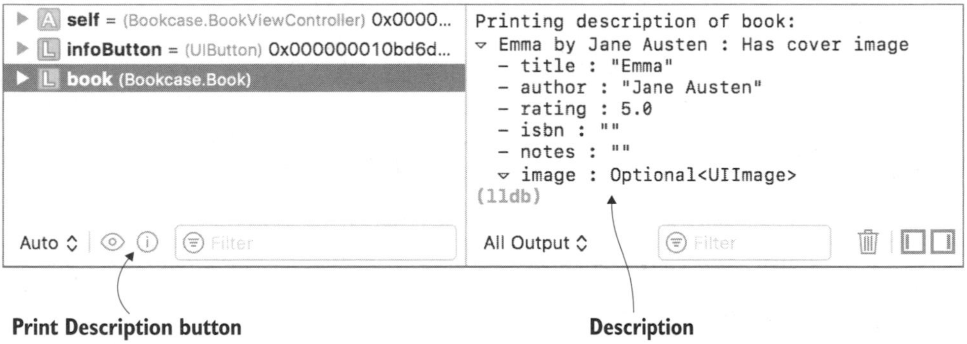

Print Description button   **Description**

Figure 15.16 Print variable description

Well, according to the output, it seems no problem exists with the book object. You'll have to continue execution and save the book to see if the problem is happening there.

But first, what's that strange `lldb` message that crops up in the console?

15.4.7 *Examining a variable with LLDB*

The console is much more than an area for receiving debug logs and outputting print messages. It's a window into the powerful command-line debugger called *lower-level debugger* (LLDB), and the lldb message is a prompt for you to enter commands.

Many debugging features in this chapter are GUI representations of lower-level commands that are available to you as command-line commands in the console.

For example, the Print Description button you used to explore details on the book object uses the LLDB po command under the hood.

1 Use the po command to examine the book variable. Type the following after the lldb prompt and press the Return key:

```
po book
```

You should see the same description appear for Book that you saw for Print Description (see figure 15.17).

If you want to go beyond the default description of a variable and print the underlying implementation of an object, use the p command.

2 Use the p command on the book variable.

```
p book
```

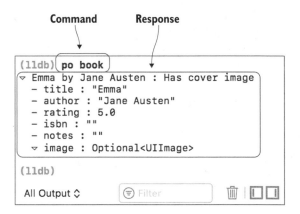

Figure 15.17   LLDB command po in the console

See figure 15.18 for the result from the p command. This time, you should see a much more detailed output of the contents of the book variable.

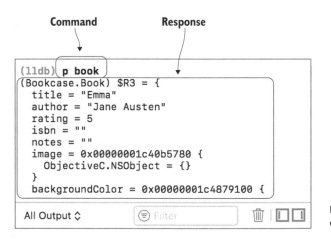

Figure 15.18   LLDB command p in the console

We've barely scratched the surface of what's possible with LLDB. Apart from online documentation, you can use LLDB's `help` command to get a comprehensive listing of debugger commands.

For a change, let's use LLDB to resume program execution.

3 Type `c` after the `lldb` prompt, and press Return. The program should continue.

4 Tap Save, to test saving this book.

Once again, the app should pause execution right after generating a book to save. Let's use one final technique to examine the contents of the book to save.

15.4.8 *Examining a variable with data tips*

Believe it or not, there's yet another way to examine the contents of your variable, and this time, you don't even need the variables view or the console!

With app execution paused, you can point your cursor in the source editor at a variable you want to examine, and a *data tip* for that variable will pop up. From there, you can open the variable the way you did in the variables view, select to show Quick Look, or select the Print Description button.

1 Point to the `bookToSave` variable now. A data tip for the variable should appear.

2 Select the disclosure triangle, open the variable, and examine its contents (see figure 15.19).

Notice that this time, the `image` property of `bookToSave` is equal to `nil`. You seem to be getting closer to the problem!

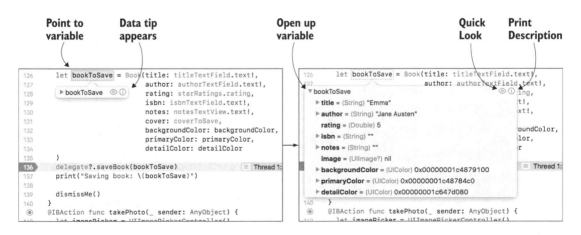

Figure 15.19   Examine a variable with data tips

15.4.9 *Solving the save problem*

Why would the image property be nil? Look at how the bookToSave object is generated—the cover image comes from the coverToSave property. Okay, where's this property set?

A quick search for the coverToSave property uncovers the problem. The coverToSave property is only set in two places: when the user selects a photo or image for the book or when the booksService returns an image after the user scans a barcode. What about books that already have an image? The coverToSave property is never set.

1 In the viewDidLoad method, after unwrapping the book object, set the coverToSave property. Check first that the book *has* a cover image, to avoid setting the default cover to the coverToSave property.

```
if let book = book {
    navigationItem.title = "Edit book"
    bookCover.image = book.cover
    if book.hasCoverImage {
        coverToSave = book.cover
    }
    …
```

2 Run the app again, select a book with a cover image, and save it. This time (fingers crossed!) the book cover image should stick around. Hooray! Good job, detective—problem solved. You can remove your two breakpoints now.

3 To remove the breakpoints, click on them, and drag them to the right. They should disappear—in a puff of smoke!

15.4.10 *Examining a variable in summary*

Many methods exist for examining the contents of a variable, each with their own advantages, as shown in table 15.2.

Table 15.2   Examining a variable

Element	Best for
print	If you prefer to not pause execution of your app
NSLog	If you want timestamps on your console logs and a log history
Quick Look	If you want a visualization of the variable's contents
Data tips	If you're short on screen space and prefer to hide the debug area, or if you prefer to explore variables in the context of your source code
p command in LLDB	If you need information beyond what the default description returns for the variable
Variables view	If you want a visual representation of the hierarchy of variables in your app

15.5 Debugging playback with gauges and instruments

Let's check out your friend's next piece of feedback.

> *I used a cool third-party framework to detect a nice color palette in the cover art of each book, to use in styling the table view cells and the book edit form. I've also added properties for these colors in the* Book *class. The app seems to freeze, though, for a couple of seconds when you add an image. Is there something you can do about that?*

Sounds like quite an interesting addition to the app that your friend has contributed; see figure 15.20 to see it in action.

Add photo

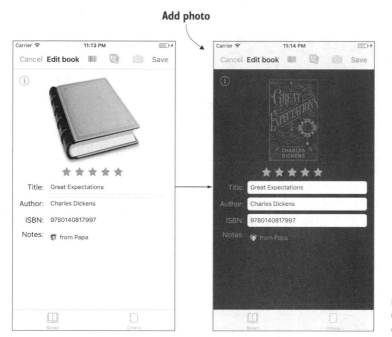

**Figure 15.20
Color detection
of the book image**

The freezing interface isn't so useful, though!

If your app is having playback problems such as a stuttering or freezing interface, the cause may be that you're performing long operations in the main thread and therefore blocking your interface from updating.

Let's explore this theory with the debug gauges.

15.5.1 Debugging playback with debug gauges

If your app is experiencing performance issues, it can be a good idea to look at your app's use of system resources. One way to do this is with the *debug gauges* that you can find in the debug navigator. The debug gauges give you a good summary of how your app is using the device's CPU, memory, disk access, and network calls. You can click on a gauge to get a more detailed report on your app's use of this system resource.

You're going to examine your app's use of the CPU when adding an image to diagnose why the user interface is freezing temporarily.

1 Run your app, and select the Debug Navigator.
2 Select the CPU gauge from the debug gauges, to display the CPU report.
3 Select a book, and add an image. You should see something like figure 15.21.

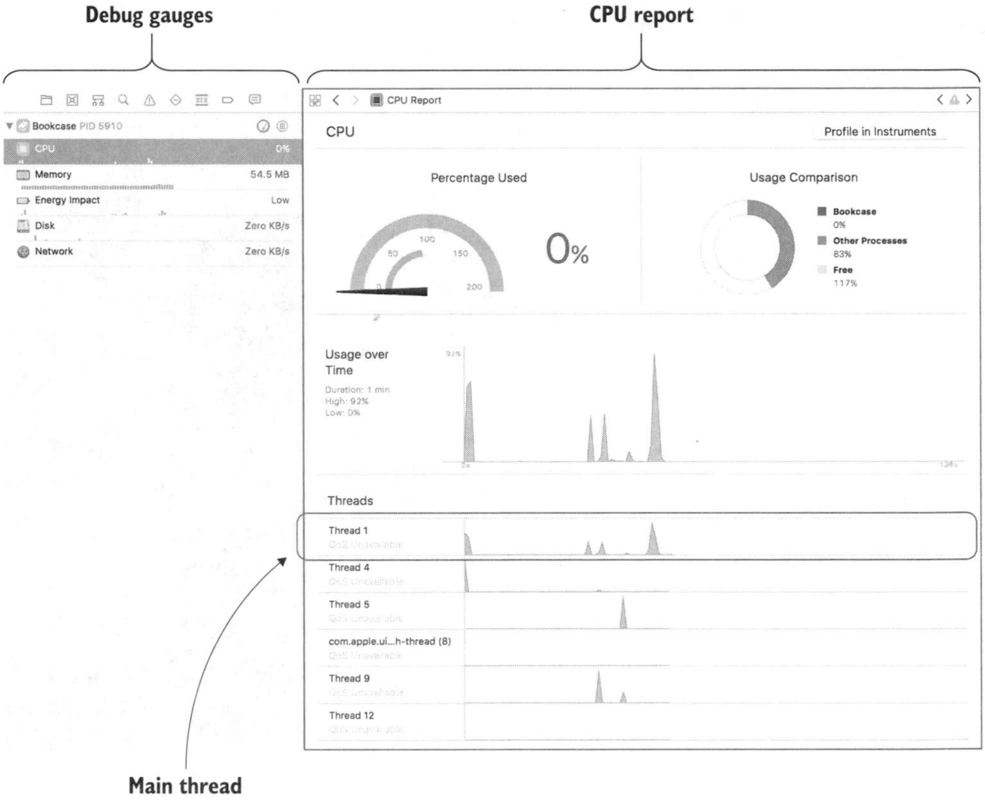

Debug gauges   **CPU report**

Figure 15.21   Debug gauges and CPU report

Note that the majority of the work is going on in thread 1. Thread 1 is also known as the main thread and is where the user interface is updated. As you've seen, if your app is busy working on a time-consuming algorithm such as image color detection in the main thread, the app's user interface will be prevented from updating and responding to user interaction.

It has become clear that a certain operation that your friend introduced needs to be moved to a background thread. But which operation? You could spend time hunting down this method in the code, but you have yet another debugging trick up your sleeve!

15.5.2 Debugging playback with instruments

Xcode provides developers with a library containing debugging tools called *instruments* that build on and supplement the performance and testing tools that are available in debug gauges.

To get a feel for instruments, we'll have a look at the *time profiler* instrument. The time profiler measures how frequently your app performs different processes. You could use the time profiler to find any long-running processes that could be holding up the main thread.

Although you could open the time profiler up by selecting Xcode > Open Developer Tool > Instruments > Time Profiler, you have a shortcut right in front of you in the CPU debug report—at the top-right corner is a *Profile in Instruments* button.

1. Select the Profile in Instruments button. Xcode will offer to transfer or restart the debug session.
2. Select Transfer.
3. The time profiler opens and automatically begins recording the time spent on various processes in your app.
4. Back in the simulator, add an image to a book again.
5. Once the image has been added to the book, you can select the Stop button in the time profiler. The processes that you want to debug have been profiled, and now you can explore the time profiler (see figure 15.22).

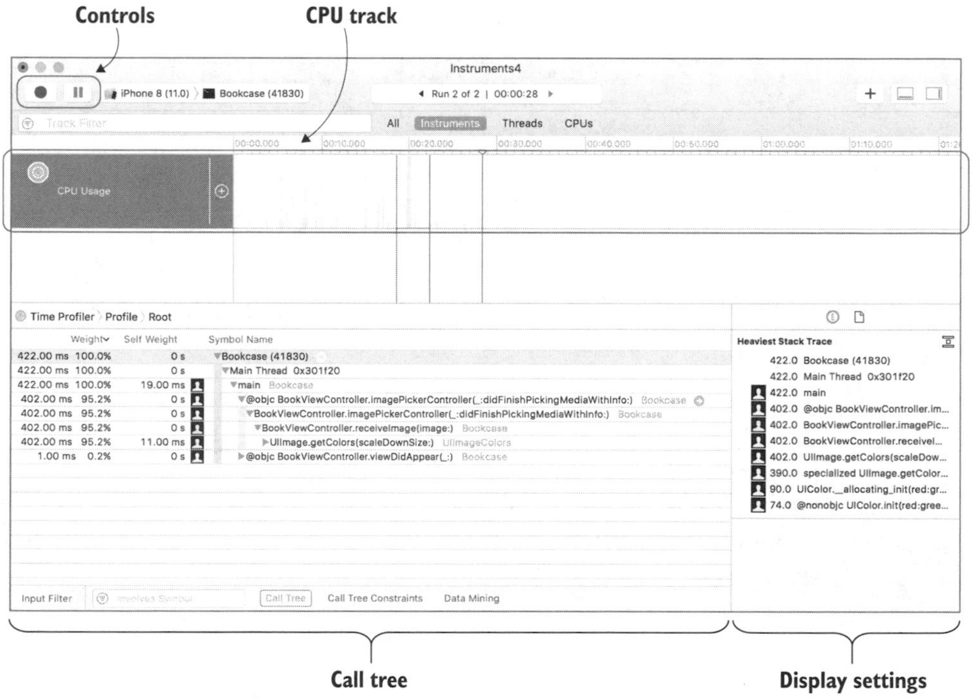

Figure 15.22   Time profiler

While you were recording your app, the time profiler sampled CPU percentage usage (indicated in the CPU track) and call stacks (detailed in the call tree) at regular intervals. Each call in the call tree indicates what's called a *weight*, which is an approximation of the amount of time spent in this process.

6 Because you're interested in finding problems in your own code rather than Apple's, select the Call Tree menu in the bar along the bottom, and check Hide System Libraries.

7 Now, your detective work involves digging down through the call tree hierarchy, following the process with the greatest amount of sample time. You should find a clear path in the main thread down to the receiveImage method in the BookViewController class, which in turn calls the UIImage object's get-Colors method.

8 Double-click the line that reads BookViewController.receiveImage. This will show you the problem line of code, indicating the number of samples recorded containing this process (see figure 15.23).

Figure 15.23   Time profiler

If there was any question which line of code was taking up processing time, it seems to be resolved now! This line definitely needs to be moved to a background thread.

9 Select the Open in Xcode button at the top right of the time profiler. This should take you straight to the problem line of code, ready for you to solve the problem.

15.5.3 *Solving the playback problem*

Now that you know for sure what was causing the app to freeze, let's move it to a background thread.

1 Move the `getColors` call to a background thread using Grand Central Dispatch.

2 Move the `receiveColors` call to the main thread, so that it can update the user interface.

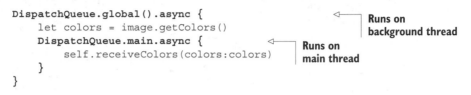

3 Run your app again and add an image to a book. You should find that the app no longer freezes while the colors are being detected in the image. You're free to interact with the app, and when the algorithm has finished its work on a background thread, the colors in the interface smoothly animate to the colors detected in the image. Nice!

I think you're ready for your final debugging challenge!

15.6 *Debugging the user interface*

I added a nice little three-page help section to onboard the app using a page view controller. It automatically triggers when you first open the app, and you can re-open it with a Help button. There should be a title, blurb, and image, but for some weird reason though, only the images are displaying.

Again, this is a nice improvement that your friend has contributed. However, as mentioned, there's a visual issue—the title and blurb for each page aren't appearing. Your friend sent through an image showing how the help pages *should* look, and how they *do* look (see figure 15.24).

Your friend isn't a fan of the storyboard and has set up the three pages entirely in code. These three view controllers make use of convenience methods in a structure called `InstructionFactory` to perform the repetitive tasks of building their interface. They then use a convenience method in another structure called `ContentLayoutMachine` that automatically sets up their auto layout constraints.

It's all sophisticated, but what's going wrong—where's the title and blurb?

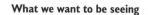

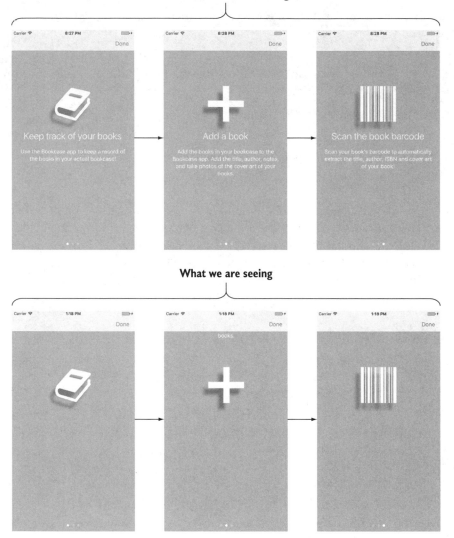

Figure 15.24   Help page view controller

Onboarding and page view controllers

It's a good idea to walk your users through how to use your app. This sort of introduction is called *onboarding* your users. Frequently, onboarding requires multiple pages, and the most common approach for displaying these pages is with a page view controller. Rather than the default page turn, it's more common to use a scroll transition style and a page control at the bottom of the screen, indicating the page you're currently viewing.

Pages are represented by view controllers, and the next and previous pages are loaded, ready for the user to scroll to them.

Your friend has been kind enough to set up such a page view controller for you in the Bookcase project, but for future reference, these are the general steps you'd take:

1 Add a page view controller to the storyboard that's connected to a custom class that subclasses `UIPageViewController`.
2 In the `viewDidLoad` method, set the initial view controller to display with the `setViewControllers` method.
3 Adopt the `UIPageViewControllerDataSource` protocol, set the data source, and implement data source methods that return the next and previous view controllers.
4 Also implement data source methods that return the number of pages, and the number of the initial page.

15.6.1 Debugging the user interface with the Debug View Hierarchy

When there's a visual problem with your app, a good place to look for answers is the *Debug View Hierarchy*. The Debug View Hierarchy helps you visualize your app's interface and interact with it by separating the layers of the interface and rotating them in 3D space.

You'll use the Debug View Hierarchy to see if you can get a better idea of what's going on in the interface of the help pages.

1 Run the app, and select the Help button.
2 Back in Xcode, select the Debug View Hierarchy button in the debug bar (see figure 15.25).

Figure 15.25 Debug View Hierarchy button in the debug bar

The app will automatically pause. A rendering of the views in your app will appear in the editor window with controls below it for adjusting the view. A hierarchy of views will appear on the left in the Debug Navigator. The object and size inspectors become available in the inspector panel, with additional information on currently selected views (see figure 15.26).

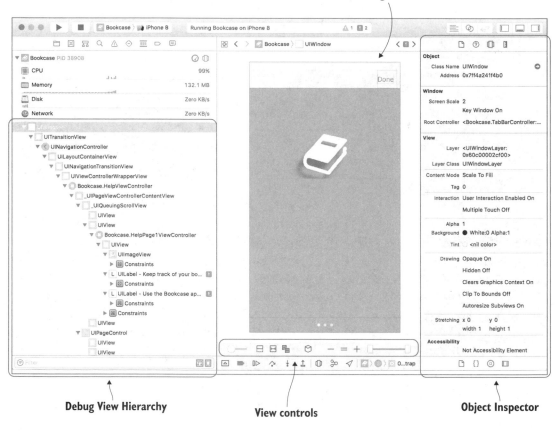

Figure 15.26   Debug View Hierarchy

This is where it gets interesting!

3 Click on the rendering of views and drag to the right. The layers will separate and rotate in 3D orientation, giving you a clearer perspective on what's happening in the scene (see figure 15.27).

Orient to 2D **Orient to 3D**

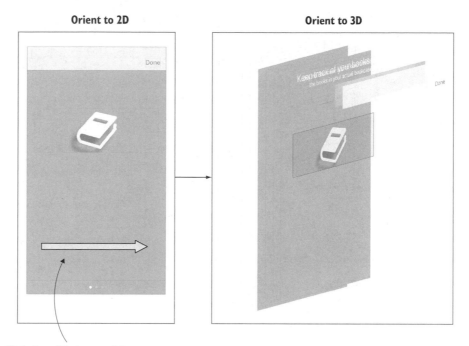

Click-drag 2D view to right

Figure 15.27   Debug view oriented to 3D

That's interesting! Two text labels are hiding behind the navigation bar. They must be the title and blurb that you're looking for! But what could be causing the layout issue?

4   Select one of the labels. If you find it difficult to select, you can use one of the two sliders in the view controls. The slider on the left adjusts the spacing between views, and the slider on the right adjusts the range of visible views.

The label should automatically highlight in the view hierarchy. Notice the purple exclamation mark beside the view. This indicates a runtime issue with this view.

5   To get more clues on this issue, open the Issue Navigator.

15.6.2 *Debugging the user interface with runtime issues*

The Issue Navigator gives you more detail on any pending issues. Until now, you've probably only noticed build-time issues, but Xcode can also report *runtime* issues. Ambiguous layouts, problems with threading, and problems with memory allocation can all trigger runtime issues.

Let's examine the runtime issues to further diagnose the problem with your app's layout.

Select the Runtime Issues tab in the Issue Navigator. You should find that several labels have ambiguous vertical positions (see figure 15.28).

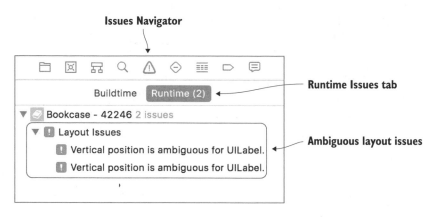

Figure 15.28   Runtime issues

Select one of the issues and open the Size Inspector. Look at the *Constraints* section. In addition to reiterating the layout issue, the existing constraints are specified. The description of the ambiguous layout issue makes sense; there doesn't appear to be a constraint specified for vertical position! See figure 15.29.

Now that you know that certain views aren't being provided with vertical position constraints, you have an idea of the problem to look for in the layout code.

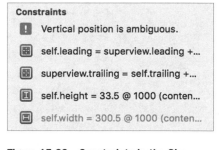

Figure 15.29   Constraints in the Size Inspector

15.6.3 Solving the user interface problem

1 Open the `ContentLayoutMachine.swift` file where your friend defined the layout for the help pages.

It appears that the `verticalLayout` method your friend wrote loops through all the views in the page, attaching their `topAnchor` to the `bottomAnchor` of the `previousView`:

```
static func verticalLayout(to rootView: UIView,views: [UIView]) {
    ...
    var previousView: UIView?          <--- Declares
    ...                                      previousView optional
    for view in views {
        if let previousView = previousView {
```

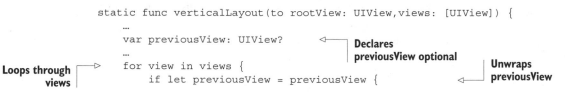

```
        constraints += [view.topAnchor.constraint(    |  Attaches top anchor
            equalTo: previousView.bottomAnchor) ]      |  to previousView
    }
    ...
  }
  ...
}
```

Going through the logic, you see a significant problem. The `previousView` is never set, so the constraint is never added!

2 Set the `previousView` at the end of the `for` loop:

```
static func verticalLayout(to rootView:UIView,views:[UIView]) {
    var previousView:UIView?
    for view in views {
        if let previousView = previousView {
            constraints += [view.topAnchor.constraint(
                equalTo: previousView.bottomAnchor) ]
        }
        previousView = view              ◁──┐  Sets previous
    }                                        │  View
}
```

Vertical constraints should be added to views now, pinning them to the previous view.

3 Run the app to check, and select Help. The help pages should appear as expected, and if you open the debug view hierarchy, you shouldn't find any run-time issues. Hooray!

✅ **CHECKPOINT** If you'd like to compare your project with mine at this point, you can check mine out at https://github.com/iOSApp-DevelopmentwithSwiftinAction/Bookcase.git (Chapter15.2.Debugged). Don't forget to run `carthage update` to update third-party code.

Well, you solved all the bugs your friend reported in their email, detective. Congratulations! But what was that your friend said about testing?

15.7 *Testing your app*

It's so easy to make changes to your app to make a minor fix or improvement, only to realize later that you've inadvertently caused a major problem elsewhere in your app. Solving one problem can create another, or, like your friend earlier in this chapter, even resting your hand on the Z key for a second could cause it to crash!

Testing your app manually but comprehensively after every small change would be a tedious prospect. Xcode provides you with the tools for automating this testing process.

Xcode can perform two types of tests:

- *Unit tests* test that your code is doing what it's intended to do.

- *UI tests* test that your app is doing as expected from the perspective of the user interface.

Within both categories, Xcode can focus from two perspectives:

- *Functional*—Is it working correctly? For example, in a calculator app, does 2+2 = 4?
- *Performance*—Is its performance acceptable compared against a benchmark time? For example, in a calculator app, is a complex calculation taking a reasonable time to process?

Let's add tests to the Bookcase app to help prevent the sort of bugs you've seen so far in this chapter and to keep the app working in tip-top shape!

15.7.1 *Testing for functionality*

Let's start by adding unit tests to test that the `BooksManager` is sorting and searching the `books` array correctly.

Tests are performed in special targets in your project: one test target for unit tests and another test target for UI tests. Targets can contain multiple test *classes*, which are useful for grouping related tests. Each test class can contain multiple test *methods*, each performing a single test.

When you create a project, the project option screen gives you two checkboxes to set up your project with unit tests and UI tests. Selecting these checkboxes automatically adds appropriate testing *targets* to your project and a test *class* containing test *methods*.

Open the Test Navigator to see the tests that come in your project by default (see figure 15.30).

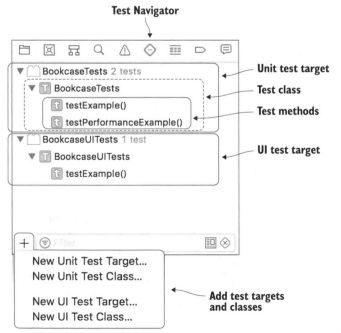

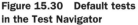

Figure 15.30   Default tests in the Test Navigator

If by chance you didn't select the testing checkboxes when you created your app, don't despair—it's easy enough to add test targets to your project. Select the + symbol at the bottom of the Test Navigator, give the target a name, and select the target to be tested. A test class will automatically be created with the same name as the target.

Let's use the same menu to add another test class (see figure 15.30) to test the `BooksManager` class.

1 Select the + symbol, and then select New Unit Test Class.
2 Name the test class "BooksManagerTests." A unit test class will appear with two default test methods: `testExample` and `testPerformanceExample`.
3 You can delete these two default test methods.

SETTING UP YOUR TEST CLASS

To `perform` tests on the `BooksManager` class, you first need to set it up. To have complete control over the test data, it'd be a good idea to set that up in the test class, too.

You may have noticed your test class has a `setup` method. This is a good place to specify any code that you want to run before each test method. This'll be the perfect place to instantiate the `BooksManager` and pass in test data to the `books` array. Because you know that these variables will necessarily be instantiated prior to the test methods, you can confidently set these to implicitly unwrapped optionals.

1 Set up the `BooksManager` and test data.

```
var booksManager: BooksManager!
var bookDaVinci: Book!
var bookGulliver: Book!
var bookOdyssey: Book!

override func setUp() {
    super.setUp()
    bookDaVinci = Book(title: "The Da Vinci Code",
        author: "Dan Brown", rating: 5, isbn: "", notes: "")
    bookGulliver = Book(title: "Gulliver's Travels",
        author: "Jonathan Swift", rating: 5, isbn: "", notes: "")
    bookOdyssey = Book(title: "The Odyssey",
        author: "Homer", rating: 5, isbn: "", notes: "")
    booksManager = BooksManager()
    booksManager.addBook(bookDaVinci)
    booksManager.addBook(bookGulliver)
    booksManager.addBook(bookOdyssey)
}
```

NOTE You've probably noticed a `teardown` method as well. You can specify any code you want to run *after* each test method here.

You'll see errors basically on every line, for example: *Use of undeclared type 'BooksManager'*.

By default, files in one target don't have access to files in another. If you select the BooksManager file in the Project Navigator, and select the File Inspector, you'll find that this file is only set to be accessible from within the Bookcase target (see figure 15.31).

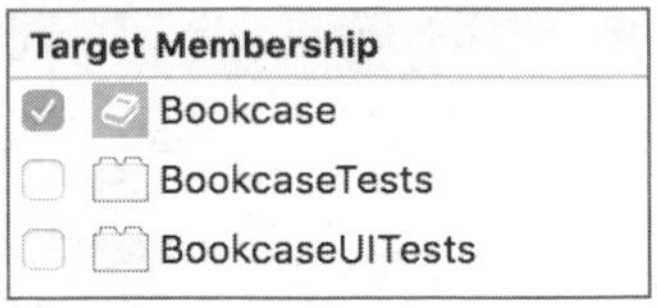

You *could* add test target membership checking the checkboxes in figure 15.31 for *every file* your test class needs to access, but there's a much quicker and easier solution! You can give your test class access to your app target files by simply *importing* the app target with a @testable attribute.

Figure 15.31   Books-Manager.swift target

2 Add a *testable import* at the top of your BooksManagerTests file to make classes in the Bookcase target visible to your test target.

```
@testable import Bookcase
```

The errors should go away, and you're ready to start filling out your test methods.

ADDING TESTS TO YOUR TEST CLASS

Let's start by creating a test method that tests that the booksManager is sorting the books correctly by *title*.

1 Add a method called testSortTitle.

```
func testSortTitle() {
}
```

2 Because you want to test sorting by *title* in this method, set the sortOrder property in the BooksManager to title.

```
booksManager.sortOrder = .title
```

Great, so your test method is set up, but how does it perform a test?

To create a test, first consider what you're expecting as the correct result. In this case, after sorting by title, you would expect that the books array will be sorted in a certain order: "Gulliver's Travels," "The Da Vinci Code," then "The Odyssey."

In Xcode, you express this expectation with what's called an *assertion*. The basic assertion is expressed with the XCTAssert method. This method requires a Boolean expression—if it returns true, the test has passed. Conversely, if it returns false, the test has failed.

3 Assert the order of the sorted array:

```
XCTAssert(booksManager.getBook(at: 0) == bookGulliver)
XCTAssert(booksManager.getBook(at: 1) == bookDaVinci)
XCTAssert(booksManager.getBook(at: 2) == bookOdyssey)
```

That's it—you're ready to run your test! Because your method starts with the word "test," Xcode automatically recognizes that it's a test method and indicates this with a diamond beside the method.

4 Hover over this diamond, and it should become a Play button. Click on this Play button, and the test method you just created should run.

   If the test is successful, the diamond will display a green tick, while an unsuccessful test will display a red cross (see figure 15.32).

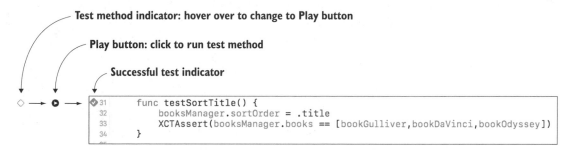

Test method indicator: hover over to change to Play button

Play button: click to run test method

Successful test indicator

```
31    func testSortTitle() {
32        booksManager.sortOrder = .title
33        XCTAssert(booksManager.books == [bookGulliver,bookDaVinci,bookOdyssey])
34    }
```

Figure 15.32   Test method

Several assertion methods expand on the basic `XCTAssert` method, performing various common test assertions such as equality, inequality, greater than, less than, and so on.

5 Add another test method to test the sort by author function. This time, use the `XCTAssertEqual` method:

```
func testSortAuthor() {
    booksManager.sortOrder = .author
    XCTAssert(booksManager.getBook(at: 0) == bookDaVinci)
    XCTAssert(booksManager.getBook(at: 1) == bookOdyssey)
    XCTAssert(booksManager.getBook(at: 2) == bookGulliver)
}
```

6 This time, run both tests in this class by selecting the Run test button next to the class declaration. You should end up with two successful tests. You can also see your successful and unsuccessful tests in the test navigator.

CHALLENGE   Create a functional test method to test searching the `books` array. You'll find my solution in the repo coming later in this chapter!

Great! If you make changes to your app now, you can be sure by running your tests that your books should still sort and search correctly.

15.7.2 *Testing for performance*

Unit tests aren't only about whether a unit of code is correct or incorrect—*performance* unit tests permit you to accurately analyze the efficiency of a unit of code. Performance tests run a unit of code 10 times and give you the average execution time.

Let's add a performance unit test to analyze the efficiency of the image color detection algorithm that your friend introduced.

1   As you did in the previous section, add a new unit test class called `UIImage-ColorDetectionTests` to test the `UIImageColors` framework, and remove the default test methods.

2   You're going to need an image to detect colors. Add an image variable and set it up in the `setUp` method.

```
var image: UIImage!
override func setUp() {
    super.setUp()
    image = UIImage(named: "book")
}
```

To analyze the performance of a unit of code, run it in a closure passed to the `measure` method.

3   Create the `testColorDetection` test method, and measure the performance of the `getColors` method.

```
func testColorDetection() {
    self.measure {
        self.image.getColors()
    }
}
```

Because this `UIImage` extension comes from a third-party binary framework that's not compiled by Carthage for testing, the `@testable` attribute won't work.

4   Instead, select the `UIImageColors` framework in the Project Navigator, and check the `BookcaseTests` target in the File Inspector to make this framework available to your unit tests.

5   Run the test by clicking the Play button beside the test method. An average time will appear after the `measure` closure, along with a gray diamond.

6   Click to the left of the Play button for more information about performance (see figure 15.33).

7   Select the Set Baseline button in the performance result.

Future tests will now be based on this baseline. If something changes in this third-party code in the future, and it becomes significantly less efficient than this baseline, you'll know about it when this performance test fails.

Click to set result as baseline for future tests

Average time

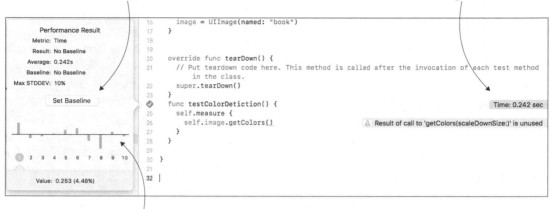

Performance result

Figure 15.33   Performance result

Silence the warning!

Because you're only testing the performance of the method, you aren't interested in the returned result. The Xcode compiler finds this strange and warns you of the unnecessary function call. To silence the warning, you can explicitly ignore the result by assigning it to an underscore:

```
_ = self.image.getColors()
```

15.7.3 Testing your user interface

User interface testing tests your app from a different perspective than unit testing. While functionality and performance can still be tested, UI testing shifts the focus from testing units of code to testing the user experience of your app.

Let's explore UI tests by creating one to test a user experience in your app. If you select the Info button in the book edit form, the ISBN field should appear. If you select the Info button again, it should disappear. Let's test that this functionality is working correctly.

UI tests are created in a separate target to the app and unit tests.

1   Find the `BookcaseUITests` test target that was generated when the Bookcase project was created, and open the default test class `BookcaseUITests`.

2   Create a new test method called `testToggleISBN`.

Your test class accesses the application via the `XCUIApplication` object, which is launched by default in the `setUp` method. You can use this object to access interface elements in various ways. For example, to get a reference to the Add button in the navigation bar, you could type

```
let addButton = XCUIApplication().navigationBars["Books"].buttons["Add"]
```

This gets a reference in the application to the navigation bar with the title Books, and then within the navigation bar finds a reference to the Add button. With this reference, you can now simulate the user tapping the button.

```
addButton.tap()
```

This is great, but with all this syntax, all you've achieved is a button tap. What happens when you want to test a longer and more complex user experience with multiple interactions? Setup would be a time-consuming and frustrating process.

Fortunately, Xcode allows you to *record* a user experience live and automatically convert to UI test sequences of code. If you entered the `addButton` code, delete it now. You're going to set up this UI test by recording it!

3 Ensure your cursor is inside the `testToggleISBN` method, and press the Record button (see figure 15.34).

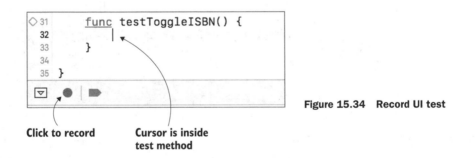

Figure 15.34   Record UI test

Click to record   **Cursor is inside test method**

The app will launch, and the Stop Recording button will replace the Record button in the debug bar.

4 Select the Add button. A UI test action will automatically be added to the `testToggleISBN` method:

```
XCUIApplication().navigationBars["Books"].buttons["Add"].tap()
```

5 Now that you're in the book edit form, select the Info button. Again, Xcode will automatically add this action to your test, even refactoring the first line to set up a convenience variable to hold the application object:

```
let app = XCUIApplication()
app.navigationBars["Books"].buttons["Add"].tap()
app.scrollViews.otherElements.buttons["More Info"].tap()
```

To check that the ISBN field has been toggled, you'll need a reference to the ISBN field.

6   To find how to reference the ISBN label, click on it. You'll find that Xcode once again has refactored your code, setting up a property to hold the elements in the interface:

```
let elementsQuery = app.scrollViews.otherElements
elementsQuery.buttons["More Info"].tap()
elementsQuery.staticTexts["ISBN:"].tap()
```

Great, with little effort on your part, you know how to reference the ISBN field! You can stop the recording now, because you're going to finish writing the test yourself!

7   Press the Stop Recording button. You're going to refactor the test yourself. You only tapped the ISBN field to get a reference to it.

8   Remove the line tapping the ISBN label and instead use the reference to determine whether the ISBN label exists in the interface prior to tapping the Info button. You can do this with the exists method:

```
elementsQuery.staticTexts["ISBN:"].tap()
let isbnExists = elementsQuery.staticTexts["ISBN:"].exists
elementsQuery.buttons["More Info"].tap()
```

Now, you're ready to make an assertion. Tapping the Info button should have toggled the existence of the ISBN field in the interface.

9   Confirm that the ISBN field's existence has toggled with a call to XCTAssert-NotEqual.

```
XCTAssertNotEqual(elementsQuery.staticTexts["ISBN:"].exists, isbnExists)
```

You've set up your first UI test!

10 As you did with unit tests earlier in the chapter, run the test by tapping the Play button beside the method.

The app will run in the simulator, automatically performing the actions defined in the test method. With any luck, it should eventually highlight a successful test with a green tick.

Accessibility

For a user interface to be testable, its interface elements need to have *accessibility* enabled. But even if accessibility wasn't required for UI testing, it's still best practice to ensure that your interface is accessible.

(continued)

Select an interface element and open the Identity Inspector. There, you'll find the accessibility panel. Here, you can provide a *label* to describe the element, a *hint* to describe the result of interacting with the element, and a unique *identifier* for the element.

Accessibility

Accessibility ☑ Enabled
Label ⟦Label⟧
Hint ⟦Hint⟧
Identifier ⟦Identifier⟧

Beneath these properties are a number of trait checkboxes, such as *Button*, *Selected*, *Image*, *Search Field*, and *Static Text*. These properties give the operating system a better understanding of how the element is expected to behave.

Adding accessibility properties to the visual elements in your app will open them up to be described by the VoiceOver accessibility app, and enable users with impaired vision to use your app.

✔ **CHECKPOINT** If you'd like to compare your project with mine at this point, you can check mine out at https://github.com/iOSApp-DevelopmentwithSwiftinAction/Bookcase.git (Chapter15.3.Tested).

15.8 Summary

In this chapter, you learned the following:

- Different methods exist for examining the contents of a variable, each with their own advantages. Check table 15.2 for a summary.
- Debugging in Xcode is a massive topic, and the tools available for exploring your app are extensive. One chapter can't cover everything—if you'd like to explore further, check out the memory graph debugger, instruments tools, and type "`help`" into the `lldb` command line.
- Use *functional* tests to test that something does what it should, and use *performance* tests to confirm that a process is taking an appropriate amount of time, compared with a baseline.
- Unit tests test from the perspective of units of code, while UI tests test from the perspective of the user experience of your app.
- Ensure that the elements in your app are accessible.
- For further reading on testing, check out Apple's documentation on testing at https://developer.apple.com/library/content/documentation/Developer-Tools/Conceptual/testing_with_xcode. Look at how to perform *asynchronous* testing.

Part 4

Finalizing your app

Finally, your app is nearly ready to publish to the App Store! But first, there are a couple of things that need attention.

In chapter 16, you'll look at distributing your app to beta testers—a source of invaluable feedback before you launch your app. You'll also look at the process of setting up a home for your app in the App Store and what is technically involved in publishing your app.

In chapter 17, you'll find a number of links to resources and further information that will help you continue your journey in iOS app development.

Distributing your app

What's the point of all this work perfecting your app if you're going to keep it to yourself? At some point, you'll most likely want to share your awesome new app with the world.

But, wait! Before you do, it's a good idea to get beta testers to give your app a good run-through. Their feedback will be invaluable—not only for finding obscure bugs, but also to provide you with a more subjective perspective of user experience with the app.

You can put your Swift hat away for now. In this chapter, we'll look at distributing your app. Along the way, we'll explore

- Joining the Apple Developer Program
- Signing identities and provisioning profiles
- Developer account site and iTunes Connect
- Beta testing and TestFlight
- Building a home for your app in the App Store

16.1   *Joining the Apple Developer Program*

Exciting days—your Bookcase app is feeling ready to distribute to beta testers. Then, after you tweak the app based on beta feedback, the App Store awaits!

The first thing you'll need to do before you can distribute your app is join the Apple Developer Program. You may have already done this, because it was mentioned in chapters 1 and 12 (you needed membership to utilize iCloud). But if you haven't joined yet and you hope to distribute your app on the App Store, now might be the time to bite the bullet!

To enroll in the Apple Developer Program, click on this link and follow Apple's instructions: https://developer.apple.com/programs/enroll/.

If you can demonstrate you have or are part of a legally registered company, you can enroll as an *organization* using your company's name. If not, you'll need to enroll as an *individual*, using your legal name.

16.1.1 *Signing into Xcode*

To make the most of your membership, you need to ensure that you've signed into your Apple account in Xcode.

1 Select Xcode > Preferences, and select the Accounts tab. If your Apple account is listed under Apple IDs, you should be good to go! (Unless your session is expired—not to worry, you'll need to log in again.)

2 If you don't see your Apple account listed, select the + button at the bottom left of the window, and select Apple ID to add your personal Apple account to Xcode (see figure 16.1).

3 In the unlikely case that you haven't yet set up an Apple ID, select Create Apple ID now.

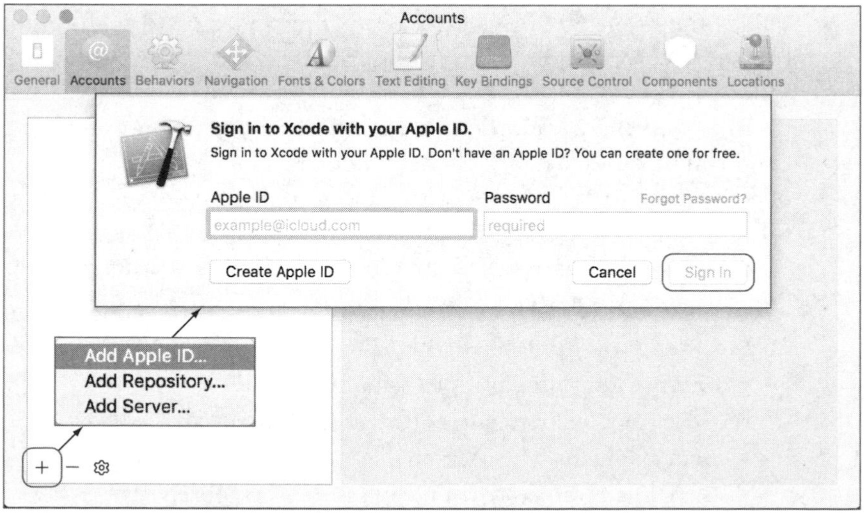

Figure 16.1   Adding Apple ID to Xcode

4 You can now sign in to your account (see figure 16.1). You should see your Apple ID appear in the Accounts tab.

16.1.2 Code signing your app

Apple has security measures in place to ensure that apps have the correct permissions to be installed on devices. These measures ensure that apps are

- Unaltered
- From a trusted source (that is, Apple)
- Developed by a developer authorized by Apple

These security measures are carried out on your app using a process called *code signing*.

EXPLORING YOUR SIGNING CERTIFICATES

To code sign your apps, you'll need what's called a *signing certificate*, which identifies you as a developer. Let's explore your signing certificate.

1 Select your Apple ID in the left column.

A list of app development *teams* that you belong to will appear on the right. You'll automatically be assigned a team connected to your Apple ID. If you've enrolled in the Apple Developer program, your role will be listed as *Agent* (see figure 16.2).

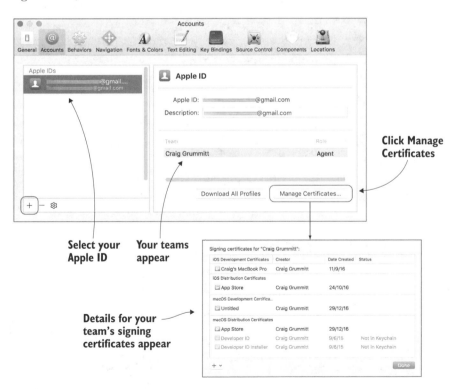

Figure 16.2 Teams and signing certificates

2   Select your team, and select Manage Certificates. A popup will appear with details of your team's signing certificates. You may or may not see signing certificates appear in this section. Don't worry if you don't see any—you'll set these up now.

You need two types of signing certificates for iOS:

- *iOS Development* allows you to test your app on devices and is free.
- *iOS Distribution* allows you to distribute your app to beta testers and the App Store. You need to join the Apple Developer Program to receive this signing identity.

Apple Developer Program team roles

As an individual member of the Apple Developer Program, your team can only consist of yourself, but if you enroll as an organization, you can add more people to your team.

Different *roles* are available to define access privileges for different members of the team:

- *Team agent*—That's you! There's only one team agent who has all access privileges.
- *Team admins*—They can do much that an agent can do, with a few exceptions such as renewing membership or creating certificates.
- *Team members*—They have limited access.

You can read more details of team roles in Apple's app distribution guide at http://mng.bz/Ou8U.

CREATING YOUR IOS DEVELOPMENT SIGNING CERTIFICATE

If you don't see an iOS Development signing certificate, it hasn't yet been generated. Let's generate your iOS Development signing certificate now.

You *could* tap the + button right now and create one, but believe it or not, an even easier way exists! Xcode will automatically generate a development signing identity for you when you select your team in a project's settings.

1   Open the Bookcase project.
2   Navigate to the project's settings for the app target.
3   In the General tab, find the Signing section, which should already be set to Automatically Manage Signing.
4   In the Team combo box beneath it, select your team. An iOS Development Signing Certificate will be automatically created for you, and appear below (see figure 16.3).

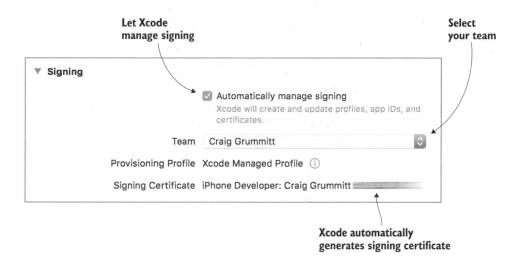

Figure 16.3 Project target signing preferences

NOTE Though the signing certificate is called *iPhone* Developer, it's relevant to all of iOS.

Signing identity vs. signing certificate

You may occasionally in iOS see mention of a signing *identity,* and wonder—is that the same as a signing certificate? Well, both are used to authenticate you in the code-signing process but a subtle difference exists:

- Your signing identity is stored locally in your Mac's keychain. It contains two encryption keys: a public key and a private key.
- Your signing certificate contains only the public key. It's included in an app's provisioning profile (more on that coming up), and once you've joined the Apple Developer Program, it's also stored remotely on Apple's servers in your Developer account.

CREATING YOUR IOS DISTRIBUTION SIGNING CERTIFICATE

Of course, using a development provisioning profile to test your app on a device that you can connect to your computer is important, but the power in iOS development is distributing to *any device in the world,* such as via the App Store. To do this, you also need a *distribution* signing certificate.

Luckily, creating your distribution signing certificate is also straightforward, now that you're enrolled in the Apple Developer Program.

1 Open the Accounts tab in Xcode preferences again and select your Apple ID.
2 Open the Manage Certificates popup again to see your signing certificates.

3 Select the + button.

4 Select iOS App Store.

That's it—your Distribution certificate is ready to go!

CREATING A DEVELOPMENT PROVISIONING PROFILE

To install your app on devices, it must be bundled with its authorization details in what's called a *provisioning profile*. Let's look at the three types of provisioning profiles:

- A *development provisioning profile* is used with a development certificate. Generally, you'll use this to test apps on local devices during development.
- An *ad hoc provisioning profile* is used with a distribution certificate to manually distribute to beta testers.
- A *store provisioning profile* is also used with a distribution certificate to distribute your app to the App Store.

The easiest way to create provisioning profiles is to let Xcode manage signing and generate them for you automatically. Behind the scenes, a provisioning profile contains

- An *App ID* for your app. If Xcode is managing signing for you, your app's App ID will be automatically determined for you. Two types of App IDs exist:
  - *Wildcard* App IDs are the default, and make it possible to group more than one app with the same App ID. Wildcard App IDs are specified with an asterisk.
  - *Explicit* App IDs explicitly identify your app. Apps that use app services such as *In-App Purchase* or *iCloud* automatically use an explicit App ID, which is generated from a combination of your team ID plus your app's bundle ID (which is initially generated from your app's organization ID and your app name).
- *Signing certificates* for each developer in your team.
- *Device IDs* that the app is authorized to be installed on. In development or ad hoc provisioning profiles, device IDs must be registered for an app to be installed on them. That's easy enough—by plugging in a device and running the app from Xcode, your device will automatically be registered in the provisioning profile. Later, we'll look at adding devices for beta testers.

Figure 16.4 shows the contents of a development provisioning profile.

Figure 16.4   Development provisioning profile

You might notice errors appear indicating that Xcode can't create a provisioning profile for your app (see figure 16.5).

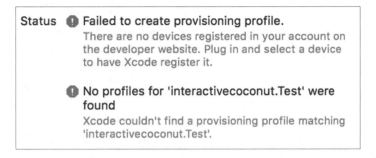

Figure 16.5　Provisioning profile errors

Apple requires that your account be associated with at least one iOS device before Xcode can generate provisioning profiles for your apps. This is easy enough to solve:

1 Plug an iOS device in.
2 Select to run your app on the device rather than the simulator.
3 Run your app. The errors should disappear, the provisioning profile will be generated for you automatically, and the Bookcase app will run on your device.

CHECKING YOUR CERTIFICATES

With a few steps, you've created a development signing identity and certificate, a device ID for your iOS device, and an App ID and development provisioning profile for the Bookcase app. Wow! To be sure it all works as expected, let's check Apple's records of this information on their servers.

1 Open your Developer account site at https://developer.apple.com/account.

The Developer account site is where you'll find many relevant links for managing your Developer account with Apple, along with additional resources such as documentation and forums. In this chapter, we'll look at two sections that also happen to be the main links highlighted:

- *Certificates, Identifiers, and Profiles*, where you can view and manage these assets.
- *iTunes Connect*, where you'll manage and submit apps to the App Store or distribute them to beta testers.

2   Select Certificates, Identifiers, and Profiles now. You're automatically brought
to the Certificates section. Here, you'll find your iOS Development and Distribution Signing Certificates (see figure 16.6).

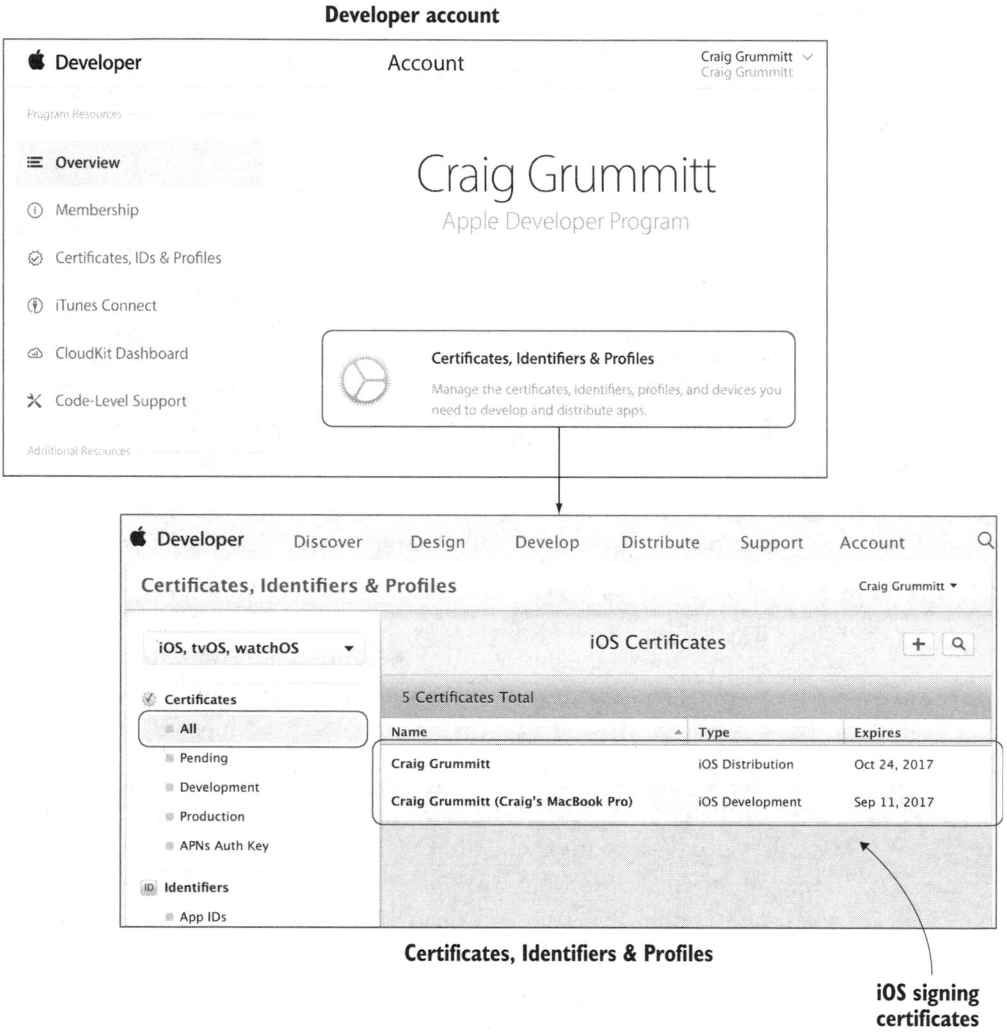

Developer account

Figure 16.6   Checking your certificates

While you're here, let's look at the ID Apple has automatically generated for
your app.

3   Select App IDs in the Identifiers section on the left. You should find that an App ID for the Bookcase app has automatically been registered by Xcode for the Bookcase app, including your own bundle ID (see figure 16.7).

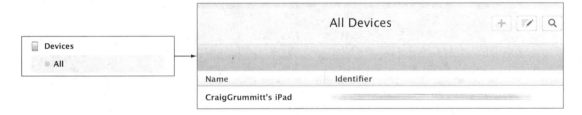

Figure 16.7   Checking your App IDs

4   Select All in the Devices section. You should find that your iOS device has been registered (see figure 16.8).

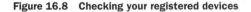

Figure 16.8   Checking your registered devices

TIP   It's usually easier to let Xcode handle automating code signing for you, but it's possible to create a signing certificate, register an App ID, register a device, or even generate a provisioning profile right here in the Certificates, Identifiers, and Profile center. Sometimes there may be reason to do so. If you wanted, for example, to restrict certain registered devices from installing an app, you'd need to generate a custom provisioning profile.

Let's check how Xcode stores your signing details locally.

5   The same way you did earlier, open Xcode > Preferences > Accounts, navigate to your Apple ID in the Accounts tab, and select Manage Certificates on your team.

You should now see your development and distribution certificates; this indicates that these identities have been generated and stored locally in your keychain.

That's it! You're all signed up and ready to start distributing your new app.

16.2   *Setting up an app in iTunes Connect*

Before distributing your app either via the App Store or TestFlight, you need to create a *record* for it in iTunes Connect. Later, you'll upload a build of your app from Xcode to the app record that's ready for distribution.

---

iTunes Connect

iTunes Connect is where Apple developers can manage their apps, users, and finances. You'll use iTunes Connect more and more as you start distributing your apps via TestFlight or the App Store. Do a little exploration and familiarize yourself with iTunes Connect—you'll find seven sections:

- *My Apps*—Create, manage, and submit your apps, and edit their metadata. This is also where you'll manage your TestFlight builds.
- *App Analytics*—iTunes Connect has built-in analytics data to help you keep tabs on user engagement, sales, crashes—even how often your app has been viewed in the App Store.
- *Sales and Trends*—Details of sales and downloads, showing trends over time.
- *Payments and Financial Reports*—Download reports of any payments to you by Apple.
- *User and Roles*—Add iTunes Connect users to your team and modify their roles. You can also define your internal and external TestFlight testers here. Take note: somewhat confusingly, your team and their roles in iTunes Connect are different than your team and their roles in the Apple Developer Program. If you're an individual member of the Apple Developer program, you cannot add members to your Apple Developer team, but you can add members to your iTunes Connect team.
- *Agreements, Tax, and Banking*—A little admin may be necessary here. If you want to develop paid apps or accept in-app purchases, you'll need to accept the iOS Paid Applications Contract and enter your tax and bank information.
- *Resources and Help*—This section is a great place to learn more about distributing apps using iTunes Connect.

---

1 Open your Developer account site (https://developer.apple.com/account), and navigate to iTunes Connect (see figure 16.9).
2 Select the My Apps section.
3 Select the + symbol to add your first app record to iTunes Connect.

Developer account

iTunes Connect

Figure 16.9  iTunes Connect

4   Fill out the form to create a new app (see figure 16.10.)

- *Platforms*—Specify the iOS platform, of course!
- *Name*—This is a unique name for your app in the App Store. Because I called dibs on the name "Bookcase," you'll need to find another, sorry!
- *Primary Language*—The language that your app will default to if your app hasn't been localized into the user's language.

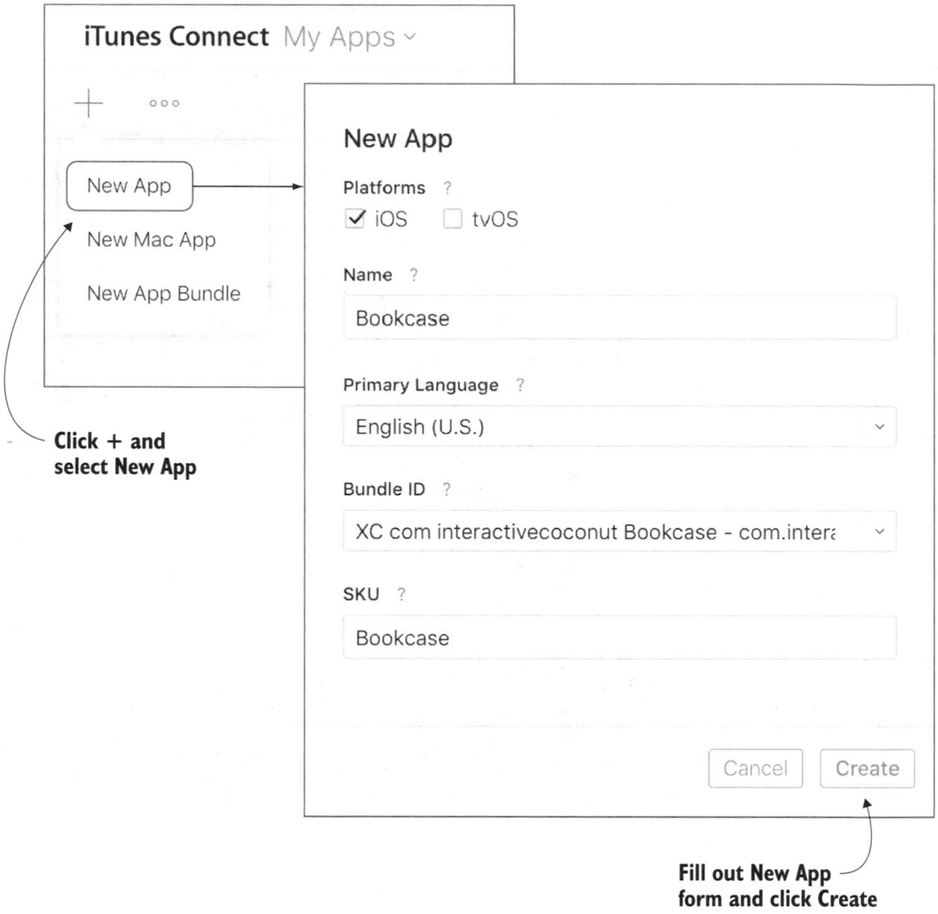

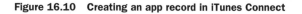

Figure 16.10   Creating an app record in iTunes Connect

- *Bundle ID*—Look for the bundle ID that matches your project's bundle ID in its General settings in Xcode.
- *SKU*—The SKU is purely used as an identifier among your apps and can be an identifying text of your choosing that needs to be unique among your apps. Make sure it doesn't contain spaces and doesn't start with a hyphen (-), period (.), or underscore (_).

5 Select Create. You should now have a brand-new app record in iTunes Connect.

16.3 *Uploading your build to iTunes Connect*

To distribute your app to the App Store or TestFlight, you need to upload it to its app record in iTunes Connect. Let's upload a build of the Bookcase app to iTunes Connect now.

1 Building an archive of your app is the first step toward all means of distribution. Archive your app in Xcode by selecting Product > Archive. If the archive option is unavailable, ensure you either have Generic iOS Device or your actual device selected for the active scheme.

After archiving the app, Xcode will automatically open the Organizer, a program for managing your app archives.

2 With your app and archive selected, select the big blue Upload to App Store button. (I think this button title is a little confusing—you're actually uploading to iTunes Connect, from where you can later submit the app to the App Store if you like.)

3 You're asked to confirm your App Store distribution options. You can choose to include bitcode, which allows Apple to optimize your app when necessary. You can also choose to strip the Swift symbols, further reducing your app's file size.

4 You're next given the opportunity to manually manage code signing if you so wish. Most likely, you'll want Xcode to automatically manage code signing.

1. Select app   2. Select archive   3. Click Upload
                                                to App Store...   4. Select App Store
                                                                        distribution options
                                                                        and click Next

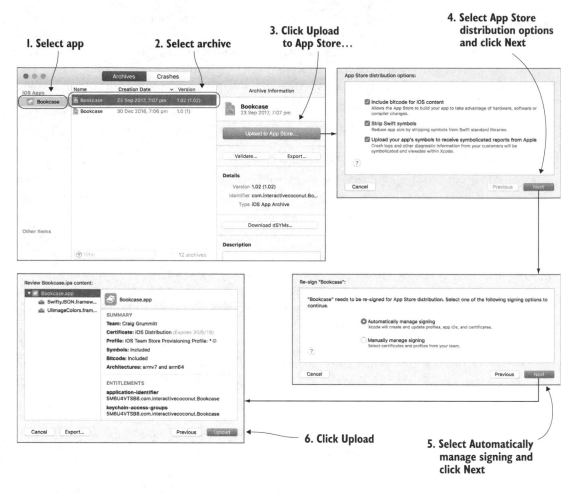

6. Click Upload   5. Select Automatically
                       manage signing and
                       click Next

Figure 16.11   Uploading build to iTunes Connect

5 Finally, you'll need to reconfirm the upload (see figure 16.11).

6 You may be prompted that codesign wants to access a key in your keychain, so select Always Allow. Xcode will prepare your app archive for uploading, which could take several minutes. iTunes Connect will then take time to process your app. You'll receive an email when it has finished processing.

7 Open the Bookcase app within My Apps in iTunes Connect, and select the Activity tab. This is where you'll find the following:

- *All Builds*—Details of builds you have uploaded.
- *App Store Versions*—The status history of versions of your app on the App Store.

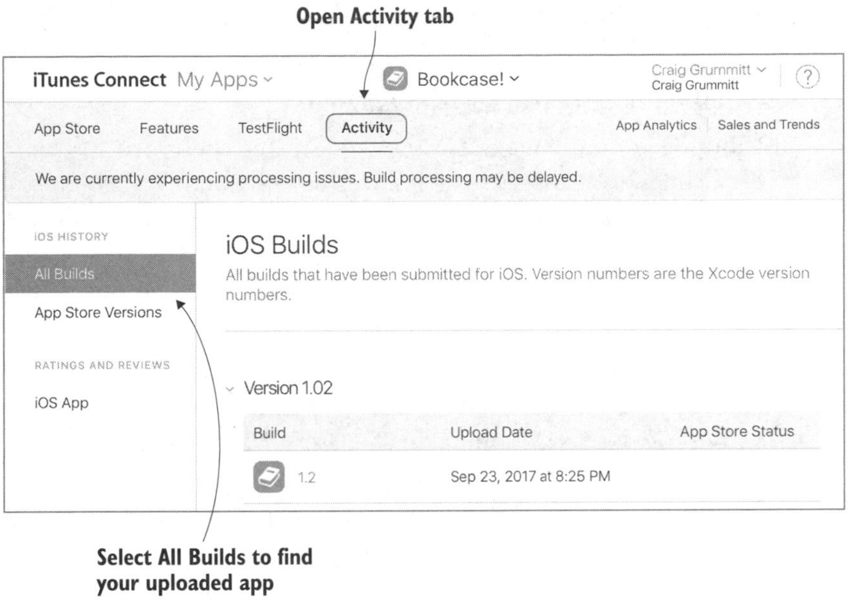

Open Activity tab

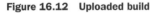

iTunes Connect My Apps ⌄		📗 Bookcase! ⌄		Craig Grummitt ⌄ Craig Grummitt	?
App Store Features TestFlight		**Activity**		App Analytics Sales and Trends	

We are currently experiencing processing issues. Build processing may be delayed.

iOS HISTORY	**iOS Builds**
All Builds	All builds that have been submitted for iOS. Version numbers are the Xcode version numbers.
App Store Versions	
RATINGS AND REVIEWS	
iOS App	⌄ Version 1.02

Build	Upload Date	App Store Status
📗 1.2	Sep 23, 2017 at 8:25 PM	

Select All Builds to find your uploaded app

Figure 16.12   Uploaded build

- *Ratings and reviews*—Available after launching your app on the App Store. You should find your build listed in the All Builds section. When it has finished processing, it should have an upload date (see figure 16.12).

Your app is another step closer to distribution. It's time to hear from your beta testers!

16.4   *Distributing your app to beta testers*

Before you send your new app into the wider world via the App Store, it's a good idea to get feedback from your app's intended audience. Beta testers can give you a whole new perspective on your app—they might find bugs or problems by using the app differently than you expected or tested for; they might give you ideas for improvements that you never considered; or perhaps they might even confirm that you're on the right track.

There are three ways to distribute your app to beta testers:

- Distribute your app manually using an ad hoc provisioning profile.
- Distribute via TestFlight, using iTunes Connect.
- Distribute via a third party, such as Microsoft's HockeyApp, or Twitter's beta by Crashlytics. We won't cover third-party approaches in this chapter.

TestFlight and third-party tools offer more automation in the process of distributing to beta testers. Apps distributed via TestFlight can also be installed on a vastly greater number of devices.

In this chapter, we focus mainly on distributing via TestFlight, but for those curious about the manual approach, here's a quick overview.

16.4.1 *Distributing to beta testers manually*

Distributing your app manually bypasses the TestFlight process using iTunes Connect by exporting your app as a file, and then distributing this file to beta testers—for example, via email—to install on their devices. Previously, this was the only option provided to you from Apple, until TestFlight was introduced.

Let's explore the manual approach by distributing the Bookcase app. Follow these steps:

1   *Add devices*—Because beta testers' devices probably won't be physically connecting to your computer, you'll need to manually add their device IDs to the list of authorized devices online in your Certificates, Identifiers, and Profiles center.

  To get the device ID, also known as the *unique device identifier* or *UDID*, you need to ask for it. A handy guide for helping beta testers find their UDID in iTunes can be found at whatsmyudid.com.

  If you can access an additional device to experiment with, add its device ID in the Certificates, Identifiers, and Profiles center now. Select All in the Devices section, tap the + symbol, and enter the device's name and UDID.

2   *Archive the app*—Similar to uploading to iTunes Connect, you'll want to build an *archive* of your app. Select Product > Archive in Xcode with Generic iOS Device or your iOS device selected as the current scheme.

  After archiving the app, Xcode will automatically open the Organizer. Instead of uploading to iTunes Connect here, you want to generate a file to distribute to your beta testers.

3   *Export the app*—Select your Bookcase app's archive and select the Export button. Select Save for Ad Hoc Deployment. Choose your team and select Export, choosing a local folder to export to (see figure 16.13).

4   *Distribute the app*—Great, you should now have a file with extension *.ipa*—that's your app! It's a compressed file like a zip, but with a .ipa extension. You can now distribute this file to your testers, via email, for example.

A tester can then open the app in iTunes on their Mac and install it to their device. After testing your app, ask them to send you their feedback.

Some developers prefer this approach as it places all of the control of the process in the developers' hands. But it does have drawbacks:

- Your tester will require a reasonable degree of technical literacy. Finding their device's UDID to send to you can be challenging, and the request itself can even sound a little strange, or worse, suspicious. Even installing the app from the app file can be a complicated process if you're unfamiliar with it. Don't forget, beta

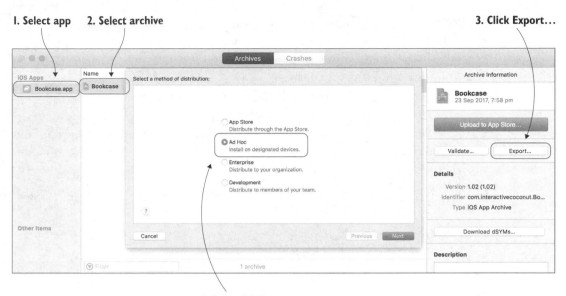

1. Select app　　**2. Select archive**　　　　　　　　　　　　　　**3. Click Export...**

4. Select Ad Hoc

Figure 16.13　Exporting archive

testers are generally testing your app for you as a favor. Any obstacles that make the process laborious or confusing could discourage them from doing it at all.

- A limitation with this approach is that it can register only 100 iPad and 100 iPhone devices.

16.4.2　*Distributing to beta testers with TestFlight*

TestFlight streamlines the process of beta testing. Developers upload their betas to iTunes Connect and add their beta testers, and Apple handles the rest. Invitations to install your app are automatically sent to your beta testers, and your app installs on testers' devices with a click of a button in the TestFlight app on their device. Developers don't need to concern themselves with requesting UDIDs from testers and can keep track of which testers have installed or opened their app.

TestFlight defines two types of beta testers:

- *Internal testers* have specific roles within your team, but are limited to 25 internal testers per app.
- *External* testers are generally kind people willing to test out your app but who don't have a role within your team. This role has a much more generous limit of 2,000 beta testers per app. Great! But there's a catch—you're required to submit your app for Apple's approval before distributing to external testers.

Let's distribute the Bookcase app to an internal tester now. An internal tester must first be added as an *iTunes Connect User* in your team.

ADDING AN ITUNES CONNECT USER

1 Open iTunes Connect again.
2 Open the Users and Roles section. You'll find three tabs in this section:

- *iTunes Connect Users*—Add users to your team on iTunes Connect. Specify their role within your team to define their level of access.
- *Test Flight Beta Testers*—Manage your internal and external testers here.
- *Sandbox Testers*—Test *In-App Purchases* or *Apple Pay* without generating any actual financial transactions with sandbox test accounts that you can create here.

3 You'll find that you're already listed in the *iTunes Connect Users* tab. Tap the + button to add another iTunes Connect User (see figure 16.14).

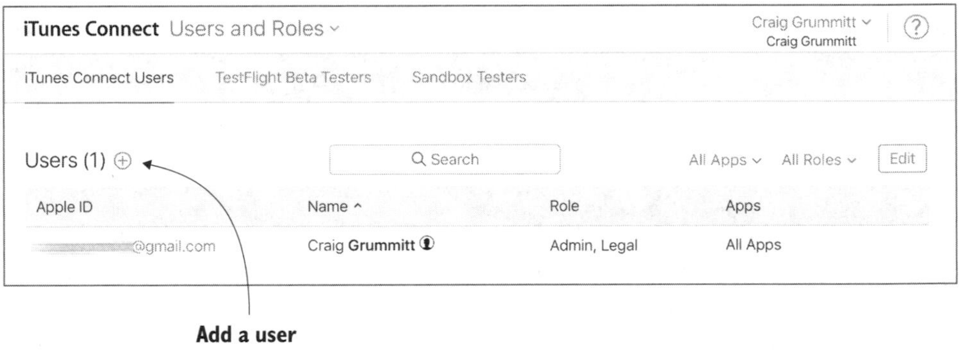

iTunes Connect Users and Roles ˅

Craig Grummitt ˅
Craig Grummitt

iTunes Connect Users   TestFlight Beta Testers   Sandbox Testers

Users (1) ⊕

Apple ID	Name ^	Role	Apps
＿＿＿＿＿@gmail.com	Craig **Grummitt** ⓘ	Admin, Legal	All Apps

Add a user

Figure 16.14   iTunes Connect Users

4 Enter the user's name and email address, and select Next.
5 Specify the user's role in iTunes Connect, and optionally limit their role to specific apps. When selecting different roles, you'll see the privileges the user will have access to. Make sure you give your new user either an admin, app manager, developer, or marketer role, as only these roles can become internal testers.
6 Select Next (see figure 16.15).
7 Optionally, specify which notifications your new user should receive, and then select Save. Your new user will receive an email and be able to activate their account. When they're all set up, you can add them as an internal tester.

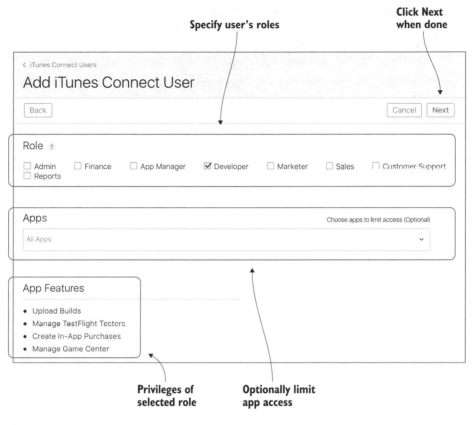

Figure 16.15   iTunes Connect Users

SET UP AN INTERNAL TEST

Now that you've created your app record on iTunes Connect, uploaded a build of your app, and set up an iTunes Connect user, it's straightforward to create an internal test and add an iTunes Connect User as a tester.

1 Within your app in iTunes Connect, open the TestFlight tab, where you can edit general test info and manage your internal/external tests and testers.

2 Select Add iTunes Connect Users. Here, you can add internal testers.

3 Select the + symbol to add an internal tester, and in the pop-up, select the tester(s) you want to invite to test your app.

4 Select the iOS tab where you can select a version of your app to test. You should see an app version that was generated automatically when you uploaded your build.

Apple requires you to specify whether you use encryption in your app.

5 Select Provide Export Compliance Information to provide details of encryption in your app. Because the Bookcase app doesn't use cryptography, select No. The version of the Bookcase app that you have selected should appear with the message "Ready to Test." Your app is now ready for internal testing.

6 Select Start Internal Testing. That's it! See figure 16.16 for a visual summary of the steps in creating an internal test.

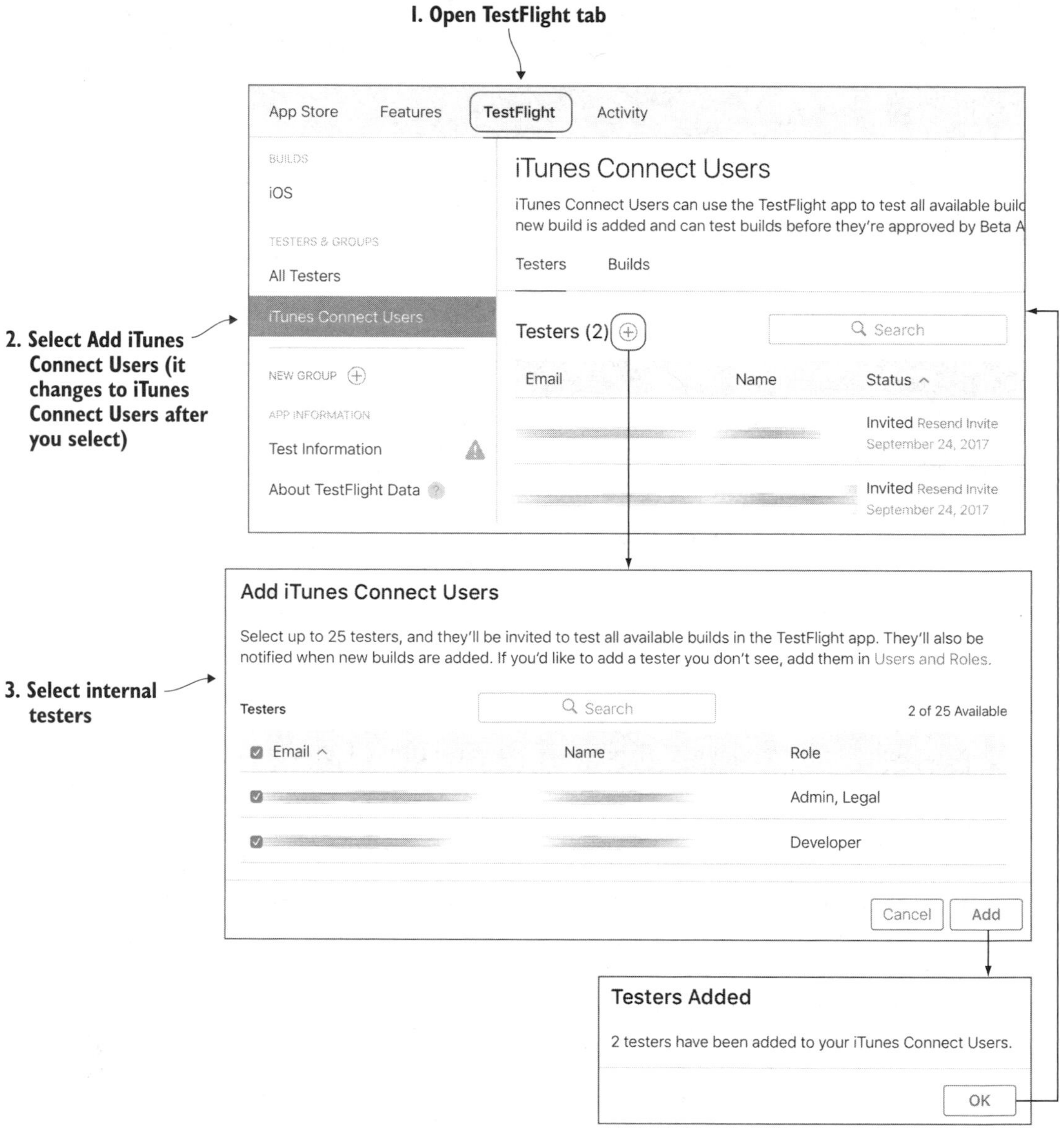

Figure 16.16 Creating an internal test in TestFlight

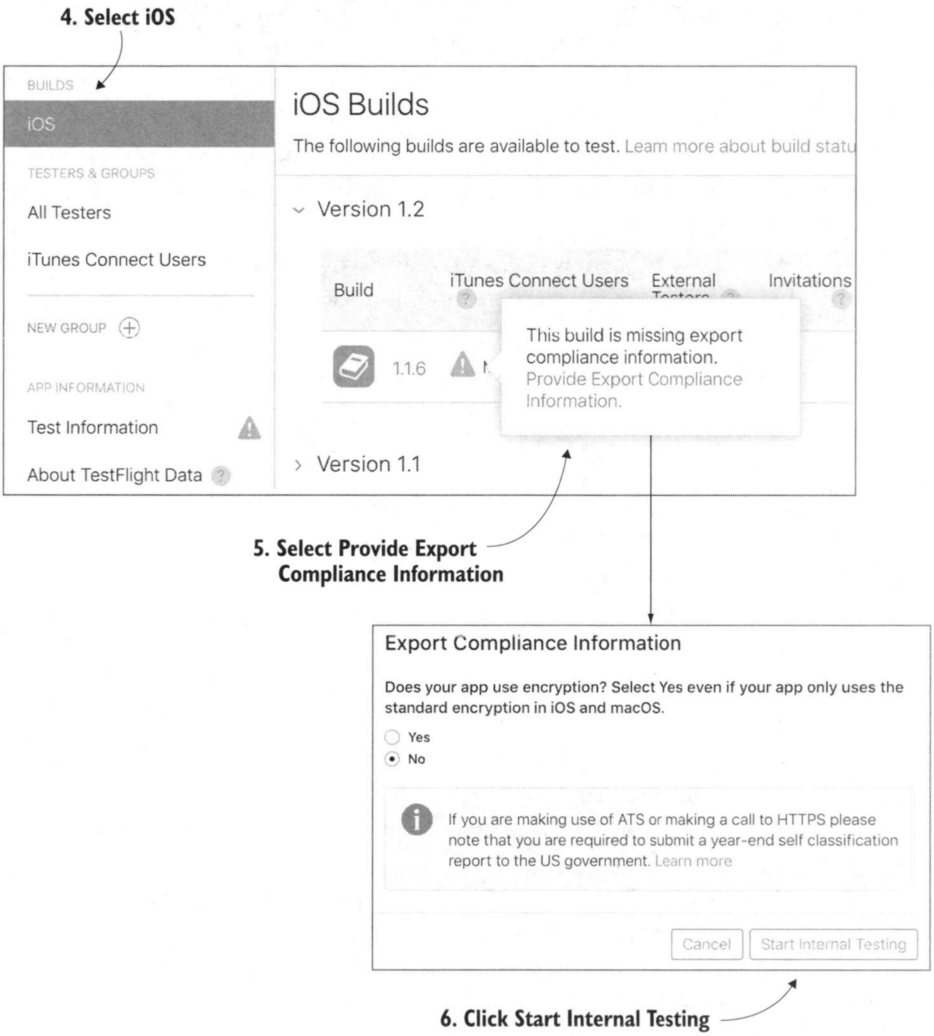

4. Select iOS

iOS Builds

The following builds are available to test. Learn more about build statu

BUILDS
iOS

TESTERS & GROUPS
All Testers
iTunes Connect Users

NEW GROUP ⊕

APP INFORMATION
Test Information ⚠
About TestFlight Data ⍰

∨ Version 1.2

Build	iTunes Connect Users ⍰	External Testers ⍰	Invitations ⍰

1.1.6 ⚠ N

This build is missing export compliance information.
Provide Export Compliance Information.

〉 Version 1.1

5. Select Provide Export Compliance Information

Export Compliance Information

Does your app use encryption? Select Yes even if your app only uses the standard encryption in iOS and macOS.

◯ Yes
⦿ No

ⓘ If you are making use of ATS or making a call to HTTPS please note that you are required to submit a year-end self classification report to the US government. Learn more

Cancel   Start Internal Testing

6. Click Start Internal Testing

Figure 16.16   Creating an internal test in TestFlight, continued

Your testers will automatically receive an email inviting them to test your app. They'll receive instructions to first install the TestFlight app on their device, which will manage installs of new test apps.

SET UP AN EXTERNAL TEST

External testers are an entirely different species from your internal testers. They may be friends, family, or colleagues you've asked to help out. Or maybe you put the call out on Twitter or one of the many beta tester community websites. They're unlikely to be familiar with your app, so they make the perfect testers for how your app will be received when it makes its way to the App Store.

Setting up an external test is similar to setting up an internal test, except for a few differences:

- Because external testers aren't likely to have seen your app before, you need to provide them with additional information about the app, and what you'd like them to look out for.
- Because Apple will review your app before you can distribute to beta testers, you need to give Apple reviewers additional information about the app and who to contact if there's a problem.
- Because beta testers aren't part of your team, you need to provide a name and email address for each.

Let's get started—your Bookcase app won't test itself!

1 If it's not selected already, select the TestFlight tab within iTunes Connect.
2 Select Add External Testers.
3 Create an External Testing Group for this app.
4 Select the + symbol to add new testers. In the pop-up, select the tester(s) you want to invite to test your app. Because there can be up to 2,000 beta testers, rather than add each tester's details individually, you can upload a CSV file with their details or specify testers from another one of your apps.
5 Select the Builds tab for this group.
6 Add a build of your app to test.
7 Provide more information for Apple reviewers, including a demo account if your app has a login.
8 Provide more information for your beta testers. This is your opportunity to let your testers know what sort of information you want from them. I find that testers are more likely to give a thorough response if you structure your questions in a numbered list.
9 Select Submit for Review. The build of the Bookcase app that you selected should appear with the message "Waiting for Review." This review can take a few hours or even a day or two. When your app comes out of Apple review, you'll have the opportunity here to select Start Testing. As with internal testing, emails will be sent out to all your testers with instructions for how to install your app via the TestFlight app. See the steps involved in setting up an external test in figure 16.17.

10 While you wait for the app to be reviewed, you can flesh out the Test Information tab, for example:

- *Beta App Description*—What's this app about? Be as succinct as possible!
- *Marketing URL*—Where can they learn more about the app?
- *Review Notes*—any additional notes to help expedite the review.

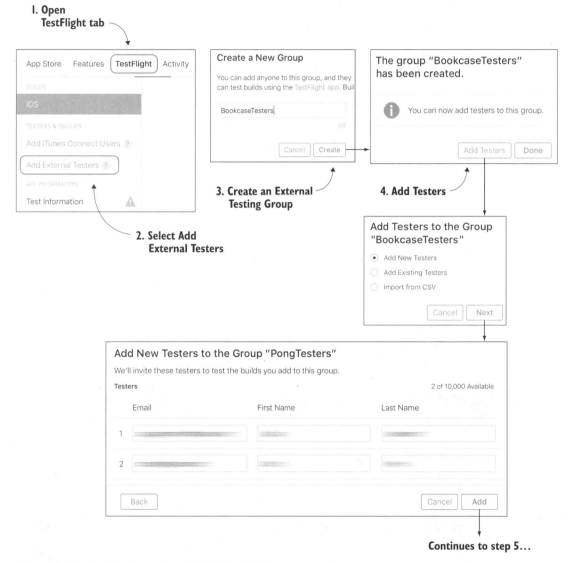

Figure 16.17   Creating an external test in TestFlight

5. Select Builds tab   **6. Add a build to test**

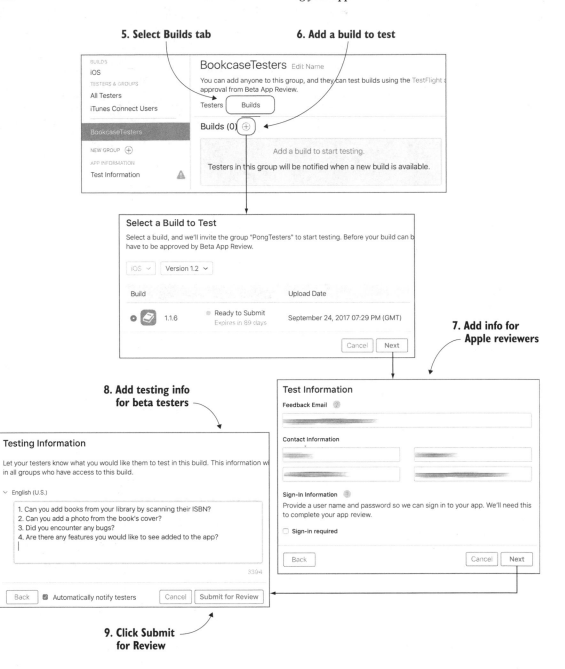

7. Add info for Apple reviewers

8. Add testing info for beta testers

9. Click Submit for Review

Figure 16.17   Creating an external test in TestFlight, continued

That's it! If you do need to make any changes to the beta test information, you can go into the Test Information tab. You can also specify an optional privacy policy there as well.

It's now your job to sit back, wait, and hope that you get good, productive feedback from your beta testers. When you have all the feedback you expect, make any necessary changes and finishing touches to your app, because the next step is the big one!

16.5 *Distributing your app to the App Store*

After what's probably been months of development and testing, congratulations! You're finally ready to distribute to users worldwide via the App Store. Let's get started!

If you've been following along with distributing your app via TestFlight, you should already have set up an app record in iTunes Connect. If not, you need to go back and do this step before distributing an app to the App Store.

If you're happy with one of the builds you've already uploaded as a beta, you're free to distribute that version to the App Store. You can also upload a new build if you prefer—go back to the *Uploading your build to iTunes Connect* section of this chapter if you need a refresher.

You now need to fill in, at a minimum, any required fields for your app in iTunes Connect.

1   Open *the App Store* tab. You'll find three tabs here that you need to fill out:

- *App Information*—Fill in any general information related to your app.
- *Pricing and Availability*—Set up a price for your app.
- *Platform Version Information*—Fill in information specific to this version of your app.

2   Select App Information. See figure 16.18 for a peek at the editable fields in this tab.

Here, you can fill in the following:

- *Name*—You've already specified this in the beta test process, but you have another opportunity to rename your app every time you submit your app to the App Store.
- *Privacy Policy*—Although including a link to a privacy policy is listed as optional, several types of apps require this, such as apps for kids or with subscriptions.
- *Language*—At the top right of the app info tab, you'll see the language you're currently editing the app info in. For me, this says *English (US)*. Select this to open a combo box listing all the possible different languages you can localize your app info into. Add a version of your app info in a different language by selecting one of these languages.

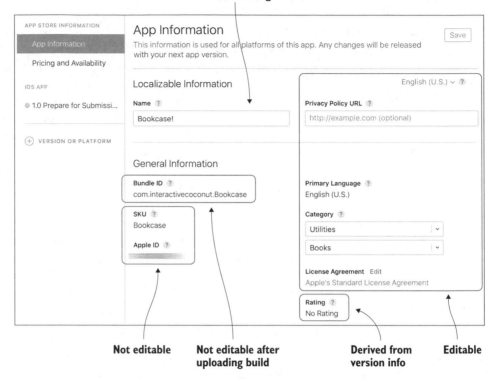

Figure 16.18   Editable fields in App Information

- *Primary Language*—If your app info supports more than one language, you can change the primary language here at any time.
- *Category*—You need to find an appropriate category and, optionally, secondary category to describe your app. Choose wisely as the category is one of the ways users may discover your app. For the Bookcase app, I'd go with *Utilities* and *Books*.
- *License Agreement*—It's possible to customize the End User License Agreement here. Apple's standard EULA is generally sufficient.
- *Rating*—This refers to the age appropriateness of your app and is derived from version information that you'll set shortly. Other app details such as Bundle ID, SKU, and Apple ID aren't editable after creating the app record.

3   Enter data in the necessary App information fields, and select Save when you're done.

4   Select the Pricing and Availability tab.

Here, you can specify the price *tier* of your new app. This price tier will display the applicable amount that the user will pay in your local currency and automatically convert to the user's local currency. Select Other Currencies to see how much your app will be priced in a specific price tier in different currencies. (Apple will take royalties of 30% out of that amount.) You can go back and change the price of your app later, or even schedule price changes here. Once you've set the price, you can optionally set the availability in various countries and discounts for educational institutions.

5   Set the price tier of your app. If you're feeling generous like me, set it to Free! The defaults will be fine for the other options. Select Save when you're done (see figure 16.19).

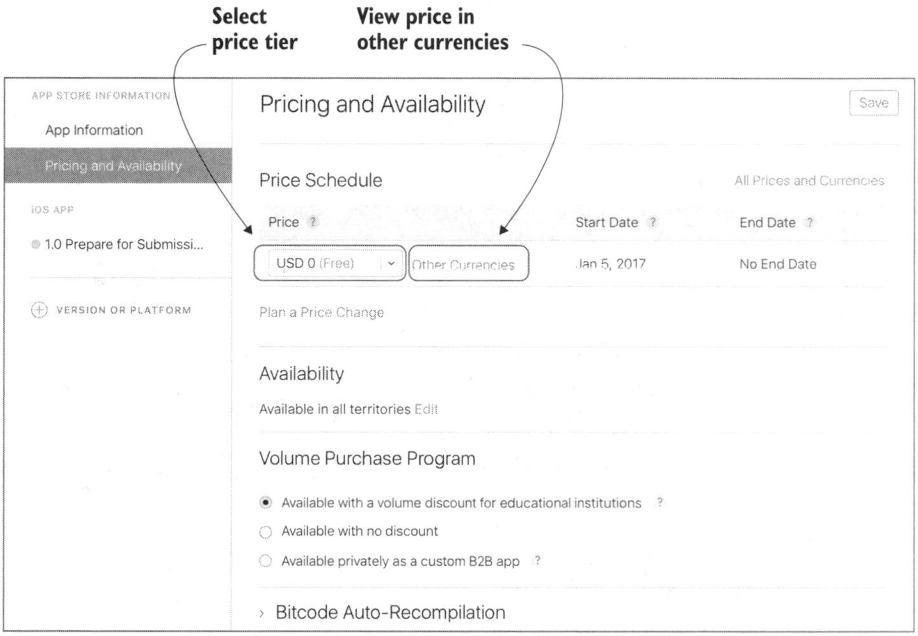

Figure 16.19   Selecting the price tier for your app

NOTE   Don't forget, if you do want your users to pay money for your app, you'll need to fill out the necessary agreements, tax, and bank details in the *Agreements, Tax and Banking* section.

Below the Pricing and Availability tab, you'll find a *Platform Version Information* tab, represented by a version number and the status of your app. You'll probably see your app's current version listed with *1.0 Prepare for Submission.*

6   Select the Platform Version Information tab. Some highlights include these:

■   *App Preview and Screenshots*—You can drag a 30-second demo video and up to five screenshots of your app onto this section. You'll need to provide at least one screenshot of your app in both the 5.5-inch iPhone and the 12.9-inch iPad if you want the app to appear in these stores. If your app varies significantly between different device types—say, the iPhone SE version is significantly different from the iPhone 7 version—you should provide additional screenshots using Media Manager (see figure 16.20).

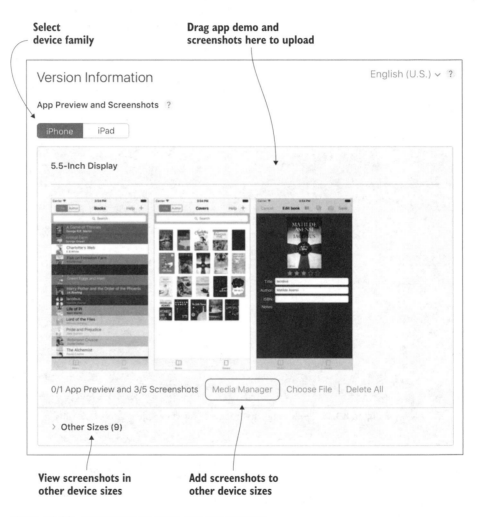

Figure 16.20   Uploading app demo and screeenshots

TIP If you don't have all the devices you need screenshots for, don't worry—you don't necessarily need to access a physical device for screenshots. If you can demonstrate the app's functionality sufficiently on the simulator, you can save screenshots directly to your Mac's desktop using Command-S.

- *Description*—The description of your app should be engaging, accurate, and succinct. Apple recommends a short descriptive paragraph followed by a list of your app's most interesting features.
- *Promotional text* gives you the opportunity to update the users on any news regarding your app. Unlike description, promotional text for a version can be updated after submission.
- *What's new in this version* gives you the opportunity to let users know what has been resolved or improved in the latest version. As you're looking at the first version of this app, this field is irrelevant and won't be available.
- *Keywords*—These help determine where your app appears in search results. It's important to consider your keywords carefully—you have only 100 characters available. Be sure to use commas to separate keywords; spaces are unnecessary and a waste of characters. Including both the plural and singular of the same word is also a waste of characters because Apple includes both versions by default. Because your app name is automatically a search term for your app, including it as a keyword is also a waste of characters.

TIP   A whole discipline called App Store Optimization (ASO) has sprung up out of the need to improve the visibility of your app in the App Store, and keyword optimization is a vital ingredient of this discipline. If you want to look into this more, you might consider checking out one of the many third-party ASO tools out there.

- *Support URL*—A URL your users can go to for help if something goes wrong.
- *Marketing URL*—An optional URL with additional information about your app. See figure 16.21 for the next section of the form.

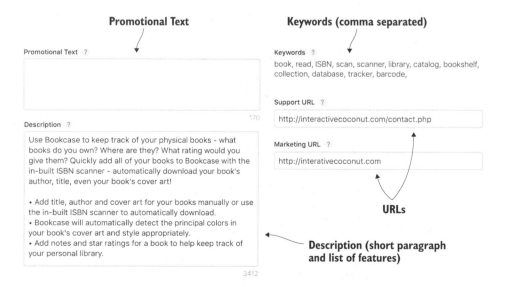

Figure 16.21   Adding description, keywords, and URLs to Version Information

- *Build*—Add a build of your app to the version that you uploaded to iTunes Connect.
- *App icon*—You'll need to upload a 1024 x 1024 image of the app icon here. (Back in chapter 13, you downloaded a folder of different sizes of the same icon for the Bookcase app. You should find the appropriate-sized image in this folder.)
- *Version*—Best to follow common convention for version numbers; 1.0 is the default for the first version of your app.
- *Rating*—Apple will determine your app's recommended age rating for you based on your responses in a pop-up as to how frequently your app may contain types of mature content, and whether it contains unrestricted web access, or gambling and contests. You can also specify here whether your app is made for kids, and, if so, which age group.

NOTE Apps intended for kids do have specific requirements, such as requiring a privacy policy and potentially requiring a "parental gate," a task at an adult level that would prevent children from accessing parts of the app not intended for children, such as in-app purchases.

- *Version Release*—After Apple approves your app (fingers crossed!), you need to specify what happens next. Should it automatically be released, choose whether to manually release it, or perhaps you want to schedule a release date. There's a lot to this form, and I haven't listed every field. Among other things, you'll also find a *Copyright* field, additional information for Apple's review team, and *What's New in This Version* for new versions of the app.

7 Fill out the platform version information form for the Bookcase app.

8 After completing all fields, select Save, and the Submit for Review button should become available.

TIP Before choosing the Submit button, it might be a good time to review Apple's Common App Rejections page at https://developer.apple.com/app-store/review/rejections/ and double-check that your app doesn't breach any of Apple's guidelines. You can find a full list of Apple's App Store Review Guidelines at https://developer.apple.com/app-store/review/guidelines/.

9 Now, take a deep breath, and select Submit for Review!
  Sigh. You'll find yourself taken to yet *another* form. Thankfully, this is only a couple of Yes/No questions regarding content rights (that is, whether your app contain third-party content) and an identifier (called IDFA) used by advertising services. If your app doesn't contain advertising, you can safely say no to this question.

10 When you've answered these questions, take another deep breath, and select Submit. This time, it's for real!

Your app will now go to Apple's review team, where it will probably take a couple of days to process. To get a better idea of how long of a wait time to expect, you can check an unofficial average at appreviewtimes.com.

16.6 Summary

In this chapter, you learned the following:

- Though it's possible to create signing certificates, register App IDs and devices, and generate provisioning profiles in the Certificates, Identifiers and Profile center online, it's generally easier to let Xcode handle it all for you.
- To distribute an app to the App Store or Test Flight beta testers, you need to create an app record in iTunes Connect and upload a build from Xcode.
- Internal TestFlight beta tests have a limit of 25 testers who have a role within your team. External TestFlight beta tests have a much higher limit of 2,000 testers, but require Apple's approval before distributing to testers.
- Be sure to check Apple's Common App Rejections page before submitting your app to the App Store to avoid problems.

What's next?

17

Congratulations! You've followed the Bookcase app on the long journey from a basic idea through to publication on the App Store.

17.1 *Further learning*

Along the way, we've covered dozens of Swift and iOS concepts, but the learning doesn't stop here. First, don't forget there were important resources that we looked at in this book:

- *Swift*—Continue to work on your Swift expertise with the book from Apple, *The Swift Programming Language* (http://mng.bz/6fKi).
- *iOS Human Interface Guidelines*—Ensure your app follows Apple's human interface guidelines (http://mng.bz/g9dI).

Other resources and tutorials you should be aware of include these:

- *WWDC videos*—Apple's extensive library of videos from their Worldwide Developers Conference (http://mng.bz/i030)
- *Guides and sample code*—Straight from Apple (http://mng.bz/eo56)
- *Apple API reference documentation*—http://mng.bz/2Jr9
- *iOS Frameworks*—A comprehensive list of all available iOS frameworks (http://mng.bz/D5cb)
- *raywenderlich.com*—A comprehensive library of iOS books and tutorials

Many more iOS concepts are available for you to explore as you continue your journey as an iOS developer. Depending on your personal goals, these could include

- *Mapping and location services*—http://mng.bz/3N31
- *Split view controllers*—Display your content in two panes if it's in an appropriate size class (http://mng.bz/d96M).
- *Local and push notifications*—https://developer.apple.com/notifications/.
- *Attributed strings*—Define text styles (font, style, color) on ranges of characters within a string (http://mng.bz/t078).
- *WebKit*—Display web pages in your app (http://mng.bz/LH0a).
- *Social*—Integrate your app with social media such as Facebook or Twitter (http://mng.bz/vw0h).
- *Internationalization*—Add translations or localizations of content, such as dates or number formats (http://mng.bz/893x).
- *Accessibility*—Ensure your content is accessible to all users, including those with impaired vision, hearing, or mobility (http://mng.bz/3B9c).
- *In-App purchases*—Add premium content within your app that requires payment (http://mng.bz/x9hi).

If you're interested in developing games, there's plenty to sink your teeth into:

- *SpriteKit* (http://mng.bz/gIqu) is a great place to start for building 2D graphic interfaces, while *SceneKit* (http://mng.bz/er3J) is generally more relevant for 3D.
- *GameKit* (http://mng.bz/8Hef) *and Game Center* (http://mng.bz/0DUQ) are for building multiplayer games, high score tables, and setting achievements.
- *Metal 2* (http://mng.bz/R433) is a lower-level framework you may want to look at if graphics performance is critical for your game.

There are also several third-party services that are worth looking at:

- *Advertising*—Though Apple no longer provides an advertising framework, other third-party services can help you monetize your app through advertising. You could start with MoPub (https://www.mopub.com/), Google's AdMob (http://mng.bz/PQhV), or Vungle (https://vungle.com/) for video ads.
- *Analytics*—In addition to the app analytics that iTunes Connect provides, you can find several third-party services that use event tracking to provide additional information about user behavior within your app. These include Yahoo's Flurry (www.google.com/admob/), Google's Analytics (http://mng.bz/Ltv6), and Mixpanel (https://mixpanel.com/).
- *Cloud services*—In this book, you've looked at iCloud, but many other options exist for cloud-based services and data persistence, such as Realm (https://realm.io/), Dropbox (http://mng.bz/faGt), Firebase (https://firebase.google.com/), and Google Cloud (https://cloud.google.com/).

17.2 *One more thing!*

Oh, there's one more thing, and to break tradition I'm afraid it's bad news. Hopefully, you're sitting down. It's about the Bookcase app you've been working on. There's no easy way to say this: someone has already launched an extremely similar looking app on the App Store. The nerve! Even down to the same app icon. You can check it out at https://itunes.apple.com/us/app/bookcase!/id1191400786?ls=1&mt=8.

Oh well, I'm confident you have another absolute winner of an app idea taking shape in your mind right now. You probably even had it before you started reading this book!

It's over to you. What are you waiting for? Go for it!

I'd love to hear about your experience, your app, and launching it on the App Store. Tweet me (@craiggrummitt) a link to your app on the App Store, and I'll add it to the list of reader's apps at the companion site for this book, iosappdevelopmentwithswift .com.

Most of all, enjoy yourself. If you're excited about your app, chances are others might be too! Good luck!

appendix A
Project settings

Apple engineers provide app developers with an exceptional degree of configurability for their projects and apps. On the flip side, all these customizable settings can be intimidating—the build settings alone could contain approximately 300 customizable fields!

We'll take a short tour of project settings, but don't be alarmed: it's not necessary to understand the detailed implications of every setting you see. In many cases, leaving them at their default is the best option.

If you select the project itself in the Project Navigator, you'll see the project editor (see figure A.1). Here, you can edit the settings for your project or your target. The Projects and Targets column on the left shows what you're currently editing, and shows that in addition to your app target, Xcode by default created two targets for your unit and UI tests. You'll find that you'll most often be editing the settings for your main app target.

Along the top of the project editor, you'll find the Settings tabs, where you can choose which settings you wish to edit in the settings pane.

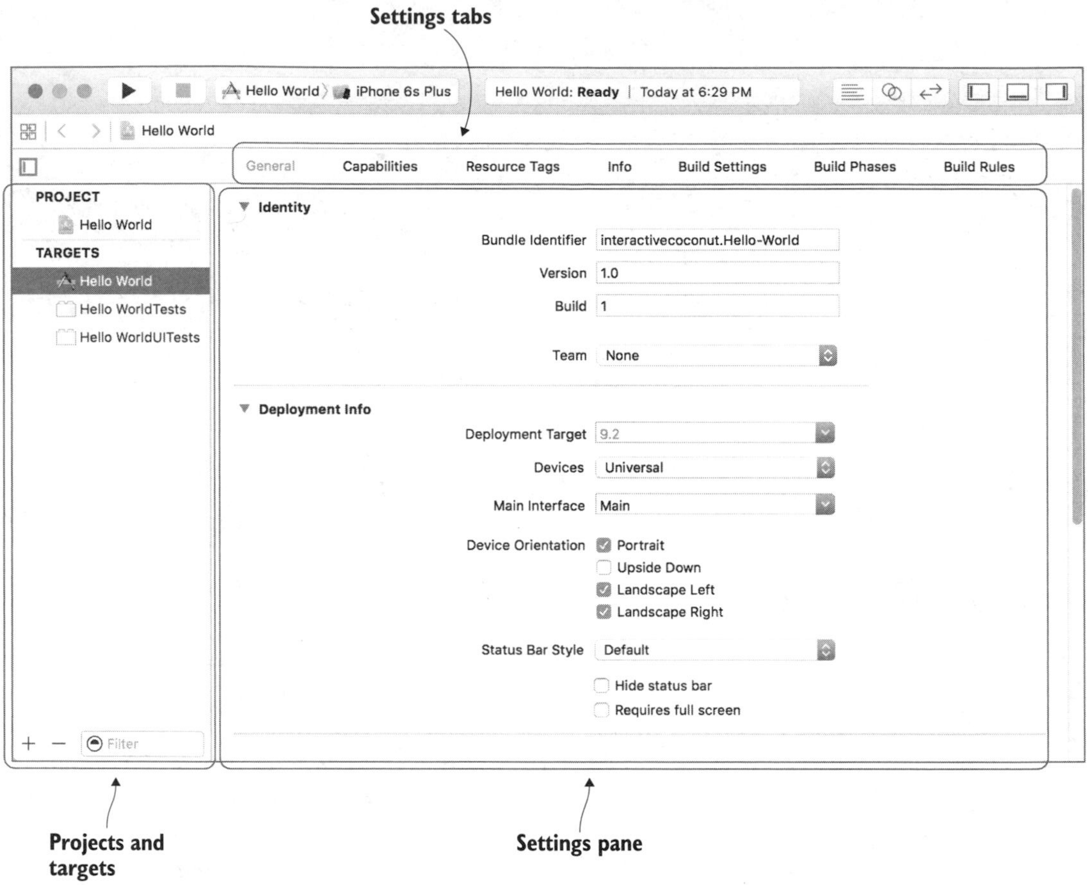

Settings tabs

Figure A.1   Project editor

Below the figure, labels read: **Projects and targets** and **Settings pane**.

A.1   *General*

In the main target's General tab, you'll find the most commonly needed settings (see figure A.1).

You'll recognize several of these from when you created your project, along with a few more:

- *Deployment Target*—Minimum version of iOS your app will work on
- *Device Orientation*—Which device orientations your app is designed to work in
- *Status Bar Style*—The look of your status bar, including whether it should be there at all
- *App Icons and Launch Images*—Where Xcode can find the app icon and launch screen

NOTE All the settings in the General tab are in fact generated from other tabs. In earlier versions of Xcode, this tab was called Summary, which was perhaps a clearer indication that this tab summarizes the most relevant information from all the tabs. Not to worry though, any changes you make here will automatically update elsewhere, and vice versa.

A.2   Capabilities

In the Capabilities tab, you can include Apple app services that aren't included by default. These include iCloud, push notifications, and Game Center. Look at the capabilities available—it's interesting to look through the list of app services Apple provides to you that could add value to your app.

We looked at adding iCloud and push notification capabilities in chapter 12.

A.3   Resource tags

Here, you can assign tags to certain resources such as data files or images. These resources are then excluded from the main app bundle and can be downloaded when they're required or on demand. This is a great way to keep your app size down.

A.4   Info

The Info tab defines and configures your app's final executable file, or *bundled executable*. You saw several of these settings already in the General tab, and modifying them in either place updates the other. All the info settings are also hardwired to a file you may have noticed in your Project Navigator called *Info.plist*. This is a special type of file called a *property list* that contains a hierarchy of key-value properties. If you open the Info.plist file in the property list editor, you'll notice that it contains exactly the same information as your main target's Info tab, but in a different order.

When you create an Xcode project, Info.plist is generated with all required properties, but during development of your app you may need to add keys to this list for different purposes.

Several properties in the Info.plist file are by default derived from elsewhere. You can spot these because they're surrounded by brackets and prefixed by a dollar sign. For example, Bundle Name is derived from $(PRODUCT_NAME), which is defined in Build Settings.

We modified the Info.plist file in chapter 13, to request permission to use the camera, and again in chapter 14, to add app transport security.

A.5   Build settings

Build settings are the instructions Xcode follows to build your app. Though hundreds of settings are available in the main target's build settings, the good news is that most of the time you'll leave these settings at their default values. However, at times you'll need to modify a build setting, so let's be sure you know your way around.

TIP Select a setting to learn more about it in the Help Inspector.

A.5.1 Changing your build settings for configurations

By default, settings are divided into two categories under Configurations: Debug and Release. These configurations are defined in the Info tab for the project (see figure A.2) and can be used to apply different rules to your build settings, depending on whether you're building for an internal debug or archiving your project as ready for distribution.

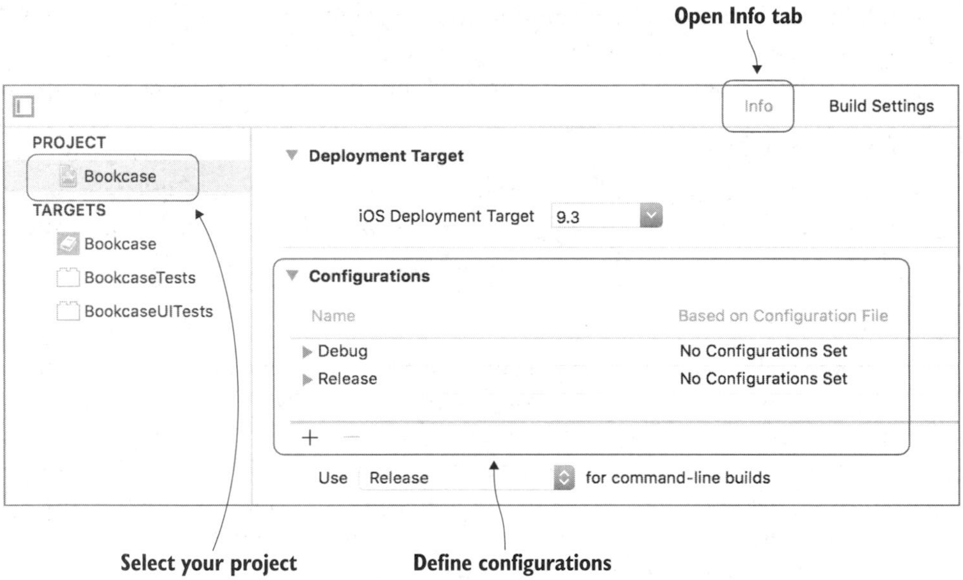

Figure A.2 Configurations

Most of your build settings are the same for both debug and release, but it's possible to change a build setting for a specific configuration. Let's say you want to change the app icon for debug and release builds (see figure A.3).

1 Open the build settings for the target and point to the app icon setting. You'll notice an arrow appear at the left of the line. Tap on this arrow to open the setting's configurations.
2 Click on a debug or release configuration setting to specify a different value.
3 Once a setting's configurations contain different values, it will display the text *<Multiple values>*.

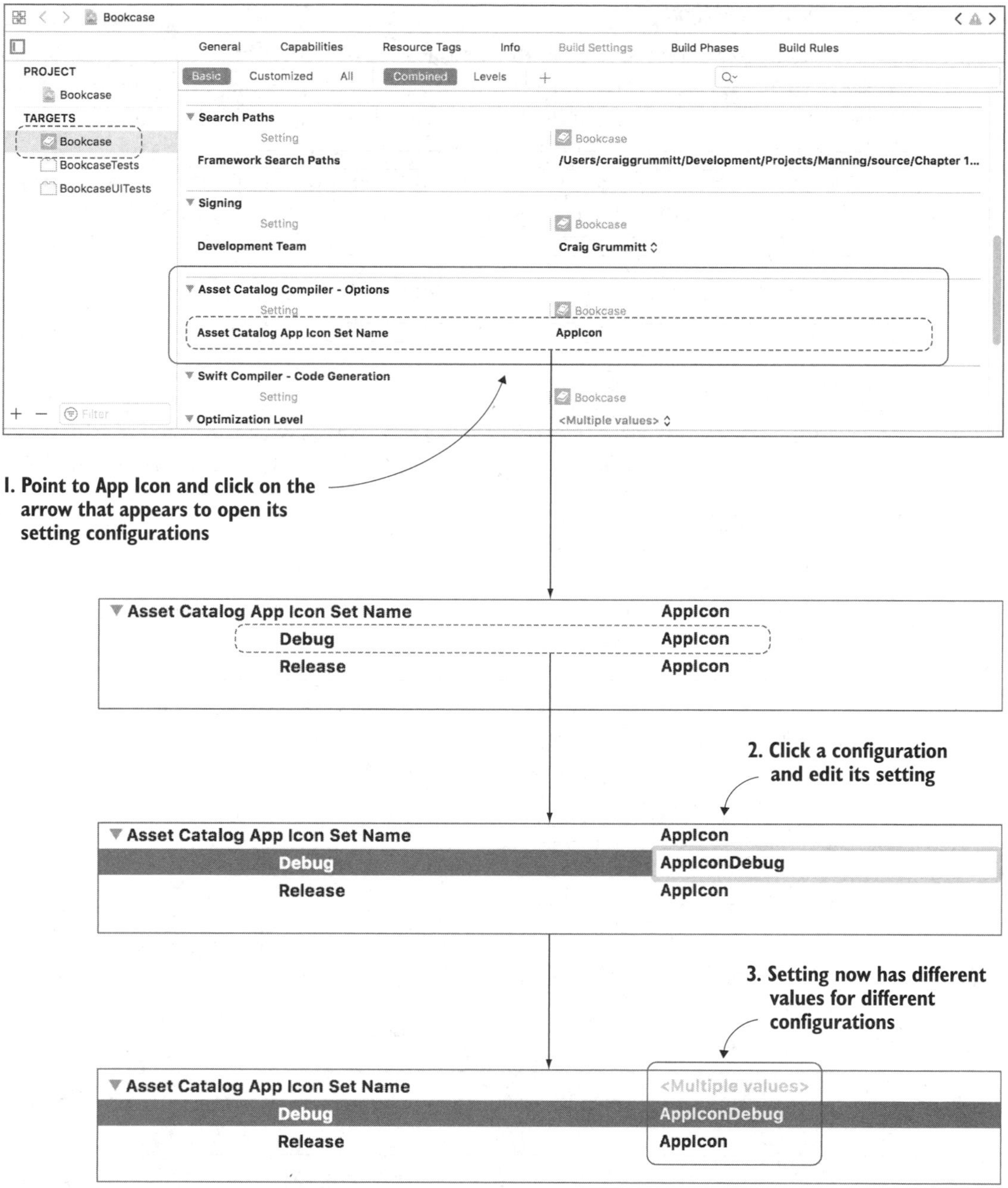

1. Point to App Icon and click on the arrow that appears to open its setting configurations

▼ Asset Catalog App Icon Set Name	AppIcon
Debug	AppIcon
Release	AppIcon

2. Click a configuration and edit its setting

▼ Asset Catalog App Icon Set Name	AppIcon
Debug	AppIconDebug
Release	AppIcon

3. Setting now has different values for different configurations

▼ Asset Catalog App Icon Set Name	<Multiple values>
Debug	AppIconDebug
Release	AppIcon

Figure A.3 Edit build setting for a configuration

A.5.2 *Filtering build settings*

Build settings aren't necessarily all determined at the target level. If a specific build setting hasn't been customized for your target, that setting will be inherited from your project. Similarly, if a specific build setting hasn't been customized by your project, it will be derived from the built-in iOS default.

At the top of the Build settings window, you'll see two sets of buttons that help you to explore these relationships. First, you'll see three options that filter *which* build settings appear:

- *Basic*—Shows you only the most basic build settings
- *Customized*—Shows only the settings that have been customized at the target level
- *All*—Shows all settings

Be careful not to have Basic or Customized selected when searching for a setting from the search field; though the setting may exist, if it's not basic or customized, it may not appear.

Next, you'll find two options (see figure A.4) that determine *how* the build settings appear:

- *Combined*—This is the default view, showing you the current status for each build setting, regardless of where in the hierarchy it's being set.
- *Levels*—This view of the build settings highlights in columns where each build setting is being set in the hierarchy—at the *target, project,* or *iOS default* level. The Resolved column is the equivalent of what you see in the Combined view. The resolved value for each setting is represented in the hierarchy with a green rectangle.

Figure A.4 Filters and Combined/Levels views for build settings

A.6   *Build phases*

The build phases define the phases Xcode steps through when building your app. Table A.1 describes them in more detail.

Table A.1   Build phases

Build phases	Description
Target Dependencies	Relevant for more-complex projects, where a target may have another target as a dependency.
Compile Sources	Defines any source files (that is, any Swift files) that Xcode needs to compile. When you add a Swift file to your project, it's automatically added to compile sources.
Link Binary with Libraries	Instructs Xcode to link this app to a library or framework. There are many libraries and frameworks provided by Apple, or you can select a third-party framework by selecting Add Other. This section corresponds to the Linked Frameworks and Libraries section in the General tab.
Copy Bundle Resources	Here, Xcode will copy any resources your app requires, such as images, audio, data, or even storyboards. When you add a resource to your project, it's automatically added to this build phase.

Sometimes, Xcode makes mistakes when automatically detecting a file's category (compile sources, frameworks and libraries, or copy bundle resources), and if something seems to go wrong after you add a file to your project, it can be a good idea to verify that Xcode has made correct assumptions about the file in your build phase settings. We looked at adding files to your project in chapter 5.

In addition to the default steps, you can add other steps to the build phases, such as copying files or running a script. We added a run script in chapter 14 to copy frameworks downloaded via the dependency manager Carthage.

A.7   *Build rules*

The Build Rules tab defines how different file types are processed by Xcode. The default behavior for file types is probably fine for your projects, and it's unlikely you'll need to make changes here.

appendix B
Swift syntax cheat sheets

Variables and constants

```
var aVariable = 0
let aConstant = 0
```

DATA TYPE ANNOTATIONS

```
var aString: String
var aBool: Bool
var aInt: Int
var aDouble: Double
```

DATA TYPE INFERENCE

```
var bString = "A String!"
var bBool = true
var bInt = 3
var bDouble = 3.0
```

CLARIFY DATA TYPE

```
var cDouble: Double = 3
```

CONVERT DATA TYPE

```
var dDouble = Double(3)
```

PROPERTY OBSERVERS

```
var score = 0 {
  willSet {
    // Score will be updated
  }
  didSet {
    // Score was updated
  }
}
```

STRING INTERPOLATION

```
var message = "You scored\(score)"
```

Collections

ARRAYS

```
var emptyArray: [String] = []
var arrayOfInts = [3, 1, 2, 5]
arrayOfInts.append(4)
```

DICTIONARIES

```
var emptyDictionary: [String: String] = [:]
var dict = ["A": 1, "B": 2, "C": 3]
dict["D"] = 4
```

SETS

```
var emptySet: Set<String> = [] //empty Set
var setOfStrings: Set = ["A", "B", "C"]
setOfStrings.insert("D")
```

RANGE OPERATORS

```
let closedRange = 1...3 // include 3
let halfOpenRange = 1..<3 // exclude 3
```

FOR-IN LOOPS WITH RANGE

```
for index in 1...3 {
    print("\(index) banana")
}
```

FOR-IN LOOP

```
let distances = [3, 1, 2, 5, 4]
var returnDistances: [Int] = []
for distance in distances {
    returnDistances.append(distance * 2)
}
```

Collections (*continued*)

COLLECTION HIGHER ORDER FUNCTIONS

```
print(distances.map( { $0 * 2 } ))
// [6,2,4,10,8]
print(distances.filter( { $0 >= 3 } ))
// [3,5,4]
print(distances.reduce(0, {$0 + $1} ))
// 15
print(distances.sorted(by: { $0 > $1 } ))
// [5,4,3,2,1]
```

Tuples

```
var card1: (Int, String)
card1 = (7, "?")
card1.0 = 3
print("\(card1.0) of \(card1.1)")
// The 3 of ♥
```

TUPLES WITH ELEMENT NAMES

```
var card2: (number: Int, suit: String)
card2 = (number: 10, suit: "?")
card2.number = 5
print("\(card2.number) of \(card2.suit)")
// The 5 of ♠
```

RETURN A TUPLE FROM A FUNCTION

```
func pickCard() -> (number: Int,
                    suit: String) {
    return (number: 2, suit: "?")
}
```

DEFINE TWO VALUES AT ONCE USING A TUPLE

```
var (number, suit) = card1
var (number2, suit2) = (13, "?")
```

SWAP TWO VALUES USING TUPLES

```
var coin1 = "dollar"
var coin2 = "penny"
(coin1, coin2) = (coin2, coin1)
```

Enumerations

```
enum AEnum {
    case aCase
    case bCase
}
let aEnum = AEnum.bCase
```

SWITCH STATEMENT WITH ENUM

```
switch aEnum {
case .aCase:
    print("Do a thing")
case .bCase:
    print("Do b thing")
}
```

Control flow

WHILE

```
var num = 1
while num < 100 {
    num += num
}
```

REPEAT WHILE

```
repeat {
    num += num
} while num < 200
```

Functions

```
func aFunc() {
    // Do something
}
```

FUNCTION RETURNS VALUE

```
func bFunc() -> String {
    // Do something
    return ""
}
```

FUNCTION WITH PARAMETERS

```
func multiply(a: Int, b: Int) -> Int {
    return a * b
}
multiply(a: 1, b: 2)
```

FUNCTION WITH PARAMETERS WITHOUT ARGUMENT LABELS

```
func add(_ a: Int, _ b: Int) -> Int {
    return a + b
}
add(1, 2)
```

ARGUMENT LABEL DIFFERENT FROM PARAMETER NAME

```
func subtract(_ a: Int,
              from b: Int) -> Int {
    return b - a
}
subtract(3, from: 5)
```

DEFAULT PARAMETER VALUES

```
func greet(with planet: String = "World") {
    print("Hello \(planet)")
}
greet()              // Hello World
greet(with: "Mars") // Hello Mars
```

VARIADIC PARAMETERS

```
func add(_ numbers: Int...) -> Int {
    return numbers.reduce(0, {$0 + $1})
}
add(3, 2, 5) // 10
```

Functions *(continued)*

OVERLOADING FUNCTIONS
```swift
func display(text: String) {
    print(text)
}
func display(num: Int) {
    print(num)
}
```

OVERLOADING OPERATORS
```swift
func +(left: Int, right: Int) -> Int {
    return left - right
}
print(3 + 2) // 1! Crazy, right?
```

Closures

METHOD RECEIVES CLOSURE
```swift
func use(num: Int,
         with calc: (Int) -> Int) {
    calc(num)
}
```

PASS CLOSURE TO METHOD
```swift
use(num: 10, with:
    { (num: Int) -> Int in
        return(num * 2)
    }
)
```

SHORTHAND CLOSURE
```swift
use(num: 5, with: { $0 * 2 })
```

TRAILING CLOSURE
```swift
use(num: 6) { $0 * 2}
```

Optionals

```swift
var w: Int?
var h: Int?
(w, h) = (5, 10)
```

FORCED UNWRAPPING
```swift
print("Rect area is \(w! * h!)")
```

OPTIONAL BINDING
```swift
if let w = w, let h = h {
    print("Rect area is \(w * h)")
}
```

OPTIONAL PARAMETER, GUARD LET
```swift
func getSquareArea(w: Int? = nil) -> Int {
    guard let w = w, w > 0 else
    {
        return(0)
    }
    return(w * w)
}
```

TERNARY CONDITIONAL OPERATOR
```swift
print("Width is \(w != nil ? w! : 0)")
```

NIL COALESCING OPERATOR
```swift
print("Width is \(w ?? 0)")
```

IMPLICITLY UNWRAPPED OPTIONALS
```swift
var width2: Int!
```

OPTIONAL CHAINING
```swift
//: ### With a two-dimensional array:
var pos = [["O", "X", "O"],
           ["X", "X", "O"],
           ["X", "O", "X"]
]
//: ### With optional chaining:
if let firstPos = pos.first?.first {
    print("Top left is a \(firstPos)")
}
```

Protocols

```swift
protocol AProtocol {
    func aFunc()
}
protocol BProtocol: AProtocol {
    var computedProp: Int {get set}
}
```
Inherits protocol

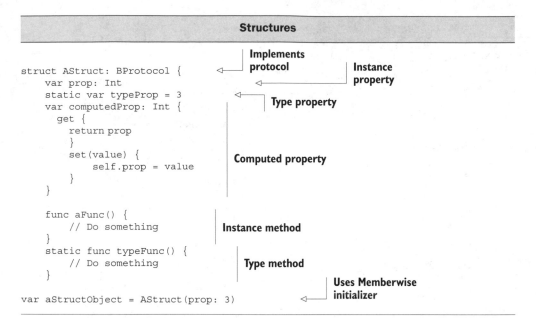

Structures

```
struct AStruct: BProtocol {                    Implements protocol
    var prop: Int                              Instance property
    static var typeProp = 3                     Type property
    var computedProp: Int {
      get {
        return prop
        }
        set(value) {                           Computed property
            self.prop = value
        }
    }

    func aFunc() {
        // Do something                         Instance method
    }
    static func typeFunc() {
        // Do something                         Type method
    }
}
var aStructObject = AStruct(prop: 3)           Uses Memberwise initializer
```

Classes

```
class AClass {
    var prop: Int
    lazy var lazyProp = AClass(parm: 3)        Lazy stored property
    init(val: Int) {
        self.prop = val                        Designated initializer
    }
    convenience init() {
        self.init(val: 0)                      Convenience initializer
    }
    func bFunc() {
        // Do something
    }
}
var aObject = AClass(val: 3)
aObject.prop
aObject.bFunc()
                                               Subclasses Class;
class ASubClass: AClass, AProtocol {           implements protocol
    func aFunc() {
        // Do something
    }
    override func bFunc() {
        // Do something                         Overrides method
    }
}
```

DOWNLOAD You can download these cheat sheets as playgrounds here: https://github.com/iOSAppDevelopmentwithSwiftinAction/CheatSheets.git.

index